HIDDEN DEPTHS

Robin Waterfield

HIDDEN DEPTHS

The Story of Hypnosis

BRUNNER-ROUTLEDGE
New York - Hove

Published in 2003 by
Brunner-Routledge
29 West 35th Street
New York, NY 10001
www.brunner-routledge.com

First published in the United Kingdom in hardback by Macmillan, an imprint
of Pan Macmillan Ltd.

Cover design: Pearl Chang
Cover photo: Pendulum © Corbis

Brunner-Routledge is an imprint of the Taylor & Francis Group.

Printed in the United States of America on acid-free paper.

10 9 8 7 6 5 4 3 2 1

Library of Congress Cataloging-in-Publication Data

Waterfield, Robin, 1952-
    Hidden depths : the story of hypnosis / Robin Waterfield.
        p. cm.
Previously published: London : Macmillan, 2002.
Includes bibliographical references and index.
    ISBN 0–415–94791–X (hb) 0–415–94792–8 (pb)
1. Hypnotism–History. I. Title.

    RC495.W345 2003
    154.7'09–dc21
                                                            2003011033

To my *karass*

Code the world with the fugitive light

'Animal magnetism is the most significant discovery ever made, even if, for the time being, it brings more enigmas than it solves'

Arthur Schopenhauer, *Sämmtliche Werke* IV

'Mesmerism is too gross a humbug to admit any farther serious notice. We regard its abettors as quacks and impostors. They ought to be hooted out of professional society'

Thomas Wakley, first editor of the *Lancet*

'All sciences alike have descended from magic and superstition, but none has been so slow as hypnosis in shaking off the evil associations of its origin'

Clark Hull, *Hypnosis and Suggestibility*

Contents

List of Illustrations

Every effort has been made to contact copyright holders of pictures reproduced in this book. If any have been inadvertently overlooked, the publishers will be pleased to make restitution at the earliest opportunity.

Acknowledgements

As usual, I have incurred many debts in the course of writing this book. Above all, I must acknowledge Rupert Heath and Peter Marshall, who between them were the prime movers of the project. This is very much my Cornish book, mostly written during a glorious two-year sojourn on the Lizard Peninsula; but it is hard to know who or what to thank (apart from my parents for their great generosity) when love of a place has been for so long so deeply rooted in one's being. In London, Jeremy Trevathan has been a warm and encouraging editor, and Tony Bickford deserves the title 'patron of the arts'. Tom Bell is a paradigm of the doctors of the future, who will include hypnosis in their arsenal; he was extremely generous with his time and advice. It is a pleasure to acknowledge the help of my bibliophile friend Robert Temple, who let me browse through his wonderful collection of nineteenth-century works on hypnosis. Thanks as always to Richard Leigh, for his constant willingness to share his enormous knowledge of fine literature. Simon Anderson-Jones and Charles Drazin pointed me in the direction of a number of films, and Simon lent me a whole stack of them too. Brian Lancaster was a superb professional reader and made many valuable suggestions. Melvin Gravitz and David Spiegel kindly sent me offprints of articles (accompanied by recommendations for further reading in David's case), and Megan Kerr tracked down some American court cases. My thanks to Bernard Carr for steering me towards the library of the Society for Psychical Research. Not all those I interviewed could be named, but I owe thanks for their time to Ron Alexander ('Sleepy Sam'), Tom Bell, Sally Gilbert and Dennis Moore. Then there are debts for board and lodging during my research trips to London and in the States: here I must mention Martin Buckley and Penny Lawrence, Stela Tomasevic and Jurgen Quick, Rod Thorn, and especially Michael Brown and Sylvia Kennick Brown – not forgetting Emily Cheng Li. Family debts are of course too many to list; in this case they range from my son Julian, for his knowledge of Hebrew, to my partner Ingrid Gottschalk, for depth of emotion and breadth of physical space.

Preface

It is 1784. You are in a dimly lit salon in a mansion in a prosperous section of Paris. The room is presided over by a tall, slightly overweight man dressed in a purple cloak trimmed with lace and embroidered with occult symbols. Other sigils decorate the walls and heavy velvet curtains cover the windows, allowing just the odd ray of sunlight in to strike the thickly carpeted floor, and hardly a sound penetrates from the street outside. Melodious piano music can be heard softly from another room. You and a number of other Parisians are seated around a large, low tub, and there are other such tubs in the room, three for the rich and one for the poor. However, there are few poor people at their tub, since it is fashionable Paris that is fascinated by this new science. Movable iron rods stick out through the cover of the tub and have been bent at right angles, so that from where you sit on chairs around the tub you and the others can hold the rods, or apply them directly or by means of an attached rope to an afflicted part of the body. The other end of these rods, you have been informed, are resting in phials of magnetized water, and these phials in turn stand in a pool of water containing magnetized iron filings. The wizard, who is none other than Franz Anton Mesmer, calls this contraption a *baquet* (which just means 'tub'), and explains that it, or the attentions of an individual healer such as himself, can restore the lost balance of the magnetic fluid which pervades the universe and animates all living creatures, and whose disturbance is ill health. The group of clients grasp the rods and wait in silence. The atmosphere in the room grows very intense. Occasionally Mesmer or one of his assistants prowls around the room. To complete his appearance as a wizard, Mesmer carries a wand, with a metal tip. He inspects the woman next to you, passes his hands behind her back without touching her, points the wand at her, and she goes into convulsions. Her body begins to jerk, and her breathing is shallow and uneven; a flush comes over her face and neck. Finally she collapses gently to the floor, coughing up phlegm. Assistants calmly come and take her away to another room, which you can see is lined with mattresses and soft silk drapes. Mesmer follows to attend to her, now that she is on the road to health.

★

It is 1850. You are in the comfortable and cluttered drawing room of a well-to-do self-styled doctor. He sits you down in a straight-backed chair, and pulls up another chair opposite you. If you are a woman, you are chaperoned, and he delicately places your knees to one side of his; if you are a man he sits with his knees between yours. He feels rather too close for comfort, but you are here of your own free will to be mesmerized, and so you submit. He asks you gently to relax, and tells you that you have nothing to fear. Then silence falls. He makes a few sample passes over your hands, from the wrist to the fingertips, drawing his hands close to the skin, so close that you can feel the warmth of his hand, but never quite touching. To your surprise after a while you feel a faint coolness and tingling. Satisfied, he then proceeds to take your right hand in his left hand, and your left hand in his right hand, in a special grip that involves pinching the balls of your thumbs, and he asks you to stare intently at one of his eyes. He returns your gaze without blinking for some minutes; you can feel him exerting his will to some end which is mysterious to you. You begin to feel a strange sensation of heaviness and drowsiness. Without speaking a word, he begins to make passes with his hands over your forehead and eyes and down to your neck. Your eyelids begin to feel very heavy . . . and that is the last you remember clearly for a while.

★

It is 5 May 2000. I am in the surgery of Tom Bell, who is currently a candidate for the chair of the British Society of Medical and Dental Hypnotists. He is a general practitioner from Okehampton, who uses hypnotherapy in his practice. His office combines comfort and professionalism; there are reassuring medical tomes on the window-sill, and light prints by Gilbert Ster on the walls, along with a number of family photographs. The room is light and sunny, and the bird-song outside contrasts with the noises of a busy medical practice from the corridor. In contrast to the intense quiet of the scenarios from the eighteenth and nineteenth centuries, Tom talks throughout the procedure, peppering his sentences with key words and phrases which remind me that I am calm, relaxed and in control. His tone of voice is quiet but authoritative, and I notice that he rarely uses negatives such as 'not' and 'don't', but finds ways to express himself positively. He gets me to close my eyes and talks me through a standard relaxation exercise, familiar from yoga, drama and antenatal classes, in which I progressively relax my whole body from toes to scalp. Once I am somewhat relaxed (a state which is unusual for me at the best of times, and especially today since one part of my mind is constantly exploring, looking at Tom's technique, and placing what's happening in the context of this book), he completes this phase by suggesting that my eyelids are so comfortable and heavy that I can't open them, and then deepens the trance by having me picture a blackboard on which a hand writes the sequence of numbers from 100 downwards, with the numbers gradually getting fainter and fainter, until they fade out altogether. To my astonishment, at his suggestion that there is a helium-filled balloon attached by a string to the index finger of my right hand, I feel a distinct tug on the finger, and gradually, as Tom continues to talk me through it, my arm rises slowly and effortlessly into the air until my hand is at shoulder height. But this is all just an experiment, so the exercise ends shortly afterwards, with no therapeutic suggestions implanted, except for the idea that I will be able to feel the tug on the finger whenever I like and use it as a trigger to go to a peaceful, relaxing place in my mind. My hand is returned to my thigh, and I count myself down into wakefulness.

*

The last of these descriptions is taken from my own experience; the second is based on a practical manual published in 1851 and written by George Barth: *The Mesmerist's Manual of Phenomena and Practice, with Directions for Applying Mesmerism to the Cure of Diseases, and the Methods of Producing Mesmeric Phenomena; Intended for Domestic Use and the Instruction of Beginners.* The first is based on eyewitness accounts of Mesmer's practice. All three fall into the province of the history of hypnotism, but obviously hypnotism has not stood still since its invention or discovery at the end of the eighteenth century.

This book tells the story of hypnotism, a practice which has attracted the most extravagant praise and the most acidic vitriol for at least 200 years. I am not a practising hypnotist or hypnotherapist, nor am I an academic psychologist or a doctor. This book is a work of reportage about something which, if even half the claims made for it are true, deserves the attention of medical science to a far greater degree than it has yet received. It appears to offer a gentle, non-invasive method of treating a wide range of ailments, and yet it has been abandoned on the margins of medicine. Indeed, in some cases it appears to deal with causes where normal medicine deals only with symptoms, to be able to go deeper and further than normal medicine. Here is a dramatic case of hypnotic healing, well documented and authenticated because it is a recent case; it hit the headlines in the early 1950s.

In 1951 a young doctor, Albert Mason, was presented with a terrible case of ichthyosis, a hereditary disease in which the patient has fewer sweat and sebaceous glands than usual, so that his skin is dry and scaly. In this case the body of the patient, a sixteen-year-old boy, was all but covered in a thick, black, smelly, hard layer of dried skin, which occasionally cracked open in places to ooze a bloody serum. The boy had had the condition since infancy, and conventional medicine was at a loss. He had endured two skin-graft operations, but in each case the new skin had soon taken on the foul appearance of the rest of his body. Dr Mason, perhaps not realizing that hypnosis was not supposed to be able to deal with congenital diseases, offered to try hypnosis. He hypnotized the boy, in front of a dozen sceptical doctors, in the hospital at East Grinstead, Sussex. He planted the suggestion that his left arm would clear. Five days later the blackened skin became crumbly and fell off to reveal reddened but otherwise normal skin underneath. Within ten days the arm was clear. Mason then worked on other parts of his body, achieving similarly astonishing results; his success rate ranged from good to remarkable. The boy was then taught self-hypnosis to maintain the improvement. The case was written up with the laconic brevity typical of many medical articles, in the bastion of traditional medicine, the *British Medical Journal*, for 1952, and three years later Mason was able to write a follow-up article reporting that the improvement seemed to be permanent.

It is in fact still a major bone of contention whether hypnosis can treat organic or structural ailments rather than psychosomatic ones. Where psychosomatic illnesses are concerned, there are so many thousands of success stories that one can get blasé about them. So let's make a sceptical assumption. Let's assume that Mason's patient underwent spontaneous remission – that the disease would have improved of its own accord, as in fact sometimes happens in their teens to children who contract ichthyosis young. It still remains the case that Mason achieved a significantly high success rate, and with significant speed; it still remains the case that conventional medical science had tried its best and failed. It still remains the case, then, that hypnosis can be a powerful weapon in a doctor's arsenal, and that it should be brought into the mainstream as quickly as possible.

As sometimes happens, science is actually behind the times on this. A great many ordinary people – you and me – know perfectly well that hypnotherapy (and some other so-called 'alternative' therapies) works. Nearly everyone knows someone who has been to a hypnotherapist for, perhaps, nicotine addiction. Many people have also seen, live or on TV, the astonishing effects produced by stage hypnotists such as Paul McKenna, and have little doubt that something real is going on, even if it seems inexplicable. This is the world this book explores. The past story of hypnotism is fascinating in itself, but it also may be of no little importance for us and our futures.

Introduction

Hypnotism is a fascinating subject, its history littered with quirky individuals (in both fact and fiction) and odd or remarkable stories. The subject takes us from the flakiest end of alternative medicine to the frontiers of experimental science, and from entertainment to healing. Most extraordinarily, precisely the same ranges are encapsulated right from the start of modern hypnosis, in the life and work of Franz Anton Mesmer. We will meet tales of remarkable healing, and heavy science (lightly treated); we will meet famous individuals from real life and storybooks, such as Mesmer, who gave his name to a whole new healing art and whose work was press-ganged into the political rhetoric of the French Revolution; Emile Coué with his famous saying, 'Every day, in every way, I am getting better and better'; Freud, who made extensive but often unsuccessful use of hypnosis in his early years; Svengali, the character from George du Maurier's 1894 novel *Trilby*, who exerted an evil influence over the innocent and ambitious Trilby O'Ferrall (and who, with his pointed beard and dark, staring eyes, has often cropped up in films and has spawned a host of lesser literary lookalikes); Grigoriy Rasputin, the Mad Monk of Russia; Milton Erickson, probably the most famous modern hypnotherapist, who could hypnotize a person with a handshake or by tapping the top of a table, or just by altering his tone of voice in specific ways. Did you know that the 1955 James Dean film *Rebel Without a Cause* was based on a medical book of the same name describing the case history of a psychopathic criminal and his successful treatment through hypnosis? Did you know that Rachmaninoff was helped over depression and 'composer's block' by hypnosis? That Stalin, perhaps aware of the power of hypnotism through his own carefully stage-managed rare appearances, and his repetitive and rhythmical speech style, banned the practice throughout the Soviet republics in 1948?

This is a book about the history of hypnotism in the West. I do not cover any of the related arts of the East, such as those practised by Indian fakirs. There is plenty of material from the West, enough for a much longer book than this one. Moreover, it is not clear that many Eastern practices should be counted as hypnotism, and in some cases there has been influence from the West to the East. For instance, a booklet I once saw on Indian hypnosis contained instructions and ideas which would have been familiar to any Western practitioner; since it is clear that these methods evolved in the West, because we can trace their history, it follows that the Indian booklet was written in imitation of Western practices.

In addition to telling the story of hypnosis and the characters who crop up along the way, there will be two main sub-themes in the book: first, what hypnosis can teach us about the powers and further reaches of the human mind; second, the degree to which hypnotic techniques have become absorbed in and reflect everyday culture. Under the latter heading I mean to include not just questions such as whether advertisers can be said to hypnotize us, but also the fact that hypnosis seems to reflect, in each era, the interests and predispositions of the era. For instance, from the time of Mesmer to the middle of the nineteenth century professional science was still young enough to be nervously aware of its limitations, and so the budding medical establishment, anxious to confirm its credentials, attacked Mesmer and his followers with particular acrimony. Or again, in periods when there is a revolt against technology (as with the early Romantics) or scientism (as today), hypnosis becomes a focus of the revolutionary party. In the middle to late nineteenth century there was a conflict between two groups of thinkers about hypnosis – the occultists and paranormalists, and the scientists and therapists. At the same time, mesmerists in general aligned themselves with Protestants against Catholics, because they tended to welcome scientific progress as a revelation of God's handiwork. And mesmerists also aligned themselves with reformers in a number of other spheres. Just as Mesmer himself was made something of an icon by partisans of the French Revolution, so in nineteenth-century England mesmerism was seen by its opponents as a working-class invasion of medicine, which was of course restricted to those with the money for education.

I do not intend this book to be a debunking of hypnosis, but a work of reportage which will allow me to present the views both of those who do debunk hypnosis and of those who believe in its real existence. Assuming that there is such a thing, I will make a fair assessment of what it is and what it can and cannot achieve, what its medical and psychotherapeutic uses and potential are, its history and ramifications. In fact, since the impression most people have of hypnotism (either because they have been duped by popular myths, or because they are die-hard rationalists) is that it is something wacky, it will be a major part of my purpose to prove that this is not so – that hypnosis has a great deal to offer, especially in therapeutic contexts, and that its value should be more widely recognized.

But why should people believe that there is no such thing as hypnosis? After all, we can see a hypnotized subject plunge his arm into a bucket of icy water with no discomfort, just because he has been told that it is tepid; conversely, we can see him screw up his face in pain on tentatively lowering his hand into tepid water, because he has been told that it is icy-cold. He may hallucinate that he is dancing with Marilyn Monroe, or smell the scent of a room full of imaginary flowers. He can remember events from his childhood which he had long forgotten, and even re-enact them. On the therapeutic side, hypnotherapists have achieved remarkable results in a wide range of ailments, and both major and minor surgery have been carried out on hypnotized patients.

All these phenomena, and all the many other marvels we will come across in the book, seem to be a clear case of mind over matter. And there's the rub. There are a number of people, academics above all, who simply do not believe in the existence of mind. They think that this is a naive belief held by the rest of us, and that the phenomena attributed to our minds are best explained otherwise. In philosophy they are called 'positivists' and in psychology 'behaviourists'. The mind they regard as a 'ghost in a machine' – the machine being the body. Where hypnosis is concerned, they might maintain, for instance, that hypnotized subjects are merely very suggestive people who are anxious to please the hypnotist, and who therefore play out the role in ways that conform to their ideas of the kind of behaviour that is expected of them and in response to often unconscious cues given them by the hypnotist.

Part of the problem is also that ever since the early days of hypnosis its practitioners and supporters have made fanciful claims for it. In the nineteenth century it was frequently claimed that a suitably sensitive hypnotized subject could see things clairvoyantly by projecting her spirit elsewhere; in recent years there have been a number of cases of supposed recall of past lives by regressing a hypnotized subject back past his childhood, past birth, past conception . . . and into the wild blue yonder. These are two extreme cases, but many practitioners have been guilty of making less radical but still far-fetched claims for their favourite art. And this in turn has attracted the wrong kind of response, in which overly sceptical investigators have thrown out the baby with the bathwater – rejected hypnosis as a whole in rejecting such extreme claims. By and large science has been unfair to hypnosis: it has been dismissed to the margins, where it can safely be ignored and left in the hands of amateurs – which then, in a vicious circle, increases the scientists' justification for dismissing it.

One of the main reasons the story of hypnotism is important, and deserves to be told, is that it is concerned with the essential human quality of suggestibility. This word often carries negative connotations, as if it meant 'liability to be manipulated by others', but it is not a faculty we could do without. No one is always active; we are also acted upon. We could not sustain relationships with family and friends otherwise. And suggestibility is also closely linked to other important abilities, such as imagination, empathy and feelings in general; tests have shown that the best hypnotic subjects are often those with vivid imaginations, who can put themselves in a situation or someone else's shoes.

There are a number of good books on hypnosis, but a lot of them are academic or partisan. Yet it is a subject that demands more accessible treatment, especially today with an audience which is likely to be open-minded and curious about such matters. The historical approach taken in this book will allow the reader a general overview of the subject in all its manifestations. In the meantime, lacking accessible treatments, the subject is surrounded by myths and misconceptions. Here are some of the most common:

1. You're asleep when you're hypnotized.
2. You're unconscious when you're hypnotized.

3. People with strong wills can't be hypnotized, only weak-willed people.
4. Hypnosis is the dominance and manipulation of gullible people by the hypnotist.
5. Hypnosis is a mysterious magical power.
6. A hypnotist can make people commit immoral or illegal acts when they're hypnotized.
7. People can be hypnotized at long distance, or over the phone or TV.
8. People can remain in trances for a long time, perhaps a lifetime.
9. People can be woken up only by the person who hypnotized them. So what would happen if the person who hypnotized them were to leave or drop dead of a heart attack?
10. Hypnosis can cure almost any ailment.
11. Hypnosis is dangerous: it can cause after-effects ranging from headaches to psychosis.
12. Hypnosis is unchristian. It is the work of the devil, and while hypnotized your soul can be possessed by the devil.
13. Hypnosis, especially self-hypnosis, is the same thing as meditation.
14. Under hypnosis people can accurately recall things that happened earlier in their life, or even in earlier lives.
15. Under hypnosis people gain paranormal powers.
16. Under hypnosis people can be made to tell the truth.

Most of these fears and fantasies about hypnosis will only be dispelled once hypnosis is properly understood. Although the primary focus of this book is the history of hypnosis, an understanding of hypnosis will emerge through the pages and by the end of the book every single one of the above statements will, implicitly or explicitly, have been shown to be wrong. It is a great pity that hypnosis has become surrounded by so much fear, since in quite a wide range of ailments and problems it is actually a very safe form of therapy – far safer, for instance, than the pharmaceutical and interventionist form of medicine most commonly practised in the West today.

We need a working definition of hypnosis. Unfortunately, no such definition can be non-controversial and agreed upon by all the experts. Here is a rapid survey of the main contenders in the bid to define hypnotism: magnetism (de Puységur, etc.), monoideism (Braid), a form of sleep (Liébeault, Vogt, etc.), nothing but a state of passive suggestibility, with selective attention and reduced planning function (Bernheim, Gauld), hysteria (Charcot), a form of dissociation (Janet, Myers, James, Sidis, Prince, Hilgard, etc.), a loving, possibly Oedipal, relationship with the therapist (Freud, Ferenczi), a state of inhibition between sleep and wakefulness (Pavlov), nothing but task-motivation (early Barber), nothing but an imaginative response to test-suggestions (later Barber), nothing but a goal-directed, role-playing fantasy (White, Spanos, Sarbin and Coe), activation of the implicit memory system (Spiegel).

Faced with this welter of definitions, it has to be borne in mind that nothing about hypnosis is uncontroversial, and that these various definitions depend on various theories of what is going on, psychologically and neurologically, and these in turn depend on the approach taken by the particular researcher (behaviourist, occult, etc.). In other words, no one really knows what hypnosis is; this is part of the attraction of the view that there really is no such thing. All of the current theories may be wrong, or none of them may be wrong, while all giving a partial picture.

I am not qualified to add to the confusion by coming up with a new definition of hypnosis. In this book I will be less concerned with its definition than its phenomenology. Phenomenology is the descriptive study of some facet of human experience in order to make it intelligible. That is, from our point of view it doesn't matter whether there is such a thing as the hypnotic state, which is different from any other state of consciousness. All that matters is that something unusual is going on, that we can trace the history of this unusual something, and that as a result of this unusual something people can have all sorts of experiences, including being cured or relieved of a number of disorders. Hypnosis should still be acknowledged as a powerful therapeutic tool, since access is gained to the client's subconscious and imagination. So in this book I will begin, at any rate, by using the term 'hypnotism' or 'hypnosis' to mean precisely whatever the experts want it to mean, whether that is no more than 'relaxation and suggestibility', or as much as 'a specific altered state of consciousness'.

The phenomenological model I have adopted for this book is as follows. Hypnotism or hypnosis is the deliberate inducement or facilitation by one person in another person or a number of people of a trance state. A trance state is (briefly) one in which a person's usual means of orienting himself in reality have faded, so that the boundaries between the external world and the inner world of thoughts, feelings, memories and imagination begin to dissolve. The ensuing altered state or states involve passivity and lack of initiative, a decrease in normal critical thinking and hence a tolerance for incongruous situations ('trance logic'). The subject is highly compliant to incoming suggestions and capable of role-playing; he has focused, selective perception; he allows his imagination greater freedom than usual, and fantasies are experienced, or memories re-experienced, with vivid intensity; he is capable of a certain range of unusual physical and mental feats, is susceptible to alterations in perception and memory, and tends to behave in a way he thinks appropriate to the role he is being asked to perform.

All these phenomena of hypnosis can be summarized under three headings: absorption, dissociation and suggestibility. The hypnotized person tends to become highly involved in whatever he is perceiving, imagining or thinking; he separates out aspects of his experience that would normally be processed at the same time (so that, for instance, the raising of an arm can seem to be involuntary, as if the arm was controlled by something other than oneself); and his responsiveness to social cues is increased, which leads to an enhanced tendency to comply with hypnotic instructions. It is worth stating from the outset that this does not mean that the subject has given up his will to the hypnotist, but just that he has suspended his critical judgement for a while. In the hypnotic state, the subject must be capable of speech and action, which is to say that he or she must not be merely asleep or unconscious. Importantly, I would add that the participation of the subject or subjects must be by their consent (which is not quite the same as saying that the subject must be willing, because there may be no conscious act of will involved): you cannot hypnotize someone if they have not at some level agreed to be hypnotized.

This model is simultaneously broad and narrow, in different respects. It is broad enough to include, for instance, entrancement by incantation, if it involves the direct and deliberate action of an operator on a consenting subject, and in other ways conforms to our model. But it excludes phenomena such as enchantment where the bewitched person was not aware of being deliberately worked on. It is common in 'primitive' societies for a person experiencing a run of bad luck to attribute this, retrospectively, to an enemy having bewitched him, but this is not hypnotism because the victim was not aware at the time of being enchanted, and there was no direct interaction between operator and subject. The model also excludes the so-called trance states involved in, for instance, watching TV or in driving a car ('highway hypnosis'). Every driver knows the experience of looking back on a journey and saying to herself: 'I know I passed through Newcastle, but I have no memory of having negotiated the traffic, the lights, the roundabouts and so on. How did I do it?' Personally, I'm not sure I would identify this as a trance state at all, because otherwise it becomes all too easy to say that almost all our states of consciousness are trance states: am I in a trance state now because I am focused on writing this book? This seems a misuse of the word; and anyway these states are not hypnotism, above all because there is no operator.

Self-hypnosis is another legitimate special case, provided the same person deliberately acts simultaneously as operator and subject. This proviso is necessary to distinguish self-hypnosis from mere day-dreaming or relaxation. The important point here again is this: not all trance states are hypnotic states. But in so far as in this book I am dealing with historical cases from the past, my focus is not really on self-hypnosis. After all, how could I or anyone know whether an ancient Egyptian, say, had hypnotized himself? The subjective element of self-hypnosis will more or less rule it out of this book.

One thing I do want to exclude from the start is animal hypnosis. People have induced hypnosis in a wide range of animals, by a wide range of methods, from repetitive stimuli (e.g. stroking, swinging the animal back and forth), to pressure on certain body parts (especially the abdominal region), to tipping the poor creature upside down. There are some impressive effects in the animal kingdom which seem to resemble hypnosis. In his book *The Red Hourglass: Lives of the Predators*, for instance, Gordon Grice vividly tells how a particular kind of wasp, called a tarantula hawk, hypnotizes its prey, a tarantula, which would otherwise make short work of it. But we have no way of knowing whether the spider is really hypnotized. Does it have the mental powers to be hypnotized in any way that makes a meaningful parallel to a human being? Does any animal have the kind of powers that can be shut down and focused, made more suggestible and so on? I doubt it. It is a common fallacy to attribute to animals human characteristics based on behavioural traits which resemble those of humans. We even do the same with plants. When you brush the leaves of *Mimosa pudica* it curls up in a way that can only be described as shy, but it would be a bold person who said that the plant was actually shy. In the animal kingdom there are many behavioural characteristics that resemble a hypnotic state: for instance, they go rigid, pretending to be dead, to deter an enemy. But we have no need to postulate the kind of sophisticated psychological processes in animals that might lead us to say that they can be hypnotized. Any reader who wants more information about animal hypnosis should read Ferenc Völgyesi, *Hypnosis of Man and Animals*; he claims to have hypnotized just about every major species of creature on earth.

In the course of this book I will touch on phenomena and practices related to hypnosis, but the focus will be on practices which satisfy the criteria of the model I have just outlined. One implication of the model needs to be brought out right from the start, since it will play a considerable part in the history of hypnosis. I have described the hypnotist as the operator, and the other party as the subject. In other words, the hypnotist is active, and the subject is passive. This is not surprising – no more surprising than the fact that we put ourselves into a passive state when we visit the doctor or go into hospital. 'They are the experts,' we think. 'They'll tell us what to do.' To this extent hypnosis involves the imposition of the will of the hypnotist on the subject, and the subject allows himself to be in a suggestible or open frame of mind. This extent is perhaps not very large – it does not license the idea of the evil, manipulative hypnotist – but it remains true that there is *inequality of will* between operator and subject. A hypnotized subject can snap out of his trance any time he chooses, but while he is entranced he is in a state of heightened suggestibility, more open than usual to the suggestions of the operator (within certain parameters laid down by the subject's long-term moral and social conditioning). This passive suggestibility is what I mean by the idea of inequality of will; the subject makes fewer choices than usual, leaving many such decisions up to the operator.

One thing hypnosis is not is sleep. It's true that the word is derived from the Greek word *hypnos*, meaning 'sleep', but this is because the closest analogy to hypnosis in familiar experience is sleep. But there are differences, the most important of which is that when hypnotized you are aware of incoming sensory data, such as the hypnotist's voice, and can carry on a conversation. In fact, because you are focused on the hypnotist's voice, to the virtual exclusion of a great deal of other stuff that would normally be distracting you, you're more awake than at other times, and you may well feel an increased vigilance.

The main thing that misleads is the term 'hypnotism'. Almost every book I've read credits the Scottish physician James Braid with the coining of the term in his 1843 book *Neurypnology*. Even this is not strictly accurate, since Braid had already used the term 'hypnotic sleep' the year before, in an open letter sent to the Reverend Hugh McNeile (or M'Neile) on 4 June 1842. In this letter he seeks to defend himself against the charges of satanism which McNeile had brought against him (while not naming him), and to distinguish hypnosis from its precursor, animal magnetism, which he declares to be founded on 'a gratuitous assumption, unsupported by fact'. In an incidental way, he describes the 'stupor' into which his subjects have been put as 'hypnotic sleep'.

However, although Braid certainly popularized the term in the English-speaking world, and may have invented it independently, it had been in use some thirty-five years earlier in France and was a favourite of the French writer Etienne Félix d'Hénin du Cuvillers (1755–1841), a mesmerist with a classical bent, who edited the important journal *Archives du magnétisme animal*, issued from 1820–3. Braid later came to regret the term, since he came to associate hypnosis not so much with sleep as with fixation. So he coined another word, 'monoideism', but it never caught on. By the same token, although stage and fictional hypnotists talk about the ending of the trance as 'waking up', if hypnosis is not a form of sleep, talk of 'waking up' is incorrect and misleading, and some modern hypnotists prefer the term 'dehypnotization'. I'd be prepared to bet that it doesn't catch on either.

The story of hypnosis is an adventure story. As a species, we are endowed with curiosity. We climb mountains, explore the depths of space and the oceans; we split the atom just to see what happens, and then we have to take responsibility for the results of our curiosity. We deny this curiosity at our peril, running the risk of stagnation or attempting the impossible task of turning back the clock. Hypnosis has for many years been one of our main tools for exploring the further reaches of the mind, and it remains true today that we know less about some of the workings of the mind than we do about the moon. Without wishing to sound too like a cheap stage hypnotist – and I hope your eyelids are not already getting heavy – I would like to take you on this historical journey.

1

Hypnosis in Fact and Fiction

When you stop to think about it, it's very strange that at a few well-chosen words quite a number of us – perhaps all of us – can fall into a sleep-like state in which we are more open than usual to suggestions from a person we trust, and capable of some unusual mental and physical feats. It is an oddity, a reminder of the extraordinary capacities and capabilities of the human brain and mind. I would like the reader to keep this in mind throughout: you are bigger than you think you are, capable of more than you imagine. In a book of this length, the facts about hypnosis may start by repetition to seem ordinary. They are not. Since these extraordinary phenomena are produced by the human mind, it follows that the human mind – yours and mine – is extraordinary in its capabilities.

Although my main purpose is to tell the story of hypnotism from a historical perspective, it will help to devote a preliminary chapter to laying some ghosts and building some bridges. There are two topics to cover: what people generally think of hypnotism, and what actually happens.

Popular Conceptions of Hypnotism from Fiction

Everybody has heard of Svengali. You can even look him up in a dictionary, since his name has entered the English language. My Chambers dictionary gives the following definition: 'A person who exerts total mental control over another, usually for evil ends.'

George du Maurier, the creator of Svengali, was actually a successful cartoonist for *Punch*. One day, late in the 1880s, he outlined to his friend, the American novelist Henry James, the plot of a story. James was impressed and told him he ought to write it down. 'But I can't write!' protested du Maurier, and offered the plot to his friend. Henry James refused, saying that it was too valuable a gift, and so it was left to du Maurier himself to tell the tale, which was published in 1894 as *Trilby*.

Trilby tells the story of Trilby O'Ferrall, a young artist's model in Paris. Three young English art students are in love with her, and she becomes engaged to one of them, William Bagot (who is nauseatingly called 'Little Billie' throughout the book). But their relationship breaks down and she falls into the clutches of Svengali, a Jew (Jews were often thought in Victorian times to have mesmeric powers), gaunt and grim, with a pointed beard and dark, staring eyes. Svengali, from Hungary, is a musician, and by the use of hypnotism he turns Trilby, who has a resonant speaking voice but is tone deaf, into an outstanding singer.

The book is not as melodramatic as the many film versions of it would have one believe, except in du Maurier's own illustrations. Nor is mesmerism as pervasive in the story as in the films. Svengali displays his hypnotic power early in the book by alleviating a neuralgic pain from which Trilby is suffering. A little later he tries to hypnotize her again, against her will, as a way of gaining control over her, because he wants to marry her, and is foiled only by the bluff Englishmen, who look after her and are deeply suspicious of Svengali. So when Svengali and Trilby reappear, later in the book, as a married couple, the great diva and her manager, we know he's been up to his tricks. In the middle of a triumphant tour of Europe, Svengali dies in the theatre, Trilby's gift fails her and she makes a laughing stock of herself; she can sing only when entranced and fixed by his eyes. After Svengali's death, her former life as an international star seems totally unreal, only vaguely remembered, if at all. She remembers only his kindness to her, not his bullying and physical violence. 'There were two Trilbys', as du Maurier puts it in the book – or, in psychological parlance, her hypnotized self was dissociated from her waking self.

Du Maurier's novel was a huge success on both sides of the Atlantic, selling over 200,000 copies in the first year alone. Trilby's songs from the book were sung by socialites at parties, and the book was soon turned into a stage play. But the plot is not as original as du Maurier might have pretended to Henry James. It's not just that a number of earlier novels had featured an evil, manipulative mesmerist or hypnotist. James Braid, the Scottish doctor who exploded the myth of magnetism and introduced hypnotism, wrote in 1850 of how he hypnotized a musically incompetent girl and took her through some of the most difficult exercises in the repertoire of Jenny Lind, the soprano, known as the 'Swedish Nightingale', who was conquering the world at the time. Moreover, in Alexandre Dumas's *Memoirs of a Physician*, first published in French in 1848, Joseph Balsamo mesmerizes Lorenza Feliciani, after saving her from rape, and marries her while she is under his spell. She, too, manifests two different personalities: in a trance she loves her husband and is grateful to him for rescuing her from the bandits; but when 'awake' she hates him and longs to be allowed to go to the convent where she was heading when she was set upon by the bandits.

But the success of *Trilby* has made Svengali the prototype, and the deepest spell cast by him has been over future fictional treatments of hypnosis, and hence over the minds of generations of audiences. Unwittingly, we have all taken in false beliefs, such as the two perpetuated by du Maurier, that a person can be kept in a permanent hypnotic trance and that we can be made by a hypnotist to do something we would not ordinarily do. The evil Medina in John Buchan's 1924 thriller *The Three Hostages* also keeps his victims in a permanent trance. Total dominance of will through hypnosis features prominently in numerous cheap thrillers, but also in more upmarket treatments. Cipolla, the deformed and boastful conjuror and stage hypnotist of Thomas Mann's *Mario and the Magician* (1930) likes to impose his will on members of the audience even to the extent of humiliating them. In Somerset Maugham's slightly ponderous tale *The Magician* (1908), the evil Haddo (a character based on Aleister Crowley, whom Maugham knew) hypnotizes Margaret in order to revenge himself upon her fiancé by taking her away from him. His will completely dominates hers, and the evil in him brings out the latent evil side of her nature. At one point in Peter Carey's excellent *Jack Maggs* (1997) the hypnotist's control over his subject's will is so total that the subject, implausibly, cries out: 'Let me wake up!'

The Russian monk Rasputin was evidently a larger-than-life

character, and over the years has become even more so in various
fictional treatments. In the 1966 *Rasputin, the Mad Monk* (a poor
movie salvaged only by Christopher Lee's efforts in the title role), he
gets women to stare into his eyes: 'Look deep into my eyes. Think
only of me. Listen and obey.' They are putty in his hands, to satisfy
his sexual appetite and his ambition. He even uses hypnosis to get a
woman with whom he has grown bored to commit suicide. To
many people's minds Rasputin, Svengali and even Dracula merge,
because of the similarity of their treatment on film: the camera pans
in on their piercing eyes – never better than in the original 1931
Dracula film, starring Bela Lugosi, or in the 1932 *Svengali* with John
Barrymore. But, at the risk of spoiling the fantasy, I'm sorry to have
to say that in actual fact Rasputin did not practise hypnotism. Not
only did he consistently deny that he did so, but in February 1914 –
that is, towards the end of his life (he was assassinated in December
1916), long after he had become famous for his healing powers – he
took lessons from a hypnotist called Gerasim Papandato, nick-
named the Musician, because he was afraid his powers were waning
and he wanted to supplement them by learning hypnotism. But
I doubt that future film-makers will let the truth stand in the way of
a good story.

   Fiction has steadily perpetuated the idea that women are more
liable to be entranced than men. The sexual undertones of this are
rarely brought out into the open (or are at least treated with some
delicacy, as in Maugham's *The Magician* or Henry James's 1874 short
story 'Professor Fargo'), but *The Power of Mesmerism: A Highly Erotic
Narrative of Voluptuous Facts* (1880) is a piece of anonymously written
Victorian pornography which goes all the way. The hero of the
book has learnt hypnotism at school, and throughout the book
uses it to seduce others, until the licentious side of their natures has
been awoken enough for hypnotism and convenient amnesia to
be unnecessary. Within a few pages he has had sex with his sister,
mother, father and school friends – often in threesomes and four-
somes. And so the wearisome book proceeds. Where films are
concerned, Barbra Streisand remarks at one point in *On a Clear Day
You Can See Forever* (1970) to her hypnotist (Yves Montand): 'That's
quite a weapon you've got there. I mean, you guys must have one
glorious night after another.'

The fascination of film directors with hypnotism is shown by the fact that as early as 1909 D.W. Griffith, who is best known for his slightly later masterpieces *The Birth of a Nation* and *Intolerance*, made a film called *The Criminal Hypnotist*. No copies of this movie exist, unfortunately. The earliest extant film in which hypnotism plays a major part is the 1919 *Das Cabinet des Dr Caligari*, directed by Robert Wiene. This atmospheric classic of expressionist cinema reflects both the main ideas of *Trilby* – the evil hypnotist and permanent entrancement.

Dr Caligari appears as a fairground huckster, offering to predict the future through his somnambulist, Cesare, who has reputedly been kept entranced for twenty-five years. But Caligari also uses Cesare to carry out murders. Things go badly wrong when Cesare fails to murder Jane Olsen, the girlfriend of the film's hero, Francis. Her beauty wakens him from his trance, and he soon drops dead. Caligari is chased by Francis back to the insane asylum of which he turns out to be the head doctor. Francis recruits the help of the other doctors; they search his office and find indisputable evidence that the doctor took control of a somnambulist patient, in order to try to repeat the experiments of a mad monk of the eleventh century called Caligari, who toured with a somnambulist called Cesare, and to test the theory that a somnambulist may be made to commit murder. The doctor is hauled off in a straitjacket to join the other patients. But there is a final twist: it turns out that Francis and Jane are actually inmates of the hospital. These are all the fantasies of a pair of paranoid patients!

Other fictional treatments are even more alarming or macabre. In 'A Tale of the Days to Come' (1927) H.G. Wells gave a fore-taste of the brainwashing scare of the 1950s, the ludicrous consequences of which will entertain us in a later chapter. Wells speculated that in the future the art of hypnotism will be able to change a person's character permanently (or at least until the change is reversed by the original hypnotist) by effacing or replacing a person's ideas and feelings, so that she has no memory at all of an element of her former life (in this case, the existence of a lover whom her father considers unsuitable, which is why he brought in the hypnotist).

In Conan Doyle's 1885 short story 'The Great Keinplatz Experiment' (later to be plundered by H.F. Heard for the plot of his

1944 novel *The Swap*) Professor von Baumgarten believes that the
phenomenon of clairvoyance proves that the mind can separate
from the body, and that it does so during hypnotism. He simultaneously hypnotizes his young assistant Fritz von Hartmann and
himself to see if in its disembodied state his spirit can see Fritz's
spirit. But the experiment goes ludicrously wrong when the two
minds reincarnate in the wrong bodies. The scary 1964 movie *Devil
Doll* takes this idea of transposing souls to a more bizarre level; the
story depends on a stage performer using hypnosis to steal a young
woman's soul and transfer it to the dummy he uses in his ventrilo-
quist act.

The possibilities hypnosis holds – in fiction, at any rate – for
baffling the authorities have often been exploited in fictional media.
For instance, in the 1972 film starring Robert Redford, *The Hot Rock*,
the employee of a bank is hypnotized to help a gang of thieves rob
the bank, the idea being that the bank employee would then forget
all about his involvement and appear genuinely innocent to the
police. For a similar reason, in the 1949 movie *Whirlpool*, directed
by Otto Preminger and starring Gene Tierney and José Ferrer, the
hypnotist (played by Ferrer) hypnotizes *himself* to commit a murder!
Or again, the virtual unassailability of the murderer in Michael
Connelly's tense 1996 thriller *The Poet* depends on his hypnotic
abilities. But as we will see later in this book, hypnosis would be at
best an erratic tool for criminals.

Another myth perpetuated by fictional treatments has been that
hypnotism involves or bestows supernatural powers. This is familiar
not just from *Das Cabinet des Dr Caligari* and from countless Dracula
movies, but more insidiously has appeared in children's fiction.
T.H. White's 1957 children's adventure story *The Master* is an example
of this. The Master has the ability to hypnotize people (male and
female, children and adults) and enter into telepathic communication with them while they are hypnotized; they can't communicate
in this way unless they are under his spell – the trance they are in
gives them their special powers.

In *On a Clear Day You Can See Forever*, Barbra Streisand sits in on
a psychology lecturer's demonstration of hypnotism, and is accidentally hypnotized herself, leading to comic consequences. Every time
she hears the word 'Wednesday', she takes off a shoe. Or again, in

the 1956 musical *The Court Jester*, Danny Kaye is hypnotized by a scheming courtier, and there is plenty of excellent comic play with the idea that a mere snap of the fingers can change him from his timid real personality to his daring hypnotized alter ego. Both these movies trade on another popular fallacy about hypnosis – that a trigger word (like 'Wednesday') or action (like a click of the fingers) seeded by a hypnotist will work whoever says it or does it. This is not so: only the hypnotist himself or a limited number of people he himself has specified could affect the subject's psyche in this way, and then only with her cooperation.

In analysing fiction like this I run the risk of spoiling the fun. 'It's fiction,' you say. 'Of course I don't take it seriously.' But that's where you're wrong. The lighter the book or film the lighter the conscious attention given to it – and these are precisely the circumstances in which ideas sneak in under our guard and become lodged in the mind as if they were the truth.

Stage Hypnotism

Another main source for popular conceptions and misconceptions of hypnotism has been the practice of stage hypnotists. There is a high degree of continuity between the performances of the earliest stage mesmerists and 'electro-biologists', and those of today. The techniques are similar, the phenomena more or less identical.

It is mostly from stage hypnotism, which is essentially a form of showmanship, that we get our image of the hypnotist as a flamboyant and authoritarian figure: 'You will go to sleep *now*! You are under my spell!' He will wave his arms around as if dealing with a quasi-physical electrical or magnetic substance; he will employ theatrical tests to check whether the punter has been hypnotized, such as the arm-levitation test, or the hand-clasp test, whereby the subject locks her hands together and is told that she cannot pull them apart. Then he will put his subjects through the most extraordinary (and sometimes demeaning) manoeuvres. Partial or total catalepsy, when a part of the body or the body as a whole is made rigid, is a popular choice. The most famous form of this is the trick known as the 'human plank', when a subject is put into catalepsy and suspended between two chairs, with his head resting on one chair and his ankles on the other. At this point the hypnotist's beautiful assistant, or a member of the audience, will be asked to stand on the rigid hypnotized person, or, even more dramatically, a piece of stone will be put on a cushion on the subject's stomach and then smashed with a sledge-hammer. Then he will make a couple of them carry on a conversation in Martian, or forget how to count to ten, or have a man nurse a baby.

Hallucination is another hypnotic phenomenon commonly exploited by stage hypnotists, so that a subject might be made to dance with a broom, thinking it is Marilyn Monroe. Anaesthesia is another, in which a subject is made to endure something that would otherwise be painful, even to the extent of sticking needles through her arm, burying her hand in icy water, or something like that. Anosmia – loss of the sense of smell – allows subjects to take a whiff of ammonia under the illusion that it is attar of roses. A skilful stage hypnotist will have several subjects up on stage at once, each performing a different act. Then he may well make use of post-hypnotic suggestion, telling the subject (or victim), for instance, that every time he hears a bell he will act like Elvis Presley.

Stage hypnotists have to do all this, because they are, first and foremost, entertainers. Even if they start with a gentle relaxation technique, they will move on to more flamboyant suggestions as soon as they can. The examples I've given are mostly fun, but there are also a good many shows which are designed to humiliate the subjects, especially in a sexual or lavatorial context. 'You have lost one of your breasts. As you walk back to your seat, you must look for it' – that kind of thing. But there is one secret of stage hypnotism that should be revealed: many of the subjects are not really hypnotized.

To the serious-minded student of hypnotism, who wishes to produce a hypnotic show for entertainment purposes, it is recommended that he forget all about trying to be a legitimate hypnotist . . . Experience has shown . . . that the hypnotic show must be faked, at least partially so, to hold audience interest and be successful as an entertainment.*

In his autobiography Mark Twain tells a story about a charlatan stage hypnotist who came to his home town when he was a child. Twain went night after night, and eventually summoned up the courage to go up on stage and be one of the hypnotist's subjects, in order to perform all kinds of bizarre and degrading acts. But he was not hypnotized, and he faked various performances, with the hypnotist at each stage crying out to the audience: 'Of course, I just told him to do that. He is under my spell!'

For obvious reasons, a stage hypnotist does not have time for a full hypnotic induction, which takes time and patience. This too gives a false idea to the audience – the idea of omnipotence: 'Look at that guy! All he has to do is touch them on the shoulder and they fall asleep!' This in turn leads to the fear that a stranger could hypnotize you all of a sudden in a train and take advantage of you in some way. If you see this kind of performance on TV, it is very likely that the induction has taken place beforehand, to save time and because it is illegal to show a hypnotic induction on TV (at any rate, in Britain), in case it works on people in their front rooms, and in case people all over the country start practising on their friends and relatives. 'Dad, you are finding that you want to increase my allowance,' says the teenage son!

A performer in a theatre or club, however, might employ a shortcut, such as pressing the carotid artery near the ear, which rapidly induces a pseudo-trance, more accurately described simply as dizziness, since it cuts off the blood supply to the brain. More commonly, he will have planted in the audience one or two 'horses' – associates who are either really good hypnotic subjects or good actors. When the hypnotist invites members of the audience up on stage, these horses will go up first. The hypnotist will either hypnotize them, or pretend to; in either case, once he has found out by some simple tests who among the others are suggestible, he will keep them on stage and dismiss the rest, because the suggestible ones will happily imitate the horses. They may be hypnotized, or

* Sources for quotations can be found on pages 426–31.

they may believe themselves to be hypnotized, but in any case, being self-selected, they are happy to go along with the show, for fun. Even the 'human plank' trick can be carried out by anyone, I'm told – though perhaps not for quite as long as a hypnotized subject might do it.

In other words, the conditions for a successful stage act are as follows. First, those who go up on to the stage are already prepared to listen to the hypnotist. Second, a simple test eliminates those who are not readily susceptible. Third, nervous expectation heightens suggestibility. Fourth, advance publicity has stressed the hypnotist's powers and made people more inclined to be hypnotized by him. Fifth, seeing one person go under increases the chances that the next will and so on by the domino effect. Sixth, there may well be an element of peer pressure, if one has friends in the audience.

If you're in the audience watching a stage hypnotist at work, you might well suppose that his subjects, who are more or less making fools of themselves, are completely unconscious of what they are doing. This is not so, and it introduces us to a recurrent theme of this book: you cannot compel someone, under hypnosis, to do what she would not otherwise have done. You can lower a person's inhibitions or (to say the same thing from another angle) bring out her latent talents, but that is all, and the reason is that there is a part of you, including your conscience, that remains alert. If someone is prepared to make a fool of himself, he is just saying to himself: 'It's just for a laugh. I'll go along with it.' If he is asked to do something too preposterous or humiliating, he will find a way to refuse.

The American psychologist George Estabrooks tells an odd story:

> A stage operator was demonstrating in the local theater. One of the audience, a dignified member of the community and a deacon in his church, turned out to be a very good subject. The hypnotist had him stand on his head, bark around the stage on all fours, take off a goodly portion of his clothes and give, in general, a very humiliating exhibition. He then awakened his subject who just as promptly knocked him down.

In order for this to happen, the subject would have to be very easily hypnotizable. In a light trance, you are still wholly conscious, and so cannot be made to do things you would rather not do. In a deep trance, you are more open to the suggestions of the hypnotist, but a part of you is still alert, as is shown by the fact that the deacon in this story knew what was going on. In all probability, the good deacon could have resisted, and would have done if asked to do something totally outrageous, but went along with the suggestions for a laugh, only to feel so embarrassed afterwards that he released his tension by lashing out.

In a later chapter I will touch on the question whether there is any danger, apart from embarrassment, in stage hypnotism. For now my point has been to show that we get some false ideas about hypnosis from these shows. Nevertheless, these shows are not unimportant. Historically, at times when hypnosis has been out of favour in medical or academic circles, stage performers have kept the art alive and the public interested. And the public is interested. If you see a good performer at work, it is amazing, and it helps to show that there is more to the human mind than is apparent.

Hypnotism and Christianity

I need to devote a section to this topic here, in the first chapter, because many people, whether they have simply been brought up in a nominally Christian society, or are practising Christians, believe that their Church condemns hypnotism as morally reprehensible or even spiritually dangerous. Other religions, such as Judaism, have nothing to say about it, but there has been some condemnation from the ranks of Christianity. It was not always so. In the last century, when it was believed that the ecstatic feats of mesmerized clairvoyants proved the existence of the soul and of higher realms, many people rediscovered their Christian roots as a result. In the pages of fiction, this is exactly what happened to Dr Minoret in Honoré de Balzac's *Ursule Mirouet* (1842). Balzac, who practised magnetism himself, evidently did not feel that hypnotism and Christianity were incompatible – and if he was right in supposing that hypnotism reveals the objective existence of transcendent realms, then of course they are not incompatible.

Still, even in the nineteenth century, there were those who were concerned. The Papal States in Italy held out against hypnosis longer than most countries, and it became such a fad that worried Catholic clergymen from all over Europe wrote to the Vatican asking for guidance. In 1856 Cardinal Vincenzo Macchi responded: 'The ordinary of each diocese must do his utmost to avert the abuses of magnetism, and to bring them to an end, so that the Lord's flock may be preserved from the attacks of the enemy, that the faith may be maintained in its integrity, and that the faithful committed to their care may be saved from the corruption of morals.' By 'abuses' he meant that magnetism, a purely physical phenomenon (or so the Vatican assumed), should not be used as an explanation for things that are supernatural. In other words, magnetism was fine as long as it was used as a therapy, but employing it to produce paranormal phenomena was a sin. This has remained the Vatican's position, and was reiterated by Pope Pius XII in 1956, who suggested that hypnotism should be regarded the same way a Catholic regards medicine.

In reality, the various Churches have always tolerated a division of opinion over hypnosis (except for Christian Scientists, who unanimously condemn it). At the same time that some clerics were condemning it as satanic in the nineteenth century, others were busy practising it. A group of Catholic theologians in Germany at the start of the nineteenth century held out great hopes for the combination by priests of pastoral care and mesmerism. Samuel Wilberforce, Bishop of Oxford and later of Winchester in the latter half of the century, immersed himself in the subject and could find nothing irreligious in it. In fact, he held that its very power meant that Christians should study and practise it, in case it fell into the hands of unbelievers. Since its healing powers seemed almost miraculous, even a physical healing was heralded by some priests who practised mesmerism as a spiritual event, which would help their parishioners, not condemn them to hell. The hierarchical aspect of mesmerism – the apparent imposition of one will on another – suddenly took on a spiritual dimension, as priests in mesmerizing members of their congregation claimed to be vehicles for God's will, and to be doing no more than Jesus and a number of others had done in healing the sick. But other clerics and religious philosophers only found a reason to try to distinguish mesmerism from miracles.

Many from the fundamentalist and evangelical churches claim, in a most misinformed way, that hypnotism opens you up to the devil. It is not a new accusation. At the beginning of the nineteenth century the case was put stridently by the Abbé Wendel-Würtz, and in the middle of the century in Britain the charge of satanism from a Liverpool preacher called Hugh McNeile provoked a famous response from James Braid. Most of their arguments do not deserve the name, but are sheer rant. But if I had to guess where they're coming from, I'd point to the fact that traditional Christian practice would involve going as far as one can on one's own conscious resources, and then handing over in silence to God. But hypnotism can take one further than one's own conscious resources, and therefore seems to oust God. This is not a problem with hypnotism alone, but with psychology in general, ever since the discovery of the unconscious and methods of tapping into it – and indeed there are elements in the Christian Churches who are suspicious of psychology too.

The idea that someone who is hypnotized has been taken over by the devil seems to me so irrational that I will not even dignify it with commentary, except to point out that interpretation of trance states has always been subjective. The dancing frenzy – St Vitus's Dance – which gripped the Low Countries and northern Italy in the fifteenth century was attributed to diabolic possession (or, in Italy, to the bite of the tarantula), despite the obvious good it did to relieve the poor of their misery. On the other hand, Shaker trances were taken to be a sign of possession by God.

Later in the nineteenth century hypnotism was closely bound up with spiritism and other occult practices, and this might raise Christian doubts about hypnosis. But (assuming for the moment that occultism is evil) if occultists made use of hypnosis, that no more makes hypnosis bad than an evil use of a car, to injure someone, makes cars bad.

As usual, most of the objections to hypnosis stem from a combination of ignorance and outmoded views. For instance, you hear the argument that you should submit your will only to Christ, since any other influence might be diabolic. But hypnosis does not involve abandoning your will or self-control. In fact, many people talk about hypnosis giving them back control of their lives, if it has helped cure them of an addiction. Modern hypnotherapy is consensual, not authoritarian, and it is not the hypnotist's purpose to rob her patient of his will power, but to channel his will power towards the therapy. In any case, this is a most unrealistic or idealistic objection. Of course it is true that a Christian has surrendered her will to God or Jesus, but that does not mean that she does not surrender her will on plenty of other occasions to others too. If she refuses to surrender her will to a dentist or a doctor, she is going down the route of Christian Science; she should never watch TV, in case she is influenced by an advertisement, or read anything but the Bible and so on and so forth. Christians do not go through their days in a state of complete submission to God; they go through their days just like everyone else, but with a background awareness, occasionally fanned into stronger life, of God's presence. On a daily basis, then, they are just as liable to external influences as the rest of us. No one's life is as monolithic as this objection presumes.

If some Christians or religious people of any persuasion are worried about hypnotism simply because it may entail the planting of suggestions, they are on very weak ground. All of us, all of the time, are being bombarded by suggestions, and mass meetings such as church services are one of the most potent methods of implanting and reinforcing suggestions. The only element of genuine concern is that (unless the visit to the therapist is prompted by something purely physiological) values are likely to play an implicit part, and a New Age therapist may be assuming a set of values some of which clash with Christian values. In that case, the patient has two alternatives: she can either accept the therapy without taking on board the values (after all, she will be conscious throughout the process), just as she can enjoy a movie without accepting its values; or she can find a Christian hypnotherapist, and there are plenty of them, since far from all Christians are as narrow-minded as those who find hypnotherapy objectionable.

The fear of being in a suggestible state can be combined with the simple human fear of being in a state about which little or nothing will be remembered afterwards. But spontaneous amnesia in hypnosis is very rare; most commonly a hypnotherapist will give you the choice to remember as much or as little as you want, or can handle, to help the healing process.

I hope that after reading this book Christians will see that there is nothing to fear in hypnotism, and that its healing properties make it a practice it would be unwise to deny to sufferers.

The Hypnotist

If flamboyance and authoritarianism are no longer in vogue (except in fiction), what are the basic techniques of modern hypnosis? They vary somewhat from therapist to therapist and practitioner to practitioner, but share the common feature of bearing little resemblance to the fictional and stage methods we've been looking at. This is also the place to mention that hypnotism has been accepted as a valid therapeutic technique by both the British Medical Association (in 1955) and the American Medical Association (in 1958).

Look them up in the *Yellow Pages* or on the Web; visit a New Age fair; contact one of the umbrella organizations of hypnotherapists. There are a lot of hypnotists around. He may be your doctor or dentist, who finds hypnosis a useful alternative to drugs, or uses it to extend his 'bedside manner' to get a patient to relax. He may be a specialist hypnotherapist, with initials after his name signifying that he has been awarded a certificate by (in America) the American Society of Clinical Hypnosis, or (in Britain) the London College of Clinical Hypnosis or the British Hypnotherapy Association. There are plenty of other such bodies – perhaps it is time for some unification. But you should certainly look into the hypnotist's credentials, make sure that he or she is affiliated to some such organization, and even check out the organization itself. Hypnotic treatment is likely to be pretty expensive, so you should take these precautions before committing yourself.

The hypnotist is unlikely to have an intense, staring gaze, or to be wearing a star-spangled cloak. Nevertheless, the respect in which fact and fiction come closest – though not really very close at all – is in the person of the hypnotist. By this I mean that some of the traits of the fictional or stage hypnotist are exaggerations of the real-life person. As explained in the Introduction, there is bound to be inequality of will between the hypnotist and his client, in the sense that you are to a degree putting yourself in his hands. Now, you are going to put yourself in his hands only if you trust that he is going to do you good, and you will feel this trust only if he exudes an aura of confidence. In other words, while he is unlikely to have a domineering personality, he will have enough self-assurance to put you at your ease, just as any expert in any field must. But it will be the self-assurance of someone you can trust to act as your guide, not of someone who will attempt to dominate you.

Confidence, then, is one essential quality of a successful hypnotist. Another is patience, because it may take some time to put a subject under. He will also have created a comfortable and comforting environment, designed to put his clients at their ease, with muted colours, few sharp edges, no bright lights. He might also, without the client's knowledge, use artificial means to make the client feel at home. One common such technique is mirroring, in which the therapist adopts the same posture, breathing, tone of voice and so on as his client, or in general uses body language, to make him feel that the hypnotist is someone just like him, someone he can trust. Recent studies have shown that body language and tone of voice are far more important than the actual content of speech in establishing a connection between people. One way or another, without making a fuss about it, the hypnotist will throughout the session be intently focused on you, the client, and sensitive to the slightest gesture or twitch which might indicate resistance or the opposite, and give him further clues as to what is going on.

A hypnotist uses suggestions, and this is a word which will recur countless times in this book. The subject responds to the hypnotist's suggestions, but that does not mean that he is suggestible in the sense of 'gullible', nor does the fact that psychologists rate our 'hypnotizability' (as they call it) on scales of 'susceptibility' bear any such implication. There are basically three kinds of suggestion that the hypnotist might make: suggestions designed to induce hypnosis ('Your eyelids are feeling heavy'), suggestions during hypnosis to be acted on immediately ('You will hear no sound except the sound of my voice') and suggestions during hypnosis to be acted on later ('After you wake up, you will no longer feel any craving for a cigarette'). These last suggestions are called 'post-hypnotic suggestions'. They are not, as the term might imply, suggestions given after the hypnotic session, but suggestions given during the session which take effect after the session is over.

Techniques of Induction

In his autobiographical *Moab is My Washpot* comedian Stephen Fry recounts how he visited a hypnotist to get him over his fear of singing in public.

> The business of being put in a trance seemed childishly simple and disappointingly banal. No pocket watches were swung before me, no mood music or whale song played in the background, no mesmeric eyes bored into my soul. I was simply told to put my hands on my knees and to feel the palms melt down into the flesh of the knees. After a short time it became impossible to feel what was hand and what was knee, while miles away in the distance rich, sonorous Hungarian tones told me how pleasantly relaxed I was beginning to feel and how leaden and heavy my eyelids had become. It was a little like being lowered down a well, with the hypnotist's voice as the rope that kept me from any feeling of abandonment or panic.

Or here is Whitley Strieber's account:

> The process of becoming hypnotized was pleasant. I sat in a comfortable chair. Dr Klein stood before me and asked me to look up at his finger, which was placed so that I had almost to roll my eyes into my head to see it. He moved it from side to side and suggested that I relax. No more than half a minute later, it seemed, I was unable to hold my eyes open. Then he began saying that my eyelids were getting heavy, and

they did indeed get heavy. The next thing I knew, my eyes were closed. At that point I felt relaxed and calm, but not asleep. I was aware of my surroundings. I could feel my face growing slack, and soon Dr Klein began to say that my right hand was becoming warm. It got warm, and then he progressed to my arm, and then my whole body. I was now sitting, totally comfortable, encased in warmth. I still felt as if I had a will of my own, a sensation that was never to leave me.

This well highlights the essential difference between real life and fiction. Modern hypnotism is consensual and permissive, gentle rather than authoritarian. All hypnotism must be consensual to a degree: you cannot be hypnotized unless you want to. In fact, it is arguable that the hypnotist's role is not to *do* anything as such, but just to facilitate your own spontaneous entry into a trance state. All hypnosis may be self-hypnosis. A light trance is perfectly sufficient for most therapeutic purposes, so that you will easily remain aware of what is going on. It is all rather relaxing and comfortable, like falling asleep in a warm bed as a child.

There are phases to the induction. First, the therapist will put the client at his ease and allay his doubts and suspicions, by discussing what he wants and expects to get out of the treatment, by explaining what is involved in hypnosis (especially if the client has expectations based on TV and fiction), and generally by establishing rapport with the client. Then he will ask the subject to be quiet and to focus on his voice. This is an important part of the induction procedure: as the famous Russian psychologist Ivan Petrovich Pavlov (1849–1936) found, the exploratory apparatus of animals, including humans, is essential to maintaining a state of general alertness and to orienting oneself within reality. So the hypnotist must close down our exploratory apparatus somehow, in order to reduce our alertness. Since the eye is the basic human exploratory apparatus, eye-closure is generally the first milestone in the induction of hypnosis. At the same time the hypnotist is ensuring that the input received by eye and ear is monotonous, because if we know what is going to happen next – if the input is boring enough to be predictable – that relaxes us, in the sense that we feel no sense of expectation, and our sensory sentinels can doze. The hypnotist may also get the client progressively to relax his whole body, starting with his toes and ending with the head. He may arouse the client out of his light trance and get him to talk about it, inspiring confidence, before repeating the procedure.

At some point the hypnotist will apply one or more tests to check whether the client is hypnotized; the most common tests used are the eye-closure test, hand-clasp test, postural-sway test and hand-levitation test. These are perfectly straightforward: in the hand-levitation test, for instance, the hypnotist suggests to the subject that his hand is so light that it floats up into the air. If the subject's hand does then float up into the air, the hypnotist knows that the subject is hypnotized. For the subject, it is a peculiar feeling, I can assure you. You know what is going on, but somehow can't be bothered to stop your hand rising up off your knee, though you know you could if you tried. The postural-sway test is a little more dramatic. The client is instructed to stand up and make herself rigid, like a board. The hypnotist pushes her gently from behind, making her sway, and then tells her that when his hand is removed she will find herself being drawn backwards. So he pushes her and withdraws his hand – and she finds herself rocking backwards on to the hypnotist's waiting hands. These tests are likely to be employed as much as anything to convince the client that something is going on, but in fact a skilful therapist already knows how susceptible any given client is likely to be, and in any case has enlisted the client's support, which is the single most important factor in susceptibility.

Some hypnotists prefer to use a device, rather than just the relaxing effect of their voice. The subject might be asked to stare fixedly at a bright object, and after a while the therapist will suggest that the patient is feeling sleepy. Whatever the induction technique, the therapist will then use suggestive procedures to deepen the trance. A common method is to get the client to visualize a set of stairs leading downwards ... downwards ... deeper and deeper. This will be repeated as often as is necessary during the process, if the trance seems to be getting shallower. Techniques seem all to be equally effective, so it depends on which ones the hypnotist and the client feel comfortable with. Further tests might be employed to check that the client is still entranced. For instance, the hypnotist might suggest that there is a mosquito in the room and the client will report (at the time and after the session) that he heard its whine.

There is no difficulty waking someone up from a trance; on the contrary, the usual difficulty is keeping him in a trance. The hypnotist will probably simply suggest that the client 'Wake up now', or he may reverse one of the procedures: 'You are climbing back up the stairs you went down earlier. When you reach the top stair you will wake up.' One common waking-up instruction has the hypnotist counting backwards from five to one, at which point the subject wakes up, ready to implement whatever suggestions he and the hypnotist have agreed on during the session.

Even if you are left alone, you will still come round from the hypnotic state. You will either fall into natural sleep, or wake up, and whichever of these happens is unlikely to take long. In a classic experiment psychologists Martin Orne and Frederick Evans hypnotized one batch of subjects but had others simulate hypnosis; the hypnotist left the room on some pretext; before long all the hypnotized subjects had come around, but those who were just pretending stuck it out for the whole half hour of the hypnotist's absence, because that is what they thought a hypnotized person would do.

At the end of the session, the hypnotist will talk his client through the procedure, and is likely to give him an exercise in self-hypnosis to do at home to reinforce the beneficial effects of the session. This might be as simple as: 'Every time you feel a craving for a cigarette, close your eyes, count to ten, and picture yourself jingling the extra money you have in your pocket as a result of not smoking.'

Methods of Treatment

There are treatments without end, and I'll just be scraping the surface here. There's more in Chapter 11. The method of treatment is likely to depend on the school to which the therapist belongs and the problem the client wants to solve. But nowadays most hypnotherapists are empirically trained rather than school trained, and so he is likely to use a range of treatments, culled basically from a Freudian or a behaviourist quiver. Freudian or psychodynamic methods are good for allowing the origin of problems to be brought to the surface, examined and explained, so that the undesirable effect can be made harmless. Behaviour-modification techniques are good for breaking ingrained habit patterns which contribute to problems. Then at the end of the treatment the therapist might suggest some reinforcing method, such as self-hypnosis or visualizations, with or without affirmations and positive thinking. Ideally each case will be judged on its own merits, and treatments tailored to the client's particular nature and needs, rather than the therapist's being so committed to a school that she cannot use techniques outside of that school.

Regression is a common technique, and has featured in films such as the 1946 Oscar-winning *The Seventh Veil*. In regression the therapist takes you back to your childhood, to uncover the origins of some syndrome or problem that you have. What caused that fear of spiders? Why did you originally start to stammer? In regression you can see the start of the problem, and begin to untie the knot.

I like the Freudian anagram technique: the hypnotized patient is told to imagine a box containing all the letters of the alphabet. She takes a handful of the letters, throws them into the air and watches them land. Those that land face up will form a word (so the therapist instructs) which will be related to the patient's problem. There are similar techniques, such as being taken through a symbolic journey, in which the things you encounter – a gate, an animal – are symbols with mental and emotional values. These are all ways for the therapist and client to see what is going on deep in the unconscious, so that measures can be taken to deal with whatever the problem may be. Sometimes being brought face to face with the roots of a problem can cause what is known as 'abreaction' – a cathartic, emotional reaction such as weeping. If such a thing occurs, the therapist will gently guide the patient through it, and show her why it happened.

Behaviourist measures can seem quite drastic. In order to deal with a phobia, the therapist will take advantage of the ability of a hypnotized subject to visualize things vividly. Suppose you have a fear of spiders: you will gradually be brought to the point, over a series of images, to where you can cope with spiders crawling on your stomach, perhaps. Or aversion is a technique whereby you are trained to associate a habit like smoking with something unpleasant, until you are put off smoking. These are techniques for 'reframing' – locating something that was perceived as a problem inside a new frame of reference, one in which it is no longer a problem, or at least less of one. As the old saying goes, an optimist perceives as half full a glass which a pessimist perceives as half empty: they have different frames. Since there is a connection between thinking and emotion, and between emotion, breathing and bodily posture, working on any of these can help to bring about the required change. Some therapists literally displace the problem. Milton Erickson once got a woman who was scared of flying to imagine a plane trip on which there was plenty of air turbulence, and to let her fear slide out of her and on to her seat. She had shed it; it was no longer part of her.

Although the patient appears to be will-less, letting the therapist stand in for his will, I would rather say that the patient is distracting his will, akin to the Zen practice of acting through non-action. If you confront a problem head-on, you treat it like an adversary, which gives it power, and makes it harder to get rid of. But if you sideline the problem, or treat it in an avuncular fashion, as the manifestation of the spoiled child within you, so to speak, its hold over you is lessened. This is passivity, but not will-less passivity. Having said that, however, it is likely that direct, authoritarian approaches will work better in cases where the patient has chosen to come to the therapist, for treatment for addiction, perhaps, while indirect, permissive, reframing techniques will work better for more deep-rooted psychological problems. The former approach is for the hypnotist to implant the direct suggestion: 'You will find that your craving for cigarettes has gone.' On the latter approach, the hypnotist might seed in the subject's mind ideas and pictures which represent how much healthier and wealthier he will be if he quits smoking.

Once the subject is hypnotized, suggestions will be seeded. Suggestions can be of various kinds, especially either direct or indirect. Let's say that you have gone to the therapist because you want to quit smoking. Then, as an example of direct suggestion, the hypnotist may say: 'When you wake up you will find that you no longer want to smoke.' Indirect suggestions are more subtle. The therapist might say something like: 'I wonder how good you're going to feel about not smoking tomorrow?' On the face of it, this is an innocuous question, but by lightly emphasizing the words *'how good you're going to feel'* the suggestion is implanted in you that you will feel good if you quit smoking.

Like all therapists, a hypnotherapist needs to get feedback from his patients. Like all therapists who are dealing to any extent with the mind, they find it hard to get reliable information from their patients. In the very nature of the unconscious, the material is not readily available to the patient, so how can she communicate it to the therapist? In the 1930s the famous hypnotist Leslie LeCron developed a technique called 'ideomotor signalling' that has come to be very widely used. The patient rests his hands on his thighs. He is asked to designate specific uses for the four fingers of his dominant hand. The reason he is asked to make the choice is that it is vital to have his agreement. So, one finger is for saying 'yes', another for saying 'no', a third for saying 'I don't know', and a fourth for saying 'That's none of your business' – or at any rate: 'I don't want to answer that right now.'

Now LeCron found – and his findings have been confirmed by countless hypnotists since – that these fingers could act independently of the conscious mind. Consciously, a subject might answer 'yes' to a question, while his 'no' finger rises of its own accord into the air. And so this is a way for hypnotherapists to tap into the unconscious of their patients. It has even been used to evoke responses from patients in a coma. If this sounds freaky, and reminiscent of automatic writing, that is quite right. Hypnotists – sober academics in prestigious universities – regularly use automatic writing in their experiments. This doesn't mean they claim to contact the dear departed and transcribe spirit messages, but they make use of a kind of extension of ideomotor signalling. They get their subjects to express in writing what's going on below the threshold of consciousness.

The Hypnotic Trance and What it Feels Like

Over the last couple of centuries, various theorists have been quite sure that there are seven – or nine, or four, or whatever – phases of trance. In actual fact, things are rather more fluid, and it is hard to discern the border between one phase and another, but there are tests that can be applied to determine depth of trance. The depth to which the client is hypnotized depends partly on his or her susceptibility, and partly on the skill of the hypnotist, but more on the particular therapy involved. For treating nicotine addiction, for instance, no more than a light or medium trance is necessary; for performing surgery, hopefully something deeper will be achieved!

For practical purposes, hypnotists may outline five stages of increasing depth of trance: the hypnoidal state, light trance, medium trance, deep trance, somnambulistic state. The term 'somnambulism' is a hangover from the late eighteenth and early nineteenth century, and since it means 'sleepwalking' it is inaccurate, but it has been perpetuated in the literature on hypnosis. 'Sleep-waking', a term which also has a long history, might be a better alternative. Since a regular hypnotic subject soon develops shortcuts to reach the full hypnotic state, the different stages of deep hypnosis are easiest to observe in a novice subject. If you've been hypnotized yourself, you may have noticed different phases in yourself. A light trance feels like being relaxed, but in a deeper trance, impressions are fresher, imagery is more vivid and so on.

What's happening, as the trance deepens, is that our generalized reality orientation is fading. Every situation every one of us encounters at any second of the day is actually unique. There has never been exactly this time before; even your front door has never been in exactly this light before. One of the main reasons that childhood is a time of wonder is that children are constantly meeting events they have never seen before, which strike them afresh. As we get older and our egos become the focal point of our lives, we assimilate new situations with old ones, accepting second best. Each of us develops a frame of reference, a world view, which we use to assess events and experiences. Those which don't fit in are often rejected, while the rest are slotted into a preformed category. Psychologists call this our 'generalized reality orientation' or GRO. It's not a bad thing: it enables us, for instance, to recognize that a movie is not real life, because we have a context in which we know that the movie is just a movie. One of the main things that happens in hypnosis is that our GRO fades in favour of a special, temporary orientation. The more the GRO fades the deeper the trance. The fading of the GRO involves a reduction in our critical faculties, so that things like fragmentary memories which might not normally impinge on our minds are accepted. That, to continue with the example of memories, is how recall can be enhanced by hypnosis. More generally, it is how we become more open to the suggestions the hypnotist puts to us.

Since the GRO is our filtering and editing mechanism, as the trance deepens and the GRO fades you get more in touch with unconscious regions of the mind. The unconscious is the basement of the mind. Far from everything down there is bad, but there are dusty corners where odd and potentially dangerous things lurk, all one's primitive impulses and desires. Everything we do not want to face about ourselves and the world has been shoved into one such corner. Every memory that we have is stored somewhere, capable of reconstruction. Everything of which we are not immediately conscious is by definition in an unconscious part of the mind. The conscious mind is characterized by everything that is immediately accessible; its relation to the unconscious mind is somewhat like a person taking a torch down into the cellar: we can use our consciousness to illuminate, or gain access to, areas of the unconscious mind. But the point is that the unconscious is taking in, storing and processing information on its own, even when it is not illuminated by consciousness. One scientist has put it like this: 'The Unconscious is not unconscious, only the Conscious is unconscious of what the Unconscious is conscious of.' Hypnosis is a good way of bringing into consciousness material from unconscious regions, and so facing and reframing such material.

I'm not a very good hypnotic subject myself, but I can fairly easily go into a light trance, and in that state one of the primary subjective impressions is a peculiarly ambiguous feeling. On the one hand, you are certain that if you chose to you would not go along with the hypnotist's suggestions, and you can easily see through his ways of getting you to do something; on the other hand you think to yourself: 'I might as well go along with it for the sake of the experiment.' So the feeling is 'Shall I or shan't I?', and this feeling persists throughout. Clever therapists use this state of slight confusion, which we could call 'parallel awareness', to seed powerful therapeutic ideas into the subconscious, while the conscious is preoccupied with the confusion. In a different context – he was at a spiritist séance – the Irish poet W.B. Yeats described the feeling perfectly. He found that his hands and shoulders were twitching: 'I could easily have stopped them,' he later wrote, 'but I had never heard of such a thing and was curious.'

From the outside, the behaviour of a hypnotized person may be no different from that of a person in a normal state. From the inside, though, interesting things are going on. The most usual feelings are: relaxation; diminished awareness of outer events and increased immersion in an inner world; a general feeling that one's psychic processes have somehow been extended, despite a narrowing of focus; boredom (a decrease in associative activity), leading to increased vividness or forcefulness or interest of certain systems of ideas, particularly those introduced by the hypnotist; relative immobilization and fixation on a single sensory experience (e.g. the rhythm of the hypnotist's voice, which may become depersonalized from the hypnotist herself); time-distortion and partial amnesia, so that a half hour passes like five seconds; a dream-like effortless flux of experience; a dream-like illogicality ('trance logic'), so that anomalous situations are taken for granted. If you were to ask someone in a deep trance what she was thinking, she might well answer: 'Nothing.' In fact, she is listening, waiting for the next suggestion from the hypnotist.

Who Can Be Hypnotized?

The American hypnotherapist Milton Erickson used to say that if someone was not hypnotized, that was a failure of the hypnotist, because everyone is susceptible. Who can resist the infectious enthusiasm of a crowd? Who is not stirred by martial music? Try watching a gripping thriller on TV and not tensing up and sitting on the edge of your seat. We like to conform and to be accepted by others. We don't like internal or external conflict. All these are pressures that make us suggestible. Hypnosis is defined by some as a state of heightened suggestibility. Even if this is inadequate as a full definition, it is certainly true that heightened suggestibility is a vital component. Since we are all suggestible, we are all susceptible to hypnosis.

But we are not all susceptible to the same degree. In the Introduction, I said that there were three key components of hypnosis: absorption (or focal attention), dissociation and suggestibility. 'Highs' – highly hypnotizable people – are simply those who are good at all three of these things. The first faculty, the ability to be absorbed or imaginatively involved in tasks, is interesting. It means – and this is important – that hypnotizable people are those who are good at deploying their attention. We can all be put into a light trance, but in about 10 per cent of cases it would take so many repeated attempts to do so that it is just not worth the effort, and so we can say that for all practical purposes about 10 per cent of the population are unhypnotizable. About 30 per cent can readily enter a light trance; about 35 per cent can go into a medium trance; and about 25 per cent can go into a deep trance (though others place this figure as low as 5 per cent).

Academics make use of 'susceptibility scales', multi-question tests to assess hypnotizability by both objective and subjective standards. I know of eighteen of these scales (the Stanford Hypnotic Susceptibility Scale, the Harvard Group Scale of Hypnotic Susceptibility, etc.), and I don't propose to weigh up their pros and cons, except to say that one of their chief benefits is that they have given some stability to psychological experiments on hypnosis. You can make up groups of subjects who score the same on the same scale of measurement, prepare control groups of 'highs' or 'lows' and so on.

If a hypnotist insists on using just a single technique, he will sometimes fail, because not everyone is susceptible to the same technique. He has to be flexible. Even reluctant patients, with whom all other procedures have failed, may be put under by a confusional technique, in which, for example, a lot of suggestions are given in rapid succession about different parts of the body feeling light or heavy. I will briefly look at other ways of overcoming resistance in a later chapter, when I talk about the work of Milton Erickson, because this was one of his special gifts.

It is often said that children between the ages of seven and fourteen are more susceptible to hypnotism than adults, with a peak at around nine or ten years of age. There may also be some truth in the modern perception that fantasy-prone individuals, those who are capable of losing themselves in a book or a film or a private fantasy, and who played highly imaginative games when they were children, are more susceptible than the rest. Hypnosis involves dissociation, and fantasy-prone people find it easier than the rest to dissociate, to separate off a part of themselves into imaginary zones, while the outside world becomes less real.

There does seem to be good anecdotal evidence that it is hard to hypnotize people who are insane. The more a subject can concentrate on a single sensory input, such as the hypnotist's voice, without getting distracted, the easier the induction of hypnosis will be. This perhaps explains why crazy people are hard to hypnotize. But don't worry: if you aren't a good hypnotic subject, that doesn't mean you're crazy!

Hypnosis is not a single phenomenon; it may well be a combination of a number of things, including the ability to fantasize and play roles, that makes a person more susceptible. If it has this complex nature, it would be foolish to look for simple correlates between susceptibility and personality types. In Victorian times, people were convinced that women were easier to hypnotize than men. Recent tests have not confirmed this finding; it was due to nineteenth-century prejudice about women being the weaker sex, along with the notion that hypnosis involves the dominance of will.

Contrary to the popular view that you have to be stupid to be hypnotized, there is evidence that hypnotizability is correlated with intelligence, or at least with the ability to concentrate. But the idea is put to great comic effect in the 1949 film *Abbot and Costello Meet the Killer, Boris Karloff*. Costello is suspected of murdering people in the hotel where he works as a bellhop. Karloff, a mystic, tries to hypnotize him, but Costello is just too stupid to be hypnotized. Self-esteem is actually a more important variable than intelligence: those with a low self-esteem are going to be harder to hypnotize, presumably because they are either more apprehensive, or less curious about exploring themselves and less willing to be treated.

On the whole, then, it has turned out to be hard for psychologists, try as they might, to correlate susceptibility with personality types. It used to be thought that hypnotizable people are more in touch with their right brain than the rest of us. Briefly (except for left-handed people), the right side of the brain governs the left side of the body, and spatial and holistic functions, while the left side governs the right side of the body, and verbal, logical, linear thinking. We draw actively on the left side, but have to surrender, as it were, to the right side. One might expect an artist to rely more on the right side of the brain, and a university professor on the left. For most of us, the left side is dominant. Some recent experiments on people who are good hypnotic subjects have indicated that they are significantly better at right-brain tasks than non-hypnotized people.

However, more is going on in the brain during hypnosis apart from the shift to the non-dominant hemisphere. This shift does not seem to occur in all cases, but more in those who are highly hypnotizable. Moreover, the dominant hemisphere is also activated during hypnosis: which hemisphere is activated depends probably on the kind of task the hypnotized person is being set. This suggests that hemisphere-shifting may not be an explanation in itself, but part of the general capacity of highly hypnotizable people to shift from one state to another – to dissociate. Work is still in progress on the relations between brain activity and hypnosis. For instance, early research seemed to suggest that hypnotizable subjects were those who could easily enter the alpha state. Brainwaves in the alpha spectrum (8–13 Hz) are 'the noise the brain makes when it is alert but doing little' – for instance, when someone is awake but has her eyes closed. But now it seems that the slower theta rhythm (4–7 Hz), associated with a deeper level of drowsiness, is more typical of hypnotizable subjects and perhaps of hypnosis in general.

Experimental findings have suggested that people can get better at being hypnotized, as if it were a skill that could be learnt. But in the experience of working hypnotherapists this is due to the overcoming of initial resistance. It is not so much that their patients learn a task as that they become less fearful and suspicious of the therapist and his practice. Another view – a powerful and interesting theory – suggests that we are all easier to hypnotize when our natural bodily rhythms are in relaxing mode.

Is it possible to resist hypnotism, perhaps as Kim did in Rudyard Kipling's novel, published in 1901, by reciting multiplication tables to himself to keep his mind off the hallucination he was being asked to see? Of course it is. You have to want to be hypnotized, otherwise it just isn't going to work. There are ways of overcoming resistance; as I said, Milton Erickson was a master at this. But in order for him to have successfully overcome resistance, the client must have unconsciously wanted to be hypnotized, however much his conscious mind was protesting.

Sometimes resistance to hypnotism can take quite extreme forms. On a famous occasion in 1978, during the World Chess Championship, defector Victor Korchnoi claimed that Russians from the camp of his opponent, Anatoly Karpov, were trying to hypnotize him from a distance, to put him off his game. But this was probably paranoia – a probability that is increased by the consideration that Korchnoi took to wearing one-way reflecting spectacles, to deflect any rays that they might be beaming at him, and to carrying a Geiger counter to detect such rays! Karpov won anyway.

The Phenomena of Hypnotism

Hypnotic phenomena can be divided into various categories. First, there are alterations in involuntary muscles: your breathing may deepen, your stomach gurgle, your eyes water, a few muscles twitch, your heart and pulse rate increase or decrease. You will feel listless, and your arms and legs may feel heavy. These phenomena are easy to understand. They are features of the light trance, or simply of relaxation. But as the trance deepens, more extraordinary phenomena begin to manifest: alterations in voluntary muscles, alterations to the senses, delusions of the senses and certain psychological phenomena. These phenomena are not unique to hypnosis by any stretch of the imagination: they can all occur spontaneously, or may be produced by drugs, for instance. But they do all occur through hypnosis, and have played an important part in the story of hypnosis through the ages.

Changes to Voluntary Muscles

Catalepsy is the state when a muscle or group of muscles becomes rigid or hard to move. Many hypnotists say, quite early on in the induction: 'You cannot open your eyes. However hard you try, your eyelids are as if glued shut.' This eye-closure test is one of the ways in which a hypnotist can tell whether the induction has been successful. The muscles of the eyelids have become cataleptic. Full-body catalepsy is when the whole body goes rigid, and this is what stage hypnotists exploit in the trick I've already described called the 'human plank'. In between, it is possible for the hypnotist to suggest catalepsy of the arm or leg or whatever. The opposite effect, abnormal plasticity, is also sometimes induced.

Other alterations in the voluntary muscles are *relaxation*, as a natural result of settling comfortably into the hypnotic environment, and *increased muscular performance*. The famous British psychologist

J.A. Hadfield tested the strength of three men under normal, waking conditions. Their average grip was 101 lbs. He then hypnotized them, and told them that they felt weak; their average grip fell to only 29 lbs. Still under hypnosis, he suggested to them that they were very strong – and their average grip rose to 142 lbs. They had been able to increase their strength by about 40 per cent. The applications of this to sports hypnosis are plain. Although plenty of other researchers have been able to test this phenomenon, it does not seem to be an invariant phenomenon of hypnosis, and many psychologists now believe that any extra strength is given by the subject's increased motivation, rather than by anything intrinsic to hypnosis itself. However, in favour of trance states enhancing such abilities are reports that entranced shamans can perform astonishing feats of strength.

Changes to the Senses

There are two main kinds of alteration which can affect any of the senses. First, they can become super-acute. The technical name for this is *hyperaesthesia*. Sometimes the effects are quite remarkable, and may explain some of the apparent paranormal phenomena so beloved of nineteenth-century researchers. A hypnotized subject, for instance, may appear to be able to detect words written on a piece of paper he has never seen, when it is being looked at by someone else; what he is actually doing is reading the reflection of the words in the other person's eyes. Stage hypnotists used to take handkerchiefs from several members of the audience, shuffle them up and get their subject to return them to their owners: perhaps the subject was using a heightened sense of smell. Tiny differences in temperature have been accurately noted, and differences of weight as small as a few grains have been detected. What is remarkable about all this is not the ability in itself. If you blindfold yourself and walk around a strange room, you will find that in a few days you can begin to use your hearing to tell where the obstacles are. So hyperaesthesia is within the capability of anyone. But what is remarkable is the speed with which hypnotized subjects gain the ability. Perhaps this is a result of the narrow focus of attention.

The other important changes to the senses are *analgesia* and *anaesthesia*. The first term is generally used for local loss of sensation, and the second for unconsciousness, with its byproduct of total loss of physical sensation. This phenomenon is familiar from TV and stage shows. We all know that a hypnotized subject can be pricked with a pin or burnt with a cigarette and not feel a thing. The stage uses are obvious, as are the medical ones, particularly in the days before reliable anaesthetics, or with patients who are allergic to anaesthetics, or who prefer to avoid chemicals. Before inducing anaesthesia, a hypnotist will probably test the patient's susceptibility by inducing what is called 'glove anaesthesia' – that is, anaesthesia restricted to the hand – or 'sleeve anaesthesia' on the whole arm. This ability not to feel pain is probably the freakiest and, in a medical context, the most important of the phenomena of hypnosis, and I'll return to it from time to time in this book.

Delusions of the senses are *hallucinations*. Hallucinations may be either positive or negative. A positive hallucination is perceiving something that isn't there; a negative hallucination is failing to perceive something that is there. Both kinds of hallucination are easily induced by the hypnotist's suggestions. Again, this is a favourite of stage hypnotists: 'You are holding a bunch of flowers. Why don't you go and offer it to that girl over there?' Hallucinations can sometimes be induced by post-hypnotic suggestion too. Their chief therapeutic use is to induce abreaction, the cathartic emotional release I've mentioned before. Suppose a patient is afraid of spiders; hallucinating spiders may force him to face this fear and overcome it. In Ambrose Bierce's 'The Realm of the Unreal' (1890) hypnotized people see things and even whole episodes that never took place. Although the phenomenon of hypnotic hallucination is well established, it requires the operator's suggestion, and cannot happen as instantaneously and as unprompted as in Bierce's short story.

Various Psychological Phenomena

The most important psychological change – so important that it is often considered definitional of hypnosis – is *hypersuggestibility*. In fact, since very few hypnotic phenomena are spontaneous, but only occur at the suggestion of the hypnotist, you could say that most of them depend on increased suggestibility.

Time-distortion: Along with catalepsy, this is the other most common spontaneous phenomenon of hypnosis. Half an hour passes as though it were five minutes. Sometimes, time-distortion can lead to the ability to perform supertasks. In one experiment, a woman successfully counted 862 cotton balls in three seconds. She even had time to check under the leaves of the plants to make sure she hadn't missed any.

Superlearning and creativity: Experiments behind the Iron Curtain in Soviet Russia suggest that hypnotized subjects can learn between 120 to 150 new words in a foreign language in an hour. The teacher has to speak in a special way, alternating gentle speech with a commanding tone of voice, and a background of soothing music helps create the environment within which such superlearning can happen. A more reliable way of using hypnosis to improve learning, however, is to get the client to relax, and to remove the anxiety or whatever it is that is blocking learning. In this way, latent talents can be revealed. The evidence as to whether hypnosis can enhance creativity is currently ambiguous. One of the most intriguing theories is that of psychologist Pat Bowers. She argues that hypnosis triggers networks in the brain which are beyond our conscious control (leading to the feeling of effortlessness which hypnotized subjects often experience). In these deep networks new associations are made, and the making of new associations is just another way of describing creativity.

Spontaneous age-regression: I have already mentioned the use of age-regression as a therapeutic technique, but it is worth mentioning that it can occasionally happen spontaneously during a hypnotic trance. Just as Marcel Proust found the taste of madeleine the trigger for recall of events in the past, so in a trance something can trigger the memory of childhood, and the subject will find herself there. It is easy for the hypnotist to recognize when this has happened, because the subject's voice and phrasing will become more childlike.

Paranormal phenomena: Occult researchers, especially in the nineteenth century, supposed that paranormal phenomena could be the result of tapping into the deeper layers of the mind under hypnosis: the most common such phenomena which were supposed to happen were telepathy, precognition (seeing into the future) and clairvoyance. Nowadays, however, these are generally discounted. If such phenomena exist, they are not manifested markedly more by hypnotized subjects than by others. However, if it could be shown – and the idea is not in itself implausible – that hypnosis increases the ability of subjects to enter the non-focused state, similar to daydreaming, which parapsychological research has shown improves the chances of psi abilities, then the relation between hypnosis and paranormal abilities would have to be reassessed.

I should briefly mention here the phenomenon of triggering psychosomatic healing and even achieving control of some organic functions, such as bleeding, bodily temperature and salivation. These are genuine phenomena of hypnosis, and are so important that I reserve discussion until Chapter 11, when I will go in far more detail into modern hypnotherapy and the theories about how it works.

Hypermnesia and Amnesia

Hypermnesia is the phenomenon whereby a hypnotized subject can remember things he couldn't consciously recall. I'll have more to say about memory in Chapter 8, but for the time being I have a suggestion as to what the mechanism is. As I've said, hypnosis involves a reduction in the critical faculty. Fragments of memory that would usually be considered too approximate and unreliable to be taken seriously can now get through the critical filter, and are taken to be accurate. Hypermnesia is very hit and miss, then: you might remember something that really happened, or you might still be unable to remember something, or you might mistake a false memory for truth.

Amnesia is another famous phenomenon of hypnosis, with much use made of it in fiction and films. Unfortunately for the fiction-writers, though, spontaneous amnesia is actually quite rare, and is mostly confined to those who can enter a very deep trance. More commonly, the therapist might induce suggested amnesia for some therapeutic purpose. Spontaneous amnesia is no more weird than forgetting your dream the morning after; you know you've been dreaming, but can't quite put it into words or pictures. One teenager

I interviewed who was hypnotized by a stage hypnotist and made to perform unusual but not degrading actions, such as curling up into a foetal position, said that afterwards she didn't remember much about it, until friends said: 'Don't you remember doing such-and-such?' She described the experience, in this respect, as a bit like the morning after a night of heavy drinking. The occurrence of spontaneous amnesia may sometimes be related to the fact that the deeper you go, the more likely you are to touch on material that has been repressed into the unconscious, which the conscious ego does not want to look at; alternatively, it may be brought on by autosuggestion, in the sense that some subjects believe that amnesia is usual, and so induce it in themselves.

Post-hypnotic Suggestions

It is remarkable that a person can act, some time later, on a suggestion seeded during the hypnotic session. All the other hypnotic phenomena we've discussed can be induced post-hypnotically, especially negative and positive hallucinations. Post-hypnotic suggestion is, of course, popular with stage hypnotists, who tell a hypnotized subject that even after they wake up, when they hear the word 'Thursday' they will jump to their feet and wave their hands in the air. The trigger word is then deliberately introduced. A good stage hypnotist will have several subjects all simultaneously responding differently to different trigger words. The therapeutic use is to suggest to a client who wants to give up smoking, for instance, that he will find the taste of cigarettes disgusting. It has often been noted that subjects who act on a post-hypnotic command find their own justification, if they can, for what they do. At a simple level, if you were told to scratch your left knee, you will genuinely feel an itch there which needs scratching; in more complex cases, if you were asked to open a book at a certain page and read it, you might say that you were trying to find a passage of which you are particularly fond.

Post-hypnotic suggestion is not infallible. If a subject is asked to carry out an action at a specific time, he may not carry it out at all, or he may carry it out at a different time, or only the impulse to carry it out may arise. The subject *always* has the choice whether to go along with the suggestion. But it works more often than not. It is arguable that at the time of carrying out a post-hypnotic suggestion, a subject is back in a trance state, similar to the alert trance state explored by psychologists such as Eva Banyai. One of the legitimate worries about stage hypnotism is that the hypnotist, having returned his victims with their implanted post-hypnotic suggestions to their seats, might then let them leave the theatre without taking steps to remove the implanted suggestion. How long might it linger? Work colleagues might be surprised to find someone jumping up and waving their hands in the air just because they said: 'What about lunch on Thursday?' Post-hypnotic suggestions can last for a long time. A hypnotherapist I have heard of told one of his patients, who was also a friend: 'When I touch you on the finger you will immediately be hypnotized.' Fourteen years later, at a dinner party, he touched him deliberately on the finger and – *clunk* – his head fell back against the chair.

Psychologists like J. Milne Bramwell have also experimented successfully with getting subjects to guess the passage of time, with only small margins of error: 'After 21,400 minutes you will perform such-and-such an action.' As William James pointed out in *The Varieties of Religious Experience* (1902) these experiments are important because they show that we have unusual talents, beyond the ordinary. There is a subconscious part of our mind, for instance, that is able accurately to assess the passage of time. Quite a lot of people know the experience of saying to themselves before going to sleep: 'I must wake up at 6.00', and, without resorting to an alarm clock, doing just that.

The Hidden Observer

I've already mentioned that psychologists researching hypnosis occasionally make use of automatic writing. Here is one such experiment, a very famous one. Professor Ernest Hilgard of Stanford University was puzzled by the fact that when hypnosis is used to block pain, the subject reports feeling no pain, but the usual involuntary indicators of pain (such as GSR, galvanic skin response) are still present. He induced sleeve anaesthesia, so that his subject could hold her arm in a bucket of iced water without feeling any pain. He asked her what she felt, and she said: 'Nothing; no pain.' But he had also asked her to use her other hand to register any pain she felt, on a scale of 1 to 10, and with that other hand, even while denying out loud that she felt any pain, she was writing a series of rising numbers, showing that the pain was increasing as you'd expect from having your hand in a bucket of iced water. Hilgard deduced from this, and from other experiments by himself and his associates, that we have what he called a 'hidden observer' – a part of us that is awake even during altered states of consciousness. The hidden observer doesn't *feel* the pain, but it is aware of the pain, which has been blocked or concealed behind a barrier of amnesia.

Hilgard himself was always very coy about the meaning of the hidden observer. He would never commit himself to saying – in fact, he positively denied – that his experiments showed that there is a deeper part of oneself that is always awake, and of which we can sometimes become aware. In fact, in his experiments he found that only about half his subjects manifested a hidden observer, and only then if they were 'highs' – people who are highly hypnotizable. He speculated that 'highs' are more adept at dissociation than most people, and so are more likely to be aware of the dissociated hidden observer.

But experimental and anecdotal evidence is mounting that everyone has a hidden observer, and this is certainly what I believe myself. Meditators know the feeling, as does anyone who has experienced what is called 'lucid' dreaming, in which you are dreaming and simultaneously aware that you are dreaming. The phenomenon of 'surgical memory', whereby anaesthetized patients hear comments passed by surgeons, especially if those comments are liable to be traumatic, is widely acknowledged in the medical community, and has led to surgeons being much more careful about what they say, to ensure that post-operative healing is helped by a positive frame of mind from the patient. Those who have been in a car accident often report that a 'higher' part of themselves seemed to click into operation, and to work at such a speed that events appeared to move in slow motion. (Perhaps this explains how the woman mentioned a little earlier was able to count so many cotton balls in such a short time.) These are all forms of dissociation. Here is part of one hypnotized subject's description of the hidden observer:

> The hidden observer is analytical, unemotional, businesslike ... The hidden observer is a portion of Me. There's Me 1, Me 2 and Me 3. Me 1 is hypnotized, Me 2 is hypnotized and observing, and Me 3 is when I'm awake ... The hidden observer is cognizant of everything that's going on; it's a little more narrow in its field of vision than Me 3, like being awake in a dream and fully aware of your actions ... The hidden observer sees more, he questions more, he's aware of what's going on all of the time, but getting in touch is totally unnecessary ... He's like a guardian angel that guards you from doing anything that will mess you up ... Unless someone tells me to get in touch with the hidden observer I'm not in contact. It's just there.

Sometimes, especially at critical junctures of your life, a pattern impresses itself upon you. 'If I hadn't gone to just that kindergarten, I wouldn't later have met Bobby's sister, who then introduced me to Martha, which led to me going to Exeter that day and meeting the woman who was to become my wife' – that kind of thing. There seems to be a hidden part of oneself that manages your activities on a lifelong scale, not in moment-by-moment detail. Although Hilgard was able to evoke the hidden observer in only about half his subjects, I guess that it is always there. Perhaps they were too used to it to think they were looking for something so familiar; perhaps it is too deeply buried and too delicate a matter to be easily perceived.

A Speculation and a Warning

In surveying the phenomena of hypnosis, something quite strange strikes me, and forces me to hazard a speculation. Hilgard's experiments on the hidden observer led him to the conclusion that the way hypnosis affords relief from pain is that it hides the pain behind what he called an amnesia-like barrier. This links three of the important phenomena of hypnosis: the hidden observer, anaesthesia and analgesia, and amnesia. Now, not only is analgesia related to amnesia, but it is also related to catalepsy. You could not hold your arm out at shoulder height for fifteen minutes if you were not inhibiting the pain. So that brings four hypnotic phenomena together in a kind of network.

Moreover, compression of time is arguably linked with amnesia. There is no such thing as 'time passing slowly'; there is only 'time passed slowly'. That is, you can only look back on a stretch of time and assess whether it passed slowly or quickly. Time is compressed, then, so that half an hour passes like five minutes, when you look back on the half hour and can remember events only for five minutes, while being amnesic for the rest. In hypnosis, it helps that your attention is narrowly focused, which limits the quantity of experienced events.

I speculate that there could soon be a kind of analogy within hypnotic phenomena to the 'unified field theory' sought after by physicists. Some single phenomenon of hypnosis will be seen to explain at once *all* the other phenomena. At the moment it looks as though the ability to dissociate or to shift states is the best bet. Most of the other phenomena of hypnosis could be brought under the umbrella by the suggestion that you make a shift to another part of the mind which involves a different kind of reasoning and a greater facility with imagery.

However, to talk like this of these phenomena, both subjective and objective, begs an important question, since it makes it sound as though the hypnotic trance is a definite, distinct, recognizable state, an altered state of consciousness (ASC) with its own signs and symptoms. This is in fact a highly controversial idea. Although it was taken for granted in the last century (and still is unthinkingly assumed in some circles) that hypnosis is such an ASC, there has been intense debate about this and related questions in academic circles in the last fifty or sixty years. In fact, it is safe to say that among professional psychologists there is probably nothing that impinges on their field that arouses more contrasting and contradictory views. They disagree not just about what hypnotism is and what is involved, but even about whether there is such a thing (some prefer to surround the word with scare quotes); they disagree about the best measures of susceptibility, and even whether such measures are worth anything; they disagree about induction techniques; they disagree about what and how much it can achieve; they disagree about whether other practices, such as acupuncture, are really hypnotism. It is so hard to prove the existence of hypnotic trance that, as a publicity stunt, the magician Kreskin (George Kresge) has offered a reward of $100,000 to anyone who can do so, and has already beaten off in court two hopeful claims. By the end of this book I won't have made you able to claim the reward, I'm afraid, but I hope to have convinced you that there is such a thing as the hypnotic state.

2

In the Beginning

In the beginning (or pretty close to it, anyway) was ... hypnosis, possibly. We read in Genesis 2:21: 'And the Lord God caused a deep sleep to fall upon Adam, and he slept.' Of course, this isn't a reference to hypnosis, although it has been cited as such by one or two over-enthusiastic writers, because even if we were to take it as literal fact, there is no mention of *how* the Lord God put Adam to sleep. He might have used drugs growing in the Garden of Eden, for all we know. But had this been relevant to hypnosis, it would also have been the first mention of hypnotic surgery, since while asleep Adam undergoes the rather painful operation of having a woman created from his spare rib!

Joking aside, one invariably reads, within the first chapter or even the first paragraph of a book on hypnotism, something along the following lines: 'Hypnotism is an ancient art, whose secrets were known to the Egyptians and Greeks, and have been transmitted down to our own times.' Of course, it is a natural tendency for enthusiasts to try to invest their favourite subject with an aura of respectable antiquity, but it is to be hoped that truth has a larger claim than such partisan concerns. Unfortunately, these statements are never supported by footnotes and references to relevant texts and authorities. We need to look at the matter afresh, which means re-examining the texts. There are few enough of these, and most are ambiguous. In short, the prehistory of hypnotism in the West, in the centuries preceding Mesmer, is poorly documented and hard to excavate.

Ancient Egypt

There are certain Egyptian paintings which show a person apparently asleep with others standing over them whose hands give the impression of making hypnotic passes. These paintings used to excite a great deal of interest in historians of hypnosis. But the interpretation of ancient wall paintings is difficult, and they would form a weak foundation on which to base any historical theory. Texts are somewhat less fluid, and there are a number of Egyptian magical texts preserved on papyrus. The most likely source of information about hypnotic practices is the famous Demotic Magical Papyrus, dating from the third century CE, which was discovered at Thebes in Egypt early in the nineteenth century, torn in two parts. Both parts, in demotic script, were bought by Jean d'Anastasy, the Swedish consul of the time in Alexandria, for his fabulous private collection, and were subsequently sold, one part to Leiden, and the other to the British Museum in London. Column 16 of this papyrus contains the text of a divinatory rite, which is typical of a number of practices preserved on this important papyrus. It begins with instructions for the careful preparation of the lamp which is to be used in the ritual. Then it goes on:

> You take a boy and seat him upon another new brick, his face being turned to the lamp, and you close his eyes and recite these things that are written above down into the boy's head seven times. You make him open his eyes. You say to him: 'Do you see the light?' When he says to you, 'I see the light in the flame of the lamp,' you cry at that moment, saying 'Heoue' nine times. You ask him concerning everything that you wish.

What is going on here is typical of divinatory practices around the ancient Mediterranean world. Someone (here a 'boy', which perhaps means a slave) in a trance state is asked questions; because he is in a trance state, he is assumed to have contact with the world of the gods (as they thought dreamers did, for instance), and so his answers are taken to be significant. It has been said that this illustrates the technique of self-hypnosis using a light as a source of fixation, but it takes a certain amount of audacity to maintain such a view. At first the boy has his eyes closed, so he is clearly not hypnotizing himself by means of the lamp at this point. Subsequently, when he has his eyes open, he is only asked 'Do you see the light?', and there is nothing in the text to indicate that he is using the lamp for self-hypnosis at this point either. It's possible, but far from certain. At the same time, it's clear that the boy's interrogator is only an interrogator, someone who is consulting the gods to see what message they have for him, and that there is no question of his being an external hypnotist.

Practices similar to the one implied in this ancient Egyptian text continued for many centuries. For instance, we can find it referred to by Apuleius of Madaurus in his defence speech *Pro Se De Magia* (sections 42ff.), which was written in the second century CE, although rather than using a lamp, his seer (who is again a boy) is lulled into a trance by means of spoken spells or certain unspecified scents. Or, much later, the Elizabethan magus John Dee used Edward Kelley as his means of contacting the astral and angelic realms. Kelley would 'scry' (look into a mirror or a crystal ball or a pool of black ink) and tell Dee what he saw there. No one assumes either that Dee had hypnotized Kelley, or that Kelley had hypnotized himself; Kelley simply reported what he saw, and our Egyptian boy may just have used the flickering lamp to conjure up images suggestive of answers to the questions put to him. There may be no reason not to call this a trance state – but there is also no particular reason to call it a hypnotically induced trance state. The most interesting aspect of this Egyptian text for this book is that the belief that entranced subjects can contact the world of the gods, however that is envisaged, will recur in the nineteenth century and beyond; the persistence of the belief is remarkable.

The similarity between the ancient Mediterranean divinatory practice just described and the modern phenomenon of 'channelling' (which is also a descendant of nineteenth-century spiritualist mediumship, and of possession in religions such as voodoo) is striking. A 'channel' appears to go into a trance and then through him or her there speaks an alien entity, often supposed to be from another planet or another plane of existence. Later in the book we will see that in Victorian times interest in mesmerism and passion for spiritism went hand in hand; but at this stage we can conclude that channelling on its own is not a form of hypnosis. A person may be hypnotized or may hypnotize herself to act as a channel; but it is not necessary to be hypnotized to act as a channel.

I cannot resist concluding this section by debunking the idea, commonly found among tourists and others, that other ancient Mediterranean seers, such as the Pythia at Delphi and the Sibyl at Cumae, relied on drugs to attain their divinatory trance state. There is no evidence for this whatsoever. One even hears it said that at Delphi narcotic fumes would arise from the depths of the earth through a crack in the floor of the shrine – but no such crack has ever been discovered. In fact, the Egyptian text translated above gives us a more accurate idea of how these priestesses worked: they relied on their own resources to go into a trance.

Mesmeric Passes in the Old Testament?

In 2 Kings 5 we hear about Naaman, a Syrian general who had contracted leprosy. One of his slaves, a captive Israelite girl, tells his wife, her mistress, about the miracle-worker (she would have called him a *nabi*) from her native land called Elisha. 'He would certainly be able to cure your husband's leprosy,' she says. Naaman gets the Syrian king to send a letter to the Israelite king, along with a great deal of money and valuables. Elisha is happy to comply, and suggests that Naaman comes to Israel. But when Naaman does so, Elisha tells him – by messenger, not even in person – to wash seven times in the River Jordan. Naaman is not best pleased: what advantage does this river have over rivers back home? He's convinced that Elisha has some trick up his sleeve: 'He will surely come out to me, and stand, and call on the name of the Lord his God, and move his hand up and down over the place, and recover the leper' (2 Kings 5:11). His servants persuade him to try the washing anyway – and it works.

But what was Naaman expecting? The Hebrew word translated as 'move up and down' is also translated, in the King James version, as 'strike'. Was Naaman then expecting physical contact? Most probably not: the root of the original Hebrew word is *nuf*, which commonly refers to some kind of rhythmical movement of the hands, such as waving. The Greek translators of the Old Testament, some centuries later, rendered the Hebrew word by the Greek verb *epitithenai*, the usual word for the laying-on of hands. But this was an interpretation, perhaps influenced by the kind of hands-on faith healing which was current in their day. Naaman, however, seems to have been expecting the *nabi* to make some healing passes over the affected part of his body. But although passes have been common in hypnosis and hypnotherapy, their presence does not constitute hypnosis. We would need, in addition, evidence of the induction of trance, and of course there is no such evidence.

Fundamentalist Christians have been known to cite Deuteronomy 18:10–11 as a biblical prohibition of the practice of hypnosis. The text reads: 'There shall not be found among you any one that maketh his son or his daughter to pass through the fire, or that useth divination, or an observer of times, or an enchanter, or a witch, or a charmer, or a consulter with familiar spirits, or a wizard, or a necromancer.' The only two categories of prohibited practice which might be relevant are using enchantment and charms; but neither of them are hypnosis. In any case, this translation of the terms, from the King James version, is far from secure. Here is the New International version: 'Let no one be found among you . . . who practises divination or sorcery, interprets omens, engages in witchcraft, or casts spells, or who is a medium or a spiritist or who consults the dead.' Clearly no mention of hypnosis there. An eminent professor, an expert on Hebrew and a practising Christian, has concluded that reference to these verses by Christians wanting to condemn hypnosis is 'exegetically indefensible'. What he means is this. The word translated 'charm' in the King James version and 'cast spells' in the New International version comes from the Hebrew root *ḥbr*, which means 'to attach, join, or bind'. Since people who have spells cast on them are bound – spellbound – the word also means 'to enchant, or cast spells'. It does not refer to hypnosis.

Curiously, Christian objectors to hypnosis appear to have missed the way this verse more plausibly supports their case. The word translated as 'observer of times' is *me'onen*. Now, the Talmud (at Sanhedrin 65b) gives an alternative interpretation of this word: 'The sages say it means one who holds the eyes', because they link *me'onen* to the Hebrew for eyes, *einayim*. If this interpretation is correct – and note that it is only one possible interpretation – and if it therefore refers to some hypnosis-like practice (perhaps the evil eye, which I discuss below), then the text could be understood as condemning such a practice. But the 'ifs' here have piled up; there is really no plausible case for reading the verse as banning hypnosis. In any case, it could be read as banning evil uses of a number of practices, but not as banning therapeutic uses of any of them.

There are myths, folk tales and legends from all around the world about how certain demonic or supernatural figures entrance humans and put them to sleep for a number of years. But magic sleep or forgetfulness, however caused – by the gods, music, wand, or charms – is not a hypnotic trance. This is what makes it nonsense to say that Genesis 2.21, with which I started this chapter, is a reference to hypnosis.

Here endeth, inconclusively, the lesson from the Old Testament.

Incubation

The other feature in the ancient world which chiefly excites the imagination of some writers on hypnotism is the practice of incubation, spending a night or two at a religious sanctuary. This took place in Egyptian temples as well, especially those of Isis and Serapis, but it is not certain that the practice originated in Egypt, as is often carelessly assumed; we have no evidence for incubation in Egyptian temples at a very early date, and it may have spread to Egypt from Greece. Certainly, our best evidence comes from Greek temples, and especially the temples of the healer-god Asclepius, though the same or similar practices occurred also at shrines sacred to Trophonius and Amphiaraus.

Suppose you were suffering from an ailment – though not an incurable one: the temple priests were canny enough to recognize that too many failures would challenge the reliability of the god's healing. One of the methods to which you might resort was incubation in the temple of the healer-god. After purifying yourself and making an offering at the shrine's altar, you entered the sacred centre of the temple and lay down to sleep. During the night, you hoped to have a significant dream, which would indicate what you had to do to cure your ailment. If it didn't come in the first night, you might stay as long as you could afford to, until the appropriate dream came along. Once you had dreamt your cure, you made a thanksgiving offering at the temple (which might typically be a terracotta sculpture of the part of your body that had been affected; hundreds of these sculptures have been recovered), and went on your way. You were not required to pay a fee, though no doubt many grateful patients did, and the whole procedure was carried out in a highly matter-of-fact fashion.

Though Epidaurus held the most famous temple of Asclepius in the Greek world, there were other eminent sites at Athens, Corinth and Troezen on mainland Greece; on the island of Cos; at Lebena in Crete; and at Pergamum in modern Turkey. Here are a couple of sample temple records of cures, found on inscriptions at the Epidaurian temple.

> There came as a suppliant to the god a man one of whose eyes was so blind that it consisted of no more than the lids, which were entirely empty and contained nothing. Some people in the temple laughed at him for being so foolish as to think that he would see with an eye that was not there. Then he had a dream while he was asleep; after boiling some herbs, the god seemed to prise apart the lids and pour in the medicine. At daybreak the man left the temple seeing with both eyes.

> A man had a stone in his penis. He dreamt that he was having sex with a handsome boy. Along with his seminal discharge he ejected the stone, which he picked up and carried out of the temple in his hands.

Not all the dreams healed you immediately; sometimes they suggested methods of treatment which you were to go away and carry out. A certain Marcus Julius Apellas, for instance, who was suffering from chronic indigestion, was given in a dream a long list of actions to perform – not just a special diet (cheese and bread, celery and lettuce), but also a regimen including running, sprinkling himself with sand and pouring wine over his body before entering the baths. In his dream he asked for a less complex way of curing himself, and had another dream in which he smeared his body with a paste of mustard and salt. After waking up he tried a mustard-and-salt poultice on his stomach, and the pain was cured.

The dreams were invariably direct and comprehensible by the dreamer, so that there was no need for interference by the temple priest or officials. Reporting his own experience, the second-century sophist Aelius Aristides says that even his doctor yielded his own professional opinion to the clarity of the dream (*Sacred Discourses* 47.57). It is important to remember that dreams were assumed to be god-given. They are, after all, mysterious – hence the continuing fascination of dream-interpretation dictionaries and so on. The practice of interpreting dreams as god-given messages is taken for granted in ancient Western literature, from Homer (*Iliad* 1.62–8) onwards.

Because dreaming was held to be as close as a mortal person got to direct contact with the gods, dreams were not seen (as nowadays we tend to see them) as stories, but as a series of symbolic still photographs. As a result the Greeks had become quite sophisticated at classifying dreams, and at giving the kind of thumbnail and superficial interpretations that modern dictionaries still give. In fact, this is another practice that goes back to ancient Egypt. A papyrus in the British Museum (BM Papyrus 10683), which dates from around 2000 BCE suggests, among many other things, that it is good to dream of eating donkey-meat, because it means promotion, but bad to dream of copulating with a female jerboa, because it means that a judgement will be passed against you! Such stock interpretations were known in the Greek world, and in the second century CE Artemidorus of Ephesus travelled around the Mediterranean to compile his dream dictionary from more ancient sources.

Incubation is a fascinating subject: after all, here we have evidence of hundreds of miraculous cures. What is one to do? Dismiss them?

That would be foolhardy, and a clear sign of prejudice: in trying to understand ancient cultures, we do not so cavalierly dismiss other pieces of evidence which are more to our liking. Should we explain them as spontaneous remission? But surely there could not be so many. It is possible that there was embroidery of the facts, from either or both of the patients and the priesthood, for the greater honour of the god; but even allowing for a certain degree of embroidery, a solid residue of miracles remain. Two factors are relevant, I think. First, it is worth remembering that in all likelihood many patients will just have improved rather than being totally cured, and that in many cases the ailment with which they presented in the first place was not very severe. Second, faith healing and the cure of psychosomatic illness cannot be ruled out in a number of cases. The patient's faith would have been enhanced by the sight of the records of previous cures up on the walls in and around the temple – precisely the records that are still our main evidence for the cures, and a couple of which I quoted just now. In Chapter 11 I will return to the topic of how optimism and expectations can cure even organic illnesses.

However, when the topic of hypnotism was in everyone's minds in the nineteenth century, and it was seen that it could have remarkable therapeutic value, people began to assume that it must have been involved in Asclepius' temples, and the idea has been perpetuated in many a tome on hypnosis. But it is clear from this brief survey of the subject that there is not the slightest possibility that hypnosis was involved. It could only have happened if there was interference from the temple officials, such that they could induce a trance in a patient and suggest that he was cured. But there is no evidence that the temple officials were involved except to administer the temple, and in purely managerial capacities. In Aristophanes' *Wealth* a witness sees the god healing a patient in the temple, and some writers have supposed that one of the priests disguised himself as the god and went around at night treating the entranced patients. But a comic play is hardly good evidence for this, and no scholar of ancient Greece believes that this is what happened. All the evidence shows that the god was seen in a dream world, not in this world; given the strictures of staging a play, Aristophanes projects the dreamt god into concrete reality.

Nor is there any evidence of hypnotic chanting, as has been suggested. In very rare cases one of the temple officials, the *zakoros* (who was sometimes a trained physician as well), might interpret an obscure dream – but if this is interference, it is interference after the event, and constitutes no kind of evidence for hypnosis. Nor is there any evidence of self-hypnosis. Incubation in some form survives under the auspices of the Church at shrines such as Lourdes and St Anne de Beaupré, but I have never seen any suggestion that hypnosis or self-hypnosis is going on there.

Further Evidence from Ancient Greece and Rome?

Aristotle's pupil Clearchus, writing perhaps at the end of the fourth century BCE, told a story in one of his works, *On Sleep*, of how a magician with a 'psychopompic wand' drew the soul out of a sleeping boy, leaving his body inert and insensitive to pain. This is suggestive, but should be treated with caution. In the first place, *On Sleep* was a fictional dialogue; in the second place, the actual work does not survive, and this report exists only as a fragment (fr. 7) in Proclus, an author writing 750 years later; in the third place, it looks as though the boy was already asleep, rather than being put to sleep by hypnosis; in the fourth place, the boy seems to have remained asleep, rather than being in the receptive hypnotic state.

The Greek statesman Solon, whose constitutional reforms were so important that the Athenians dated the beginnings of their experiment in democracy from the time he was in power (594 BCE), was also a rather good poet. Only fragments of his poems survive, but in a long one preserved by John of Stobi in the anthology he compiled in the fifth century CE, there are a number of lines on various professions, usually making the point that in all of them good is mixed with bad; farmers, for instance, have to work extremely hard to make a living. At one point Solon turns his attention to healers:

> Others, who understand the work of Paion [the physician of the gods, later identified with the god Apollo], with all his drugs, are healers. But their work too is imperfect, because often a small ailment turns into a major illness which no gentle remedy can relieve, while someone else, who is riddled with terrible and serious diseases, is cured all at once by the touch of a hand.

Apart from the fact that there is no evidence of the induction of a trance, this should not be adduced as evidence of hypnotherapy in ancient Greece. The lines are usually taken out of context, but it is clear that the 'touch of a hand' is almost an accidental remedy, not a special technique. Hypnotherapy would be signposted as a special technique.

In his tragic masterpiece *Bacchae* the fifth-century Athenian dramatist Euripides talks of how in a state of religious ecstasy the followers of Dionysus pierce their cheeks with pins without feeling pain or even bleeding, and in the climax to the play the Bacchants hallucinate that the king of Thebes, Pentheus, who is resisting the introduction of this barbaric religion into civilized Greece, is a lion cub, and they tear him apart. Although this play is often mentioned in books on the history of hypnosis, it would certainly be a dangerous precedent to think of religious ecstasy as a hypnotic state.

Much more promising are a couple of lines (313–14) from the Roman comic playwright Plautus' *Amphitryo*, which was written about 195 BCE. It was based on a lost Greek original, but the extent of the borrowing is uncertain. The god Mercury, in confrontation with a slave called Sosia, says: 'What if I were to touch you with gentle strokes, so that you fall asleep?' Despite appearances, however, this is not evidence of hypnotism. Mercury is a god, a supernatural agent; sleep, and occasionally death, were regarded as creeping slowly over one, from head to toe or the other way round. So this is only a way of describing the process of falling asleep naturally, ascribing it to the influence of a god.

Another careless reference to an ancient text by modern writers on hypnosis, anxious to find mention of their art in classical times, has been to what the first-century encyclopedist Aulus Cornelius Celsus says about Asclepiades of Bithynia, a medical writer alive a couple of hundred years before Celsus. It is said that Asclepiades used to lull madmen to sleep by making hand passes over them. Even a glimpse at the original text would have shown that this is a load of rubbish. Celsus reports that Asclepiades used to practise 'rubbing' or 'massage' (*frictio*) for a number of ailments, but that such rubbing (as opposed to gentler anointing) is unsuitable for acute diseases, 'except to induce sleep in madmen' (*On Medicine* 2.14.1–4). The idea that rubbing can produce sleep (and not just in madmen) is also attributed to Asclepiades at 3.18.14. The reference is clearly to a hands-on technique of dispelling pain and fever, or of calming a patient down, and therefore bears no true relation to hypnotic or mesmeric passes. Pliny the Elder, who famously died during the eruption of Vesuvius in 79 CE, talks of curing certain diseases – burns and rheumy eyes – by the application of magnets (*Natural History* 36.25.130), but magnetic healing has a long history in the West, and is not in itself evidence of mesmerism, let alone hypnosis.

There is no further evidence of any practices suggestive of hypnosis in either ancient Greece or Rome. In the area of magic, there is a great deal of continuity between Egypt, Greece and Rome, such that it makes sense to talk of the ancient Mediterranean world in general. So it is not surprising that, for all the centuries of its history, Rome should not throw up any new evidence. They simply continued the same practices. Of course, there was a lot more to ancient Mediterranean magic than the couple of practices I have mentioned. They used talismans, spells, incantations, charms and so on – but none of these could conceivably be construed as hypnosis, so I have ignored them. Spells and incantations might come close to hypnosis if they were cast by an operator in the presence of the subject, but in fact they were cast secretly, remotely, at a distance from the subject. For instance, if someone had been bitten by a snake, the local healer would chant in the field where the incident occurred, but the sick man remained home in bed. The only respect in which these practices draw at all close to hypnosis is that they may require passive suggestibility in the subject. However, it is interesting to note in passing that magic was far more pervasive in the ancient Mediterranean world than many scholars would have us believe. It is, of course, a dark subject, and so it is usually over-looked in cultural histories of the period, but comparison with the cultures of any other country shows that it must be taken into afolk ccount.

Was Jesus a Hypnotist?

This is the claim put forward by Ian Wilson in his book *Jesus: The Evidence*. Actually, he wasn't the first to make the claim, although he writes as if he were. It can be found, for instance, in William J. Bryan's *Religious Aspects of Hypnosis*, written some twenty years before Wilson's book. Bryan claims that what is called in the Bible 'casting out devils' is hypnosis, and also that Jesus used hypnosis for all kinds of healings; but he undermines his case by failing to provide any evidence. He simply paraphrases a number of cases of healing from the New Testament, and calls them hypnotism. He doesn't argue for the thesis. All cases of faith healing are termed cases of hypnosis or self-hypnosis, let alone any cases where the laying-on of hands is involved. The casting out of spirits by hypnosis is more or less what happens at one point in Noël Coward's 1941 play *Blithe Spirit*, but I'm not sure anyone has tried it offstage.

Wilson's thesis is just as thin as Bryan's, although he at least makes an attempt to argue the point (while admitting that his argument is 'circuitous'). First, he describes hypnotism in a deliberately broad manner, as a therapeutic method in which a belief system is imposed on the patient in order to effect a cure. This is a good description of faith healing, but that is not the same as hypnotism. As for 'imposition', Wilson adduces the authority with which Jesus consistently spoke while healing. So is anyone who speaks with authority and wields charisma a hypnotist? Only if that is the case might one be able to describe Jesus as a hypnotist. Second, Wilson makes much of the fact that the few cases where Jesus is reported to have failed in a healing (as in Mark 6:1–6) took place in his home town. Wilson says: 'The significance of this episode is that Jesus failed precisely where *as a hypnotist* we would most expect him to fail, among those who knew him best ... Largely responsible for any hypnotist's success are the awe and mystery with which he surrounds himself, and these essential factors would have been entirely lacking in Jesus' home town.' But this does not make Jesus a hypnotist: exactly the same (if true) holds for faith healers too.

Here is a typical healing performed by Jesus, as reported in the Gospels:

> And there was in their synagogue a man with an unclean spirit; and he cried out, saying, Let us alone; what have we to do with thee, thou Jesus of Nazareth? Art thou come to destroy us? I know thee who thou art, the Holy One of God. And Jesus rebuked him, saying, Hold thy peace and come out of him. And when the unclean spirit had torn him, and cried with a loud voice, he came out of him. (Mark 1:23–6)

Where is the hypnotism in this? Clutching at straws, and in the spirit of rationalistic dismissal of the miracles, Wilson goes on to claim that Jesus never really turned water into wine, but hypnotized the guests at the wedding at Cana (John 2: 2–11) to believe that they were drinking wine rather than water, that the transfiguration was a hallucination induced by hypnotic suggestion, as were the disciples' visions of the kingdom of God, and that post-resurrection sightings of Jesus were induced by suggestions planted by Jesus in his hypnotized subjects while he was still alive. This is all extremely flimsy. While I must confess to disbelief – or at any rate amazed incredulity – where Jesus' miracles are concerned, and therefore to a tendency to look for more plausible explanations, I can see no evidence at all that Jesus was a hypnotist.

The Evil Eye

There is a certain folk belief which crosses all geographical and temporal boundaries. It can be found even today, and not just in places such as the Philippines, but also, closer to home, in some of the Greek islands or Sicily; it is particularly prevalent, I have found, in Turkey and Corsica. This is belief in the evil eye. It is said that someone with the evil eye can cause another person to fall ill (since contagion is thought to be transmitted by the eyes) or to become immobile. There are traces of this belief in English phrases such as 'Looking daggers at someone' and 'If looks could kill . . .' And in general, of course, we attribute a great deal of potency to the eyes and to looks: the eyes are the carriers of curses or charms, attraction or repulsion. At the height of the European witch-hunt in the sixteenth and seventeenth centuries, supposed witches brought to trial were often required to keep their backs turned to the judges, lest they bewitch them with their gaze.

Literature from all over the world warns the man who would be chaste to avoid meeting a woman's eye. The ambiguity between attraction and repulsion, life (through sex) and death, is present in the Latin term used throughout the Middle Ages for the evil eye – *oculus fascinus*, the bewitching eye. And *fascinum* might mean 'bewitchment', or in other contexts refer to the penis. Phallic gestures are still the most common means used to ward off the evil eye, but there are others. In many cultures it is or was believed that if you praise a child you then have to curse him, or find some other way – such as spitting in his face – of defending him against the evil eye, to which children are particularly vulnerable.

In the ancient Greek and Roman world, there are enough references to make it certain that the belief was pervasive. Even wolves and certain snakes were considered to have the evil eye. You could say that the mythical and monstrous gorgon Medusa is the evil eye writ large, with her ability to turn men to stone, even after Perseus chopped off her head. Pliny the Elder attributes the evil eye to certain Scythian women, who are distinguished by having double pupils (*Natural History* 7.2.16–18). Fifty or so years later, Plutarch was composing his urbane *Table Talk*, in which he recounts the learned discussions held over various dinners at which he was present; he devotes a whole chapter to the question of the evil eye, which he attributes to certain emanations which are given off by the whole body, but by the eye in particular. Some are beneficent, but some are harmful, and these can injure those who are especially vulnerable, such as children.

There are numerous references in the Bible, in both testaments, to magical practices (most of which are 'abominations unto the Lord', as at Deuteronomy 18:9–15). The evil eye is mentioned specifically at Deuteronomy 28:54–8, Isaiah 13:18, Proverbs 23:6 and Mark 7:22. Proverbs 23:6, for instance, recommends that we refrain from the bread and the 'dainty meats' of someone who has an evil eye – probably good advice! The frequency with which belief in the evil eye occurs in the Bible guaranteed lively debate throughout the Middle Ages. In his *On the Natures of Things* 2.153 the British writer Alexander Neckam, who died in 1217, speculated that evil rays can emanate from a person's eyes and cause 'fascination' (which is the usual medieval term). He claimed that the way to cure a child who had been subjected to the evil eye was to have its nurse lick its face.

With rather more psychological profundity, it was common to explain the phenomenon of fascination as due to one person's will dominating another. So one of the dominant figures in medieval learning, the thirteenth-century writer Albertus Magnus, cites eminent Arabic authorities in his attempt to justify his theory that fascination is a case of occult influence exerted by one man over another (*On Sleep and Waking* 3.1.6). It is because man's mind is of a higher order than matter that it can act upon it; similarly, one person's mind may dominate that of another person. In another work, which was either written by Albertus Magnus or in imitation of him, the author proposes 'that superior intelligences impress inferior ones just as one soul impresses another . . . and by such impression a certain enchanter by his mere gaze cast a camel into a pit.'

In later centuries it became more common to deny or explain away phenomena such as fascination, but it was perfectly acceptable earlier, and the theories could get quite complex. Nicolas Oresme, for instance, a French divine of the fourteenth century, proposed that the imagination of some people could be so intense that it could alter their bodies; this alteration then affected the surrounding air, and ultimately other bodies. Even such pseudo-scientific explanations are preferable to the retrograde step taken by many Christian writers of the period, who simply attributed all such phenomena to demons and either left the matter there, or at the most allowed the efficacy of Christian incantations.

There seems little reason not to think of the evil eye, or

fascination, as an early trace of hypnotism. It satisfies the criteria. Both an operator and a subject are involved, and there is inequality of will (as I called it) between them. There is (or is supposed to be) a deliberate attempt on the part of the fascinator to dominate the subject, and no doubt if one came from a culture in which belief in the evil eye was prevalent, there would be a strong element of suggestibility to enhance the effect. But there are two features of fascination which do not sit easily with our ideas about hypnotism. In the first place, it is the *evil* eye; it can be used only for malign purposes – including the satisfaction of lust, says Marsilio Ficino (1433–99). The idea that it might be used for good, for healing, does not seem to have occurred. In the second place, it is used only for limited purposes – basically, causing illness, bad luck, or immobility. There are no traces of the familiar phenomena of hypnosis, such as amnesia and anaesthesia.

These differences between medieval fascination and modern hypnosis can easily be explained. There is no trace of technique among the medieval fascinators. It appears to have been a gift with which you were born (or cursed); it appears to have happened rarely and at random, with no continuity of research, or passing on of technique from one practitioner to the next. But it is only when there is such continuity that knowledge of hypnosis can grow, as it did in the nineteenth century. The wide variety of uses to which hypnosis can be put were only gradually discovered. The familiar phenomena of amnesia, anaesthesia and so on depend on the operator planting suggestions in the mind of the subject, and the discovery of hypnotic suggestion also had to wait until the end of the eighteenth century. If we add to all this the climate of superstition of the Middle Ages, with witches and amulets, periapts, spells and occult forces, it is not surprising that fascination should be assumed to be used only for evil purposes. The Church was constantly having to battle against what it saw as satanic forces, which were preserved above all in the folk heritage. And so hypnosis became the evil eye, and the world had to wait several centuries for a more balanced view of the practice and its possibilities.

Glimpses of Hypnosis in the Middle Ages

Although fascination was considered a dangerous and evil ability, and was never used for healing, there were other, non-hypnotic means of healing, such as incantation, and it is interesting to note that medieval theorists were already speculating along lines that seem to have been confirmed by recent research on the placebo effect and on the therapeutic properties of visualizations. So the French medical writer Oger Ferrier (1513–88) claimed that incantations and so on work thanks to the confidence of the healer and the patient. His contemporary, Georg Pictorius von Villingen (c. 1500–69), in his *Physical Questions*, explained that incantations could sometimes more effectively cure diseases if they were accompanied by the use of the imagination of both the enchanter and the enchanted. A little later, with rationalism beginning to rear its head, one finds claims such as that made by Pierre Gassendi (1592–1655), a French scientist who denied that incantations work in themselves, but accepted that they might inspire the patient with confidence. The great scientist and occultist Paracelsus (1579–1644) also stressed the power of the imagination to affect the body: 'The spirit is the master, the imagination the instrument, the body the plastic material.'

This emphasis on imagination and confidence is striking. Physicians of the time believed that the imagination could cause healing or disease as follows: an image creates an emotion, the emotion affects the humoral balance of the body for better or worse. Given this notion, it is not surprising to find that they were able to recognize the existence of psychosomatic disease, to argue that placebos such as talismans were effective, and to use methods such as musical therapy, which works directly on the emotions, to heal some cases. The great medical theorist Galen of Pergamum, of the second century CE, whose ideas held sway for 1,000 years and more, even argued that it works both ways. Not only does an image cause an emotion, but an emotion can cause an image and so one can use the analysis of dreamt images to diagnose the underlying emotion and get back to the basic humoral imbalance. It was only when Descartes forced a complete separation between mind and body that natural recognition of the psychosomatic origin of some illnesses began to wane, before being rediscovered and put on to a modern scientific footing in the twentieth century.

But this is a digression, since we have decided that incantations are not hypnotism. Slightly more suggestive is the talk by Peter of Abano (fl. 1300) of cures being effected simply by strength of will. This sounds like autosuggestion, and he also defines sorcery as 'taking possession of a person's powers so that he loses self-control'. But, like all these medieval authors, he fails to illuminate us with talk about specific techniques and practices, so that we are left guessing. Part of the problem is that they are all Christian writers, and they did not want to draw attention to supposedly occult practices.

While we're in this period of history, I should mention that in *The Three Hostages* John Buchan attributes considerable knowledge of hypnotism to the famous thirteenth-century astrologer and physician Michael Scot. I have not been able to confirm this at all. I suspect, then, that Buchan simply chose the name of Scot at random for his own fictional purposes.

Anyway, given that there is evidence of the practice of hypnotism in the Middle Ages, in the evil eye, some more tantalizing texts slot into place. Here are the most important, in chronological order. The best one is also the earliest: a certain Theophilus, in his *Breviary of Diverse Arts*, quoted in the thirteenth-century encyclopedia *Lumen animae* (*The Light of the Soul*), is reported as remarking how difficult it is to wake someone up when they have been put to sleep by enchanters and thieves. He doesn't say that they were drugged; he clearly takes for granted that people could be and were put to sleep by unscrupulous people. This surely is certain evidence of the practice of hypnosis, although details of the theory (if there was one) and the practice are lost.

In the light of Theophilus' testimony, other glimpses start to sound like relics of hypnosis. Nicolas Oresme (whom we have already met) told in *Quodlibeta* 2 and 44 how incantations can make men beat themselves, or unyoke their horses and put the yokes on their own necks. In the light of modern stories about the absurd things hypnotized people can be persuaded to do, this looks significant. However, Oresme adds, in fairness, that he has never personally witnessed any magicians getting people to do such things.

Another fragmentary glimpse is provided by Giorgio Anselmi, a philosopher from Parma, who was alive in the middle of the fifteenth century. In his *Astronomia* he makes a careful distinction:

> *Haustus* is more powerful than fascination. This is the phenomenon whereby through incantations or spells or invocations a man is so thoroughly bound that nothing gets through to him, and it is as if he has lost the use of his senses, and is dull and mindless, and for whole days at a time he seems to be absent, as though he had been drained of all his physical and mental strength.

This is interesting. Anselmi associates *haustus* with fascination, except that fascination uses only the eyes, whereas *haustus* uses speech. Could a practitioner of *haustus* have used rhythmic speech, as many modern hypnotists do? Unfortunately, there is no further trace of *haustus* as a distinct practice, and we don't even know whether the spells were to be chanted by the operator while the subject was actually present. The word *haustus* gives us no further clue: it literally means 'drawing' or 'draining' (as in our word 'exhaustion'), so what is important about the experience for Anselmi is that it leaves its victim in a zombie-like state, with his powers drawn out of him.

There was a phenomenon familiar in the Middle Ages of a magician conjuring up illusory castles and so on for the amazed entertainment of the audience. We might be tempted to attribute this to mass hypnotism – or even think that the audience had been snacking on the local mushrooms – but we are lucky to have preserved a number of the spells required for creating this illusion (recently published by historian Richard Kieckhefer in *Forbidden Rites: A Necromancer's Manual of the Fifteenth Century*), and hypnotism is not involved at any stage; the operator has no such contact with his audience, but apparently works on his own in all sincerity to create the illusion.

Conclusions

This, unfortunately, is all the evidence there is – and it is a far more thorough survey than one usually meets in books on hypnosis. It does seem safe to conclude that what we call hypnosis was known in the medieval world, at any rate, even if not in the ancient world. But even in the medieval world, evidence is scarce and hard to assess. This paucity of evidence may not be an accident of time. It may in fact be the case that there was no tried-and-tested, handed-down technique, but rather the accidental and therefore piecemeal discovery of how to induce trances in people.

But even the disappointingly negative features of this chapter bring home two important conclusions. The first is simple: evidence for the induction of trance states is no more evidence for hypnosis than, say, evidence for the ingestion of narcoleptic drugs is evidence for hypnosis. To repeat: not every trance state is a hypnotically induced state. In February 1999 I saw a brilliant production of Shakespeare's *Tempest* at the Barbican in London, directed by Adrian Noble. Now, as everyone knows, there is plenty of enchantment in the play; both Prospero and Ariel have the ability to put others into a trance. Ariel is even trapped on this earth because the person who originally put a spell on him has since died – a trace of the same superstition that survives as one of the supposed dangers of hypnotism. In this production Prospero, for instance, made various hypnotic passes over Miranda in order to entrance her. Shakespeare himself left no stage directions, so we have no way of knowing how the scene would originally have been enacted; but I think we can be reasonably sure that hypnotism would not have been his model, as it was for Noble.

The second conclusion is a word of caution. I started this chapter by putting down the over-enthusiastic attempt to lend respectability to hypnotism by giving it a long history, with little regard for the facts. I end by expanding the same topic and casting doubt on what I call 'hypnotic imperialism'. This is the tendency of some theorists of hypnosis to attempt to explain too many phenomena as hypnosis. In particular, there has been considerable discussion of whether acupuncture is a form of hypnosis. There are certain similarities – for instance, the acupuncturist likes to build up rapport with a patient, and to get her to relax – and it is interesting (though not conclusive) that the same people who can derive benefit from acupuncture are also those who are most hypnotizable. But current evidence suggests that there is a reasonable physiological basis to acupuncture: it works by stimulating the body's nervous system and encouraging endorphins, our natural painkillers, to help in the healing process. The most convincing evidence is that experiments have shown that hypnosis does not reduce pain in animals, but acupuncture does. This shows that acupuncture has a physiological basis, and is not identical to hypnosis.

Hypnotic imperialists are perhaps misled by the extended use of the term in common parlance: 'I was so hypnotized by the film that I didn't notice the time passing.' But this is a metaphor, not a statement of fact. Alternatively, they may have been misled by the kind of over-broad definition of hypnotism one occasionally comes across in which *any* attempt to gain a person's attention and make them do something or act in a certain way is seen as hypnotism. John Grinder and Richard Bandler, founders of neurolinguistic programming, are arch-imperialists: 'If you think of hypnosis as altering someone's state of consciousness, then any effective communication is hypnosis,' says Connirae Andras in the preface to their book *Trance-formations*. Perhaps the worst – or do I mean the silliest? – case of hypnotic imperialism that I have come across is William J. Bryan's book *Religious Aspects of Hypnosis*, which I have already mentioned. Bryan defines prayer as 'a state of hypnosis in which the mind is super-concentrated on God', God is described as a hypnotist, and religious services are described so that they seem hypnotic. Bryan is writing not just as a hypnotherapist, but as a totally sincere Christian. He is misled by his basic premiss, that hypnosis has to be an emotional experience, similar to the emotions aroused in religion. The relation between hypnosis and religious practices such as meditation will occupy us in a later chapter. In the meantime, we can turn from the slender evidence of the ancient and medieval world to more modern times.

3

Franz Anton Mesmer

The beginnings of hypnosis in the West are, as I said, hard to excavate. But as we hack our way through the jungle, we suddenly come across a clearing with the remains of complete edifices. They are covered in creepers and weeds, to be sure, but one ruin is particularly prominent, towering above the rest. This tower represents Franz Anton Mesmer. In his chequered career as a healer, he encapsulated in miniature the whole range of the future history of hypnosis, from flamboyant showmanship to serious medicine, and from wacky theorizing to the limits of science (such as they were in his time). Was Mesmer a charlatan or the prophet of a new medicine? The jury is still out.

Early Life

Franz Anton Mesmer was born on 23 May 1734 in Iznang, a small village near Radolfzell, in the beautiful country around the western end of Lake Constance in Swabia, which is now part of Germany (just – the border with Switzerland is close), but was then a province of the Austro-Hungarian Empire. His father was a gamekeeper, and Mesmer was one of a number of children. He went to school at Dillingen, in Bavaria, and then went on to the University of Ingolstadt in 1752. He studied theology there, but there is no record that he ever graduated, and he was certainly not ordained. No one knows what he did between 1755 and 1759, but perhaps he was studying at some other university, because by the time he entered the University of Vienna in 1759 he had, or claimed to have, a PhD.

At Vienna he studied law for a year before transferring to medicine, the subject that would occupy him for the rest of his life and make his fame and fortune. We have no information to enable us to read between the stark lines of these early data. He changed his major topic of study twice: is this the sign of a flighty mind or a desire to gain a broad educational background? He ended up with medicine: was this the result of vocation or desperation? How did he support himself financially for thirteen years of study? Perhaps he had a patron, because his father was not rich; perhaps he took odd jobs to keep himself in food and textbooks.

Mesmer graduated on 20 November 1765. The medical school required a dissertation, as well as regular examination papers, and the title of his was *De influxu planetarium in corpus humanum* (*On the Influence of the Heavenly Bodies on the Human Body*). This inevitably sounds to us today like an occult treatise, unsuited to a medical degree, but in fact it was strictly scientific. The question Mesmer tackled was the effect of gravitation on human beings, and his hypothesis was that there is a universal gravitational fluid, which acts as a medium through which the planets may influence life on earth. Modern hackles rise: are we in the realm of astrology? In fact, Mesmer was contemptuous of astrology, or at least astrologers. The idea of a universal fluid seems more than a little far-fetched. But in its day reference to a universal fluid, even as an unsubstantiated hypothesis, would not have seemed unscientific: scientists posited various arcane fluids to explain a number of natural phenomena (such as light, gravity, heat and electricity), and as candidates for a universal fluid the world had already been offered ether, phlogistic fluid, vitrious fluid and resinous fluid. Only twenty-five years later, shortly after the period of Mesmer's greatest success in Paris, Luigi Galvani first noticed that the thighs of dissected frogs twitched when lightning flashes in the sky, and then found that they also did so when stimulated by a direct electric current. The scientific world went mad for electricity, and few had any doubt that it was the universal animating force of the world and all its parts.

This was the era when Erasmus Darwin imagined he had evidence that plants felt mother love, and when jolts of electricity delivered by the popular Leyden jar were thought to have curative properties. It was also the era of work that we would today recognize as scientific, from people such as Antoine-Laurent Lavoisier and John Dalton, Jean-Baptiste Fourier and Joseph Priestley; but the number and variety of scientific beliefs being published made it hard for the layman to distinguish fact from fiction. And the layman was interested; this was an era of popular science like no other, when balloon flights were of more interest than the imminence of political revolution, and the latest theory of the universe was discussed in the streets as well as the salons of the aristocracy. But in fact – and oddly, given that he was awarded the degree – Mesmer's thesis was entirely unoriginal, and even in places an act of plagiarism. Perhaps the requirements for a dissertation were not as stringent then as now; perhaps (as in the ancient world) plagiarism was seen as a compliment not a crime; perhaps his examiners were unfamiliar with the work from which Mesmer plundered whole sentences and a complete list of case histories.

This work was Richard Mead's *De imperio solis ac lunae* (*On the Rulership of the Sun and Moon*, 1704). Mead was an English doctor who moved in the highest circles of English society, and was the personal physician to both Queen Anne and Isaac Newton. Most of the forty-eight pages of Mesmer's dissertation are taken up with physics, and contain a summary of Newton's theory of gravitation and tides, followed by an unacknowledged précis of Mead's application of this to the human body. Mead postulated that there was a 'nervous fluid' in the body which was affected by the gravitational pull of the sun and moon. Mesmer postulated a universal gravitational fluid which exists as the medium of gravity, since the heavenly bodies would be unable to exert any influence on one another in a vacuum, and which therefore transmits the influence of the planets on to human bodies as well as everywhere else. Mesmer adapted Newton's theory of tides to the human body and before long he would be claiming to be able to create tides in the human body by magnetism.

Throughout his life Mesmer liked to see himself – and liked others to see him – as an original thinker, a misunderstood genius. In actual fact, though, his dissertation was derivative and his theories were not startling in the context of their times. Anyway, armed with a degree from a medical school as good as any in Europe, Mesmer set up a practice in Vienna, the rival of Paris as the European capital of culture. Before long, he had worked his way up to the highest levels of society, chiefly by the fortunate marriage, on 10 January 1768, to the wealthy widow Maria Anna von Posch, whose first husband had been a government official. The wedding was a splendid affair, conducted in the fourteenth-century St Stephen's Cathedral by the Archbishop of Vienna, Cardinal Migazzi, but the marriage was not blessed with happiness. He found her stupid and dull, but presumably this downside was more than offset by her positive qualities: she gave him money and respectability. She already had a teenage son, Franz, and Mesmer never had any children of his own.

Maria's father gave them a large house at 261 Landstrasse, in the most prosperous district of Vienna, overlooking the Prater park. Here the couple lived in the grand style; attached to the house was a garden large enough to be laid out with avenues and statues, a belvedere and so on. Mesmer added laboratories and a small concert hall. He was musical, playing the clavichord and cello very competently, and specializing in the arcane glass harmonica, an instrument consisting of a series of different-sized glass bowls – a development of the method of making music by tapping tumblers filled with varying quantities of water. The American statesman and scientist Benjamin Franklin is credited with the invention of the glass harmonica, but this is not the only way in which his path and Mesmer's were destined to cross.

As well as making music himself, Mesmer turned himself into something of a patron of the arts. He soon became friends with Christoph Willibald von Gluck and Joseph Haydn, but his most famous friendship was with Leopold Mozart, who was in Vienna promoting the talent of his son, twelve years old in 1768, Wolfgang Amadeus. Leopold Mozart and Mesmer were on good terms, and saw quite a bit of each other over the years, whenever the Mozarts were in town. A 1773 letter of Mozart to his wife in Salzburg gives us a glimpse of the relationship: 'I did not send a line by the last post for there was a big musical rout at our friend Mesmer's house ... Our host plays Miss Davies's glass harmonica vastly well. He is the only person in Vienna who has learned to perform upon this instrument, and he possesses a far more handsome glass machine than was Miss Davies's own. Wolfgang has played it too.' (The instrument was known as 'Miss Davies's glass harmonica', because an English woman, Marianne Davies, had become famous as a performer on the instrument. At concerts, her sister Cecilia used to sing along with her.)

In September 1768, not long after the *Wunderkind* had arrived in the city, Leopold was frustrated in getting an opera of his son's performed in public on a large scale. Mesmer kindly offered the little theatre in his garden, and this place then goes down in history as the site of the first performance of a Mozart opera. The young genius composed *Bastien and Bastienne* specially for the occasion. Later, however, he did not repay his debt to Mesmer in kind: the only direct reference in his works to Mesmer's theories is a piece of burlesque. Towards the end of the first act of *Così fan tutte* Ferrando and Guglielmo, in disguise, have pretended to swallow poison, in an attempt to persuade Fiordiligi and Dorabella of the sincerity of their wooing. Despina, the girls' servant, who is in on the whole charade (the men are in disguise in order to try to win a bet with Don Alfonso, who does not believe the girls will remain faithful to them), comes in disguised as a healer, carrying a huge magnetic stone with which she revives the two men. Despite the superficially complimentary words – 'This magnetic stone should give the traveller pause. Once it was used by Mesmer, who was born in Germany's green fields, and who won great fame in France' – the whole scene is supposed to be played in a comic fashion. Depending on how the stone was shaped and wielded, the scene could even be made comically obscene. The opera dates from 1790, by which time it had become popular to ridicule Mesmer and his theories; even though, as usual, it was Lorenzo da Ponte, not Mozart himself, who wrote the words to the opera, it looks as though Mozart was pandering to the audience's expectations and whims in allowing his librettist to get away with this ridicule.

Breakthrough: Fraulein Oesterlin

Since we have no record to the contrary, we may presume that at this time Mesmer's medical practice consisted of the usual methods – leeches and bloodletting, blistering, purgatives, sedatives and so on. He was getting on for forty years old, a tall, stout man, with broad shoulders, somewhat coarse features, an imposing presence and the kind of bedside manner that went down well with his wealthy clients, provided he could curb his enormous ego and short temper. But in the early 1770s it came to his attention that the Astronomer Royal to the imperial Austrian court, Father Maximilian Hell, was experimenting with the healing properties of magnets. This was greatly facilitated by the fact that in 1750 John Canton had discovered how to make artificial magnets by rubbing iron or steel. Magnets were suddenly more widely available, and didn't have to be dug out of the ground, but could be shaped and sized to one's purpose.

Healing through magnets has a long history, dating back at least to ancient Greece, and it had been promoted, closer to Mesmer's times, by various luminaries. Paracelsus (Theophrastus Bombastus von Hohenheim, 1493–1541) had hypothesized that we possess a magnetic power by which we can attract healthy or diseased effluvia from a body; the magnetic 'virtue' is stronger in the healthy than the weak. Johannes Baptiste van Helmont had discussed magnetic healing in *De Magnetica Vulnerum Curatione* (1621), as had the Jesuit Athanasius Kircher (1602–80), Robert Fludd (in *Philosophica Moysaica*, 1637), and William Maxwell in *De medicina magnetica* (c. 1650). Maxwell went so far as to claim that all illness is the result of a defect in the vital magnetic fluid of the body, and that these defects can be rectified by restoring the appropriate quantity of magnetism. Hell was far from the first to practise healing with magnets.

Mesmer had a hysterical patient called Francisca Oesterlin, a friend and companion of his wife. She suffered, in Mesmer's own words, from 'constant vomiting, inflammation of the bowels, stoppage of urine, excruciating toothache, earache, melancholy, depression, delirium, fits of frenzy, catalepsy, fainting fits, blindness, breathlessness, and lameness'. It's hardly surprising that melancholy and depression are on the list! Some of Leopold Mozart's letters add that she was frequently at death's door, and nothing but skin and bones. Mesmer had tried all the usual remedies, but to no avail. Finally he turned to Hell, and ordered some magnets from him. In July 1774, he made Oesterlin swallow a drink infused with iron and then attached three magnets to her, one on her stomach, the other two on her legs. Oesterlin went into crisis: she felt waves of energy pulsing through her body and threw a fit. After several sessions, though, she was cured, and the cure seems to have been permanent. At any rate, we have a 1781 letter of Leopold Mozart from Mesmer's house saying that Oesterlin was plump and well, and the mother of two fine babies – she had married Mesmer's stepson.

It looks as though this cure struck Mesmer like a bolt of lightning. He was a convert, an enthusiast; the course of his life was changed for ever. Away with conventional medicine: he had discovered a universal panacea, a way of helping nature to bring about the state of ideal health. But if this was the first of Mesmer's magnetic cures, it was also the first of many professional quarrels. Hell wrote an article, to which Mesmer took great offence, pointing out his part in Oesterlin's cure. Mesmer replied that Hell's magnets had little to do with it, since magnets themselves are not the agents of cure, but simply channel the universal magnetic fluid into and through the patient's body. The magnetic fluid is what animates a body and is responsible for health and disease; if it is in equilibrium, we are healthy, and disease is disorder of the fluid. The presence of the magnetic fluid in us gives us 'animal magnetism' (which simply means 'vital magnetism'), more if we are healthy, less if we are ill. If health is the correct balance of the magnetic fluid in us, it is the healer's job to channel the universal fluid into the patient's body to effect a cure. And he claimed that this is what he had always believed, since his days as a medical student at university. In other words, somewhere along the line in Mesmer's mind the 'gravitational fluid' of his dissertation had become 'magnetic fluid'.

Hell suggested testing Mesmer's theories by magnetizing just one of a number of bottles of water and asking a patient to pick out the correct bottle time and time again. The patient should instinctively know which is the correct bottle, because of her bodily need for extra magnetic fluid. Needless to say – and as he would later too – Mesmer refused to carry out any such experiments. In his view the fact of the cure was all the evidence anyone should need to recognize the supreme importance of himself and his discovery to humankind. Throughout his life he would dress his theories up in scientific language and say things like 'Observations have shown that . . .', when he had carried out no laboratory tests at all.

Exorcism or Magnetism?

Further magnetic cures followed (and perhaps some failures too, though we don't hear of those). Mesmer found he could 'magnetize' other substances – paper, glass, water, etc. – so that all these things could act just as effectively as magnets themselves as conductors of magnetic fluid and as instruments of healing. This only confirmed his argument with Hell: the magnets themselves are not important. He gradually came to believe that he himself was a particular channel for the magnetic fluid – that his animal magnetism could produce the same effect on people as real magnets or magnetized substances – and he began to use hand passes to redistribute the fluid in the patient in a healthy way, and to guide it if necessary to the ailing part of the body. He also realized that the patient was more likely to get better if there was good rapport between him and her, and even that physical contact was not always necessary, just speaking with authority. On occasion, then, he found that he could heal through a wall, but it never occurred to him that this was due to the power of suggestion: throughout his life he remained a convinced materialist, so that if he could heal through a wall, that was because the fluid was powerful and fine enough to pass through solid objects.

'There is only one illness,' Mesmer would grandly declare, 'and only one cure.' Illness is caused by blockage of magnetic fluid (witness hardening of the arteries, stiffening of the joints, aches and pains), and to cure is to free the blockage. The patient will often experience a crisis point when the fluid reaches equilibrium (it had been standard medical theory since the time of Hippocrates in ancient Greece that the transition from illness to health is marked by some kind of crisis). This crisis is due to the fact that the magnetic fluid in the patient's body has solidified, so to speak, and a sudden push is needed to restart the healthful process. This push is provided by the magnetizer. The crisis takes the form of a fit: physical convulsions, weeping, hiccups or uncontrollable laughter, a tight feeling in the throat and chest, a feeling of cold and then of heat, sweating – that kind of thing. In some patients the crisis passes quickly; in others it lasts up to three hours.

Mesmer is sometimes criticized because, despite the blunt maxim that there is only one illness and only one cure, throughout his life he continued to prescribe certain medicines, both for himself and for others. But in fact these medicines are largely purgatives, which is consistent with his theory of blockage and unblockage. He once told Charles d'Eslon, his foremost disciple in Paris, that medicines were effective only in so far as they were conductors of the magnetic fluid. Perhaps he felt that over time he had identified the drugs which were such conductors and employed only these: there would be nothing inconsistent in this.

Emboldened by his successes, and wanting to gain official recognition for his methods and theories (a goal that he and his disciples would pursue, more or less futilely, for years), he sent a paper outlining his work round to various European medical academies. The only one to respond, however, was the Berlin Academy of Sciences, on 24 March 1775. They were extremely doubtful that Mesmer could magnetize non-metallic substances and found it unlikely that his methods had any true therapeutic value.

A test case for Mesmer's materialism occurred later that year. Mesmer was visiting Bavaria, where his fame had gained him membership of the Academy of Sciences (the only official honour he was ever to achieve). He was spreading the magnetic gospel, and Elector Maximilian Joseph III asked him to investigate the work of Johann Joseph Gassner, a Catholic priest who was carrying out a great many exorcisms, though by the laying-on of hands rather than by the rites accepted by the Church. Gassner had started healing in the 1760s, in Klösterle, a small village in eastern Switzerland where he was the priest. By the middle of the 1770s he had achieved astonishing fame throughout the German-speaking areas of Europe, and people were flocking to him in their thousands. Here is an account of one of his healings:

> The first patients were two nuns who had been forced to leave their community on account of convulsive fits. Gassner told the first one to kneel before him, asked her briefly about her name, her illness, and whether she agreed that anything he would order should happen. She agreed. Gassner then pronounced solemnly in Latin: 'If there be anything preternatural about this disease, I order in the name of Jesus that it manifest itself immediately.' The patient started at once to have convulsions. According to Gassner, this was proof that the convulsions were caused by an evil spirit and not by a natural illness, and he now proceeded to demonstrate that he had power over the demon, whom he ordered in Latin to produce convulsions in various parts of the patient's body; he called forth in turn the exterior manifestations of grief, silliness, scrupulosity, anger and so on, and even the appearance of death. All his orders were punctually executed. It now seemed logical that, once a demon had been tamed to that point, it should be relatively easy to expel him, which Gassner did.

The fact that Gassner got the nun to display anger, grief and so on, is remarkably reminiscent of the displays elicited by stage hypnotists. More importantly, Gassner's patients behaved just like Mesmer's patients, and were cured just as effectively – and yet Gassner spoke only about God and evil spirits, with no reference to any material fluid, magnetic or otherwise. Mesmer's conclusion about Gassner, not surprisingly, was that Gassner, without knowing it, was making use of animal magnetism, an entirely natural process. In the sixth and fifth centuries BCE, certain Greek thinkers began to explain the awesome meteorological phenomena which had previously been the exclusive domain of the gods by reference to natural processes: it was not Zeus but the clouds that caused thunder when they clashed. This exactly parallels the clash between Mesmer and Gassner. Gassner was a 'primitive' healer born in an increasingly rationalist age; Mesmer represented the new spirit. He felt himself to be a scientist because he was attributing healing to natural rather than divine causes. Gassner fell from grace, not as a result of Mesmer's report to the Elector of Bavaria, but because the Church had long been looking askance at his practices. His fall was as abrupt as his fame. The Church and the Bavarian government proscribed his writings and banned his practice, and he died a few years later in obscurity.

Back in Vienna Mesmer won few converts among his fellow doctors. They tended to regard him as unscientific, and they were worried about reports of trance states in his patients, which sounded to them like sorcery; it was not many years since the last witch to be burnt in Europe had gone to the stake. They were also worried about the moral propriety of Mesmer's methods. The hand passes Mesmer employed often involved physical contact with the patient's body – think of it as massaging the body's supposed magnetic poles and nodes with the hands or sometimes with magnetically charged instruments. Mesmer would sit with the patient's knees between his own or with feet touching, so as to set up a magnetic polarity between healer and patient, since he believed that opposite sides of the body contained opposite magnetic poles. His patients were invariably women. The healer would run his fingers all over or around the patient's body, looking for the poles of the small magnets that together composed the great magnet of the body as a whole. Areas to be avoided were the crown of the head and the soles of the feet, because they were respectively the receptors for astral magnetism and terrestrial magnetism. The small magnets of the body kept changing position somewhat, except those in the nose and the fingers. (Mesmer prohibited the taking of snuff, in case it upset the nose's magnetic balance.) In practice, the area of the body most massaged was the upper abdomen, which was seen as the body's equator. This was bound to seem licentious to the sensibilities of the time. Nowadays we are used to doctors prodding and probing us, but that was not the way things were done in the days before the invention of stethoscopes and percussion. Rarely would a doctor press his ear to his patient's chest. He identified the illness as best he could from past experience and from questioning the patient, and then made prescriptions accordingly.

But official disapproval from the medical academies and his

fellow doctors in Vienna didn't dent Mesmer's confidence, and he continued to attract a number of patients. He set up a magnetic clinic in his own house, in which he installed baths where patients could immerse themselves or their hands and feet in magnetized water. Powerful patients began to hear of his reputation as a miraculous healer. Baron Horeczky de Horka invited him to spend some weeks at his castle in Hungary, near Rohau, where he not only helped the baron with his throat spasms, but cured a number of local folk too. An eyewitness report of his working on the baron shows the eccentricity of his methods:

> Mesmer sat on the right side of the bed, on a stool, wearing a grey gown trimmed with gold braid. On one foot he had a white silk stocking; the other, which was bare, was immersed in a tub about two feet in diameter, filled with water . . . Near the tub sat Kolowratek [Mesmer's assistant for this operation], fully dressed, facing the bed and holding in his left hand a metal rod the tip of which rested on the bottom of the tub. With his right hand he rubbed the rod up and down.

The eyewitness, Ernst Seyfert, the tutor of the baron's children, adds that he couldn't help laughing at the sight of Mesmer alternately grasping the baron's hand with one hand and his big toe with the other, presumably to polarize the magnetic fluid in his body. But for the baron, as occasionally for others among Mesmer's patients, the treatment was worse than the ailment: the unpleasant aspects of the convulsions put him off and he eventually asked Mesmer to leave.

Breakdown: The Affair of the Blind Pianist

There was in Vienna a child prodigy who was the talk of the town. Despite her blindness, Maria Theresa von Paradis was an excellent pianist and had become one of Empress Maria Theresa's protégées. She was not born blind, but lost her sight on 9 December 1763, aged three. She was talented enough on the piano not only to give concerts from an early age, and to compose a few pieces herself, but later to have Mozart write his Concerto in B Flat Major for her. Cynically or realistically, we might think that part of the reason for her fame was precisely her blindness, but her parents and those who cared for her had spent enormous amounts of time and money trying to get her cured. For ten years and more, she had been subjected to the full range of standard medical treatments, including some 3,000 electric shocks, but everything had proved useless.

Late in 1776 her parents approached Mesmer. Did he mind being the last resort, when everything else had failed? Probably not: if successful he would shine, and otherwise nothing had been lost. Early in 1777 Mesmer moved the teenager into the private clinic he had built as a wing of his house. By 9 February she claimed to be able to see outlines, and the spasms in her eyes became less. Her parents were delighted, and her father even vouched for her cure publicly, in writing. Gradually Mesmer acclimatized her to light, until she could see better and better; gradually she got used to people's ugliness, and to perspective.

Understandably, while she was at the in-between stage of learning to use her eyes, her piano-playing suffered; her touch had been secure in her blind world, but certain skills had to be relearnt with the recovery of her sight, and she had continuing problems with the assessment of distance. This worried her parents: they were receiving a good income from the Empress thanks to their daughter's skills, and if she lost those skills, the Empress might well cancel their allowance. They arranged for other doctors to examine the girl, and while these other doctors, who were already antagonistic to Mesmer, could not deny that a blind girl now could see, they poured scorn on Mesmer's methods. There may also have been hints of immorality. A beautiful young girl had been living in Mesmer's house for some time, and treated in ways that were more often maliciously misinterpreted than misused. In the phenomenon the Freudians call 'transference', perhaps the girl had become overly attached to Mesmer. Perhaps Mesmer returned her affection; he would shortly leave his wife and change his life in a way that smacks of mid-life crisis, and attraction to a younger woman is often a sign of mid-life crisis in a forty-something male.

The parents stormed into Mesmer's house and demanded their

daughter back. She refused to leave, and the mother forcibly tore her from her nurse's arms and flung her against the wall. When Mesmer went to help, the mother turned on him. The father entered with his sword drawn. By now Maria Theresa was in a terrible state, and was vomiting noisily in a corner; her parents became alarmed at this and were persuaded to leave her there. They even asked Mesmer to continue the treatment, and within a fortnight Mesmer had calmed her nerves and got her back to the point before her parents' interference. They asked to have her home for a while, promising to return her soon to her doctor, and Mesmer fell for it. The girl soon suffered a relapse, but Mesmer was refused access to her. The doctors pronounced her blind and Mesmer a charlatan. All Vienna was talking about the affair. We may guess that Mesmer's conventional wife was deeply upset with him. He was accused of fraudulent practice and ordered to give up his practice or leave Vienna.

The trouble with this account of the Paradis affair, as with most of Mesmer's work, is that we hear only Mesmer's side. Since he was an irascible man who suffered opposition very poorly, it is hard to tell how much exaggeration has gone into it. Reading between the lines, it is quite plausible to suggest that the young Miss Paradis never really recovered her sight; she could probably already see things vaguely and dimly, and was sensitive to light and shadows, and that was all. There is little in Mesmer's account to make one think that he was not simply redescribing her limited sight in a more optimistic fashion, or that she was not deluding herself into thinking that she was getting better. Her blindness was more likely organic than functional, since it is hard to conceive how a three-year-old might receive the kind of shock which would induce hysterical blindness, and it did prove to be a lifelong affliction. But if it was organic blindness, Mesmer could hardly have managed to improve it.

The City of Light

As a result of his rejection by the Viennese medical community, Mesmer grew restless and decided to try his luck in the other European centre of culture and science, Paris. At the end of January 1778 he went to Paris, without his wife (whom he never saw again; she died of breast cancer in Vienna in September 1790), but with a letter of introduction to Count Florimund Merci-Argenteau, the Austrian ambassador. He may well have entertained hopes of being patronized by Marie Antoinette, Louis XVI's queen, who was Austrian herself, the daughter of the great Empress, who had certainly heard of Mesmer. At any rate, he renewed his acquaintance with Gluck, who was in Paris and a favourite of the queen.

The Paris into which Mesmer came was a city of conflicting opinions and attitudes. On the one hand, the Enlightenment appeared to rule: Voltaire and Rousseau had just died, Diderot had completed the final volume of his massive *Encyclopédie*, science and mathematics were forging ahead in the hands of men such as Laplace, Lavoisier and Lagrange. On the other hand, there were secret societies of Rosicrucians and Swedenborgians propagating vague mystical notions, quacks selling home-brewed medicines in the streets, and the time was ripe for occultists such as Casanova and Cagliostro. It was Mesmer's tragedy that although he felt he belonged among the scientists, he would be condemned to the other class. But at a popular level his theories would easily have passed for science at the time, and even the fact that there was something 'occult' about them would not have been held against them.

In Paris his reputation – both as a healer and as a controversial figure – went before him, and he found it easy to meet influential people through his Austrian contacts. He claimed, in fact, that it was not his intention to practise healing in Paris, but that people's curiosity and the desperate plight of his first patients won him over. To many he was the prophet of a new science; to some his cures seemed to show the direct effect of God in the world, and therefore to counteract the atheism of the Enlightenment; to most he simply seemed to offer hope of a cure for their ills. In a medical context, it is not difficult to see why he was so popular: what passed for medical science at the time was invariably little more than faith healing dressed up in rationalistic language, and was usually far more intrusive and painful than what Mesmer was offering. There are actually rather few ailments that are effectively treated by the kinds of potions available at the time, or by leeches, bloodletting and purges. Nevertheless, many physicians felt instinctively that what they were offering was altogether different from folk medicine, and drew a sharp dividing line by climbing on to a high horse of overblown and ultimately unjustifiable rationalism.

Mesmer rented a large mansion in the Place Vendôme (or the Place Louis-le-grand, as it was known then). He made the acquaintance of Charles Leroy, President of the French Academy of Sciences. Mesmer wanted to gain official recognition for his theories, and since he considered himself a physicist as much as a physician, the Academy seemed the right place to start. With Leroy's help he held a couple of demonstrations in front of sceptical officials, but they were inconclusive; any effects Mesmer produced were said to be inexplicable, rather than attributable to animal magnetism. Mesmer gave up on the Academy and approached the newly formed Royal Society of Medicine, hoping that it would be more open to revolutionary ideas, but they were just as sceptical. He wrote several letters to the Royal Society, asking them to come and witness his results for themselves, but his letters remained unanswered or snubbed. It is typical of Mesmer that, although he wanted the imprimatur of these official organizations, once he had been rejected by them he cast scorn on them. He described the Royal Society as a licenser of quacks and sellers of poisons.

Having failed to make any impression on the medical community, Mesmer decided to build up a practice and convince by success. He had moved to the village of Créteil, a few miles from Paris, where the layout of the house and the rural surroundings suited his work better. Here he continued to attract lay clients and official scorn. In so far as he was concerned to make money – to keep himself in the manner to which his acquired social status in Vienna had accustomed him – he could somewhat ignore the scorn and bask in the new feeling, which he had never experienced before, of being the healer to whom patients turned first, rather than as a last resort.

Soon he had too many patients to treat individually. Reluctant to turn them away, he needed to develop some more rapid means of treating them. He found two such means: the *baquet*, described in the Preface, by which he could treat as many as thirty patients at a time, and the 'magnetic chain', in which patients held hands so that the magnetic fluid and its healing properties could pass from one to the other. Mesmer's house was thronged by up to 200 patients at a time, and most of them were paying handsomely for the cure. His dreams were coming true. He was minting money and gaining support at all levels of society. After a couple of months the need to be in the centre of things led him back to Paris, where he took a large house in the rue Coq Héron. Soon, despite the large sums he charged, he had too many patients and even this mansion could not house enough *baquets* to cope. But since he believed that anything could be magnetized, he magnetized a huge tree near the St Martin Gate and attached ropes to the branches. Up to 100 people could sit around this tree, touching the ropes to the afflicted parts of their bodies, and the tree's remarkable properties were said to be confirmed by the fact that it was the first to bear leaves in the spring and the last to lose them in the autumn. Such was the popularity of his techniques that the mere rumour that a particular tree had been mesmerized would have people running over to hug it.

Mesmer was a man of contrasts. There is no doubt that he wanted money and respect, but at the same time he was moved by a genuine impulse to heal. He was shocked by the treatment of the poor, who were either herded into huge wards in public hospitals or not treated at all since they couldn't pay. He treated them for free (as his teacher at medical school, Gerard van Swieten, had in Vienna), and to compensate charged his rich clients enormous sums. Driven not just by common humanity, but by a desperate need for recognition, he treated princesses and paupers, duchesses and dustmen, counts and cobblers. In reality, though, there were more duchesses than dustmen, because the ailments Mesmer was particularly good at treating were the kind which working people do not have the time for – nervous ailments such as the vapours. It is also undoubtedly true that many women came to Mesmer when they were not really suffering from any illness; it became a fashion, an amusement, something to talk about over tea and cards at Countess So-and-so's salon.

Some idea of the scene around a *baquet* can be gained from the report of the 1784 Royal Commission, whose work we will soon look at in more detail:

> The tableau presented by the patients is one of extreme diversity ... Some are calm, composed, and feel nothing; others cough, spit, have slight pains, feel a glow locally or all over the body, accompanied by perspiration; others are shaken and tormented by convulsions. These convulsions are remarkable in their frequency, their duration, and their intensity. As soon as one attack begins others make their appearance. The Commission has seen them last for more than three hours; they are accompanied by expectorations of a viscous matter, torn from the chest by the violence of the attack. Sometimes there are traces of blood in the expectoration. The convulsions are characterized by involuntary spasmodic movements of the limbs and of the whole body, by contractions of the throat, by spasms of the hypochondriac and epigastric regions; the eyes are wandering and distracted; there are piercing cries, tears, hiccoughs, and extravagant laughter. The convulsions are preceded and followed by a state of languor and reverie, by exhaustion and drowsiness. Any sudden noise causes the patients to start, and even a change in the music played on the piano has an effect – a lively tune agitates them afresh and renews the convulsions.

This excerpt focuses on the convulsions, but it is clear from the first two sentences that although convulsions were frequent, they were by no means universal. In fact d'Eslon, in his reply to the commissioners, claimed that of the 500 or so patients he had treated, only about twenty had experienced convulsions. Nevertheless, the commissioners were right to stress them, because Mesmer clearly expected his patients to have fits, and took that to be a sign of the crisis that cleared the way for healing. What on earth was going on? Why did so many people have convulsions? They cannot all have been epileptics, or subject to other organically based fits. There were probably three main reasons why the crisis manifested in this form. First, the Christian rites of exorcism, which had been practised for many centuries, and, as we have seen, reached a phenomenal height of popularity with Gassner, invariably provoked such fits in their subjects, and so Mesmer's patients will have expected their crises to take such a form. Within recent history there had been a craze for spontaneous healing at a saint's grave in Paris, until the king banned it as a public nuisance: the cures had often been preceded by fits. Second, it was fashionable at the time and throughout the nineteenth century for society women to suffer from the 'vapours', which involved hysterical fainting and nervous fits. Third, Mesmer's practices and the general enthusiasm for science (he cleverly modelled his *baquet* on the Leyden jar, which was popular at the time among the very aristocrats who formed Mesmer's clientele) aroused such high expectations that the eventual release of those expectations, when it came, might well have produced a nervous reaction.

Of these, the first factor is probably the main one. Expectation and mass suggestion are powerful forces. Emile Coué tells the story of how a madman injected a passer-by in the street with a liquid which caused her leg to swell. The newspapers gave the story a few lines – and within a few days dozens of other cases had been reported, too many to be true. All Mesmer needed was a few good cures, and word spread around high-society Paris in a trice: 'There's a remarkable healer in town. He's really good.' This was an age of marvels; if Montgolfier could conquer the air with his balloons, why should Mesmer not discover a panacea?

As described in the Preface, Mesmer also made use of occult trappings, subdued lighting and so on in his healing rooms. Presumably he had found by experience that these work, but he never acknowledged the importance of psychological factors in the cures, and he remained an obdurate materialist all his life. It wasn't just his detractors who obscured the importance of the psychological aspects of his healing by focusing on the question whether there was any such thing as the cosmic fluid Mesmer talked about. These were precisely the rules of the game as Mesmer saw them too.

From Paris to Spa and Back Again

Not long after his arrival in Paris, Mesmer gained his most notable convert in Charles d'Eslon. This resuscitated his hopes of official recognition, because d'Eslon was physician to the Count d'Artois, one of Louis XVI's brothers, and a member of the prestigious Faculty of Medicine, the governing body of medicine in France. Even with d'Eslon by his side, however, his hopes were to be signally dashed. In 1779 he arranged to read some or all of his famous *Mémoire sur la découverte du magnétisme animal* (*On the Discovery of Animal Magnetism*) to some representatives of the Faculty, but this got him nowhere. They were impressed by his results, but needed more research before agreeing that the causes to which Mesmer attributed his successes were the right ones. There was little point, they argued, in his displaying patients before them and treating them, when they knew nothing of the previous history of these patients and so could not assess the extent of the cures. They wanted to put in place a control experiment to see if a blindfolded person would react to a line-up of people, only one of whom would be Mesmer with his magnetic powers. Mesmer and d'Eslon might have replied that in their view everyone had magnetic powers (though some more than others), but instead they rejected the experiment out of hand. Mesmer's discovery was too important to be subjected to petty tests.

At the end of the *Mémoire* Mesmer reduced his theory of animal magnetism to twenty-seven propositions, the most important of which are the following:

1. There exists a mutual influence between the heavenly bodies, the earth, and animal bodies.
2. A universally distributed fluid, which is so continuous as to be entirely without vacuum, and is of an incomparably rarefied nature, and is by its nature capable of receiving, propagating and communicating all the impressions of movement, is the medium of this influence.

8. The animal body sustains the alternate effects [ebb and flow] of this agent, which insinuates itself into the substance of the nerves and affects them without any intermediary.

9. It is particularly clear in the case of the human body that the agent has properties similar to those of a magnet; by the same token one can distinguish within it different, even opposite poles, which can be brought into communication, changed, destroyed and strengthened . . .

10. The animal body has a property which makes it susceptible to the influence of the heavenly bodies and to the reciprocal action of the bodies surrounding it; the similarity of this property to the magnet induced me to term it 'animal magnetism'.

23. The facts themselves will show that, provided the practical rules which I shall draw up are followed, this principle can cure nervous disorders directly, and other disorders indirectly.

If a system lacks coherence, drawing up its main points as a list can disguise its lack of coherence only to a limited extent. D'Eslon thought that they had failed with the Faculty because Mesmer was too vague and obscure; he focused too much on cosmology and not enough on the concrete matter of the cures. Perhaps too he had failed to impress the Faculty because of his thick German accent. So in 1780 d'Eslon published his *Observations sur le magnétisme animal*, a lucid account of a number of cures. But this only made him too a target for abuse. He was ordered to withdraw his allegiance from this new fad, but he refused and was stripped of certain privileges as a member of the medical Faculty, which at the same time unequivocally rejected Mesmer's ideas, and bullied other members who had shown signs of interest in animal magnetism to give it up.

Mesmer was fed up, and he decided to leave Paris. Marie Antoinette herself was persuaded to try to get him to stay by offering him, in the name of the king, a substantial income per year, provided a commissioned report was favourable. Even when the king relaxed this condition to a clause that Mesmer should accept some men of the government's choice as students, Mesmer was affronted. He saw such students as spies rather than a disinterested committee. He wrote an astonishingly arrogant and paranoid open letter to the queen, in which he demanded not just the annuity she had offered but a country estate where he could continue his work. He could have got away with such a letter only because these were the declining years of the monarchy in France. It is easy to see why he was gaining a reputation as a crank.

Naturally enough, Marie Antoinette did not deign to answer, and in May 1781 Mesmer left Paris for Spa in Belgium, accompanied by a few of his wealthier patients. In Spa he perhaps hoped to pick up further patients from the various clinics, as well as restore his own health which had been battered by the stresses of Paris. He was bitterly angry and disappointed, but perhaps he also had the hidden agenda of wanting to arouse public opinion to wield against the authorities. 'If they miss me,' he might have thought, 'their protests will reach official ears.' His constant rejection by the medical authorities (which he attributed to envy, presumption and incredulity) had only hardened his determination to achieve recognition as a great pioneer and the saviour of humankind. He wanted d'Eslon to join him in Spa, but d'Eslon refused, stayed in Paris and set up his own clinic. One can sympathize with d'Eslon's position: he did not want to abandon his patients, and could not understand how Mesmer could do so. But Mesmer took offence: he thought that d'Eslon was stealing his patients, and regarded him as a traitor.

In Spa, as well as taking the waters to calm his disgruntled nerves, he wrote his *Short History of Animal Magnetism*. With d'Eslon in bad odour, his two main cronies were the lawyer Nicolas Bergasse and the banker Guillaume Kornmann, who were dividing their time between Paris and Spa. They came up with a proposal which was designed to attract Mesmer back to Paris, and to assuage his worries about losing clients and hence income to d'Eslon. They wanted to found a special academy for the propagation of animal magnetism, where Mesmer would instruct others. At the end of 1781 Mesmer returned to Paris to discuss the rules and regulations of this academy with Bergasse and Kornmann, who had prepared the way well: Mesmer found that there were more than enough people prepared to pay the exorbitant subscription to found the academy, and he gave Bergasse and Kornmann the go-ahead. He returned to Spa in July 1782, with Bergasse as his unwilling secretary; their relationship was never sound, and would soon lead to the project's collapse.

While in Spa he heard that d'Eslon had again been reprimanded by the Faculty, and had suffered the indignity of having further privileges removed. While he was pleased by his disciple's loyalty to the cause, he still felt betrayed. He raged that d'Eslon had no right to set up on his own, that he was incompetent, that he didn't know enough about animal magnetism and so on. Though there were some attempts at reconciliation, the two of them never again saw eye to eye, one of the bones of contention being that d'Eslon felt that only qualified medical men should be allowed to study animal magnetism, whereas now, with his academy, Mesmer was opening it up to anyone who could afford the fee. Finally, in January 1784 d'Eslon published a brief account of his quarrels with Mesmer and formally announced that he was setting up as an animal magnetist in his own right. By now he had been expelled from the Faculty, but his aristocratic connections guaranteed him a wealthy practice – or, as Mesmer saw it, deprived Mesmer of a number of wealthy clients. Mesmer threatened to sue him, but in the end backed down from this silly posturing.

Anyway, back in Paris at the end of 1782, Bergasse, Kornmann and Mesmer put their plans into operation: 100 of Mesmer's followers gave a subscription of 100 louis d'or each, and further money was raised from provincial societies where the charge was 50 louis d'or. They called the Parisian academy by the Masonic-sounding name of the Lodge of Harmony (later the Society of Universal Harmony). Mesmer was named Founder and Perpetual President of all the societies. Members were sworn to secrecy: they were not to divulge Mesmer's instruction (which took place not only in classes, but also by the reading of his written works), nor set up as practising animal magnetists on their own. This last clause was presumably inspired by Mesmer's resentment of d'Eslon, because there was no rational reason for it and it went directly against the original plan of Bergasse and Kornmann, for whom the whole point of the academy was that it would teach future teachers. Torn apart by this contradiction and by the dissension between Mesmer and Bergasse, the Paris society lasted no more than two years from its foundation in March 1783.

As well as witnessing cures and learning the techniques and the theory of the action of animal magnetism on the nervous system, the students discussed the metaphysical, cosmological and political aspects of magnetism – the type of work that in 1784 would result in Bergasse's *The Theory of the World and of Living Organisms According to the Principles of Mesmer*. This book was written partly in code: over 100 of the key terms were given symbols rather than spelled out, so as to exclude non-initiates of the society. But then Bergasse was even more given to mystery than his master.

The founding members of the Paris society included some illustrious names. Of especial interest to us in this book is that all three de Puységur brothers, whom we will meet more thoroughly in the next chapter, were original members, along with some of the great names of the French aristocracy – Duc de Lauzun, Duc de Coigny, Baron de Talleyrand, and the Marquis de Jaucourt, for example. Ironically, given Benjamin Franklin's hostility towards mesmerism (as we shall see in the next section), his grandson William Temple Franklin was an early member of the Paris society. The flamboyant Marquis de Lafayette (1757–1834) was also one of the original members. He had recently made a name for himself by taking a ship across the Atlantic to offer his help in the American War of Independence and inflicting a heavy defeat on the English at Barren Hill. Mesmer encouraged this disciple of his in his enthusiasm both for animal magnetism and for the new republic across the ocean, since he saw de Lafayette as a suitable apostle of the new therapy in America. De Lafayette did talk to George Washington privately about animal magnetism, but he does not appear to have spread the word more widely than giving one or two lectures. However, Thomas Jefferson, who was then the American represent-ative in Versailles, was worried enough to send back home a number of anti-mesmerist pamphlets and copies of the negative reports of the two 1784 commissions.

1784: Mesmerism in Crisis

Mesmer was either giving up the idea of official recognition, or was biding his time, but d'Eslon, motivated perhaps by a desire to advertise his clinic, succeeded where Mesmer had failed. As a result of his requests, on 12 March 1784 Louis XVI appointed a committee from the Faculty of Medicine, who co-opted some members from the Academy of Sciences. Their brief was to investigate animal magnetism, and they chose to do so in d'Eslon's clinic, not Mesmer's. Mesmer protested, but it shouldn't have made any difference, since they were investigating animal magnetism, not personalities. In any case, the fact that it was d'Eslon who was investigated, not Mesmer, eventually worked to Mesmer's advantage. Subsequent to the commission's report, the threat to forbid the practice of animal magnetism was defused by the legal technicality that Mesmer's work had not been examined. In any case, Mesmer had always been convinced that he had more magnetic power than most people, and so could work the cures better.

The committee was chaired by Benjamin Franklin, then an old man of seventy-eight, who was one of the envoys to France of the newly recognized country, the United States of America. Franklin's position was honorary rather than active, because of his age and infirmity, but some of the meetings took place in his house at Passy. The deputy chairman was Jean-Sylvain Bailly, an astronomer and statesman, who later became Mayor of Paris until his death on the guillotine. Antoine-Laurent Lavoisier was also prominent; he was an eminent chemist who had isolated and identified oxygen in the air, and had established the principle of atomic weights and the classification of chemicals. He was a tax-collector in Paris during the early years of the Revolution, until he was sent to the guillotine on the trumped-up charge of having added water to tobacco supplies. The names of other committee members – there were nine in all – have not survived the passage of time well, but it is worth mentioning

Joseph-Ignace Guillotin, who was himself spared from beheading by the instrument he had envisaged only by the death of Robespierre.

Franklin and his colleagues on the committee were members of a Masonic lodge in Paris called the Neuf Soeurs (Nine Sisters). The membership of this lodge overlapped with that of a mystical lodge called Philalethes (Love of Truth), whose Grand Master, Savalette Delanges, had convened an international conference to consider the occult implications of mesmerism in the very month that the committee met. Reports were already coming in from the provinces that magnetized subjects were demonstrating clairvoyant abilities. The stage was set for a battle between empiricism and cumulative knowledge, on the one side, and on the other the claim that mesmerism opened one up as a sensitive to more comprehensive knowledge.

There is no doubt that the commission did an effective hatchet job on mesmerism, but there were also gaping holes in their procedures. They proved that the magnetic fluid does not exist, but oddly ignored the question of how Mesmer and d'Eslon had cured so many people. They did not want to disturb the sensibilities of d'Eslon's eminent clients – 'The distinguished patients could not be questioned too closely without the risk of annoying them' – so they experimented on themselves rather than them, but they were healthy people, so the fact that they felt no effect is, on Mesmer's own terms, no proof or disproof: their fluid was already in equilibrium. They tried to magnetize others themselves, but since they were sceptics, the healing power of suggestion was not present, and so it is no wonder that they failed. They suspected that cures might be due to spontaneous remission, and thought that convulsions could be damaging and addictive. As the 1784 comedy *The Baquet of Health* ironically puts it, when one character asks another if she is getting better: 'Much better, madame. I used never to have more than one crisis a week. Now I have two a day.'

It is hard not to reproach the commission for short-sightedness. There were hundreds of testimonials of cures available to them. It would surely have been worthwhile for them to investigate them. As the Marquis de Puységur later complained, they thought that the facts did not prove anything. All right, they dismissed animal magnetism as nonsense; but *something* was causing the cures, and as scientists they should have looked into what it was: they might have appreciated the power of suggestion. The immediate problem was that they took themselves to be scientists investigating the existence of a supposed new substance, rather than physicians looking into an effective way of curing patients. The broader problem has been well expressed as follows: 'Science is the outgrowth of human curiosity, but the trained scientist often appears to be the least curious of mortals because he has imposed upon himself such rigorous conditions for satisfying his need.'

But for all the gaps in their approach to the cures, their debunking of animal magnetism was telling. They tried to repeat Mesmer's cures under controlled conditions and found that it was only when patients could see which parts of their bodies the magnetic fluid was being directed towards that they felt the required prickling sensations and were cured. When patients knew they were being treated by an operator, they would reach the crisis in a few minutes; when they did not know, no crisis was reached, even when the magnetizer was in the same room. Conversely, blindfolded patients who believed in animal magnetism reached crisis when they believed that d'Eslon was in the room even when he was not. Or again, they had one of five trees mesmerized, and then sent a patient to find which tree would effect the cure: the patient went into crisis at the wrong tree. They falsely told a patient in an adjoining room that he was being mesmerized, with the result that he went into crisis, even though nothing was in fact going on. They tried to detect the magnetic fluid with measuring devices, and failed. They concluded that 'imagination without magnetism produces convulsions, and that magnetism without imagination produces nothing', that 'the existence of the fluid is absolutely destitute of proof, and that the fluid, having no existence, can consequently have no use'.

The committee's emphasis on imagination is odd, in an ironic fashion. They were appealing to something psychic and hardly more liable to scientific procedures than animal magnetic fluid. Perhaps this is why they did not leave imagination to carry the whole burden of their argument. While stressing it as the main factor involved in Mesmer's cures, they also noted that sometimes the magnetist would actually touch his patient, and they thought that this touching could itself be therapeutic in some cases. Finally, along with imagination and touching, they pointed out the power of imitation: the fact that one patient feels better, and goes into convulsions, is likely to provoke the same reactions in the next and so on.

As we have seen, Mesmer's system was not a pseudo-science within the framework of the science of the time. There were other grandiose and unverifiable systems around, some of which received the official blessing of the Academy. In fact, two members of the 1784 commission were enthusiastic fluidists: Franklin explained the action of electricity by appeal to a fluid, and Lavoisier did the same for heat. Yet mesmerism was condemned by the 1784 commission. Why? What kind of threat did it pose to the medical establishment? The clash between mesmerism and the 1784 committee was an archetypal clash between two paradigms. It was to be echoed many times in the following decades, not just in further French commissions (which we will look at in the next chapter), but in Romantic literature. For many Romantics the attraction of magnetism was precisely that, as a holistic theory which saw the whole universe as interconnected by the fluid that pervaded it, it ran counter to the kind of scientific theory which splintered the world and forgot the big, meaningful picture. With good reason, the commission explicitly placed Mesmer in the scorned tradition of Paracelsus, van Helmont and Kircher, who all believed in magnetic cures. This tradition was despised because it was really no more than a pseudo-scientific dressing-up of magic; in this tradition magnetism was the occult force of the universe, on which a magician could draw to effect changes in the world. Finally, it is hard to resist the notion that Mesmer was being punished for his notorious cantankerousness.

As well as the official report, they submitted a private report to the king, expressing doubts about the morality of mesmeric procedures. Pointing out that the magnetizers are always men, and the patients invariably women, who are more susceptible to touching, imagination and imitation, they didn't like the fact that the magnetizer could touch 'the most sensitive parts of the body', nor the way the healer got so close to his patient: 'Their proximity becomes the closest possible, their faces nearly touch, their breaths mingle, they share all their physical reactions, and the mutual attraction of the sexes acts with full force. It would not be surprising if their feelings became inflamed.' They deliberately described the convulsions they had witnessed in d'Eslon's clinic in a way calculated to remind the reader of an orgasm. But no action was taken on the basis of this secret report, and it remains the case that no aggrieved husband or lover ever tried to sue Mesmer or d'Eslon for fooling around with his woman.

The Faculty and Academy commission was not the only investigation to which mesmerism had to submit in 1784. The eminent botanist Antoine-Laurent de Jussieu and some others from the Royal Society of Medicine formed an independent committee, also authorized by the king, which tagged along after the main commission. The Royal Society's report agreed substantially with the main committee's findings, but de Jussieu submitted a minority report, saying that they had not investigated the causes of the cures thoroughly enough. He felt that there were still some cases that hadn't been explained away by the commissioners, and for which animal magnetism or some such cause was required.

As a result of these two reports (or three, counting the secret one), the Faculty banned any doctor from professing or using animal magnetism, and the convictions of very few even of those doctors who had been using it gave them the courage to face official banishment. Mesmer claimed that he received many letters of encouragement, but he seems to have been further embittered by the whole business. D'Eslon's response was simply to agree that the imagination plays an enormous part in the cures of animal magnetism. He also published another series of wonderful cures to counteract the negative effect of the two commissions' reports. But it was too late for him, and he died in August 1786.

This last book by d'Eslon, called *Observations sur les deux rapports* (*Remarks on the Two Reports*), was just one of a torrent of pamphlets and discussions that circulated in 1784. In newspapers too there was no more common topic than mesmerism. Just to show how popular a topic mesmerism was, consider that the printed copy of the Franklin report sold 20,000 copies within a week or two of being published. No doubt Mesmer saw the printing of so many copies as a deliberate attempt by the establishment to turn popular opinion against him. To add to his woes, Fraulein von Paradis happened to be playing in Paris that April, and she was pronounced as blind as ever. Mesmer foolishly attended the concert; everyone knew the story; all eyes in the theatre turned to him. Another event which told against him was the death of the scholar Antoine Court de Gébelin, famous for his book *Le Monde Primitif*, in which he touted the notion that ancient cultures knew of a 'primitive science' which has since been lost to us. He had been a patient of Mesmer's previously for dropsy, and had written an enthusiastic pamphlet when he thought he was cured, but now, late in 1784, he died of kidney disease. A spoof epitaph circulated, which read:

> Here lies poor Gébelin,
> Fluent in Greek, Hebrew and Latin;
> All should admire his heroism;
> He was a martyr to magnetism.

If accidental events were tipping the balance against mesmerism, in the war of words honours were more evenly balanced. There were serious discussions, testimonials from cured patients, scurrilous attacks on animal magnetism and comic plays and verses which held it up for public ridicule. The two main playwrights to enter the fray were the satirists Pierre-Yves Barré and Jean-Baptiste Radet. In their comedies *Modern Doctors* and *The Baquet of Health* they liberally accused Mesmer of charlatanism, veniality and immorality. Some of Mesmer's loyal but misguided followers attempted to disrupt these plays by showering pro-magnetic leaflets on the audience. Incidents like this kept the topic in the public mind, as also when a mesmerizing priest, Father Hervier, interrupted one of his sermons to magnetize a woman in his congregation who was having a fit. The first accounts were also arriving in Paris of the miraculous phenomena the Marquis de Puységur was getting his mesmerized subjects to display on his estate in Buzancy. Jean-Jacques Paulet wrote a pamphlet implying, by innuendo, that all kinds of sexual titillation went on at mesmeric sessions: for instance, he suggested that the bodily magnetic poles that Mesmer worked with on women were in the region of the heart (or breasts) and the vagina. The frontispiece of another such pamphlet shows a magnetist touching a woman's breasts and asking: 'Do you feel that?'

Disputes within the Society of Universal Harmony did not help matters. The feather in the society's cap, Claude-Louis Berthollet, an eminent chemist and a member of the Academy, left, publicly declaring the society and its teachings to be humbug:

> After having attended more than half of M. Mesmer's course; after having been admitted to the halls of treatment and of crises, where I have employed myself in making observations and experiments, I declare that I have found no ground for believing in the existence of the agent called by M. Mesmer animal magnetism; that I consider the doctrine taught to us in the course irreconcilable with some of the best established facts in the system of the universe and in the animal economy; that I have seen nothing in the convulsions, the spasms, which could not be attributed entirely to the imagination, to the mechanical effect of friction on regions well supplied with nerves, and to that law, long since recognized, which causes an animal to tend to imitate, even involuntarily, the movements of another animal which it sees . . . I declare finally that I regard the theory of animal magnetism and the practice based upon it as perfectly chimerical.

On the other side, the main volume of testimonials of cures came out under the title *Supplément aux deux rapports de MM. les Commissaires*. Over 100 cases are reported, some by doctors, some by the patients themselves. Although many of the cases are incomplete, with treatment still ongoing, so that the patient could report only improvement not cure, the range of ailments successfully treated is remarkable; where the disorders are identifiable they include burns, skin diseases, tumours, sciatica and fevers. It is also good evidence of loyalty to Mesmer's cause that all these patients, who invariably occupied lofty positions within society, would expose their details to public scrutiny, especially since the cures often included heavy sweating, vomiting or diarrhoea.

One of the most intelligent pro-mesmeric responses was *Doutes d'un Provincial*, a treatise written anonymously by Joseph-Michel-Antoine Servan (1737–1807). He argued that the commission had exaggerated the importance of convulsions, which were much rarer in the provinces than in Paris. In other words, the commission should have focused on cures, not crises. If they did not want to question d'Eslon's 'distinguished patients', there were plenty from lower classes available. And he pointed out that medical science was not immune to mistakes: for instance, in the past inoculation had been condemned before its value was established. Another pamphlet from the provinces, by Antoine Esmonin de Dampierre, cited Puységurian experiments on magnetic sleep. Whereas the main commission had stressed touch, imagination and imitation as the only factors necessary to explain Mesmer's results, de Dampierre argued that the production of a somnambulistic state at a distance refuted the idea that touch was necessary, and that imagination and imitation could hardly be involved in magnetizing animals and infants.

The Wilderness Years

It would be safe to say that 1784 was a year Mesmer would rather forget. Nor did the publicity, both favourable and adverse, show much sign of dying down. Not only did the pamphleteering continue, but at the Carnival of 1785 an exhibit had a clownish doctor sitting backwards on an ass making magnetic passes in the direction of people walking behind, who parodied going into convulsions.

By now Mesmer was thoroughly disgruntled with Paris, and probably suffering from one of the bouts of depression that accompanied his setbacks. He felt that they didn't deserve him; they had failed to give official recognition to himself and his great discovery. The Paris society, already torn apart by dissension, did not survive for very long, and this too must have confirmed for Mesmer that it was all over with Paris. While Mesmer was on a visit to Lyons in August 1784 (where he completely failed to mesmerize Prince Henry of Prussia, who offered himself as a sceptical guinea pig), Bergasse took over and invited non-members to come along to some of the meetings. When Mesmer returned, he accused Bergasse of breaking the secrecy contract. To Bergasse's mind, however, the secrecy clause had only been temporary, its purpose being to prevent the doctrine being too widely disseminated until private subscribers had raised enough money to pay for Mesmer's teaching, which was agreed to be the sum of 10,000 louis d'or or 240,000 livres (a domestic servant or an agricultural labourer might earn about 40 livres a year at the time). This sum had now been reached and surpassed – and so Bergasse thought the time for secrecy had passed too. 'Bergasse and Kornmann saw that amount as the purchase price for the system, while Mesmer saw it as a reward to the discoverer who was still to maintain his proprietary rights.' They fell out, and despite conciliatory moves by other members, the society fell apart. Bergasse, Kornmann and Jean-Jacques d'Éprémesnil, the most influential members, formed a splinter group, which began to propagate a political form of mesmerism, preaching the reform of society along Rousseauan lines of harmony with nature; the Revolution was looming, after all. Before long they had admitted members who had nothing to do with animal magnetism, but were purely political, such as the future Girondist leaders Etienne Clavière and Antoine-Joseph Gorsas.

Bergasse and others, such as Jacques-Pierre Brissot, read politics into mesmerism first because its stand against the medical and scientific authorities was seen as a model for resistance to and oppression by dictatorial authorities in all walks of life (and indeed the academies were seen by Brissot and his friend the revolutionary leader Jean-Paul Marat, whose scientific views had also been rejected by the establishment, as tools of the tyrannical government), and second because it provided them with 'scientific' grounds for their political theorizing: harmony with the universal magnetic fluid would restore health not only to the human body, but to the body politic of France. Bergasse overtly politicized mesmerism by writing to the popular Parlement, calling for this body to sponsor a proper investigation of animal magnetism, in the face of the hostility and intransigence of the commissions' reports. It was in this climate, with Mesmer's students calling for publication of the material and the revelation of any secrets that Mesmer was withholding (not that he had any, but he pretended he had), that one of the breakaway members took it upon himself to publish an account of the teaching. This was Dr Caullet de Veaumorel, and his book was *Aphorisms of M. Mesmer . . . in 344 Paragraphs*. In the preface de Veaumorel disingenuously expressed his hope that Mesmer, committed as he was to the dissemination of his system, would not be offended by the publication.

The most important dispute will become clear only after the next chapter. Suffice it to say here that the kind of mesmerism being practised in the provinces was very different from Mesmer's own practices. His child had grown up and taken on a life of its own. The Lyons society, for instance, was headed by the redoubtable occultist Jean-Baptiste Willermoz. On his visit there, Mesmer found himself quite out of sympathy with Willermoz, who was a Rosicrucian, a Freemason, a Martinist and the head of a ritual magical lodge. Not all the provincial societies were entirely given over to occultism, but most of them were involved with the kind of psychological, non-materialistic magnetism espoused by the Marquis de Puységur. Mesmer could only have been aggrieved when the countries that spoke his own native German proved receptive to Puységurian mesmerism, rather than his own brand. Mesmerism was introduced into Germany by Johann Kaspar Lavater (whom Mesmer met in 1787). As early as 1787 and 1789 Professor Eberhard Gmelin published two large books on magnetism without once mentioning Mesmer's name.

Following the collapse of the Paris society, Mesmer gave up on Paris and took to travelling, starting with a tour of the new provincial Societies of Harmony. It is not known how many of them he visited, but in Europe there were societies in Lyons, Strasbourg, Metz, Bayonne, Montpellier, Dijon, Nantes, Marseilles, Bordeaux, Lausanne, Nancy, Ostend and Turin. Abroad, there was one on the colony of Santo Domingo. After the death blow of the commissions' reports, it was indeed in the provinces rather than in the capital that mesmerism thrived.

This is an obscure period of his life. Per Olov Enquist's book, *The Mesmerist's Last Winter*, is a fictional account of Mesmer's life after he has left Paris, and during his wanderings in Germany. This period is indeed ripe for fictional treatment, since almost nothing is known of it. In Enquist's thoughtful account Mesmer (or Meisner, as he is calling himself) is a wild, unscrupulous, egotistic charlatan, who will resort even to murder in order to achieve his ends, and has a weakness for his female patients. These qualities of his clash with the forces of law and order, comfort and solidity, reason and science. For all his unpleasant traits, he is a gifted healer, capable of dealing in the days before depth psychology with hysterical and psychosomatic illnesses.

Leaving fiction aside, it is clear that he tried to wrap up his financial affairs in Paris, and invested most of his fortune in French government bonds, but no one knows precisely where he visited; rumours of an extended stay in England are probably false. He was abroad or at least away from Paris at the start of the Revolution. Perhaps because so many of his patients and followers had been aristocrats – although it was not just followers like d'Éprémesnil and Bergasse, but some of his adversaries who went to the guillotine too, including Bailly and Lavoisier – he found it sensible to stay away from Paris, except for a brief visit in 1792, between sojourns in Vienna in 1791 and 1793. He also spent some time in Germany staying with his publisher Michael Macklot in Karlsruhe in Baden. But in 1793 when he tried to return to Vienna, he was expelled on a partially contrived political charge. In conversation he tactlessly tried to distinguish between the extremism of the Jacobins and the justified struggle for freedom of the Girondins. But in order to be politically correct in Vienna at the time he should have condemned all the French revolutionaries, whatever their stripe. After all, the King and Queen of France had only just been beheaded, so the royal families of Europe were feeling somewhat uneasy. He was branded a radical, and spent two months in prison. After his release on 18 December 1793 he seems to have gone to Switzerland, where he lived for some years in Frauenfeld, the capital city of the canton of Thurgau.

Not unnaturally, he wanted to recover the money he had left behind in Paris. In 1798, when the new government, the Directorate, made it safe, he returned to France, hoping to be recompensed for his losses, since the value of the government bonds in which he had invested had been wiped out by the Revolution. He lived quietly for three or four years in Versailles and Paris, keeping out of touch with the animal magnetists, writing his 1799 book, *Memoir of F.A. Mesmer, Doctor of Medicine, Concerning His Discoveries*. In 1799 he wrote to the Swiss Minister of Arts and Sciences suggesting the establishment of a permanent clinic in Switzerland, of which he had been made an honorary citizen in 1798. It was the same old story. The minister wrote back: 'Your treatise on animal magnetism confirms beyond all doubt the universally accepted opinion of your brilliant and fertile imagination. But equally sincerely I cannot hide from you my reluctance to admit a physical theory not yet demonstrated by

experiment.' While assuring Mesmer that this was not 'blind prejudice', he adamantly refused to entertain the idea of a clinic on Swiss
soil.

In the end the French government granted him an annual
pension of 3,000 francs. This was enough for him to live on
comfortably, but not real compensation for the 400,000 livres he had
lost; he also complained that his wife had got through most of
his fortune in Vienna, which is not really fair, since the money had
been hers in the first place. He returned to Lake Constance, living
variously at Frauenfeld and Meersburg. He lived in retirement,
looked after by his housekeeper and a couple of other servants,
hardly aware of progress being made in the field he had started. He
did receive visitors, though, and one of them, Dr Johann Heinrich
Egg, has left us a telling account of his visit. He speaks with warmth
of Mesmer's sociability and knowledge, and of his kindliness in
treating local patients for free, but acknowledges that he had certain
pet topics to which he always returned: his own importance, the
narrow-mindedness of the medical authorities, the stupidity of current medical practices. At one point Egg asked him why he recommended river water for bathing rather than spring water, and
apparently without humour Mesmer told him that this was because
river water is more magnetic than spring water, which in turn is due
to the fact that the sun shines on it, and he, Mesmer, had magnetized
the sun. The man's egotism was also revealed by a portrait that hung
in his living room, which showed Mesmer as the genius of humanity
celebrating the victory of animal magnetism over other forms of
medicine.

Well might the Swiss minister have spoken of Mesmer's 'fertile
imagination'. For in the 1799 book for the first time Mesmer nailed
his colours to the mast of the paranormal implications of animal
magnetism. Earlier in his career Mesmer had deliberately avoided
this whole area, in his desire to establish the teaching on a scientific
basis. Perhaps he resented the success of Puységurian magnetism and
wanted to show that he knew it all along. In this book he accepts as
brute facts the ability of mesmerized subjects to diagnose illnesses
and predict their courses, and to see clairvoyantly. His explanation
is that in a mesmerized subject (as in anyone who is normally
asleep) the outer senses are asleep, but the inner senses are awake

and capable of receiving messages directly from the cosmos, which is pervaded by magnetic fluid. A magnetized subject can tap into a timeless metaphysical zone, and this is how precognition works. But even now his explanation for all this is scientific and materialist in tone, not occult: it is the ebb and flow of magnetic fluid in the body that allows the five senses to operate in a waking subject, and the inner senses to be aroused as the others become dormant in a sleeping subject.

In 1812 Karl Wolfart discovered, to his surprise, that Mesmer was still alive, and wrote to invite him to lecture to the Prussian Academy. War and an old man's natural reluctance to travel intervened, but in the end Mesmer consented to be interviewed by Wolfart at home. Wolfart was impressed by the old man's energy; he was still healing local folk. He stayed there a month, took back to Germany Mesmer's latest manuscript, and published it as Friedrich (*sic*) Anton Mesmer's *Mesmerism, or the System of Reciprocal Influences; the theory and practice of animal magnetism as a generally applied treatment which will preserve mankind*. As well as a thorough discussion of the theory and practice of magnetism, in this book Mesmer also imagines a utopian society run on magnetic principles, and criticized current conceptions of law, education and so on. This section of the book had actually been written early in the 1790s and submitted to the French revolutionaries as a model on which they could reform society – but they promptly buried it in a bottom drawer. The basis of the theory is the basis of animal magnetism: all bodies influence other bodies through the universal magnetic fluid, and awareness of this fact would get people to change their social and educational systems to take account of it.

Early in 1815 Mesmer moved to a village even nearer Iznang, the place of his birth. He died there from the effects of a stroke on 5 March.

A Faith Healer

So who was this man whose unintentional legacy would prove to be hypnosis? He was a man of contrasts: a snob who extended charity to the poor but demanded a huge fee as entry into the Society of Harmony, an avaricious man who claimed disinterest in financial gain, a man who wanted the world to know of his discoveries, but wanted to be seen to hold the real secrets himself.

His consistent refusal to allow his theories to be tested by the kind of experiments that eventually proved to be his downfall when carried out by the 1784 committees suggests that he was a charlatan, but it is hard to sustain this thesis. A charlatan is someone who knows that he is peddling falsehood, and continues to do so anyway. But Mesmer comes across as sincere – fanatical and over-concerned with money, but sincere. In all likelihood, he should be seen as a man of moderate abilities who never saw that he was working in the field of psychology rather than physics, and who became the ancestor of modern psychotherapy only because his followers developed his ideas and practices along more productive lines. There is no doubt, though, that he could perform almost miraculous cures. This is not surprising in the days before depth psychology. His miracles depended on winning the trust of the patient; there may have been nothing substantial underneath – no solid bedrock of verifiable theory – but this only makes him a faith healer. He put his stagecraft, the occult trappings and quasi-scientific mumbo-jumbo, towards the goal of increasing his own fame and wealth, but the way to this goal was paved with cures. Does the end besmirch the means?

As a faith healer in an age of reason, he served an important purpose. While the medical profession could cope (to some extent, at any rate) with regular disorders, they had no way of coping with neuroses and psychosomatic illnesses. These had formerly been part of the domain of priests, or of other channels of divinity, but the priests had withdrawn from the scene under the influence of the Enlightenment. So, whatever one thinks of Mesmer, his work did fill a genuine and important gap, until such time as psychological healing would become recognized as a crucial branch of medicine.

As an example of the kind of faith healing that had only recently fallen into disuse, consider the Royal Touch. On the assumption that kings hold their position thanks to the gods, that they have a divine right to kingship, healing power and worldly power have commonly been taken to coincide. In ancient times, for example, the touch of the toe of King Pyrrhus of Epirus (319–272 BCE) was said to cure inflammation of the spleen, and similar powers were ascribed to the Roman emperors Hadrian and Vespasian. Edward the Confessor in England (1042–66), and Philip I in France (1067–1108) were the first to use the Royal Touch. The illness the Royal Touch is supposed to cure is simply called the 'King's Evil'; the term probably covers a number of disorders which involve swelling of the neck, but chiefly scrofula (tuberculosis of the lymph nodes of the neck) and goitre. Each sufferer was touched on the head by the king or queen, who wore a glove. The glove was supposed to absorb the disease, and was later burnt, so that the upper air could disperse the disease. At each touching a priest said: 'The king touches you, the Lord God restores you.'

By association, anyone vested with a sufficiently awesome authority could heal by touching. Samuel Scot, from Hedington in Wiltshire, in the sixteenth century, was far from royal, but he was the local squire's son, and it no doubt helped that he was the seventh son of his father. If superstition didn't support your healing efforts, grandiose titles might, as was found in the late eighteenth century by the prolific healer Prince Alexander of Hohenloe-Waldenberg-Schillingfürst, Archbishop and Grand Provost of Grosswardein in Hungary, and Abbot of St Michael's at Galargia.

In its heyday, the Royal Touch was extensively used. In the five years 1660–4 Charles II touched 22,982 people. Dr Johnson was touched when young by Queen Anne, but plainly to no great effect, since portraits dating from later in his life show that his neck glands remained swollen. William III discouraged Royal Touch, and said to one applicant: 'May God give you better health and more sense!' Since all forms of faith healing depend on the patient's expectations, one can only hope, for the sake of the poor sufferer, that King William did not ruin the effect. An amusing example of the kind of scepticism that eventually did away with the Royal Touch is the remark of the arch-rationalist Voltaire, who noted that one of Louis XIV's mistresses died of scrofula despite having been well touched by the king! In France the practice fell into decline under Louis XV and died out during Louis XVI's reign – that is, during Mesmer's lifetime.

So the laying-on of hands, whether by a priest or a monarch, was a means of transmitting divine healing power. This was the case even when a layman practised it, as Valentine Greatrakes, the 'Irish Stroker', did in seventeenth-century England. He was an educated man, a member of high society, but around the middle of the century he experienced a conversion which convinced him that he could channel divine healing power. In the years following 1662 he cured not just the King's Evil, but ague (malaria) and a wide range of other ailments. Charles II was interested enough to ask to see him at work, and so did the chemist Robert Boyle. A more humble man than Mesmer, Greatrakes admitted that he was not always successful. There are several parallels between his career and Mesmer's. His method was massage, chiefly over the patient's clothes (for modesty), but sometimes under, which led to charges of obscenity. His patients too often went into convulsions before being cured (as did those of Greatrakes's contemporary in Italy, Francisco Bagnone), and, even more bizarrely, sometimes fell into such a deep trance that they were insensible to pain. Like many faith healers, his response to some patients was striking – a ploy to encourage confidence, as in the nineteenth-century cure for warts which involved rubbing them with beef stolen from a butcher's shop! In some cases Greatrakes used his own urine as a potion or salve; in another he spat on the eyes (in imitation of Jesus?). But whatever the method, he always claimed that he was only an instrument of God.

Mesmer's use of hand passes places him squarely in this tradition, with the important difference that he invoked science and impersonal mechanical forces, rather than God. To say that Mesmer was a faith healer is not to say that he can be consigned to a historical dustbin, nor does it classify him as a charlatan, nor does it license us to try to explain away his cures. Faith healing works, it's as simple as that. Certified cures at Lourdes include cases of blindness and partial paralysis brought on by childhood meningitis, organic blindness, terminal cancer and hemiplegia. Medjugorje in Bosnia is bidding fair to rival Lourdes as a place of healing. Statistical evidence is accumulating that people with religious faith are healthier than the rest of us. We cannot dismiss all of Greatrakes's cures, nor those of Mesmer.

4

Magnetic Sleep and Victor's Sister

Late in 1783 Armand-Marc-Jacques Chastanet, Marquis de Puységur (1751–1825) and one of the largest landowners in France, found himself on his estate at Buzancy, near Soissons. An officer of the French army, in charge of an artillery regiment, he was temporarily on leave. Just the previous year, in Paris, he had been persuaded by his two younger brothers to fork out the 100 louis d'or subscription to join the newly formed Society of Universal Harmony of Franz Anton Mesmer, the wizard from Vienna. In an idle moment the marquis decided to try to put into practice the little he felt he had learnt from attending the course at the Paris society.

One of his first patients was a twenty-three-year-old shepherd from his estate called Victor Race. He was extraordinarily lucky to stumble so easily on a deeply hypnotizable subject. To de Puységur's surprise, the magnetic passes he used on the young man had quite the opposite effect from what he had been told to expect, and had witnessed in Paris. Mesmer wanted his patients to go into a violent crisis, but in a few minutes Victor's head lolled and he appeared to be fast asleep. But no, he wasn't asleep. De Puységur found that he could talk to Victor, ask him questions and get replies; Victor could get up and walk, if ordered to do so by his master, while remaining in this sleep-like state; and most astonishingly of all, he appeared to have quite a different personality in this quasi-sleep state. Normally subservient and quiet, he appeared more intelligent, more of an equal, and this new person spoke about the normal Victor as a third person. While apparently asleep, his mental faculties were actually more alert than usual, and he could be woken up simply on command.

This was a different kind of crisis altogether. At first, de Puységur called it the 'perfect crisis'. The closest analogy for what he was seeing was sleepwalking, or somnambulism – a state somewhere between sleep and wakefulness, in which the subject functions in the external world to a certain extent, as a sleepwalker can negotiate a journey. So he came to call the state Victor and others entered 'mesmeric somnambulism', or 'magnetic sleep', to differentiate it from spontaneous somnambulism. Before many years had passed, further similarities between the two states had been found: the kinds of people who go into spontaneous somnamabulism make good hypnotic subjects, and both conditions involve what is called 'state-dependent memory', which is the ability, when you are again in the same state, to remember things which are otherwise forgotten.

News of the marquis's success spread fast, and hordes of peasants from his and neighbouring estates came to him for healing. Following an idea of Mesmer's, de Puységur magnetized an elm tree in the centre of the village and tied ropes to its branches to cope with the increased demand. (The elm tree, by the way, survived until 1940, when it was blown down in a storm. The local folk collected pieces of the tree, remembering that it was supposed to have curative properties.) He found that Victor was not unique: others also fell into magnetic sleep. It is worth pausing right from the start to ask why this should have happened. Why did the marquis's subjects not go into convulsions? There are a number of possibilities. De Puységur was not dealing with fashionable ladies who were liable to the vapours, but with peasants. Moreover, the labourers on his estate had no background in mesmerism: they had not heard rumours of it from Paris, and so there was no expectation that convulsions were the order of the day. It is also worth reflecting that being put to sleep is a kind of expression of subservience, and the marquis was after all dealing with people who were his subordinates, almost his serfs. Finally, the surroundings were rural, more peaceful than the bustle of the capital. Imagine the scene around the famous elm tree: in the distance is the magnificent castle of the de Puységurs, set in rolling hills covered in forests; in the foreground are homely thatched cottages; at the foot of the tree a spring bubbles up; elms have long been thought to have magical properties. It's got to be nicer to be hypnotized there, seated on the stone benches with which de Puységur surrounded the tree, than in the occult hothouse atmosphere of Mesmer's salon in Paris.

The Phenomena of Magnetic Sleep

Just as children grow and become independent human beings, so Mesmer's brainchild was taking on a life of its own, breaking free of its original limitations and setting out on a course that would lead directly to the development of modern psychiatry and psychology. Before Mesmer, someone who was mentally ill was either possessed (the intrusion paradigm) or had something physically wrong with them (the organic paradigm). Since the sixteenth century, the organic paradigm had gradually been gaining ground over the intrusion paradigm, and in fact many mental illnesses were thought to be hereditary. Mesmer unwittingly created a third paradigm. I say that he did so unwittingly, because he himself was a devoted follower of the organic paradigm. But with de Puységur's discovery of magnetic sleep, Mesmer's physiological explanation of what was essentially psychological could no longer survive. Victor Race appeared to have an alternate personality within him, which emerged when he was in magnetic sleep. This led, before too many years had passed, to a third paradigm of mental illness, the alternate-consciousness paradigm, and by the time of Freud psychologists had realized that not only mentally ill people, but all of us, have alternate streams of consciousness going on simultaneously within us. The map-makers of the mind saw that we have an unconscious, and therapists found new ways to work with their patients to uncover the contents of this other layer of the mind.

One aspect of Race's manifestation of an alternate personality proved vital in this context. When magnetized, he expressed feelings of hostility towards his sister, whom he ostensibly loved. The importance to history of Victor's sister, who was by all accounts a spiteful shrew, was that when de Puységur learnt of Victor's domestic troubles, he suggested to the magnetized man ways of alleviating the situation. This was the first practice of psychotherapy: in his magnetized state Victor revealed emotions he would not normally have revealed, and de Puységur felt able to offer him advice because Race

often expressed feelings of trust for his master. Similarly, psychotherapists today recognize the importance of that feeling of trust and find
ways to get their patients to unlock hidden emotions and reveal
painful secrets.

At a stroke the therapeutic potential of mesmerism was extended
from the bodily to the psychological realm. De Puységur developed
his psychotherapeutic theories further in reflecting on a later case,
that of Alexandre Hébert, whom he met in 1812. Alexandre was a
young teenager given to frequent violent rages, episodes in which
anything smashable in the vicinity would certainly be smashed,
people would get bitten and Alexandre would try to harm himself.
The kind and diligent marquis looked after the boy more or less on
a daily basis for some months to effect a cure. He came to believe
that mental illness was a kind of deranged somnambulism. If the
somnambulist is in rapport with a man of good will, the results will
be good; but if the magnetizer's will is bad, or if there is some other
form of disturbance in the rapport, such as breaking the subject's
contact with the real world, the result will be insanity. By 'rapport'
here de Puységur means not just the special case of rapport with a
magnetizer, but one's relationships in general; and few psychotherapists today would disagree that close relationships such as those with
one's parents may, when unbalanced, be responsible for many kinds
of mental disturbance.

De Puységur reflected at length on the degree of rapport that
quickly built up between himself and his subjects. He found he could
get Victor, and later his favourite somnambulist, a young woman
called Madeleine, to do something just by willing it. Just as it is will
that makes me raise my hand when I want to, so the magnetized
subject is like a limb or extension of the operator. Victor's alternate
personality seemed to be summoned forth, almost created, by the
marquis himself. Madeleine would fetch an object on an unspoken,
willed command; and all de Puységur had to do was order a patient
to recover and he would recover. The question of control came up
immediately: what would Victor or other somnambulists *not* do if
the magnetizer ordered it? De Puységur came to the conclusion,
however, that he could not make anyone do something they would
not normally do.

Double consciousness and rapport were not the only phenomena of magnetic sleep that de Puységur discovered through his work with Race. One day, when magnetized, Victor gave the marquis a document to look after; the next day, in an unmagnetized state, he spent ages searching for it, and was very worried that he couldn't find it. De Puységur had discovered hypnotic amnesia and state-dependent memory. He also found that Victor could remember things apparently forgotten, from his childhood, for instance – this is hypermnesia, another common hypnotic phenomenon. He thought the amnesia was due to the fact that when magnetized the subject operates with a set of senses different from our normal set, and he thought he had proof of this in the paranormal phenomena Race and others manifested.

The first of these paranormal faculties was clairvoyant therapy. Race and others could apparently diagnose their own illnesses, diagnose illnesses in others too, prescribe treatments and predict the course of disorders. Whatever one may think of all this, the reports are very convincing, for all the crudity of their medical knowledge:

A young man . . . submitted himself for examination. He was told that he suffered from the stomach, and that he had obstructions in the abdomen, arising from an illness which he had had some years previously. All this, he told us, was correct. But, not content with this soothsayer, he went straight away to another 'doctor', 20 feet distant, and was told exactly the same. I never saw anybody so dumbfounded with astonishment as this young man, who had assuredly come to ridicule rather than to be convinced.

Then there was telepathy with the magnetizer, as a result of the rapport between them, which was such that de Puységur had only to will Victor to sleep, from some distance away and without saying a thing, and Victor would fall asleep. Actually, some of what de Puységur was inclined to attribute to telepathy is more easily explained otherwise. For instance, the marquis was once absent-mindedly singing a song to himself, and to his astonishment Race then sang it out loud. This was probably due to hyperaesthesia: de Puységur was probably slightly moving his lips, and in his sensitized state Race could pick out the words. In any case, de Puységur himself did not talk of telepathy – that is my word for the phenomenon. He attributed it, at this stage, to the transference of magnetic fluid, bearing the magnetizer's will and thoughts, from the magnetizer to the subject.

As can be imagined, when in 1784 de Puységur published an account of his experiments with Race, both he and his master, Mesmer, acquired great fame throughout France. Imitation being the sincerest form of flattery, other noblemen throughout France magnetized trees as de Puységur had to keep the workers on their estates healthy and happy. Before long the phenomena, both supernormal and paranormal, which de Puységur had witnessed in his subjects were being reproduced all over France. In some cases, matters went even further: instead of just clairvoyant diagnosis, reports came in of subjects who could see details of distant events, and sometimes – in what is known as 'travelling clairvoyance' – felt themselves detach from their bodies and visit other places.

'Believe and Will'

At first de Puységur was a loyal believer in animal magnetism and Mesmer's magnetic fluid, but not for long. He had found the course at the Society of Universal Harmony unsatisfying, and felt he left just as ignorant as he went in. In 1785, at the foundation of the branch of the society at Strasbourg (where he had been posted with his regiment), he announced that the true principle of successful magnetism was encapsulated in the motto which he henceforth adopted: 'Believe and Will'. That was all the operator had to do to be effective. There may or there may not be such a thing as magnetic fluid, but it made no practical difference. Even if there was such a fluid, the operator's will was still required to transmit it: it would be passed through the magnetizer's hands on to the patient. Good will would produce good effects, bad will the opposite; all the operator needed was self-confidence, to enable him to draw on his store of healing will. Out of deference, he expressed agnosticism: 'I no longer know whether there is a magnetic fluid, an electric fluid, a luminous fluid, etc. All I know for certain is that in order to magnetize successfully there is no point at all in knowing whether a single fluid exists.' But these views of his were not fully published until the nineteenth century, and in the meantime his peers throughout France remained materialists.

As a result of these novel beliefs, he dispensed with the *baquet* and other accessories; as mechanical means of transmitting magnetic fluid, they were no longer necessary. Through this emphasis on will he was led to an anti-materialist position quite opposed to Mesmer's. In disagreeing with Mesmer like this, de Puységur was not unusual. Of course, there were some who were more orthodox, and de Puységur himself would initiate his own orthodoxy, but in reading the mesmeric literature of the end of the eighteenth and the nineteenth centuries one is constantly struck by how writers felt free to invent their own fluid or some other explanation of the phenomena.

De Puységur actually took Victor Race to Paris and showed him to Mesmer, but Mesmer was not impressed. I would like to have been a fly on the wall at that momentous meeting, the critical point at which Mesmer's star began to decline and de Puységur's to rise. One imagines that de Puységur would have been unfailingly polite, keeping his reservations to himself and trying gently to point out to Mesmer the interest of Victor's trance and the new abilities he displayed. Meanwhile, Mesmer would have stubbornly insisted on the reality of magnetic fluid and denied the efficacy of mere will. True, some of his patients had gone into a trance state, but he regarded this as an interruption or delay in the healing process, which was properly marked by crisis and convulsions. The trance state, Mesmer thought, might even be a sign of severe mental illness. De Puységur, on the other hand, came to believe that convulsions were not only unnecessary, therapeutically speaking, but may even be harmful. The whole process of healing needed more care than Mesmer had given it. And it was a stroke of genius for de Puységur to see that the trance state was a valid end in itself, not just a sidetrack on the way to a mesmeric crisis. If he hadn't done it, someone else would, but in any case modern psychotherapy begins here: Charcot and Bernheim, Janet and Freud are de Puységur's grandchildren, with Mesmer as their ancestor.

The Spread of Puységurian Magnetism

In the years immediately following de Puységur's 1784 and 1785 publications, a number of French writers such as Jean François Fournel explored the state of magnetic sleep, without adding substantially to de Puységur's findings or speculations, while others such as A.A. Tardy de Montravel tried to reconcile Mesmer and de Puységur. According to de Montravel, whose somnambulist claimed to be able to see the magnetic fluid leaving the magnetizer and entering her, magnetic sleep was just one form of crisis, a cataleptic form as opposed to the more violent convulsions.

Soon more and more magnetizers found their subjects going into magnetic sleep rather than crisis. Before long, enthusiastic experimenters had come to recognize most of the major hypnotic phenomena acknowledged today: catalepsy, amnesia, anaesthesia, positive and negative hallucinations, post-hypnotic suggestion, individual differences in susceptibility. But the claims for paranormal abilities – especially clairvoyance, somnambulistic medical diagnosis and prophecy – also persisted and grew. Ironically, for all Mesmer's stubborn materialism, he had opened the floodgates of occultism in the provincial societies.

The reality of magnetic sleep was no longer in doubt, but its interpretation was controversial. Gradually, two main schools or lines of thinking emerged. The fluidists, following Mesmer's belief in magnetic fluid, attributed mesmeric phenomena to the fact that all nature is akin, and that everything is imbued with this fluid; this means that we are all unconsciously in contact with the universe, and they speculated that in a trance we wake up to this fact. The animists had no time for magnetic fluid and attributed the trance phenomena to the separation of a higher spiritual part from the physical body. Fluidists thought that magnetism involved the transfer of magnetic fluid from the operator to the subject, while animists thought either that will alone was sufficient to explain the induction of trance, or, as among others Johann Heinrich Jung-Stilling

(1740–1817) argued, that will plus prayer did the trick. Finally, fluidists perpetuated the old mass methods of mesmerism, since for them it was a mechanical process which *baquets* and magnetized trees could transmit, while animists focused more on one-to-one treatments. However, despite these differences, there was one vital similarity: both schools still emphasized the role of the magnetist himself. For the fluidists, he was the channel for healthy magnetic energy; for the animists, it was his will and his prayers that were effective. The days were still a long way off when the consensual participation of the subject could be seen to be critical.

With interest in mesmerism waning in Paris following the 1784 reports, the spotlight fell on the provincial societies. The most energetic of these were in Lyons and Strasbourg. Both of them were founded with the help of local Masonic lodges, and de Puységur himself was a Mason (as were Mesmer, the Marquis de Lafayette, Court de Gébelin and other prominent mesmerists). There are a number of reasons for the connection between magnetic societies and Masonic lodges, but they don't amount to anything very sinister. At the most mundane level, the members of Masonic lodges were generally aristocrats, who were precisely the educated men of leisure who had an interest in the latest scientific discoveries such as mesmerism, and through their lodges had an already existing infra-structure for spreading the mesmeric gospel. Secondly, there was considerable interest in many Masonic lodges in occultism, and since magnetic sleep seemed to give its subjects paranormal abilities, it was a topic the Freemasons wanted to pursue.

The founders of the Lyons school started as strict followers of Mesmer, but soon added their own techniques, particularly the diagnostic method of 'doubling', whereby the magnetizer felt in his own body the ailment of the patient, and so was enabled to come up with an accurate diagnosis. They even practised this method on animals. They developed a unique magnetic cosmology which stressed the importance of the will of the healer in effecting cures. Before long the Lyons school gave itself over almost entirely to mysticism and paranormal phenomena rather than curing patients. It was run by Jean-Baptiste Willermoz, who was heavily influenced by his friend Louis-Claude de Saint-Martin, the most important Martinist in France. Martinism was a spiritual way – a combination of Kabbalah and Catholicism – founded by Martines de Pasqually. Saint-Martin was an early member of Mesmer's Paris Society of Harmony, and acted as a kind of consultant to several of the provincial societies, to guide their understanding and propagation of the paranormal phenomena their subjects were manifesting. One of the best ways to get a sense of the kind of work in which the Lyons society was involved is to read Edward Bulwer-Lytton's wonderful 1861 novel *A Strange Story*, in which magnetism is one of the tools of the evil magician Margrave. I don't mean to imply that Willermoz and the others were evil magicians, but the novel does give a contemporary sense of how magnetism and magic were bound together by some nineteenth-century researchers.

Or again, and to keep the scene in France, in 1891, in *Là-bas*, one of Joris Karl Huysmans's decadent novels, the astrologer Gévingey recounts how he was threatened by a notorious satanist, who used hypnotism to send his curses and poisons through the astral realms. Gévingey turned to a magical exorcist, Dr Johannes, whose first step was to call in a clairvoyant.

> He hypnotized her and she, at his injunction, explained the nature of the sorcery of which I was the victim. She reconstructed the scene. She literally saw me being poisoned by food and drink mixed with menstrual fluid that had been reinforced with macerated sacramental wafers and drugs skilfully dosed. That sort of spell is so terrible that aside from Dr Johannes no thaumaturge in France dare try to cure it.

This is the kind of way in which, in the nineteenth century, hypnosis and magic were bound together.

In 1785, de Puységur was posted to Strasbourg and while he was there he founded, along with a certain Dr Ostertag, a Society of Harmony whose express aim was to experiment with magnetic sleep in order to gain more understanding of it. Unlike their animist peers in Lyons, they remained fluidists for a long time. Ostertag used to mesmerize his subjects by getting them to stare at a glass ball, a remarkable anticipation of the fixation techniques which were developed later. The success of the Strasbourg society led de Puységur to set up two more, at Metz and Nancy. His brother Count Jacques-Maxime founded one at Bayonne, and his other brother, Antoine-

Hyacinthe-Anne, founded one in the colony of Santo Domingo (now the Dominican Republic); after the slaves revolted and established their own republic on the island, mesmerism died out or became absorbed into the local voodoo religion. Back in Strasbourg, the society gradually became more and more animist and mystical, and eventually combined mesmerism with Swedenborgism. A parallel may be found in the society at Ostend, founded by Chevalier de Barbarin. De Barbarin, a Martinist, attributed cures to God. Healing, he taught, was a result of the magnetizer's will – of his willed channelling of divine energy – and the patient's faith.

While they were relatively uncontaminated by mysticism and retained the traditional focus on therapy, both the Strasbourg and Lyons schools published a large number of case histories. It is the same story we have met before. Time after time, where conventional medicine had failed for years, the magnetists achieved cures, and did so rapidly. Although there was some discussion within their own ranks as to which ailments magnetism could and could not treat, there was a strong tendency to regard magnetism as a kind of panacea, and its practitioners boldly approached the most appalling cases. For instance, there was a lady who had for many years been in a terrible state: she had a prolapsed womb and an enlarged abdomen, suffered from dizziness and awful migraines and rheumatic pain, and had no more than irregular menstrual periods. Through magnetism and self-diagnosis she attained an almost complete recovery. The same story – and the reasons remain the same: the inadequacy of what passed for medicine at the time, and the undeniable power of faith healing.

Mesmerism in Germany

Magnetism came early to Germany, and found many gullible recipients. The King of Prussia in the 1780s, Friedrich Wilhelm II, a weak king, handed out honours and contrived policies according to the dictates of a hunchbacked somnambulist who was supposed to be in touch with higher realms. In actual fact, the only realms she was in touch with were the minds of the devious courtiers who had introduced her to the king to further their aims and gain them honours. The hunchback only fell from grace when the messages communicated to her began to conflict with the desires of the Countess Lichtenau, the king's mistress. *Omnia vincit amor.*

The chief evangelist for mesmerism in the German-speaking countries was a priest from Zurich called Johann Kasper Lavater. The first centres of Strasbourgian mesmerism in Germany were Baden and Bremen, while the chief centre of rationalist opposition was Berlin. Contrary to the mysticism of the French schools, the German schools at first tried to give magnetism an aura of scientific respectability. For instance, Luigi Galvani's experiments in Italy ('galvanizing' frogs' legs) were taken to indicate the presence in all living creatures of 'animal electricity'; this obviously supported the theory and practice of the magnetists. This respectable cloaking of mesmerism, and the fact that so far its German practitioners, such as Eberhard Gmelin (1751–1808) and Arnold Wienholt (1749–1804), had focused on therapy rather than paranormalism, led to its introduction into the rationalist stronghold of Berlin. In Berlin we meet some more of those remarkable personalities who litter the early history of hypnotism, Christoph von Hufeland, Karl Kluge and Karl Wolfart. Wolfart was the evangelist, Kluge the chronicler and theorist. Kluge's main book, *Versuch einer Darstellung des animalischen Magnetismus als Heilmittel* (*An Attempt to Present Animal Magnetism as Therapy*, 1811), is one of the most important works in the history of hypnosis. It systematized and summarized everything that was known about the theory and practice of mesmerism at the time.

Most German mesmerists totally ignored Mesmer himself: they assumed he was dead, and in any case were inclined to dismiss him as a charlatan. But Wolfart was in personal touch with Mesmer, and his clinic, constructed along the lines of Mesmer's old rooms in Paris, became the centre for mesmerism in Europe. Wolfart attracted powerful friends from high society, but the reintroduction of Mesmer into the frame led to a Berlin commission being set up to investigate the claims of mesmerism. This report was not published until 1816, because it was interrupted by war. Despite the continued opposition of the majority of the professional medical community in Berlin, the report of this commission was favourable. The same was happening at much the same time elsewhere in Europe: in Denmark, Prussia, Russia and certain areas of Italy cautious approval was given to mesmerism, provided it was in the safe hands of reputable physicians.

But it was not long before the supernatural phenomena of magnetic sleep began to fascinate the minds of German mesmerists. Early in the nineteenth century, Romanticism was on the rise, with its desire to understand the mystical forces and laws that govern the universe, and humanity's place in the world. It isn't hard to see how Romanticism and mesmerism were made to reinforce each other. The Romantics believed, for instance, in the existence of a world soul, which pervades the universe – just as Mesmer's magnetic fluid did. Novalis (Friedrich von Hardenberg, 1772–1801) postulated the existence of two distinct sets of sense organs, one attuned to external events, the other to the inner world of the spirit; the mesmerists pounced on this to explain their paranormal phenomena. Then the main Romantic philosopher, Friedrich Wilhelm Joseph von Schelling (1775–1854), saw the whole world as a set of polarities such as light and gravity, positive and negative electricity, the north and south poles of magnetism and so on. Further down the scale of these polarities, at the level of humankind, one of the most important polarities was sleep and waking, the difference being that while awake we work and strive towards individuation, but while asleep we merge with the common essence of humankind. By the beginning of the 1810s this idea had been developed until it was thought that we have two sets of nervous systems, one functioning during our waking hours, the other when we are asleep. According to Gotthilf Heinrich Schubert, writing in 1814, it is the nervous system centred on the solar plexus which gives us the ability to transcend the boundaries of time and space. Romantic philosophy developed independently of mesmerism, but German thinkers were quick to see the possibilities in magnetic sleep: the use to which they put somnambules was less for therapy and more to confirm their high-flown metaphysics.

Theoreticians abounded in Germany, but disappointingly few of them were doing original work, rather than relying on anecdotal evidence. Explanations of somnambulistic paranormal phenomena tended to follow the lines already established in France. Some were fluidists, others animists. Scepticism also made an early mark. In 1787 Privy Councillor C.L. Hoffmann of Mainz offered a reward of 100 ducats for any somnambule who could detect which of a set of randomly shuffled glasses of water had been magnetized. No one came forward to take up the offer.

From Germany, interest in magnetism spread to Russia, Holland and the Scandinavian countries, but made scarcely any impression on the Austro-Hungarian Empire. From France it had already spread to Belgium. Roman Catholic countries such as the Italian states were suspicious of magnetism, though they eventually had to give way to popular interest. However, there were few native developments: the work in these places was very derivative on the Franco-German forms of magnetism. Mesmerism went into rapid decline in Germany after about 1850, when positivism and rationalism became the dominant modes of thought.

Mesmerism in France After the Revolution

Not unnaturally, the French had rather a lot on their minds in the last dozen or so years of the eighteenth century, and the centre of mesmeric activity moved to Germany. Mob rule and riots in Paris in 1789 (including the momentous destruction of the Bastille prison on 14 July) soon spread to the provinces. France was effectively split for a while into small provincial governments, with no central focus except a common resentment of the aristocracy, whose excesses and feudalism were often outrageous. All the old political, civic and ecclesiastical structures were discarded, and 1791 was optimistically renamed 'Year One', the start of a new order for humankind. But the bloodshed (not just the execution of nobles and the royal family, but the elimination of political rivals), the frequent changes of government, and constant warfare against an alliance of most of the other European countries, brought the Revolution into disrepute, and people welcomed the relative stability offered by Napoléon's consulate, which started in 1799.

The Revolution almost put paid to animal magnetism. The societies of Universal Harmony were dissolved and many of their members were among the emigrés. Others earned ridicule by attaching themselves to Cagliostro (Giuseppe Balsamo, 1743–95), a conman who travelled around Europe peddling a supposed alchemical elixir of immortal youth and gaining recruits for freemasonry. The flood of books up to 1788 died down to the merest trickle for about twenty years, and animal magnetism survived, if it survived at all, as a result of work quietly carried on in secret. When interest began again, Mesmer himself was forgotten, presumed dead, and it was to de Puységur that the new generation of researchers looked for inspiration and theoretical framework. He was practising quietly in Soissons, as before, having kept his head on his shoulders. He had been a military commander in the revolutionary army, but the mindless slaughter sickened him and he resigned his commission. This act earned him a couple of years in prison, but after that he was able to retire to his estate and pick up his private life, including his mesmeric practice, where he had left it. He was even working again with Victor Race, and discovered that, when mesmerized again, he could remember everything from his trances twenty years earlier.

The revival of magnetism in France owes a great deal to the publication of his *Du magnétisme animal* in 1807, and to further works in subsequent years. His doubts about the existence of magnetic fluid, or any material basis for mesmerism, had by now taken deep root. He emphasized will to the exclusion of everything else, and began to show even more of an interest in the paranormal abilities of somnambules.

Another survivor was Joseph Deleuze (1753–1835), an enthusiastic pre-war magnetizer who became one of the chief spokesmen and writers in the early nineteenth century, especially after 1820, when de Puységur began to take a back seat (he died in 1825). Deleuze had been introduced to animal magnetism in 1785 when he attended a demonstration given by a young woman and, although he was not the subject, he found himself going into a trance. He was a prolific and pellucid author, who closely followed the theories of de Puységur, but was far clearer and more organized than his mentor, and was more scientific in that, for example, he rejected anecdotal evidence, laid down criteria for assessing the validity of claims made on behalf of magnetism, and followed them himself by conducting careful experiments. He also prefigured a number of later developments in hypnotism, by suggesting, for instance, that those who could achieve the deep state of somnambulism could well undergo surgery while in this state. He warned magnetizers against getting too excited by the appearance of paranormal phenomena. Throughout, his work is scholarly and sceptical. His two most important books are his famous *Histoire critique du magnétisme animal* (1813), an invaluable sourcebook for the early history of mesmerism, and a practical manual written in 1825. One of his most important contributions was to try to improve the moral reputation of mesmerism. He knew from his own experience with the young woman who had introduced him to the subject that it was possible for sexual energy to build up between operator and subject, and so, to preserve decorum, he recommended that husbands and wives should work together, and that a young female subject should be mesmerized by another woman.

In order to put things on a more formal footing, de Puységur and Deleuze became, respectively, the president and vice-president of the Magnetic Society, founded in 1813 with the help of a certain Joseph du Commun, whom we will meet again in the next chapter. Apart from arranging lectures and general publicity and public relations for the cause of mesmerism, in their brief history (up to 1820) they ran one of three contemporary French journals devoted to the subject. The journal was *Bibliothèque de magnétisme animal* (1817–19). The other two were *Annales du magnétisme animal*, which ran from 1814 to 1816, and *Archives du magnétisme animal* (1820–23), edited by Baron E.F. d'Hénin de Cuvillers (1755–1841). On the whole the standard of writing is not very good in these journals (they were mainly amateurs, not medical men), varying between inadequate reporting of case histories and well-meaning but waffly publicity articles. All this did nothing to win over the medical professionals, who remained either hostile or uninterested, and tended to attribute magnetic cures to other causes. However, certain future developments in hypnotism are prefigured in the pages of these journals: 'self-magnetization' (i.e. self-hypnosis); the use of suggestion to produce blisters; the first steps in painless surgery.

But there was also a new generation of mesmerists. One of the most important was a colourful character – too flamboyant for the likes of sober Deleuze – called the Abbé José Custodio di Faria (1753–1816), a Portuguese priest who came to France in 1813 from India, where he claimed to have been initiated as a Brahmin. He used to dress up as an Indian magician and put on displays of magnetic cures, making him the forerunner of all the mesmeric entertainers of later years. The importance of this rather vulgar showman lies in his technique: he had his subjects or patients sit in a comfortable chair and gaze fixedly at his raised hand while he simply commanded them, in a loud voice, to sleep. This practice was backed up by theory. He totally rejected Mesmer's magnetic fluid and had little time for clairvoyance and telepathy. He said that the reason mesmerism worked therapeutically was the impressionability of the subject to the operator's will (an impressionability which, more bizarrely, he seems to attribute to anaemia); the subject has expectations of what will happen, and is in a state of heightened suggestibility. In a sense, then, all hypnosis is self-hypnosis. Faria was the first to make suggestion occupy the centre of the theoretical stage. If Faria's name is familiar, by the way, that is because Alexandre Dumas borrowed it (and certain traits of the original) for the old imprisoned abbé in *The Count of Monte Cristo*.

Faria's downfall was spectacular and probably unfair. An actor pretended to be mesmerized by him and to perform some of the clairvoyant feats typical of the time. In the middle of the performance, he opened his eyes and denounced Faria to the audience as a fraud. It was unfairly assumed that if one subject could fake it, all the others were frauds too. The ruse did the actor's career no harm, because he gained the lead part in a popular farce called *Magnetismomania*, written by Jules Vernet, in which he played a mesmerizer who looked suspiciously like Faria. The abbé, though, was forced into retirement and died a few weeks later.

In every branch of science and walk of life there are people about whom you feel that if they had only lived longer they would have gone on to even greater things. In the early history of animal magnetism Alexandre Bertrand is one of these. When he died in 1831, in his thirties, he had already left a body of important work. He combined the scholarly caution of Deleuze and the insight of Faria. It was Bertrand, as much as anyone, who was responsible for the return of mesmerism from the provinces to Paris: the course of lectures on the subject he gave there in 1819 and 1820 were hugely successful, and forced the medical authorities to pay attention to the subject. Then in 1820 a magnetizer, Baron Dupotet de Sennevoy, who will later play an important part in the story of hypnosis, was invited to come and heal one of the patients in the Hôtel Dieu, one of the main Paris hospitals. The patient was a good subject and self-prescribed her cure. In 1821 the first well-publicized mesmeric operation was carried out in Paris by Dr C.A. Récamier.

Bertrand's first book was *Traité du somnambulisme* (1823), written more or less from an orthodox fluidist point of view, but by the time he wrote his second book, three years later, he had undergone a conversion, as a result of thinking more deeply about the work of Faria and his associate F.J. Noizet. In *Du magnétisme animal en France*, he argued that suggestion alone is responsible for the phenomena of magnetism, and that no fluid is needed to explain them. This explains, for instance, why subjects who merely believe they are sitting under a magnetized tree will feel the same effects and behave in the same way as those who are sitting under a genuinely magnetized tree. He made the rapport between operator and subject the central phenomenon of hypnotism, because it is rapport that makes the operator's suggestions effective, and he understood that rapport also explains why post-hypnotic suggestions work. The patient or subject, he argued, becomes open to the least suggestion of the operator, by word, gesture or intonation. Given a few more years of life he would have followed up these tentative speculations on the power of the subconscious mind to cause health and disease.

Dupotet conducted apparently successful experiments on mesmerizing his somnambule from a distance, but Bertrand thought they were badly set up, and argued that her entrancement was due to suggestion. At this time, there was generally uncritical acceptance of the marvellous phenomena of hypnosis. Bertrand was the exception – not that he didn't accept some phenomena about which we would be sceptical today, but he did at least carry out his own careful analyses of many cases of trance. As a result of his experiments, he came up with a list of what he saw as the twelve main phenomena of mesmerism:

1. Division of memory between trance and normal life
2. Time-distortion
3. Anaesthesia
4. Exaltation of imagination
5. Exaltation of intellectual faculties (e.g. hypermnesia)
6. Instinct for remedies
7. Prevision (seeing into the future)
8. Moral inertia (i.e. passivity in relation to the operator's will)
9. Communication of the symptoms of maladies
10. Thought-transference
11. Clairvoyance
12. Control by the subject over his own involuntary organic processes.

The sixth item on the list is literally just instinct – the kind of instinct that animals show when they find the right herb to chew when they are ill. It is noticeable, then, that he omits intro-vision (self-diagnosis) and medical prediction; he didn't believe that these were genuine phenomena, and argued that in most cases the subject showed little knowledge of anatomy, ascribed most ailments to 'abscesses' or obstructions, and proved incapable of predicting the course of serious diseases, only trivial ones. This showed, he claimed, that no actual prediction was involved, but rather that by autosuggestion the subject would manifest the appropriate trivial symptoms at the right time.

We have already seen that there were two main schools of thought about mesmerism at this time (with countless individual variations, to be sure): fluidism and animism. Although clearly closer to animism than fluidism, Faria and Bertrand effectively initiated a third school of thought: that suggestion is responsible not only for the induction of trance, but also for the phenomena of mesmerism. In due course of time, after a period when magnetism was again in the doldrums in France, their work would come to the attention of Bernheim and the Nancy school, and by this route would exert an enormous influence on modern thinking about hypnosis.

The French Commissions of 1826 and 1837

But the careful, quiet work of Bertrand was overlooked for a while due to the excitement of what was going on elsewhere, for instance with Récamier's famous operation on a magnetized patient. Then there were the show-stealing methods of Dupotet, who used to magnetize his patients in hospital by screaming at them to go to sleep. This kind of activity led to magnetizers being banned once more from the Paris hospitals. The pendulum was swinging either for or against the medical use of magnetism in an erratic fashion. In 1825, in order to try to put things on a sane and steady keel, a certain Dr P. Foissac persuaded the medical section of the Academy to appoint a fresh committee, especially to investigate the diagnostic abilities of somnambulists. Foissac offered to provide somnambules if they would appoint a commission to investigate the subject. There was some nervous debate as to whether they should proceed. The usual arguments were trotted out: Mesmer and de Puységur were quacks; the whole thing was faked; it was beneath the dignity of the Academy to investigate it; it had already been condemned in 1784. But a commission of eleven was appointed on 28 February 1826. The timing was right: where Mesmer had found few allies among really significant scientists, by the 1820s Laplace and Georges Cuvier were giving the science named after him cautious affidavits. Cuvier said, for instance, that two living bodies in close contact undoubtedly did communicate with each other through their nerves – that although it was sometimes hard to distinguish real physical causes from imagined ones, in this case something real was going on. Another eminent scientist gave even more explicit support to mesmerism. The 1820s saw the publication of the multi-volume *Dictionnaire de Médecine*, a work of exemplary respectability. The article on magnetism was written by Dr L. Rostan. To everyone's surprise, he showed himself to be a believer in the reality of magnetic sleep, and even described his own successful experiment in clairvoyance.

The commissioners started with Céline, Foissac's somnambule, but obtained no worthwhile results. They then tested magnetism on some patients in the hospitals, until the General Council reminded them that magnetism in the Paris hospitals was still forbidden. Starved for suitable subjects on whom to experiment, the inquiry dragged on for another five years, and even after all that time only about a dozen people were tested. None of the commissioners could himself mesmerize, so they had to rely on Foissac and Dupotet, who selected their subjects for their sensational effects. In the end, then, the committee, guided by these two enthusiasts, shifted its focus on to paranormal phenomena rather than therapeutic value, and over-looked Bertrand in favour of fluidism. They assumed that a certain something is passed from operator to subject and therefore looked for proof of this something. They found such proof not only when the operator was in physical contact with his subject, or made close hand passes, but occasionally in telepathic hypnosis as well. The kinds of paranormal and supernormal phenomena which they ratified were feats of abnormal strength, prediction of epileptic fits, diagnosis of oneself and others. The report was favourable to mesmerism. When it was presented to the Academy, some wanted to discuss it, but it was forced through on the credibility of the commissioners. This report is often cited by mesmeric enthusiasts later in the nineteenth century as a vindication of their practice, but it is clearly unsatisfactory in many ways, and is not even representative, in that it ignored the kind of magnetism that was being practised by the likes of Bertrand and Faria.

One case covered in the report was that of Mme Plantin, who in 1829 underwent an operation for breast cancer while anaesthetized in magnetic sleep. The operation, by Jules Cloquet, was apparently successful (although the poor woman died three weeks later of 'a diseased liver' – perhaps the cancer had spread, since it is clear from the description in the report that it was far advanced), but in a fashion typical of the shambles surrounding this committee, the relatives refused to allow the commissioners to visit Mme Plantin for themselves, so that they had to rely on hearsay. They were present only at her autopsy a few weeks later.

These were the days before chemical anaesthetics had been discovered. You just had to grit your teeth (unless you were undergoing a dental operation, of course) and suffer. Under these circumstances, you'd think that the benefits of hypnotic anaesthesia would be obvious, and that any medical body worth its salt would investigate the matter. But the French Academy buried its head in the sand. The problem was the old one: the startling nature of the paranormal phenomena and the fanciful nature of many of the theories caused sceptics to concentrate on debunking these rather than focusing on what was important about mesmerism.

Consequently, in 1836 a Dr Hamard decided to bring matters to a head. He anaesthetized a dental patient and got a member of the Academy, Dr M.J. Oudet, to perform the operation. Discussion followed in the Academy, with many making the implausible claim that the whole thing was a fraud. Then another physician, Didier Jules Berna, offered to convince the Academy of certain facts about magnetism, principally somnambulism, insensibility to pain and the action of his unexpressed will on the subject as shown by the loss and restoration of movement or sensation in given limbs. A commission of nine was appointed. They concluded that magnetic somnambulism did not exist, that insensibility to pain was not proven, and that clairvoyance and sympathy between operator and subject were illusory. In a final attempt, Berna tried to induce clairvoyance in a different subject, but he failed. This commission's report to the Academy was, understandably, negative. Some protested that the issues required more than just a few hours' work, on two subjects, but their voices went unheard in the general climate of hostility towards mesmerism. For roughly half a century, in France, animal magnetism was thought to have no therapeutic use, and its practice was entirely given over to showmen, and to exploration of its paranormal and mystical aspects.

For these aspects the Academy of course had no time. And they had good reason for their official disdain. In the wake of the 1837 report, C. Burdin, a member of the Academy, offered a prize of 3,000 francs to anyone, somnambule or not, who could read without using his or her eyes. This was one of the most common clairvoyant tricks of the time. The whole thing turned into a farce. Dr J. Pigeaire from Montpellier wrote to the commission about his daughter's clairvoyant gifts, and came, on their invitation, to Paris. He and his daughter gave public exhibitions, which were all successful, but when the commission insisted on its own blindfold apparatus being used,

Pigeaire withdrew his daughter from the competition. Their public exhibitions continued, however, to public acclaim; even George Sand, the aristocratic but Bohemian novelist, attended and was convinced. Professor P.N. Gerdy decided to investigate Madamoiselle Pigeaire and found – why are we not surprised? – that she could not perform when her blindfold was taped to her face, but could when a little crevice of light remained. Burdin stated his conditions more clearly: if anyone could read with eyes open and in broad daylight through an opaque substance such as silk or paper placed six inches from the face, he or she would claim the prize. Dr Hublier from Provins entered his somnambule, but she was found to be a fraud before ever reaching the commission. When faced with the book she was to read clairvoyantly, she used to plead female indisposition or tiredness or something to get the room clear briefly, and then peek at the book while everyone was out. The use of spy holes was her undoing. A third somnambule of Dr Alphonse Teste also failed in front of the commission, and in the end no one won the prize. At this point the Academy decided that it need no longer concern itself with animal magnetism.

The whole history of the study of paranormal phenomena, whether spontaneous or enhanced by hypnosis, is studded with the same problem. There may well be people – just a few – who possess genuine psychic gifts. They never claim to be able to do whatever it is that they do with unfailing reliability. The appreciation and the proper study of such gifts is spoiled by the fakes and tricksters, who are in it for the money and attention. This puts the whole subject in bad odour not just with the general populace, but with the grant-giving bodies who might finance proper research.

Paranormal Titillations in Europe

Napoléon Bonaparte, we may safely assume, was a pretty hard-headed kind of fellow. But even Napoléon Bonaparte could succumb to the craze for paranormal mesmerism to the extent of consulting a somnambulist seer about the prospects for his first campaign in Italy. Just possibly, though, he did so cynically, or to raise morale, because we also hear of him dismissing clairvoyance. He is reported to have told de Puységur: 'If your somnambulist is so clever, let her predict what I shall be doing in eight days' time and which will be the winning numbers in tomorrow's lottery.'

Interest in paranormal mesmeric phenomena conquered Europe as effectively as Napoléon, and maintained its dominance in the absence of any opposition in the form of scientific research into magnetism. In both France and Germany it was common practice to magnetize a group of patients to find which one was the best somnambulist and then get him or her to diagnose the rest; the names of clairvoyants such as Maria Rübel, Marie Koch, Mattheus Schurr, Calixte Renaux and Prudence Bernard were as well known in their countries as their contemporaries Goethe, Beethoven, Victor Hugo and Alexandre Dumas; the Vatican was flooded with letters from anxious bishops in Catholic countries asking for guidance on the matter. At the end of the eighteenth century, several books on mesmerism had been placed on the Index in Rome, but popular interest in the shows of itinerant magnetizers such as Zanardelli and Rummo, but especially the Belgian Donato (A.E. d'Hont) could not be kept down, either here or in other Italian states, by totalitarian measures such as this. The circumspection of the Vatican, however, meant that the therapeutic potential of mesmerism was the main aspect that was studied in Italy, by people such as Francesco Guidi and Pietro d'Amico, in the 1850s.

In other countries too the showmen and paranormalists did serve the purpose of keeping interest in mesmerism alive. In Holland, for instance, P.G. van Ghert's work with clairvoyance paved the way for later study of the medical applications of animal magnetism. Charles de Lafontaine travelled extensively in Europe in the 1830s and 1840s, lecturing and exhibiting; his work with psychic somnambules in Brussels ushered in the golden age of mesmerism in Belgium, and we will later see the crucial importance of his tour of England to the history of hypnotism.

Many of the stories of paranormal abilities among somnambules are hard to assess at this distance, because we don't know how strict the controls were on assessing the results. Even so, there is a fascinating mixture of gold and dross. Here are a few snapshots.

Prudence Bernard, one of the most famous somnambules of them all, continued to tour extensively in Europe, and to receive amazed acclaim, despite having been accused of fraud in Paris in the 1840s. She was subsequently investigated by Professor Wartmann of the University of Geneva. In tests she succeeded in moving a compass needle 45 degrees, apparently by sheer telekinetic will power – but then she was found to be wearing a corset whose busk was made of magnetized steel. In 1852 she took her exhibition to London, and then to Manchester, where James Braid saw her. Her main trick at this time was playing cards while blindfolded. Braid challenged her, saying that he was sure she could see through gaps at the bottom of the blindfold. He suggested a more thorough blindfold, but she refused to comply. Prudence's flamboyant mesmerist, Auguste Lassaigne, hardly inspires confidence, since he trained as a stage conjurer before discovering – and marrying – Prudence. He felt he had a sacred mission, to spread the gospel Prudence revealed when hypnotized (for she also acted as a medium) and through her, a modern Joan of Arc, to restore France to the True Faith.

In Germany Dr Franz Nick's somnambule, Miss C. Krämerin, predicted the death of the king of Württemberg on 28 October 1816. The story goes that they tried to keep it secret, fearing official repercussions, but news leaked out and led to the merry sport of court officials placing bets as to whether she had got it right, or which exactly would be the day of death. It turned out to be a couple of days later than predicted.

Dr Johann C. Valentin of Cassel worked with Caroline Ramer, who seems to have had genuine clairvoyant abilities. She saw the fall of a farm worker in Breitenbach bei Hof, four hours' journey from Cassel. They were investigated by a committee which acquitted them both of fraud.

The most famous clairvoyant of them all in Germany was the Seeress of Prevorst, Friederike Hauffe. She was born in 1801 in the remote Swabian village of Prevorst, near Löwenstein. She came to Justinus Kerner (1786–1862) on the point of death through hysterical depression and starvation. Before long, he had discovered that in magnetic sleep she displayed remarkable gifts – not just telepathy and clairvoyance, but her forte was conversing with the dead, who appeared to her (and occasionally to others around her) as ghostly figures. She predicted the future, healed the sick, spoke in a language that she claimed was the original language of humankind, and 'channelled' (as we would say now) a whole complex cosmology and theology, which accommodated magnetism. The Seeress aroused immense interest throughout Germany, and her bedside was visited by many cultured and learned men – doctors, philosophers, theologians – who discussed her revelations in all seriousness. Kerner was a notable doctor, the first, for instance, to describe food poisoning by botulism. But there is a dark side to his relationship with her. He was so bound up in his experiments with her that he found ways to keep her in an almost permanent trance for years, and even fed her laurel berries to aid her hallucinations. With hindsight, he probably hastened her death in 1829 – on a day she had accurately predicted.

Visions of ghosts became common among somnambules once the fame of the Prevorst Seeress spread. It was largely a German phenomenon, but in France there was Alphonse Cahagnet with his somnambule Bruno, who had Swedenborgian visions of heaven and angels, and Adèle Maginot, who began as a clairvoyant diagnostician of others' ills, but soon had visions of heaven and conversations with the dead. Even Deleuze, let alone Dupotet, was converted to spiritism in the end.

From Russia stories emerged later in the century of one of the most remarkable mesmeric clairvoyants of them all. Although she was practising and being studied in the 1880s and 1890s, her stories belong here, because Russia was typically thirty or so years behind the rest of Europe. She was a thirty-year-old schoolteacher, known simply as 'Miss M.', who came to the attention of Dr A.N. Khovrin of Tambov. She was magnetized for her nervous attacks, and in magnetic sleep soon manifested clairvoyance. She was tested in an impressively methodical manner. Once, for instance, nine scientists in St Petersburg each wrote a sentence on a piece of paper. All the pieces of paper were then sealed into envelopes and put into a hat. One envelope was removed without being opened and the rest were burnt. The chosen envelope was put inside another thick envelope and glued to it inside in two places. The flaps of the outer envelope were glued and stapled down, and closed with a seal surrounded by pinpricks which were visible only under a magnifying glass, and a tiny piece of hair was placed under the seal. The package was sent in a box to Khovrin in Tambov. Miss M. read the text as 'I'm convinced that you will read my letter easily and without trouble and that afterwards you will feel magnificent. Petersburg, L.G. Korchagin.' Khovrin sent the unopened package back to St Petersburg along with Miss M.'s solution. The Society of Experimental Psychology – the original scientists – verified that the seal had not been tampered with. The envelopes were opened, and the original text compared with Miss M.'s version, which was identical.

Later that year (1893) Miss M. performed the same feat under even more strict controls. She read 'There are things in this world the wisest men did not dream of' as 'There are things in this world we never dreamt of.' On another occasion, she didn't get the words, but a picture of what the words described: a burning building. On another occasion she accurately described a drawing which had been sealed inside envelopes under similar conditions. She also proved very accurate at psychometry – the psychic 'reading' of the history of places and objects – and at transposition of the senses. She was tested many times for this latter ability, and was invariably successful. In one such experiment, conducted under very tight controls by Dr Nikolski of Kiev, various solutions, including sugar, cooking salt, quinine and zinc sulphide, were poured into identical glass containers. Blotting paper was soaked in each of the solutions in turn and applied to the inside of Miss M.'s right arm. Each time she identified the taste accurately.

If I calculate the proportion of frauds to genuine psychics in Europe in the middle of the nineteenth century, I might count it as misleading to end this chapter with Miss M.'s stories, since she is the exception rather than the rule. But throughout the world, people in trance states have been thought to have divinatory and other talents and, as we have seen, the same belief became attached to animal magnetism early in its history, as soon as the Marquis de Puységur discovered magnetic sleep. I for one am certainly not inclined to say that there is nothing to it.

5

Crusaders and Prophets
in the United States

France was the original home of mesmerism, but there were close
political links between France and the United States – links that were
forged in what they saw as their shared revolutionary fervour and
tempered by the freemasonry of all or most of the major players on
both sides of the Atlantic. The consummate symbol of the close
relationship between the two countries, old and new, was the
subsequent gift by France to America of the Statue of Liberty, which
stands proudly in the bay at New York. *Liberty Enlightening the World*
(to use her full name) was designed and built in France by the
sculptor Auguste Bartholdi and the engineer Gustave Eiffel (rather
well known for his tower), and formally presented to America on
Independence Day 1884, an exact century after the critical year of
Mesmer's stay in Paris, and 108 years after America's declaration
of independence.

It is not surprising, then, to find that mesmerism tried early to
find a foothold in the new country. We have already seen how the
first pioneer, the Marquis de Lafayette, attempted to import it. He
wrote enthusiastically about Mesmer to George Washington from
Paris on 14 May 1784, and Mesmer himself followed this letter up with
one of his own to Washington, written a month later on 16 June.
Washington replied to Mesmer five months later, after he had met de
Lafayette in the States, saying cautiously and with impeccable polite-
ness that if mesmerism was as beneficial as it was supposed to be, it
would certainly do people good and bring fame to its founder. In the
meantime, in the course of his visit, the marquis had given one or
two lectures on the subject, had visited the Shaker community, since
he saw similarities between the trance state into which the Shakers
worked themselves up and the crisis inspired by mesmerism, and had

gone to see some Native American rituals, because he was not convinced that mesmerism was just a new European phenomenon, rather than a rediscovery of something older and more primitive.

But despite these speculations by de Lafayette, what attracted most of the American mesmerists was precisely its newness. They felt they were pioneers, participants in the creation of a new country, one with enormous potential; and many of them felt that mesmerism would be a useful tool in making America spiritually the most advanced nation on earth.

Perkinism

After de Lafayette, there are no further recorded visits from French missionaries of mesmerism for some thirty years, while France went through the turmoil of the Revolution, Napoléon's tyranny and constant warfare. But meanwhile, perhaps as a result of de Lafayette's visit, there was a home-grown development, in the form of what became known as 'Perkinism'.

Some time in the 1790s Elisha Perkins, a founding member of the Connecticut Medical Society, invented a 'tractor' with which he achieved some remarkable cures. His 'tractor' was made of two pieces of different metals about 2½ inches long, of secret composition, one coloured silver, one gold; when brought together they formed the shape of half a cone, split lengthwise. He claimed that this device, when waved over and around the site of an illness, could draw or extract the illness from the patient's body – hence the name 'tractor', which means 'an instrument for drawing'. He was so successful that before long he expanded his business interests to Europe, sending his son Benjamin to set up shop in London, where the tractors sold for an astonishing 5 guineas a pair. His business was no doubt helped by the publication in 1799 by J.D. Herholdt and C.G. Rafn of their *Experiments with the Metallic Tractors*, in which the authors had nothing but good to speak of Perkins's invention, which they had found to be particularly effective on horses.

The craze was short-lived, however. The tractors were not well received either by the mesmeric community or by orthodox doctors – and even the general public enjoyed the sarcasm of, for instance, the satirical verse by John Corry:

> Arm'd with twin skewers, see Perkins, by main force
> Drag the foul fiend from Christian and from horse.

In Paris Deleuze took issue with Perkins, as not being a true magnetist, while in England the reaction from the scientific community may be gauged by a book published in 1801, in which a Fellow of the Royal Society called J. Haygarth reported that he had found that a pair of fake wooden tractors, painted to look like the real things, were just as effective as the expensive model. In his book *On the Imagination, as a Cause and Cure of Disorders in the Human Body* he suggested that it was all down to the imagination of humans and the faith of horses in their masters. Perkins was expelled from the Connecticut Medical Society as a quack, and died in the New York yellow fever epidemic of 1799, valiantly trying to cure the ill with his tractors.

Three Foreign Pioneers

The next mesmeric visitor from France was Joseph du Commun, whom we met briefly in the last chapter. He settled in the States in 1815, but seems not to have undertaken much in the way of proselytizing about the new miracle treatment until 1829, when he travelled from his base at the US Military Academy at West Point, where he was a teacher, to give lectures on mesmerism in New York. Despite these lectures (which were also published in book form) he seems not to have made much of an impression. Perhaps the hostility of Benjamin Franklin and Thomas Jefferson prevented American high society from taking the matter seriously.

The breakthrough came with Charles Poyen St Sauveur, who wrote, taught and practised mesmerism in Massachusetts, where he arrived in 1834 after a short stay in the French West Indies. Poyen had come across mesmerism as a medical student in Paris in 1832. He was a sickly man, and was overwhelmed when a hypnotized clairvoyant gave him a complete list of his symptoms. It was another case of the flash of enlightenment. Poyen was a convert, and spent the rest of his short life as a crusader for the cause.

At first, though, his enthusiasm may have done the cause more harm than good. New England, and Boston in particular, was seething with reforming zeal, open to new ideas. Having witnessed slavery in the West Indies, Poyen was an ardent abolitionist, and must have seen New England as his spiritual home. But these former Puritans did not prove very receptive to Poyen's brand of showmanship. Although he came across as serious and thoughtful, his strong French accent can't have helped (not to mention the strawberry birthmark that disfigured half his face), and his notion that through mesmerism the new country could become a paradise on earth fell on deaf ears. New Englanders were more convinced that they would carve out their paradise by hard work and moral virtue.

Fed up with the relative lack of interest, and finding himself low on funds, Poyen was contemplating returning to France when he accepted an invitation to visit Rhode Island. This was the turning-point: not only were his lectures better received there than elsewhere, but he came across an excellent subject, Cynthia Ann Gleason, who was deeply hypnotizable and displayed remarkable feats of clairvoyance. He saw that she could make his lectures stand out and reach a wider audience, and so he took her on the road with him on a tour of New England, again starting in Boston, with a demonstration at the Harvard Medical School.

His shows were well received, but with some lingering scepticism: reviewers thought that he might be conning his audiences through collusion with Miss Gleason. Ever flexible, Poyen rose to the bait, and began to include in his demonstrations not only Miss Gleason's feats, but also the magnetizing of volunteers from the audience. Just like modern stage hypnotists, he would show that his subjects were impervious to pain, could sniff ammonia straight from the bottle without flinching, and were unresponsive to loud noises. Following a short introductory lecture on the history and theory of mesmerism, he would launch into these demonstrations, and sometimes even cure people of their sickness then and there on stage. Paranormal phenomena played a certain part in his performances too, though he maintained that so-called clairvoyance was actually the transference to the subject of thoughts from the operator, with whom she was in sympathetic harmony.

This new style of show was a great success in New England, and by 1837 Poyen could boast that he knew of some forty people who had experimented with the art. One of them, another Frenchman called B.F. Bugard, performed a painless tooth extraction in 1836, which caused quite a stir. After Poyen's success, there was no stopping mesmerism. This is probably due as much to a comparative lack of professional bodies to resist and denounce it, as to any independence endemic in the American mind. Poyen himself left the States in 1839 and never returned; he was actually on the point of embarking for a return trip from France in 1844 when he was overtaken by death. But his legacy lived on: one of the early American books on the topic (*The History and Philosophy of Animal Magnetism with Practical Instructions for the Exercise of its Power* by A Practical Magnetizer), published in Boston in 1843, claimed that there were already 200 practitioners in Boston alone. It had also spread to New York and Philadelphia, where it had attracted the attention of the anonymous 'Gentleman of Philadelphia' who wrote *The Philosophy of Animal Magnetism* in 1837. This book is famous not just as a very early American book on mesmerism, but because many scholars believe that the author was Edgar Allan Poe, whose fictional forays into mesmerism we will look at in a moment.

Another pioneer from abroad was the Englishman Robert Collyer, who came in 1839 originally to lecture on phrenology, which was generally a more acceptable subject. He was appalled by what he saw, especially in the field of medicine, where quackery was more prominent than anything resembling scientific medicine. 'Daily some poor unfortunate falls a victim to these murderous quacks,' he intoned. 'Their deeds of darkness and iniquity fairly outherod Herod.' He found a ready audience not only for phrenology, but mesmerism too, which he had studied in England with John Elliotson, whose career will occupy us in the next chapter. He lectured on mesmerism to great acclaim up and down the eastern seaboard, in New York, Boston and Philadelphia. Three months of nightly lectures and demonstrations in Boston led to an investigation by the city council. While falling short of actually endorsing mesmerism, they found Collyer to be sincere and not a danger, and freely admitted that *something* mysterious was going on, which was not fraud. This was presumably also the reaction of the majority of the audiences: puzzlement combined with awe.

Early American Practice and Ideology

As a result of the pioneering work of du Commun, Poyen and Collyer, mesmerism became a vogue, and indigenous lecturers and demonstrators arose to fulfil the demand. The two most famous were John Bovee Dods (1795–1872), who was such a popular lecturer that 2,000 people attended his six-lecture course, and La Roy Sunderland (1804–85), who could win the same size of audience for a *single* demonstration. Later, in 1850, Sunderland was even invited to lecture on the topic to the US Senate.

Neither Dods nor Sunderland were fluidists. It is rather hard at times to say exactly to which category they belong, fluidism or animism, and Sunderland called what he did by various names at various times, but the one which lasted longest was 'pathetism'. For a time he had worked New England as a revivalist preacher, and he was clearly a good enough speaker to be able to hold a large audience. He came across mesmerism in 1839 and swiftly made the transition from one form of entrancement to another. His technique as a performing 'pathetist' was amazingly downbeat. He would take the stage at a meeting and begin to talk about pathetism, explaining how an operator and his subject could build up sufficient rapport between them to lay the subject open to the operator's will. 'I use this term [pathetism] to signify not only the agency by which one person by manipulation, is enabled to produce emotion, feeling, passion, or any physical or mental effects, in the system of another, but also that susceptibility of emotion or feeling, of any kind, from manipulation, in the subject operated upon, by the use of which these effects are produced.' At some point he would simply declare that some members of the audience were in the 'pathematic' state. They would announce themselves by walking up to the speaker's platform, perhaps in imitation of one of his old revivalist meetings. He would then use them as subjects for the usual round of showmanlike and entertaining phenomena, including, occasionally, minor operations.

In 1843 Sunderland was publishing a magazine, *The Magnet*, out of offices in New York. The magazine's scope was comprehensive: it was 'Devoted to the investigation of Human Physiology, embracing Vitality, Pathetism, Psychology, Phrenopathy, Phrenology, Neurology, Physiognomy and Magnetism'. It is worth lingering briefly over the short-lived journal's contents, because it is typical of many of the publications (in book or journal form) that sprung up in the nineteenth century in Europe and elsewhere. In his introductory editorial Sunderland compared the misguided abuse of William Harvey (who discovered the circulation of the blood) and Galileo to what was happening to magnetism; this comparison was already a commonplace in mesmeric literature. Magnetism, Sunderland claims, is a complete philosophy of mind and matter, and especially illuminating for the light it casts on the mind, dreaming and forms of insanity. He takes some pains to distance himself from mesmeric entertainers and other popular lecturers, on the grounds that what he is offering is hard science. The body is covered in magnetic poles, manipulation of which cures diseases, calms hysteria, causes somnambulism, etc. Insanity is derangement of the poles; death is their destruction. It is easy to see the attractions of grand, all-encompassing schemes like this.

The rest of the journal is devoted to reports and correspondence about case histories and to explanations of the laws of the universe. Among the case histories is one of a lady blind from birth (though familiar with lettering through Braille) who, when mesmerized, could read from a book, though she was even better at describing her internal organs than external things. Although Sunderland reports such cases, he carefully distances himself from the many over-credulous accounts of clairvoyance, visions of the future, etc. The whole tone of the journal is cautious and crusading. For instance, Sunderland regrets the horde of popular entertainers who are sullying the name of magnetism, because one cannot expect a country brought up on such fare to place much value on the medical use of magnetism; he therefore uses the pages of the journal to report case histories which provide evidence for its medical value, and calls on moral men to take up magnetism.

The combination of enthusiasm and circumspection evinced by Sunderland's journal was to be echoed many times. In the nature of things, little evidence remains of the work of the shysters and travelling showmen, but this constant circumspection shows how prevalent they were. In the eyes of all these writers, the showmen were in danger of muddying the waters. Sunderland and the rest wanted to establish mesmerism as a valid and valuable medical practice, based on solid, scientific principles, and their defensive tone is their main means of making it clear to the medical men that they were not to be confused with their flamboyant cousins.

Among the new, scientific practitioners were men like Colonel William Stone of New York, a former ambassador to the Netherlands. Although he was converted to mesmerism by the remarkable exploits of Loraine Brackett, a clairvoyant who had been partially cured by her mesmerizing doctor, George Capron of Providence, of blindness and dumbness (caused by a blow on the head), he eschewed the more melodramatic side of things, quietly experimented on the phenomena in his home and published a careful account of them. Another responsible researcher was J.K. Mitchell (1798–1858), who in the 1840s conducted a series of sober experiments on mesmerism, looking for changes in skin temperature and pulse rate, finding what proportion of the population was susceptible and so on. He also performed a number of dental operations under hypnotic anaesthesia. He failed to find evidence of paranormal abilities or of magnetic fluid, the latter because the mesmerist's energy does not become depleted, as one would expect if the fluidic theory were correct. Even if there were such a fluid, he doubted that metals and other substances could be charged by it. He suggested that the operator brings about changes in his own nervous system which then somehow effect the subject's nervous system. Up until this last vague sentence, Mitchell seems like a forerunner of academic researchers, long before the foundation of the first psychology departments in American universities in the 1880s.

The fact that both Dods and Sunderland began their lives as ministers (Dods was a Universalist, Sunderland a Methodist) tells us immediately that Americans were attracted to the religious dimension of animal magnetism. Since sensitive subjects appeared to be able to travel beyond the confines of their bodies, it seemed to prove the existence of the soul and to show that the soul had higher powers, and could commune with the angels. Not a few people rediscovered their Christian roots as a result of investigating mesmerism, although others were led away from scriptural and dogmatic religion to something altogether more vague. Moreover, as a cure, mesmerism seemed to be treating the whole person, changing the moral character as well as healing the body. Both physical and spiritual or psychological illness were taken to be the result of being out of harmony with the invisible workings of the universe. And, to top it all, mesmerism was presented as scientific, so that you did not have to think of yourself as superstitious to believe in it. Even in the domain of religion, a down-to-earth tone of writing prevailed.

These were the kinds of ideas that were spread by the dozens of books that were published in America in the 1840s on mesmerism. Typically they would start with a plea to the reader to be open-minded, and then go on to a short history of Mesmer's work, a catalogue of cures, documented reports of telepathy and clairvoyance, and then instructions for the would-be magnetizer. The enthusiasm, the crusading tone, of much of the writing may be seen in a single example. In *Facts in Mesmerism and Thoughts on its Causes and Uses* (1842) the eminent physician Dr Charles Caldwell wrote:

> Never has there been before a discovery so easily and clearly demonstrable as mesmerism is, so unreasonably and stubbornly doubted, and so contumaciously discredited and opposed . . . Yet never before has there been made, in anthropology, a discovery at once so interesting and sublime – so calculated to exhibit the power and dominion of the human will – its boundless sway over space and spirit.

New England remained the centre of interest in mesmerism, but there were also, for instance, flourishing societies dedicated to the topic in Cincinnati and New Orleans (whose members, being largely of French extraction, maintained contact with mesmerists in France rather than in New England).

Partly under the influence of the British writer Chauncy Townshend's book *Facts in Mesmerism* (1840, second edition 1844), which became a kind of bible for American mesmerists, orthodoxy tended to distinguish five phases of trance after the normal waking state. Deep trance was only the second such phase, after a light trance, because what interested them were the remarkable phenomena of catalepsy (a third phase) and what were known as 'mesmeric consciousness' (the state in which the subject exhibited telepathy and clairvoyance, which was understood as the separation of the soul from the body) and 'clairvoyant wisdom', which involved direct contact with the mesmeric fluid itself, so that the subject's mind was temporarily imbued with its omniscience.

America quickly became a hotbed of hypnotic surgery. Although operations had been performed in both France and England, it is telling that the bulk of such surgical activity took place far from the centres of culture – in India (see the next chapter) and in numerous small towns around America. The explanation for this is that these places were remote from the canons of medical propriety, dictated by the academies. Their approach was more pragmatic: if it works, let's use it, and never mind the theory.

This pragmatic attitude colours mesmerism in the States more generally. When mesmerism first appeared in Europe, it was taken up by the privileged classes. When it was introduced into America, however, it rapidly penetrated further down the social scale. This had enormous consequences on the future progress of the art in America. If it was to flourish among the middle classes, then, in keeping with the American self-help spirit, it had to serve some practical purpose. The cures were practical, but medicine was only one compartment of life. In short, it had to offer a whole philosophy of life, because that kind of self-improvement was the vogue. Hence early lecturers such as Dods dropped the odd name 'animal magnetism' and redescribed mesmerism as 'the science of the mind and its powers', while Sunderland ended up calling the field 'electrical psychology'. In America, mesmerism became a way of exploring your potential and reframing your personal philosophy. They were attracted to its cosmology: health – not just bodily health, but health of the mind and spirit too – was a result of being in tune with the energy pervading the universe. So the mesmerists taught that mesmerism was a spiritual path, the solution to individual and to the budding nation's ills. For these men mesmerism was not a substitute for Christianity, but the means of its millenarian realization on earth. For the hundreds of ordinary men and women interested in their preaching, mesmerism was not a way of altering their relationship with God and the manifest destiny of the nation, but of establishing it on a firmer footing.

Phreno-magnetism and Electro-biology

With typical American inventiveness, in the 1840s mesmerism commonly became combined with phrenology, the belief that different mental faculties were located in different parts of the skull. So a 'phreno-mesmerist' or 'phreno-magnetist' would direct the magnetic fluid through his finger to the relevant part of the skull to provoke the appropriate form of behaviour. By stimulating the destructive area of the skull, for instance, he would provoke violence in the subject. Or he would use the subject as a guinea pig, to see which parts of the brain concealed or contained which moral faculty. This inevitably gave rise to fierce arguments, as different phreno-magnetists gained different results. It is hard to tell exactly, but phreno-magnetism seems to have been an indigenous American phenomenon, which then spread back to Europe.

Phreno-magnetism was essentially bound up with showmanship. There was little point in stimulating violence or benevolence or whatever in a subject if there was no audience there to be amazed and impressed. And, since phreno-magnetists could not make use of the same subject night after night, because collusion would then be an easy accusation, it was natural for them to make use of members of an audience.

Another American development, equally linked to showmanship, was electro-biology. This owes its rise to Dods, who recommended and practised a mesmeric technique in which the subject held a small, bimetallic disc in the palm of his hand and stared at it with fixed attention. The theory, bizarrely enough, was that electricity thrown off by the disc accumulates in the brain. But never mind the theory – the practice was a gift to prospective showmen. No expensive equipment was needed (the disc was a kind of coin made up of a core of copper or silver surrounded by zinc), nor any special skills, and you could even get your audiences to do all the work. And so a whole generation of 'electro-biologists' was born, who were the forerunners of today's stage and TV hypnotists. They travelled the States with bags of discs, which they would hand out to audiences to mesmerize them and get them to manifest as many of the extraordinary phenomena associated with mesmerism as they could. A contemporary English report of a visiting American electro-biologist says:

> Dr Darling proceeds to shew his power over the sensations of his subject. For example, he deprives one hand, or one arm, of all feeling, and renders it utterly insensible to the most acute pain; or he makes his subject feel a cold pencil-case burning hot, or himself freeze with cold, or taste water as milk, brandy or any other liquid . . . Dr Darling further controls the memory. He causes the subject to forget his own name, or that of any other individual; or to be unable to name a single letter of the alphabet, etc. etc. Moreover, he causes him to take any object to be what Dr Darling says it is, a watch for a snuff-box, a chair for a dog, etc. etc., or to see an object named, where nothing really is, as a book in Dr Darling's empty hand, or a bird in the room, where none is. The illusion is often absolutely perfect. Again, he will cause the subject to imagine himself another person, such as Dr Darling, Father Matthew, Prince Albert, or the Duke of Wellington, and to act the character to the life.

All good entertaining stuff – but not without its importance. An anonymous article in the 1849 Cincinnati *Buchanan's Journal of Man* expressed regret at the demise of the practice of hand passes and so on. Modern mesmerists, it complained, simply ordered their subjects to sleep. With hindsight, we can see that the electro-biologists' practice was closer to what we would now recognize as hypnotism, but at the time it seemed to some as though they were ignoring the welfare of their subjects, by failing to recharge their bodies with the vital magnetic fluid. Technique apart, an unexpected consequence of their demonstrations, and perhaps of audience expectations, was that they established many of the criteria by which even today hypnotists test for susceptibility and recognize that their subjects are in a trance state. Of course, they were building on the work of their predecessors in Europe, but unwittingly they established much of the vocabulary for later academic discussion. One of the main differences from their European predecessors was that they held these phenomena to be a result of the state in which their subjects fell, whereas in Europe some of them, at any rate, were held to be the product of the action of the mesmerist's will on his subject, rather than something produced by the subject himself.

This is our first real brush with showmanship and so it will not be out of place to mention Ingmar Bergman's wonderful film *The Magician*, despite the fact that this is set in Europe. The film is an intelligent, challenging and ironic portrait of life on the road for a travelling mesmerist called Vogler and his troupe in 1846. It is too complex a film to be easily summarized; suffice it to say that we are left thinking that they are probably frauds, but also in the uncomfortable position of not being entirely sure. Even though their elixirs are certainly fake, even though they are wanted by the police (we're never told what for), and even though they admit to the use of mirrors to create spiritist phenomena, in their performance they seem to alternate between mere tricks and genuine psychic feats, and it is a distinct possibility that they claim to be frauds in order to escape hostility and persecution. In a spooky scene in an attic, where Vogler takes his revenge on one of his spiteful persecutors, one is never sure if he is genuinely using mesmerism to produce hallucinations, or whether the whole thing is merely the result of clever stage management. No doubt many of America's travelling electrobiologists and mesmerists used the same combination of trickery and genuine mesmerism.

Fiction and Fears

It didn't take long before the usual fears about mesmerism arose in America. It took advantage of human gullibility, since it was fraudulent; it involved surrendering your will. A mesmerist might be able to implant secret commands into your mind. He could have his way with women. An anonymous pamphlet, *Confessions of a Magnetizer*, confirmed these suspicions. The author, claiming to be a reformed magnetizer, admitted that the rapport between himself and his female subjects or patients had laid him open to temptation, and that he had on occasion made sure that the women found him attractive too. He insisted, however, that he had never succumbed to the temptations, and merely felt it his duty to warn people of the dangers.

Learned opinion was less polarized, not simply in favour or in opposition. Ralph Waldo Emerson found the idea of being in someone else's power appalling, but recognized that mesmerism could trigger interest in the profundities of life. Nathaniel Hawthorne thought one might be able to question a mesmerized subject about matters metaphysical and cosmological, and flirted with the idea that mesmerism might be a positive force that would help put human life on a more spiritual basis, but in *The House of the Seven Gables* (1851) he holds not just the idea that the hypnotist imposes his will on his subject, but also that this is why women make the best hypnotic subjects – because their will is weaker than men's. He also perpetuates the fiction that lifelong entrancement is possible. When Matthew Maule wreaks the revenge of the Maules on the Pyncheons by hypnotizing Alice Pyncheon, after she wakes up she can function normally (with no memory of having been hypnotized), but for the rest of her life she is Matthew's to command and humiliate. While Holgrave (who is also a descendant of 'the wizard Maule', and like all the Maules has 'witchcraft' in his eyes) is telling the story, he so enters into the spirit of it that he makes the gestures and hypnotic passes Matthew Maule would have made to entrance Alice – and inadvertently starts to put Phoebe Pyncheon, his audience, into a trance. Phoebe is saved from this kind of mental rape only by the self-restraint of Holgrave. In Hawthorne's real life, his fiancée suggested in 1841 that she consult a mesmeric healer for her headaches, but Hawthorne would not hear of it. Mesmerism was manipulation, and violated 'the sacredness of an individual'. But although he despised mesmerism and any form of control, Hawthorne was fascinated by the subject and found in it a model for the kind of fiction he himself was trying to write, which would fascinate others. He wanted his readers to enter a kind of trance world of the imagination.

Edgar Allan Poe's story 'The Facts in the Case of M. Valdemar' (published in 1845 and originally entitled 'Mesmerism in Articulo Mortis') provoked huge controversy. Poe plays with the idea that a dying person may be so imbued with magnetic fluid by a mesmerist that he can remain, though dead, in a kind of suspended death for months, until released by the mesmerist – at which point his body immediately turns into a pile of stinking, putrid slime. Taking it to be factual, people seriously debated whether such a horrifying use of mesmerism was possible, and condemned it on the assumption that it was. Poe's macabre imagination had already led him to write two other short stories about mesmerism, both published in 1844 – 'Mesmeric Revelation' and 'A Tale of the Ragged Mountains'. 'Mesmeric Revelation' is simply premissed on the idea that a magnetized person may act as a medium or channel, revealing metaphysical truths, while 'A Tale of the Ragged Mountains' tells how a frequently mesmerized man glimpses in a dream-like state details of a previous incarnation.

But all publicity is good publicity. These negative reports and fears gave mesmerists like La Roy Sunderland the opportunity to set the record straight. In response to *Confessions of a Magnetizer*, which had named him in person, he stressed the many diseases for which mesmerism had proved to be effective, from blindness to coffee addiction, and the important insights it gave into the capabilities of the human mind, which seemed to have latent clairvoyant abilities. The mesmerists argued that their detractors were focusing on the superficial degrees of mesmerism, the kind of state achieved in the electro-biologists' stage shows, and ignoring the obvious interest and importance of the deeper states. To this kind of argument, learned men replied that these 'facts' about paranormal powers were subjective and unverifiable, merely the experiences of mesmerized subjects.

A couple of fictional treatments of stage hypnotism in America of the nineteenth century conveniently illustrate the opposing views. In Hawthorne's *The Blithedale Romance* (1852) there is a scene in which Priscilla, as the 'Veiled Lady', performs on stage 'in communion with the spiritual world' and in touch with 'the Absolute'. She is in a cataleptic state, her will totally under the control of the unscrupulous Professor Westervelt. Hawthorne seems to believe that such people are genuinely in a trance (although Priscilla's trance is broken by her love for Hollingsworth, an attraction stronger than the magnetism of the charismatic but flawed Westervelt). In *Alias Grace*, however, Margaret Atwood's 1996 novel, the whole thing is portrayed as a sham – effective, and harmless, but still fraudulent.

Mesmerism and the American Prophets

When mesmerism first became all the rage in America, the rash of books stressed both the medical and the paranormal potential. By 1850, however, the latter was of far more interest than the former. Physicalist theories were abandoned in favour of various adaptations of traditional lore about the soul and the spirit, or in favour of Swedenborgism, since the Scandinavian prophet was immensely popular in the States, and mesmerists were supposed to prove the reality of Swedenborg's visions. In *Mesmer and Swedenborg*, for instance, written in 1847, George Bush reckoned that although Swedenborg had communicated with angels on his own, Mesmer had introduced a method by which others could be vouchsafed glimpses of the same realms. Bush accepted all the so-called 'higher phenomena' of mesmerism, from clairvoyance to the ability to see auras, because these were just the kinds of phenomena one would expect to find in the spiritual world if Swedenborg's teachings were true. Mesmerism, in fact, had been given to the world to prepare the way for the final acceptance of Swedenborgism. For whatever reasons, peculiar to the cultural history of the developing nation, mesmerism predisposed Americans to think not only of a lower unconscious, but also of a mystical higher unconscious, and to abandon scripturally based Christianity in favour of the psychological and experiential attempt to align oneself with higher or natural forces.

It was, in a sense, Poyen's fault once again. He was the missionary who started the whole thing off by his direct influence on a couple of significant figures, Dr James Stanley Grimes (1807–1903) and Phineas Parkhurst Quimby (1802–66) and, through them, by his indirect influence on even more significant figures. By the time of this third generation, it is fair to say that mesmerism no longer played a major part in the lives or work of any of the major American prophets, but it was the original impetus that initiated the whole fascinating movement.

Quimby, a thoughtful, respectable-looking man, met Poyen on tour in Belfast, Maine, in either 1836 or 1838, and was bowled over by his demonstration and lecture. He pestered Poyen with questions afterwards, and Poyen told him that he too could become a mesmerist if he applied himself. This was all Quimby needed to hear; he left his job as a clock-maker and followed Poyen around until he felt he had learnt enough from him and could set up as a magnetizer himself. With seventeen-year-old Lucius Burkmar as his somnambulist diagnostician, he rapidly became the most famous mesmerist in America. His services were in demand wherever he went.

After a while, however, a niggling doubt began to surface: was this somnambulistic clairvoyance, or telepathy with the patients themselves? If the latter, Lucius was simply confirming what the patients already believed, and the reason the cures worked was not necessarily any particular efficacy in the herbal remedies Quimby prescribed as a result of Lucius's diagnoses, but the trust and confidence of the patient. In 1859 he moved to Portland, Maine, and set himself up in consulting rooms large enough to accommodate the hundreds of patients who came to see him. He found that he didn't need Lucius, but could cure patients himself, by putting them at their ease, sitting opposite them and staring at them until he went into a trance state. He then used psychic force to transmit healing energy from himself to the patient, and backed this up with herbal drugs.

But the doubts would not go away, and seemed to be confirmed by a discovery Quimby made. His poorer patients could not afford many of the drugs Quimby used to prescribe, and so he would recommend to them drugs which, while less expensive, were also less strong. To his surprise, he found that they were cured just as effectively, if they were cured at all. He realized it was his patients' confidence in him as a healer that was doing the trick, and so he gave up using drugs – and magnetism – and became a faith healer. He claimed not that the cause of cure was confidence, but, more radically, that illness was caused in the first place by bad beliefs. Disease, he said, was 'a deranged state of mind'. Eradication of these negative beliefs would not only cure disease, but keep one free from illness; in trying to cure the disease, doctors were taking an effect for a cause. It was important to Quimby, then, that his patients understood what the sources of illness and cure were; he would explain things to them, rather than imposing anything on them, and with this use of speech resembled a modern psychotherapist rather than one of the silent mesmerists of Victorian Britain. Magnetism could bring temporary relief, but only the right attitude could really cure. Like Coué after him, he stressed optimism (and putting the mind on higher things) as a shield against illness.

Poyen influenced not only Quimby but also Dr Grimes in Poughkeepsie. Grimes was an itinerant lecturer and demonstrator, of the same generation as Sunderland and Dods, but not quite of their stature. A tailor, William Levingston, left one of his shows with a burning desire to test his own mesmeric powers, and found that he was highly successful with a young man called Andrew Jackson Davis, who had moved to Poughkeepsie not long before, in 1839, from Blooming Grove, New York, where he had been born in 1826. Davis soon demonstrated that he had extraordinary clairvoyant powers, and Levingston toured with him around the country. In addition to the usual run of medical diagnoses and foretelling the future, the 'Poughkeepsie Seer', as he became known, was famous for channelling (to use the modern term) a vision of the divine powers and workings of the universe as a whole, which he came to see as the beginning of a new revelation for humankind. As his fame grew, he left Levingston and moved to New York to spread his gospel more effectively, and took Dr Lyon as his magnetizer and the Reverend Fishbaugh as his scribe. Before long he came to prefer a self-induced trance to one that was externally imposed, at any rate for the dictation of the vast, rambling book in 800 pages, on science, love, religion and the spiritual world, which he called *The Principles of Nature, Her Divine Revelations, and a Voice to Mankind.* 'The poverty of blood which marked poor Andrew Jackson's childhood was reflected in his spiritual life. Surely to few other seers has been granted so limited and so purblind a vision of things celestial. He was almost wholly lacking in passion, human or Divine. His ideal of conduct was an emasculated stoicism, his highest virtue a milk-and-watery benevolence, his God a progressive nebula.' But for all these shortcomings, the book was an enormous success, and ran to thirty-five editions in the thirty years following its publication in 1847. Davis's intelligence and enthusiasm shine from his eyes in contemporary portraits, and his personal magnetism helped to convince thousands of the truth of his visions.

Quimby's Disciples

Andrew Jackson Davis was only the first of the American prophets. Others soon followed, of whom the most significant and interesting was Thomas Lake Harris (1823–1906). But they made no particularly significant use of mesmerism. In Davis's case it was mesmerism that first clearly revealed his clairvoyant faculty and triggered his later career; for Harris it was more that mesmerism had primed the American public to receive his message. Nevertheless, the history of mesmerism in the United States does have this peculiar twist. In Europe, when hypnotized subjects were used as seers, they were literally 'mediums': they were intermediaries, no more than mouthpieces for higher intelligences. In America some of these seers, like Davis and Harris, claimed religious status themselves, as prophets, dispensers of a new revelation.

By far the most famous of the native American prophets was Mary Baker Eddy, the founder of Christian Science. Mesmerism certainly left its mark on her life and work. In the first place, although she later denied it (but then she was somewhat given to lying, especially about her childhood), she was a disciple of Quimby, who in fact coined the term 'Christian Science', as well as giving her the principles. Eddy's life displays a pattern of attaching herself to men (often younger) and then turning on them later and accusing them of malevolence towards her. For instance, after the foundation of Christian Science, she relied on a man called Richard Kennedy to do most of the healing, while she took charge of the lecturing. Kennedy later took her to court for not paying him fairly, and he won both the court case and her lifelong enmity. Her vehement denials that she owed anything to Quimby, whose writings she undoubtedly plundered for her *Science and Health* (1875), are simply part of this pattern. In the second place, in her later, somewhat paranoid years, Eddy was convinced that her illnesses – and indeed anything that went wrong – were due to a force she called 'malignant animal magnetism' (or sometimes the 'red dragon') being directed towards her by her enemies, so she clearly remained a believer in the efficacy of magnetism. (Even today Christian Scientists persist in calling hypnotism 'animal magnetism', and they are some of the foremost denouncers of hypnotism as unremittingly evil.) In fact, she used to keep a rotating staff of students in residence at her Brookline mansion whose major responsibility was to ward off the malicious animal magnetism generated by her enemies and to look after her household. They were not particularly successful, because Eddy was plagued by a string of court cases from patients who claimed she had overcharged them. In the third place, with their Quimby-like faith in the power of affirmative thinking, some of the practices of Christian Scientists resemble self-hypnosis.

Mary Baker Eddy was born Mary A. Morse Baker in July 1821, the daughter of a poor New Hampshire farmer, and the youngest of six children. She married a bricklayer called George Washington Glover, and moved to South Carolina, where Glover died. Mary Glover, then aged twenty-three, gave their son away to neighbours to bring up and didn't see him again for twenty-three years. Not long afterwards, she married Daniel Patterson, an itinerant dentist, but this marriage quickly broke down. In 1862, suffering from back pain, she consulted Quimby, and was cured. Quimby, as we have seen, was concerned to educate his patients, not just to cure them, and so Mary Patterson learnt all she could from the great man. In 1866 the pain returned as a result of a fall, but she healed herself, and went on to found Christian Science, beginning by advertising a course teaching people how to heal themselves without drugs, electricity and so on.

The principles of Christian Science are encapsulated in the following quotation from *Science and Health*, and the reader will immediately notice the resemblance to Quimby's teachings: 'You say a boil is painful; but that is impossible, for matter without mind is not painful. The boil simply manifests through inflammation and swelling a belief in pain; and this belief is called a boil.' In 1870 she moved to Lynn, Massachusetts, and established a practice. In 1877 she married Asa Gilbert Eddy, who died in 1882. She herself lived on until 1910, by which time there were already some 90,000 Christian Scientists in the States alone. In her later years she had delusions of divinity and in 1938 the board of directors of the Christian Science Church confirmed that she was the spiritual idea of God typified by the woman in the Apocalypse and now come to life. This belief in the near divinity of Mary Baker Eddy is reflected in some of the Christian Science practices, which include, for instance, self-healing by focusing on her teachings, which are the carriers of positive wholesome beliefs.

Christian Science has weathered well, and is still a flourishing movement, but in her day Mary Baker Eddy was no more famous than two more of Quimby's pupils, Julius and Annetta Dresser, the founders of New Thought. An impression of New Thought may be conveyed by comparing it with Christian Science. First, where Christian Science is authoritarian, regarding Mary Baker Eddy's writings as final revelations, the Dressers stressed that spiritual truths go on being revealed. Second, where Christian Science stresses the negative (disease does not exist, vigilance is necessary against malignant animal magnetism), New Thought stressed affirmation – I am well, I am perfect and so on. Third, New Thought was more flexible on the issue of cooperation with doctors. But whatever the differences, all mind-curists share the belief that mind has power over matter – a belief that was undoubtedly generated within the matrix of mesmerism.

In its day, New Thought was a massive movement, whose most famous proponents were Warren Felt Evans, Henry Wood and Ralph Waldo Trine. Trine's book *In Tune with the Infinite*, published in 1897, sold 1.5 million copies. He taught that unhappiness, illness and so on are due to our being out of touch or harmony with God. We are in fact united with God, but can fail to realize it. Affirmations, visualizations, prayer, music and breathing exercises can help to restore the balance. At first, all mind-curists used the laying-on of hands, but by the end of the century fears of manipulation and mind control by Svengali-like characters meant that it became a religion of the printed word. Mind-curists promoted not just cures, but general success in life: we are the product of our desires, therefore all you have to do is desire something strongly enough and it shall be yours – especially if you live a good Christian life. Their attitude towards mesmerism was not hostile, but rather indifferent. Evans, for instance, maintained that, since people cured themselves, there was no need for a magnetizer except perhaps to relax one and put one into a calm frame of mind.

As well as Christian Science and New Thought, a number of other mind-cure movements flourished in the States in the last quarter of the nineteenth century. There was Jewish Science, founded by Rabbi Morris Lichtenstein, which taught, among other things, a method of passing beyond the hypnotic state into a 'superconscious state'. Divine Science taught that disease was of man's own making, not God's. There was Scientific Christianity (not to be confused with Christian Science) which used scripture readings rather than Mary Baker Eddy's writings to effect faith healing. There was the Nazarene Movement founded by the Reverend Henry Blauvelt of Boonton, New Jersey, which conducted healing services in churches, and there was the Emmanuel Movement, which was part of the Episcopalian Church (or the Church of England, as it is called over here). The popularity of all such movements, including New Thought and faith healing in general, was due to a widespread dissatisfaction with physicians for their lack of sympathy and negative suggestions. Nor was faith healing entirely without its merits: it proved good for neuroses, addictions and general improvement of morale.

Whereas the majority of these movements are the grandchildren of mesmerism, and made little or no use of it themselves, the

Emmanuel Movement returned to its roots. Founded in the Emmanuel Church, Boston, in 1906 by the Reverend Elwood Worcestor and the Reverend Samuel McComb, it used hypnosis, backed up by scripture reading, prayer and teachings, and claimed a high degree of success with non-organic illnesses. Worcestor had studied psychology in Germany and France, and was a follower of the Nancy school of hypnotism (on which see Chapter 7). He would lightly stroke a patient's forehead and temples to get him to relax, before inducing a deeper trance by getting him to fix his attention on a crystal ball. Once the patient was entranced, he guided the patient's thoughts away from mundane reality towards bright realms of optimism, on the principle that the subconscious is not only suggestible and liable to moral influence and direction, but actually good in its natural state. This pure natural state could be reached by hypnosis, so that a person could become more accustomed to live in accordance with its primitive, moral and healthful dictates. The movement spread rapidly, and the two priests soon had more patients than they could handle; but the movement fell into disrepute after being attacked by the medical community as naive, unreliable and potentially dangerous, and by members of religious communities of all stripes as evil. These attacks were largely born of ignorance; Freud has shown that the subconscious is not as pure and innocent as Worcestor and his colleagues believed, but that only makes them guilty of naivety, not of dealing with the devil.

Spiritism and the Decline of Popular Mesmerism

Spiritism started in the States in 1847 with the Hydesville rappings, and within half a dozen years it had swept like wildfire through the States and into Europe too. It all began when mysterious knockings disturbed the house in Hydesville, New York, into which John Fox had recently moved with his wife and two teenage daughters. The noises soon settled into a kind of coded language, and were believed to be messages delivered by the spirit of a man who had been murdered in the house and buried in the basement, though no such body was found even when the basement was excavated, and the knocking followed the Foxes wherever they went. They came to realize that the noises centred on their daughters, so they separated them, sending Maggie, aged fifteen and a half, to her older brother David, and Kate, aged twelve, to her older sister Leah. But the noises continued in *both* houses, and soon objects started flying around the room where Kate was: hair-combs removed themselves from one old lady's head and inserted themselves in the hair of another; chairs and tables shook and turned over.

By now everyone was convinced that all this was the frenzied attempt of spirits to communicate with our world, and friends of the Foxes in Rochester evolved the system of 'spiritual telegraphy': someone went through the alphabet, and the spirits rapped the table when the appropriate letter of the alphabet was reached, to spell out words. The very first message received was one which has reverberated down through the generations of subsequent spiritists: 'We are all your dear friends and relatives.' It seemed to be possible to communicate with the dear departed. The Foxes took the show on the road, and before long there were many imitators on both sides of the Atlantic. By the 1870s there were 11 million self-professed spiritists in America alone.

It was soon discovered that some people were 'mediums', who could help the spirits manifest and communicate. Nor were enthusiasts slow to make use of mesmerism in this context, since mesmerism was believed to unlock precisely the kinds of latent faculties that might allow someone to be a medium. But the incredible excitement which spiritism generated in the States swamped mesmerism, and by the middle of the 1850s it was a dying art. Not that spiritism was alone in sounding the death knell of mesmerism, but since it occupied the same field, so to speak, it usurped the place of mesmerism in the hearts and minds of the public. At the same time, developments both at home and abroad were putting the final nails in the coffin of mesmerism. In the States La Roy Sunderland, for instance, came to much the same negative conclusions about magnetism as James Braid did in Britain, stressing that mesmeric passes and any ideas of magnetic fluid were of considerably less importance than the subject's suggestibility and the operator's will. Then before long mesmerism in America was pushed further into the background by New Thought, a revival of church-going Christianity, and the rise of psychology departments in universities, which claimed the study of the mind for themselves and denounced all fringe psychologies. A few, like William James, recognized the importance of mesmerism as a precursor of modern psychology, but most of the new researchers were too nervous of their position to be able to give it any credit at all.

The final factor was the discovery, in 1842, of the anaesthetic properties of ether. J.V.C. Smith, writing in the *Boston Medical and Surgical Journal* for 1847, celebrates the banishment of mesmerism and, incidentally, gives us a vivid picture of the practice of mesmerism in its heyday in the States:

> Before the discovery of the new use of ether, the country swarmed with traveling mesmerizers who lectured in every town and hamlet in New England – and made such high pretensions, that gentlemen who presumed to question the honesty of the vagabonds, made themselves quite unpopular with the vulgar multitude. It was one of the great boasts of the magnetizers that they could prepare the system, by their extraordinary manipulations, or by an active mental influence, so that the body would be insensitive to pain. Whole scores of silly girls were exhibited in public, on platforms, pricked with needles, had their toes crushed and teeth extracted, of all which they were represented to be wholly unconscious . . . Of late, however, the mighty boasters have disappeared . . . How can this falling off be explained by those noisy men and women who were offensively busy in propagating the marvels of mesmerism one year ago? A few remnant signs are observable about our city, like these: *'mesmeric examinations here'*, *'all kinds of diseases investigated by an experienced clairvoyant'*, etc. Which are a reproach to the intelligence of the age, to the good city in which they are to be seen, and a mortifying evidence of the ignorance that passes for wisdom.

And so mesmerism passed into oblivion in the States after a brief history, stretching only from Poyen's tours at the beginning of the 1830s to the early 1850s.

6

'Mesmeric Mania' in the United Kingdom

The whereabouts of Franz Anton Mesmer in the 1790s are more or less unknown, with the result that various rumours have sprung up over the years. One is that he spent some time in England, but I'm sure this is false; at any rate, there is absolutely no evidence to support it. The first mesmerist known to have practised in England is a man called John Bell, who had learnt the art in Paris, and lectured in London and the provinces in the middle of the 1780s. Then in 1787 or 1788 one of d'Eslon's pupils, called Dr J.B. de Mainauduc, arrived from France and began to teach, at a very high price: he charged 25 guineas for a course of fifteen lectures. De Mainauduc had previously lived in Ireland, and had been a medical student in London.

One way or another, then – through lectures or the translation of French pamphlets – magnetism was known in Britain before the nineteenth century, but it seems to have aroused little interest. Most notices of mesmerism at this time tend to be scornful, and to praise the common sense of the British people for not falling prey to such a silly fad, as their Continental neighbours had. A pamphlet written in 1790 by John Pearson, called *A Plain and Rational Account of the Nature and Effects of Animal Magnetism in a Series of Letters*, exemplifies the tone in which much of the attack was couched. For example, he imagines a politician using mesmerism to put an opponent to sleep 'by the eloquence of his fingers' or to throw him into a mesmeric crisis. If both political parties were to avail themselves of this, parliament 'would exhibit a motley scene of members sound asleep, or rolling in convulsions'. Dr Haygarth's refutation of Perkinism (discussed in the previous chapter) also brought mesmerism into disrepute. There was hardly enough interest to sustain the country through the drying up of French sources during the Revolution. The practice of mesmerism effectively died out altogether, apart from a very few isolated spots of interest, and was only really revived around 1835. The revival was largely due to the work of J.C. Colquhoun, who translated the report of the favourable Parisian commission, and wrote books of his own on the subject, knowledge of which he had acquired in Germany. These books sowed the seeds for future interest, and were the first in a torrent of pamphlets and books in the later 1830s and 1840s. The most famous and widely circulated of these books was *Facts in Mesmerism* by the Reverend Chauncy Hare Townshend (1798–1868). Townshend was a friend of Charles Dickens and other influential members of society, but it was the clarity of his book which enabled it to gain such popularity both at home and abroad.

It was largely through his influence, as well as the undeniable interest of the subject, that mesmerism was on the lips of every learned person for the best part of twenty years in Britain. Consider just a few of the Victorian luminaries (I choose those whose names are still well known today) who are known to have dabbled or experimented in it, or at least commented on it: Charles Dickens, Harriet Martineau, Wilkie Collins, George Eliot, Charlotte Brontë and Elizabeth Gaskell from the world of literature; Charles Darwin, Michael Faraday and Alfred Russel Wallace from the world of science; Samuel Wilberforce, Bishop of Oxford, and Richard Whately, Bishop of Dublin; and William Gladstone from politics.

Mesmeric Performers and Their Social Implications

But it was not only the written word which spread the gospel of mesmerism in early Victorian Britain. These books and the debate they aroused were restricted to the upper classes, to their salons and drawing rooms. A more important conductor of information to the masses was performance, by the 'small army of mesmeric performers, whose lively presentations carried the controversy to a much wider audience than could be reached through publications'. These per-formers should be seen in the context of the popularity of accessible lectures on and demonstrations of scientific subjects; the best lectur-ers, like the sophists of fifth-century Greece, travelled from town to town, and their arrival was eagerly anticipated. Canny advertising helped too. Mesmeric performances were often billed as perfectly respectable – to forestall but also to arouse the idea that a male mesmerist imposing his will on a young lady subject might be at all naughty. In Britain, as elsewhere, the popularity of these itinerant lecturers on mesmerism was also assisted by the tradition of itinerant mountebanks, vendors of nostrums, who entertained with their sales pitches as well as offering their patent medicines.

Phrenology was an especially popular subject. A host of phrenol-ogists toured the country in the 1820s and 1830s and paved the way for mesmerism, since the two subjects seemed to complement each other. The claims of mesmerism about the powers of the human mind and will seemed credible in the light of the revelations of phrenology, and both were ideally suited for public performance: phrenological demonstrators could 'read' a head, while magnetizers could place someone in a trance. Phreno-mesmerism, the combi-nation of phrenology and mesmerism, an American import, made an especially good display. Phrenologists assumed that different mental and emotional traits were located in different parts of the brain. The mesmerist, having put his subject into a trance, pointed at or touched the part of the skull that concealed, say, Veneration – and lo and behold! The mesmerized subject began to pray! A skilled phrenolo-gist would play a skull like an organ. The subject was taken very seriously, and was considered to be more scientific than mesmerism. There was even a proposal that leeches should be applied to the Larceny and Deceit areas of criminals' brains in order to suck off their criminal tendencies. Phreno-mesmerism had its more serious side, then, and we may guess that many a lecturer will have turned serious at this point to expatiate upon the limitless blessings of the whole magnetic field, which became known simply as the New Science.

The Frenchman Charles de Lafontaine (1803–88) was one of the earliest of the magnetic showmen. De Lafontaine was the black sheep of a noble French family, who wanted to become an actor before discovering that he had magnetic powers. Specializing in demonstrating hypnotic anaesthesia and deafness, he attracted large audiences in London (but less enthusiasm further north) when he toured in 1841 and 1842 with a young French boy who was his trance subject. His eccentric appearance – he dressed in black, and had a long, bushy beard and a piercing eye – and the dramatic tests he performed to prove the boy's insensibility to pain guaranteed him a ready audience, despite his difficulties with the English language. Spellbound by the subject's ability to have his arms pierced by pins without apparent pain, and to have a pistol shot ring out by his ear without hearing it, they were then introduced to some of the more arcane phenomena, such as clairvoyance, and lectured on the relationship between mind and body, and between operator and mesmerized subject. Once, a callous member of the audience, convinced that the whole thing was fraudulent, jabbed a scalpel into the boy's thigh to test his analgesia – and failed to elicit the cry of pain he had been expecting!

But more usually the lecturer would be a native Englishman, either touring the country, or one who had established a name for himself in his home town. Some achieved national fame. Spencer Timothy Hall (1812–85), originally a Nottingham stocking-maker, toured all the major towns between Northampton and Edinburgh, attracting audiences of up to 3,000 people. For a few pennies, education and entertainment could be had by anyone, whether they were gentry or common folk. Names, now long forgotten, include H. Brookes, who toured the southern counties in 1843, and W.J. Vernon, who lectured before an audience of 1,000 at the Greenwich Literary Institution, and then took his show on the road in 1843 and 1844. He had an entourage, including a doctor and two children who were his mesmeric subjects. Dr Owens would lecture on the history and theory of mesmerism, while Vernon mesmerized the children and demonstrated their powers. The twelve-year-old girl lifted a 200-lb man and read while blindfolded; the boy specialized in playing cards while blindfolded. Vernon aroused considerable controversy, and encouraged it. Like other itinerant lecturers, some of his performances took the form of debates, with votes being taken by the audience at the end. Not a few of the mesmeric showmen used their displays also as a way to advertise their abilities, in order to attract private patients. Mesmerism in the 1840s and 1850s was not restricted to public halls, but could be found in the parlours of practising therapists and the drawing rooms of high society, where mesmeric conversaziones took place. But as the 1840s wore on, lecturing gave way almost entirely to performance, debate to showmanship focusing on the more dramatic and esoteric aspects of mesmerism.

The prices charged for such performances kept them within the reach of less well-off people. Sometimes working-class men themselves, the showmen's venues were public meeting rooms and working-men's clubs, pubs and temperance halls. Part of the attraction of such displays was undoubtedly their social subtext. Since the model of magnetism was extreme inequality of will, such that the operator imposed his will on his subject, it was a short step from there, and one taken by many, to declare that the operator had moral and intellectual superiority to his subjects. In the 1830s this notion was perpetuated by the fact that the subject was invariably of lower social standing than the medical operator, but in the 1840s it became clear to people from all walks of life that they could, if they had the opportunity, mesmerize the local duke and duchess. What then became of their traditional superiority, if their will could be shown to be less than a steelworker's?

One amusing case involved Jane, the wife of the renowned Scottish intellectual Thomas Carlyle (1795–1881). Though famed for her intelligence and satirical wit, Jane seems to have been liable to the usual prejudices. The Carlyles, who had long been resident in London, arrived one day at a tea party to find a mesmerist at work, a man who, Jane later wrote to her uncle, dropped his 'h's and showed his lower nature in his animal-like eyes. He was specifically claiming, in front of his upper-class audience, that mesmeric influence consisted of moral and mental superiority. Jane rose to the bait and challenged him to try to mesmerize her. He took hold of her hand and set to work.

> I looked him defiantly in the face as if to say, you must learn to sound your H's, Sir, before you can produce any effect on a woman like *me*! and whilst this or some similar thought was passing through my head – flash – there went over me from head to foot something precisely like what I once experienced

from taking hold of a galvanic ball, only *not nearly* so violent.
I had the presence of mind to keep looking him in the face as
if I had felt nothing and presently he flung away my hand.

So who won the contest? A dead heat, I'd say. And another high-
society presence, Lady Elizabeth Eastlake, echoed Jane Carlyle when
she said that mesmerism is 'advocated by women without principle,
and lectured upon by men who drop their h's'.

Historian Roger Cooter has linked mesmerism with one of the
most important social movements of the time: 'That in the nineteenth century mesmerism was perceived in Britain as a means to
anti-establishment ideology and epistemology is nowhere better
illustrated than through the adoption of mesmerism by Owenite
socialists in the early 1840s after they had come into contact with
phreno-mesmerism.' They immediately recognized the humanistic
possibilities of mesmerism, and realized that if it was left in the hands
of the medical profession these possibilities would be lost. Over the
next few years working-class people flocked to the Owenite Halls of
Science to witness mesmerism. Owenism collapsed in the mid-1840s,
but for a few years it was one of the major instruments of the
perpetuation and popularization of mesmerism in Britain. Owenites
believed that access to education would enable the working man to
assert his own dignity and self-reliance, and they were looking for a
subject that did not already come with bourgeois baggage. Mesmerism fitted the bill. First, it was democratic: it had not been
pre-packaged for presentation to the lower classes and it appeared
to involve active experimentation by everyone. Skill, not expensive
equipment, was what was required, so that working-class men
like Spencer Hall could become professional practitioners. Second,
Owenites believed that character was determined by external circumstances, and mesmerism appeared to reinforce this idea since in the
mesmeric state the subject could not act except at the suggestion of
the operator. Third, mesmerism included a non-hierarchical spiritual
doctrine.

Mesmerists often aligned themselves with Protestants and non-
conformists against Catholics, who were more wary about scientific
progress. And mesmerists agitated in the pages of the *Zoist*, the most
important British journal dedicated to the subject, for other reforms

as well: they took a stand against animal experimentation and capital punishment, and supported reforms in education, sanitation, slum housing and prisons. Their reforming zeal sometimes became an attack on professionalism in general (especially, of course, on their enemies in the medical profession), and an espousal of the natural faculties of the working man. Spencer Hall wrote, for instance, in the first issue of his journal *Phreno-Magnet* (founded in 1843, the same year as John Elliotson's *Zoist*), that when rejected by the prejudices and snobbery of professionals, mesmerism would appear 'in quarters least expected – among the humble and unconventional masses of the country – those whose only facilities for receiving or dispensing information were the passive faculties with which Nature herself had furnished them for the purpose ... It remained for a Mechanics' Institution to be the first large conventional body that would dare to have its name identified with Phreno-Magnetism.' Mesmerism was sometimes seen as a working-class invasion of the hallowed halls of medicine, entry into which was otherwise restricted to those with the money to pay for their education.

But the greatest impulse to reform came from the educated upper classes, and was therefore often rather paternalistic in attitude. Elliotson, the supreme advocate of mesmerism in Britain, himself criticized Spencer Hall as not being sober enough to be a true champion of the New Science. Others, like Lord Morpeth and Lord Adare, still assumed the whole social hierarchy as a matter of divine right. Like most Victorian reformers, their target was the lower classes: they needed saving from themselves, and these Whig peers felt they knew just how to go about it. Schemes were hatched, for instance, to cut down the rate of divorce and domestic violence by allowing only those who were phrenologically matched to marry. Philanthropically, they dispensed mesmeric cures in the same way that others were dispensing temperance tracts. It is noticeable how (apart from mavericks like Hall) mesmerism throughout the nineteenth century largely conformed to social expectations: landowners hypnotized their labourers in France, men hypnotized women, the educated hypnotized the uneducated. Lord Adare became president of the Bristol Mesmeric Institute, while Lord Morpeth extended his sway further than Castle Howard when he was chosen as one of the governors of the London Mesmeric Infirmary, which ran from 1849 until the middle of the 1860s, with two permanent mesmerists on its staff, W.J. Vernon and Theodysius Purland. Although it may be easy now to deride such well-meaning mesmeric philanthropy, it was possible to do so even then, as when the *North of England Magazine* wittily suggested that landlords could feed the poor by entering into a state of mesmeric sympathy with them, such that when the landlords ate the poor would taste the food!

In other words, in a social context the reformist challenge of mesmerism was not strong enough to overcome the normal Victorian prejudices and assumptions. The chain of volition went one way only, downhill. As a popular ballad of the 1840s has it:

> The new Mesmeric sleep is by
> Phrenologists directable.
> They oft begin it on a boy,
> Amusing the respectable.
> Upon the rich it comes not o'er,
> They're not to it susceptible.
> They only Mesmerize the poor
> To please the more respectable.

While many mesmerists *felt* themselves to be radicals, then, and even to be ushering in a new era of peace and prosperity on earth, they did not offer a strong enough challenge to the Victorian status quo. In other contexts too the reformist possibilities of mesmerism were too ambiguous to take root. In therapy, for instance, it actually impeded reform. Through the introduction of instruments such as the stethoscope and methods such as percussion, Victorian doctors began to have the means to directly examine their patients' bodies – but only if they could get them to remove their clothes, a breach of propriety which was repugnant to many. Mesmerism, however, with its emphasis on intro-vision and clairvoyant diagnosis, was safer and more modest in this respect. Feminists too were divided. Mary Wollstonecraft denounced London magnetizers in 1792 in her *Vindication of the Rights of Women* as 'lurking leeches' who invoked supernatural powers to exploit the credulity of ignorant women; but Harriet Martineau and Mary Grove Nichols defended mesmerism as one way for women to reclaim the rights to their own bodies.

Prurient Fears

So the normal inequalities of Victorian social life remained in place, largely unchallenged by mesmerism. Men were superior to women and children, the upper classes to the lower; this superiority is displayed by a greater strength of moral will, and will is the all-important instrument of a magnetizer. 'By the exercise of this influence the operator can often overcome the voluntary power of the subject; that which he wills, the subject does . . . It seems as if there were two human organisms and but one human will whilst the subject is under the influence.' Since this was the usual assumption in the nineteenth century about the way mesmerism worked, doubts about the morality of the enterprise were quickly translated from the Continent to Britain. Could one man take over the will of another? Could he force himself sexually on an otherwise reluctant woman? At one point in Peter Carey's excellent novel *Jack Maggs*, which is set in 1837, a hypnotist's lover feels herself aroused by his control of a dangerous subject, as if submission were in itself sexual. To take just one of many contemporary examples, although the writer Elizabeth Gaskell had very little to do with mesmerism, she was of course aware of it and what was being said about it, and it was precisely this aspect, the possibility of sexual dominance, that worried her and stopped her from investigating further.

The operator exerts his will; because he is healthy, he transmits his health to the sick person (or whatever the operation may be). He can use his will to mesmerize a suitably sensitive subject from a distance. Even the passes a mesmerist makes with his hands were no longer presumed, except by die-hard magnetists, to do anything mechanically, but were simply means for the operator to focus his will and project his influence. Edward Bulwer-Lytton makes amusing hay with the idea of dominance in *A Strange Story*, to give an impression of one of his characters:

Electro-biology was very naturally the special entertainment of a man whom no intercourse ever pleased in which his will was not imposed upon others. Therefore he only invited to his table persons whom he could stare into the abnegation of their senses, willing to say that beef was lamb, or brandy was coffee, according as he willed them to say. And, no doubt, the persons asked would have said anything he willed, so long as they had, in substance as well as in idea, the beef and the brandy, the lamb and the coffee.

Sir Arthur Conan Doyle was only following all this through to its logical extension when in his 1888 short story 'John Barrington Cowles' he said: 'If there was one man in the world who had a very much more highly developed will than any of the rest of the human family, there is no reason why he should not be able to rule over them all, and to reduce his fellow-creatures to the condition of automatons.' To Conan Doyle's credit he went against the nineteenth-century trend in making the evil and strong-willed mesmerist of his story a woman. And at least one novel of the time – Isabel Romer's *Sturmer: a tale of mesmerism, to which are added other sketches from life*, published in London in 1841 – gave a mesmerist the power not just to seduce women, but even to kill.

Sexual fears were not helped by those like the eminent physician (unnamed in my source) who in delivering the Harveian Oration said: 'The impostors called mesmerists were the especial favourites of those persons, both male and female, in whom the sexual passions burn strongly either in secret or notoriously. Decency forbids me to be more explicit.' Similar prurient attacks occurred also in the Victorian quarterly reviews, the arbiters of upper-middle-class opinion, such as *Blackwood's*. But then the eccentric Baron Dupotet, who was indirectly responsible for much of the British passion for mesmerism, wouldn't have helped matters either by likening the build-up of magnetic force in an operator to a (male) orgasm:

> In his body all is in tumult. The force within reaches his skin, while his heart beats harder and harder, like a drum. When it reaches a pitch, his volcano erupts over the human landscape in an outpouring of lava and a whirlwind of sulphur. Behold! This is how you must use your desires, which are like a fire that glows and shines in you unseen. It is exactly like the act of

reproduction, except that here the emitting organ is the brain
. . . It is necessary . . . that a fire runs through you, that a kind
of erection (which is not erotic) happens that allows an emission
of the brain to depart from your being. Your hand must conduct
this animated essence, this living magnet, to the chosen surface,
and it must immediately establish the spiritual rapport and
attraction proper to it. It is not the female organ that receives
this emission . . . but purer and more active elements which the
senses cannot see.

Mesmerism and the Romantics

I have said that in the early years of the nineteenth century the
practice of mesmerism almost died out in Britain. But there were
those who retained an interest in its theory, and many of them
belonged to the Romantic movement. It was no impediment to
them that mesmerism came to England tainted with the French
Revolution – that was a positive plus. They saw Mesmer not as a
great innovator, but as someone who had found a way to harness an
immutable power, which might be identified with God or Nature.
Like many mesmerists, the British Romantics had a millenarian
streak, and thought that a new age of spirituality was imminent.
Mesmerism was seen not just as a painless method of healing,
accessible to all, but also as a means for contacting a reality higher
than the mundane one to which humans had hitherto been condemned, and as a complete new science of life, the universe and
everything. It was a new revelation, a new dispensation. It would
help us to usher in a new age of peace and fraternity. For the
Romantics, none of this meant that they were prepared to endorse
mesmerism *tout court*, but they were certainly prepared to give it a
hearing.

One of the main sources of knowledge of mesmerism for the
Romantic circle was Robert Southey's *Letters from England*, written in
1807 under the pseudonym of Don Manuel Alvarez Espriella, in order

to maintain the conceit that as a foreign visitor to the country he could be objective about its customs. Letter 51 is an 'Account of Animal Magnetism', which is in fact a summary of de Mainauduc's lectures. Although de Mainauduc was not quite an orthodox follower of Mesmer, he was a physicalist, and a great deal of Southey's Letter is taken up with a description of the cosmology and physics of magnetism. He explains how man is a microcosm of the universe, and that just as every part of the universe is giving off 'emanations' as energy is constantly circulated throughout its parts, so we humans emit particles too. The mind is superior to the body, and the will can direct these emanations as required. Free circulation of energy is health, obstruction 'must occasion derangement in the system and be followed by disease'. The theory and practice of medical healing through magnetism then follows, sometimes accompanied by details which reveal astonishing confidence:

> The pathology is soon explained. The impressions produced upon the fingers of the examiner by the stone, will be heaviness, indolence, and cold. Burns and scalds produce heavy dull pricking at first; when inflammation has taken place, great heat and sharp pricking, but indolent numbness from the centre. Rheumatic head ache occasions pricking, numbness and creeping or vermicular motion, heat if the patient be strong, cold if he be relaxed. Inflammation caused by confined wind produces intense heat, pricking and creeping; the heat is occasioned by the inflammation, the pricking by the wind acting against the obstructed pores, and the creeping by the motion of the wind from one part to another. Pus communicates to the hand of the examiner such a feeling of softness as we should expect from dipping the hand in it, but combined with pricking, from the motion which the wind contained in it makes in its endeavours to escape. Diseased lungs make the fingers feel as if dough had been permitted to dry on them, this is called clumsy stiffness. Pleurisy occasions creeping, heat, and pricking; deafness; resistance and numbness. Contracted nerves announce themselves to the examiner by a pressure round his fingers, as if a string was tightly bound round them; cases of a relaxed habit by a lengthened debilitated sensation, diseased spleen, or ovaries, by a spinning in the finger ends, as if something were twirling

about in them. The impression which scrofula produces upon the practitioner, is curious and extraordinary: at every motion which he makes, the joints of his fingers, wrists, elbows and shoulders crack. Worms excite creeping and pinching; bruises, heaviness in the hands and numbness in the fingers.

It is clear from Southey's account that part of the attraction of magnetism was that it purported to be a complete physical system of the universe, occult and therefore giving secrets to initiates. And in fact de Mainauduc's success in London was due in part to his being taken up and supported by a group of Swedenborgian mystics and alchemists. Southey thinks this is all 'quackery' and calls de Mainauduc's references to God and Jesus 'blasphemy', but nevertheless he did provide an account of mesmeric theory and practice which contained enough meat for his peers to get their teeth into.

Samuel Taylor Coleridge had a lifelong interest in animal magnetism, but could never make up his mind about it. Its influence on *The Rime of the Ancient Mariner* is obvious:

> He holds him with his glittering eye –
> The Wedding-Guest stood still,
> And listens like a three years' child:
> The Mariner hath his will.

But after attending the lectures of J.F. Blumenbach in Göttingen in 1798–9, he was convinced that there was no reality to the apparent phenomena of mesmerism, and he deleted the more overt references to it from the poem, which was first written in 1797 and 1798. However, in 1817 he heard that Blumenbach had reversed his scepticism, and this reawakened Coleridge's interest. In 1820, in a note on Southey's *Life of Wesley*, he recorded how he had investigated 'zoo-magnetism' for nine years, had read widely and never passed up an opportunity to question eyewitnesses, and yet remained uncertain, 'in a state of philosophical doubt' about it, as he would say in 1830. The 1820 note carried on:

> Were I asked, what *I* think, my answer would be that the evidence enforces scepticism and a *non liquet*; too strong and consentaneous for a candid mind to be satisfied of its falsehood, or its solvibility on the supposition of imposture or casual

coincidence; too fugacious and unfixable to support any theory that supposes the always potential, and, under certain conditions and circumstances, occasionally active, existence of a correspondent faculty in the human soul.

He quotes the German botanist Ludolf Treviranus (1779–1864) who had said to him: 'I have seen what I am certain I would not have believed on *your* telling; and in all reason, therefore, I can neither expect nor wish that you should believe on *mine*.'

In 1822 Percy Bysshe Shelley wrote a poem called 'The Magnetic Lady to Her Patient' (published ten years later in the *Athenaeum*). Shelley had been introduced to mesmerism by Southey's Letter 51, but also by Lord Byron's doctor John Polidori who was a practitioner and who was present on the famous occasion in June 1816 in the Villa Diodati when Byron, Shelley, Mary Shelley and Claire Clairmont competed to write a supernatural story – a game which gave the world *Frankenstein*. The first verse of Shelley's poem contains a poetic induction of trance:

> 'Sleep, sleep on! forget thy pain;
> My hand is on thy brow,
> My spirit on thy brain;
> My pity on thy heart, poor friend;
> And from my fingers flow
> The powers of life, and like a sign,
> Seal thee from thy hour of woe;
> And brood on thee, but may not blend
> With thine.'

When the patient – Shelley – awakens, the woman asks him for his own mesmeric diagnosis:

> 'The spell is done. How feel you now?'
> 'Better – quite well,' replied
> The sleeper, – 'What would do
> You good when suffering and awake?
> What cure your head and side?'
> 'What would cure, that would kill me, Jane;
> And as I must on earth abide

Awhile, yet tempt me not to break
My chain.'

The role-reversal – that the hypnotist is a woman and the subject a man – is remarkable for the time. In his *Shelley Papers* Tom Medwin, Shelley's friend, gives an account of the therapeutic experiments in 1820 out of which the poem grew:

Shelley was a martyr to a most painful complaint, which constantly menaced to terminate fatally [kidney stones]; and was subject to violent paroxysms which, to his irritable nerves, were each a separate death. I had seen magnetism practised in India and at Paris, and at his earnest request consented to try its efficacy. Mesmer himself could not have hoped for more complete success. The imposition of my hand on his forehead instantaneously put a stop to the spasm, and threw him into a magnetic sleep, which for want of a better word is called somnambulism. Mrs Shelley and another lady [Mrs Jane Williams] were present. The experiment was repeated more than once. During his trances I put some questions to him. He always pitched his voice in the same tone as mine. I enquired about his complaint, and its cure – the usual magnetic enquiries. His reply was, 'What would cure me would kill me' . . . He improvised also verses in Italian, in which language he was never known to write poetry.

Presumably, the enigmatic 'What would cure me would kill me' is a reference to the fact that in his day the operation for the removal of kidney stones was often fatal. In his *Life of Shelley* Medwin adds:

After my departure from Pisa he was magnetized by a lady [Jane Williams], which gave rise to the beautiful stanzas entitled *The Magnetic Lady to her Patient*, and during which operation he made the same reply to an enquiry as to his disease and its cure as he had done to me – 'What would cure me would kill me.' . . . Mrs Shelley also magnetized him, but soon discontinued the practice, from finding that he got up in his sleep, and went one night to the window (fortunately barred), having taken to his old habit of sleep-walking.

Finally, on the subject of Victorian poetry, it is worth mentioning Robert Browning, whose rather obscure poem 'Mesmerism' was first published in *Men and Women* (1855). It explores the typical nineteenth-century themes of control and especially mesmerism at a distance. Browning was acquainted with Sir Edward Bulwer-Lytton, who was familiar with mesmeric theory and practice; but more especially his wife, Elizabeth Barrett Browning, had agonized over the issues in the 1840s, eventually concluding that it was a dangerous practice.

Although other poets dealt with trance (as Keats had in 'La Belle Dame Sans Merci', written in 1819), it is striking that those who wrote poems directly about mesmerism were more taken by its clinical potential than anything paranormal. At first blush, one would have thought that the more spiritual side of mesmerism would have been meat and drink to the Romantics. Perhaps they knew less about it; Southey didn't mention it in his Letter. Perhaps they knew about it, but were sceptical. In any case, in the early years of the nineteenth century, the fire of animal magnetism was barely kept alive by a few intellectuals. It was soon to be fanned into a raging inferno by one man alone, John Elliotson.

John Elliotson

In June 1837, Dupotet came over to England, undeterred by his ignorance of the language, to demonstrate the powers of magnetism. He was an arrogant man, slightly built and missing the thumb of his right hand, scion of a noble house that had lost its wealth and position, the author of a handbook on animal magnetism which is filled with purple prose, a practising occultist and magician who was convinced that he was 'the incarnation of magnetism', as he puts it at one point in his autobiography. One of his earliest converts was an eminent doctor, the senior physician at University College Hospital, London, which he had helped to found, and the author of one of the standard medical textbooks of the day. This man was John Elliotson (1791–1868), a mere five foot tall, with intense, intelligent features. For all his great fame and dignity, he was looked at somewhat askance by many of his peers because of his presidency of the London Phrenological Society, his championship of acupuncture, and his general eagerness to experiment, to look for new and better ways of treating patients. For instance, he was one of the first doctors in the country to use a stethoscope. On a more personal level, he was the first in his circle to wear trousers rather than the knee breeches and black silk stockings which had been the hallmark of the physician, and to affect side whiskers. These mannerisms were considered signs of eccentricity, but his undoubted personal integrity won him many powerful friends and admirers, including Dickens and Thackeray (he was the model for Dr Goodenough in Thackeray's *The Adventures of Philip* and *Pendennis*).

Dupotet's demonstrations at University College Hospital (following a similar show at the Middlesex Hospital, at the invitation of Herbert Mayo) were not Elliotson's first exposure to the therapeutic possibilities of mesmerism: in May 1829 he had witnessed Richard Chenevix, a Paris pupil of the Abbé di Faria, at St Thomas's (where Elliotson had been working since 1817; he moved to University College Hospital in 1832), and his interest had been cautiously aroused. Nothing more came of this at the time, though, because Chenevix died and the climate in Britain, as we have seen, was such that there was little chance of coming across qualified magnetizers. But Dupotet soon swept aside Elliotson's caution, and Elliotson himself began to practise mesmerism at the hospital. Word of the results he was achieving spread fast throughout the medical community and London high society, but the practice aroused incredible hostility and invective. The story of the next few months reads like a soap opera of personal rancour.

Elliotson Versus the Medical Establishment

Taking a step back, we can see that Elliotson's character was a major factor in the drama. He was an irritable man, quick to perceive or imagine a slight. For instance, within a year of the foundation of the Phrenological Society of London Elliotson had resigned in a huff and formed the London Phrenological Society (in March 1824). The

famous phrenologist George Combe, an Edinburgh lawyer, wrote to
him in 1829: 'Matters of very little moment appear to affect you as if
they involved your whole existence.' Combe was undoubtedly right
– but this remark also spelled the end of his long friendship with
Elliotson. More to our purpose, Combe's remark can be seen as a
foretaste of Elliotson's relationship with the authorities of University
College Hospital and with Thomas Wakley, the editor of the newly
founded but already influential *Lancet*, another of Elliotson's friends
who felt himself forced in the name of science to turn against him.
Until the crisis, Wakley had published the proceedings of Elliotson's
London Phrenological Society, and Elliotson had been a regular
contributor on a range of subjects.

Dupotet's experiments convinced Elliotson that mesmerism was
a natural phenomenon with therapeutic potential particularly in
diseases of the nervous system and to induce anaesthesia in surgical
procedures. The *Lancet* reserved judgement, but in September 1837
published a substantial lecture by Elliotson on the subject and
detailed accounts of various ward cases in which mesmerism had
been applied successfully. Elliotson and Dupotet trained others,
especially William Wood, who after Dupotet's departure became
Elliotson's chief mesmerizer at the hospital, and his chief supporter
in the debate against the hospital authorities. By 1838 Elliotson was
devoting some of his time to public demonstrations, to the dismay
of the hospital authorities. They were uncertain about the therapeutic
value of the practice, but perfectly certain that opening up the
hospital's theatres to members of the public was not acceptable.

For his experiments and demonstrations Elliotson made use of
two of the hospital's charity patients, young Irish sisters called
Elizabeth and Jane O'Key. The teenage sisters were inpatients of the
hospital, diagnosed as suffering from epilepsy and 'hysteria', which
in this case meant that they were liable to fits, in which Jane, for
instance, changed character from modest to aggressive. They were
maidservants who had been brought to the hospital, one after the
other, in the middle of 1837 by their doctor after he had read about
Dupotet's experiments there and had tried mesmerism out on the
sisters himself, with some success. He was encouraged to do so by
the very nature of the fits, which ended in a restorative coma. The
original idea, then, was that magnetic sleep would help the girls

quickly through the troubled phase of an attack and into peaceful sleep. Elliotson was also struck by the similarity between the apparent state of mind of the girls during one of their fits and that of a mesmeric subject; physically, it was reminiscent of the crises brought on by Mesmer and his followers, and the babbling, childish speech they came out with reminded him of somnambulistic talk. In January 1838 Elliotson decided to try to produce a fit artificially, by mesmerism, and was immediately successful. Both sisters proved good at manifesting all the familiar mesmeric phenomena – up to and including diagnosis of others, intro-vision (self-diagnosis) and clairvoyance (which Elliotson saw as hyperaesthesia).

On 10 May, in provocative defiance of the hospital authorities, who had already begun to ask him to curb his mesmeric activities, Elliotson demonstrated Elizabeth O'Key's powers to a wider public. Some, such as Charles Dickens and Michael Faraday, had seen it all before, since they had been invited to private displays, but this was the first time the broader scientific community was involved, and the banks of benches in the surgical theatre – a true theatre now – were packed. Elizabeth O'Key was put through her paces and the whole demonstration was a great success. The *Lancet* gave it a favourable review, commenting that O'Key could not have been faking, unless she were a consummate actress. Further displays followed throughout the summer, until all London was buzzing with talk of them, and the O'Keys had become celebrities equal to Elliotson himself. In later years 'O'Key' became a slang term to refer, depending on the writer's proclivities, either to a clairvoyant or to a fraud.

Just like de Puységur's Victor, the O'Keys underwent a personality change when magnetized. As poor Irish maidservants, their usual modesty was to be preferred. But when mesmerized they often became on familiar terms with anyone around, joking with aristocratic members of the audience and making fun of Elliotson. Since supporters of mesmerism saw it as heralding the future of medicine (and in extreme cases the future development of the human mind towards a more holistic grasp of things), this ability it apparently had to release effrontery in the lower classes was immensely threatening to the educated upper classes who ruled the medical roost.

Elliotson's effrontery in defying the hospital authorities was equal to the O'Key's alternate personalities. The hospital tried to

undermine Elliotson's position by discharging Elizabeth O'Key, who
was his best subject. Elliotson did not mince his words, but criticized
his critics in the most strident terms. He kicked up such a fuss that
the hospital ordered the complete cessation of the use of mesmerism
in the wards. Throughout the debate, the issue was not the truth or
falsity of mesmerism, but the prestige of the hospital: Elliotson, they
felt, was bringing the institution into disgrace by advocating and
using a disreputable practice. On Friday, 28 December 1838, despite
considerable support from some of his colleagues and some of the
students, Elliotson resigned from his official posts at both University
College and the North London Hospital. He declared: 'I shall never
again enter either building.' He set up in mesmeric practice on his
own – a brave move on the part of a man who had pulled himself
up by his own abilities out of the lower middle class to rise to the
top of his profession.

'Quacks and Impostors'

The hospital's hostility towards mesmerism was aided and abetted
by Elliotson's former friend, Wakley. The *Lancet* had always taken a
keen interest in Elliotson's work at the hospital, and its reports are
very full and thorough. Most of them are too long to be reprinted,
but here is a catalogue from a report of one of his lectures of 10 May
1838:

> A severe case of periodic insanity, which had resisted all other
> treatment, was remarkably relieved by the operation of magnet-
> ism, on its second employment, and in a fortnight the patient
> was well. A child who had laboured under paraplegia and
> incontinence of urine during nine months, was perfectly cured
> by this agent. In a case of epilepsy in which a fit had occurred
> every day for nine months, the performance of magnetism at
> once arrested the fits, not one occurring during a month after
> its first application, and the patient went home well. In a case
> of delirium in a young woman who was subject to hysteria, . . .
> the patient, the second time that she was magnetised, became
> tranquil, and afterwards remained well. In a case of St. Vitus's
> dance, in which no other remedy was tried, magnetism effected

a cure. In conclusion he was enabled to state that a body of members of the Physiological Committee of the Royal Society had considered the subject to be one of such importance, that they had attended to witness its effects, and test its truth.

Some time that summer, however, sufficient doubts had entered Wakley's mind for him to set up a series of experiments at his house to test the genuineness of the O'Keys. The experiments took place in August. Elliotson first produced some powerful effects on Elizabeth O'Key by means of some 'magnetized' nickel. Wakley asked whether he could do the same, but secretly the nickel was pocketed by a friend of his, Mr Clarke, and Wakley just made passes over the girl with lead in his hands, which Elliotson had assured him would have no effect whatsoever. Nothing happened until a Mr Herring, a stooge of Wakley's, said in a loud whisper, so that the girl could hear: 'Take care. Don't apply the nickel too strongly.' At that point the girl displayed all the symptoms of a trance. Afterwards the girl left the room, and Wakley told Elliotson about the deception. The experiment was repeated, with the same results. Elliotson was puzzled, but confident that an explanation could be found. The next day further experiments were tried, and Jane O'Key consistently failed to detect or be influenced by wine glasses filled with water, or other objects, whether none of them had been magnetized, or one had, or all of them had. Her arm became paralysed by unmagnetized coins, while magnetized coins failed to produce any effect. Elliotson was clearly wriggling and finding excuses. He claimed, for instance, that even the lead induced a trance because the passes were made in the same place as the nickel had already been applied, reinvigorating the effects of the nickel.

A number of options were open to Elliotson. He could have joined Wakley in his repudiation of magnetism and apologized for having been misled for so long – but this was not likely. He could have abandoned the O'Keys in disgust, but persevered in his support for the benefits of mesmerism in general. Or he could have stubbornly persisted in believing that the O'Keys were genuine. This last course was the one he took. Along with the fact that he had staked his reputation on mesmerism, some of his stubbornness was no doubt due to the influence of his friend Townshend's book.

According to Townshend a mesmerized subject was incapable of lying. She occupied a pure, Platonic realm where Truth reigned and Deceit was banished. Some of it was also due to British class prejudice. The lower classes, from which the O'Keys definitely came, were closer to their animal natures, too naive and primitive to perpetuate such an elaborate fraud.

In a long editorial on 8 September Wakley announced:

> Careful investigation and a consideration of all the experiments have convinced us that the phenomena are not real, and that animal magnetism is a delusion; we shall, therefore, lose no opportunity of extirpating an error, which in its nature, applications, and consequences is pernicious. How does the question stand? The existence of somnambulism, and catalepsy, and delirium, is admitted on all hands; and it is an elementary truth that one human being can affect another; that the whole system can be agitated in a great variety of ways, and driven into action voluntarily and involuntarily. But all these influences act through the senses; they are submitted to laws of distance, etc., and under the same circumstances, give rise to phenomena which only differ in intensity in different individuals. The mesmerists assert that the body can be influenced independently of the intellect, independently of anything that can excite the imagination; that in this respect it is like iron to the magnet, acted upon as an unconscious thing is acted upon, and thrown into mesmeric sleep, catalepsy, motion, delirium, by an unseen waive [*sic*] of the hand, a look, a sovereign grasped for a minute, or water in which the fingers have been dipped. Now, we never declared any of these things *impossible*, we never denied the possibility of *clairvoyance*, *allgemeine Klarheit*, or the prophetic power; but we demanded evidence adequate to the improbability of the alleged phenomena. And how great is that improbability!

And a week later Wakley went on:

> The 'science' of mesmerism, like the 'science' of fortune-telling, will always carry on a precarious existence wherever there are clever girls, philosophic Bohemians, weak women, and weaker men, but it can no longer affront the common sense of the

medical profession, or dare to show its face in the scientific societies after the late exposure.

He then casts doubt on Mesmer and Dupotet, and praises the acting ability of the O'Keys. He suggests that they operated by detecting temperature differences in the metals and water which had been merely warmed by the hands supposed to magnetize them. When pasteboard was placed between Elliotson and Elizabeth, she could detect the shadows, whereas when a better blindfold was used, she got no results. He concludes: 'O'Key [that is, Elizabeth, whom Wakley takes to be the ringleader], no doubt, in the first place pitied the believers panting for signs and wonders, which the slightest exertion of her will could produce; she desired to please and astonish her dear good friends.'

Wakley certainly went overboard. Rather than concluding just that the O'Keys were frauds, he dismissed mesmerism as a whole. His attacks must have seemed devastating to Elliotson. And his former friend never looked back, but continued the barrage for some years. On 11 September 1841, for instance, he reprinted from *The Times* Elliotson's account of Elizabeth O'Key's power of foretelling death in a fellow patient at the hospital with regret that such an illustrious newspaper 'should be polluted by such odious and disgusting trash'. On 29 October 1842 he said: 'Mesmerism is too gross a humbug to admit any farther serious notice. We regard its abettors as quacks and impostors. They ought to be hooted out of professional society.' On 22 July 1848 he described mesmerism an 'odious fraud', and so on. As an ironical aside, we should perhaps note that Wakley never abandoned his devotion to phrenology.

More insidiously, late in 1838 Wakley raised the spectre of sexual malpractice in relation to mesmerism by recounting a tale, current in France, that a mesmerist had seduced a woman – and not just a common woman, but the daughter of a wealthy banker. Wakley, however, no longer believed that there was any such phenomenon as the mesmeric trance, so he maintained that the girl was duped by her unscrupulous seducer into giving way to him. He now characterized mesmeric passes as 'indecent assaults' and the men who visited hospital wards to witness Elliotson's displays as 'libidinous'. His thunderous conclusion was:

Mesmerism, according to its advocates, acts most intensely on nervous and impressionable females. What father of a family, then, would admit even the shadow of a mesmeriser within his threshold? Who would expose his wife, or his sister, his daughter, or his orphan ward, to the contact of an animal magnetiser? If the *volition* of an ill-intentioned person be sufficient to prostrate his victim at his feet, should we not shun such pretenders more than lepers, or the uncleanest of the unclean? Assuredly the powers claimed by Mesmer will eventually prove their own ruin. In endeavouring to raise themselves above ordinary mortals, they lay claim to attributes and powers which must place them, forever, beyond the pale of civilized society.

The charge of sexual impropriety was attached more personally to Elliotson in an anonymous pamphlet published in 1842, called *Eyewitness, a Full Discovery of the Strange Practices of Dr Elliotson on the Bodies of His Female Patients*.

By the time of his resignation at the end of 1838, then, Elliotson was under attack from two directions within the medical establishment, and certain members of the religious community were joining in with accusations of witchcraft. Indeed, the persecution of Elliotson does smack of a witch-hunt, and in retrospect we want to ask why mesmerism aroused so much anger. It would be comfortable to believe that Elliotson's medical peers knew that mesmerism was false and attacked it as reputable scientists. The truth, however, is rarely so clear-cut:

Why has some knowledge been accepted by the medical community and other knowledge rejected? Most historians of medicine have assumed that knowledge-claims are eventually accepted if they correspond to scientific truth, and rejected if they do not . . . In this view, rational scepticism or misguided opposition sometimes prevails for a short period after the announcement of a discovery – the classic example being the resistance to Harvey's discovery of the circulation of the blood – but in time truth prevails. In contrast to the heroes of science, purveyors of false knowledge are usually portrayed as unscrupulous charlatans or befuddled eccentrics . . . If, however, one looks critically at why certain knowledge-claims were rejected by nineteenth-century medical men, one discovers that there are other factors than objective truth or falsity that determine whether knowledge is accepted or rejected by medical men.

Elliotson never claimed that mesmerism was a panacea, but he did claim that it was a very important therapeutic tool for neurological disorders and as an anaesthetic. In due course he would cite scores of cases of patients suffering from hysteria, epilepsy, etc., who had been treated unsuccessfully time and time again by conventional methods such as bleeding and cupping, and who were then treated successfully in a short time by mesmerism. And its anaesthetic applications were remarkable. Why, then, was it not greeted with interest but with hostility?

First, it needs to be noted that the hostility was not universal. The prolonged and personal attack on Elliotson by the *Lancet* was certainly an assault by the medical establishment, but the establishment was divided. The *Medical Times*, a rival to the *Lancet*, continued to print papers and letters on the therapeutic benefits of mesmerism, but this was as much as anything to spite Wakley. In fact, the *Medical Times* was in the minority, and Wakley was not alone in his attacks on Elliotson and mesmerism. The eminent physician Sir John Forbes (1787–1861), FRS and physician to the Queen's Household, whose attitude towards mesmerism was usually quite generous, launched an attack in the April 1839 issue of the *British and Foreign Medical Review*, saying that medicine had been afflicted by 'paroxysms of credulity'. Mesmerizers were either charlatans, or the dupes of unscrupulous people, or unscrupulous people themselves, or highly principled fanatics. He clearly had Elliotson in mind for the last category.

Mesmerism undoubtedly did constitute a challenge and a threat to medical men. This was a critical period in the history of medicine; for the first time, there was the prospect of professional standards and guidelines being put in place to guarantee quality. Medical men had a poor reputation as drunkards, womanizers and grave-robbers, and so a reform movement had arisen to correct these weaknesses. It was proposed that there should be a single supervisory body which would register all medical practitioners, standardization of medical education, and criminal sanctions against unlicensed practitioners. In other words, the medical profession, as a profession, was still young and vulnerable, and resented the fact that mesmerism fell outside this three-pronged reforming attack. The charge of 'quackery' was liberally sprayed around – it was not only mesmerists who were stuck with this label. Basically, a 'quack' was anyone who claimed to be able to cure something without understanding the reasons why his cure worked. Mesmerism was especially threatening, then, precisely because it came with a grand theory, which challenged the exclusivity of medicine's claim to knowledge. The only response was to dismiss mesmerism as fraudulent. Oddly, though, some physicians added that any successful mesmeric cures were the result of the patient's imagination: 'It is a measure of the commitment of orthodox medical men to a purely somatic explanation of disease that they could consider mesmerism a hoax if they were convinced that it worked through the imagination, regardless of its efficacy,' remarks historian Terry Parssinen, drily.

Mesmerism was also a challenge because its practitioners could set up shop without years of special training and formal education. So, for instance, the *London Medical Gazette* for 23 August 1844 didn't spare the scorn in saying that mesmerism 'admits the humblest and most insignificant, unrestrictedly for a time, into the society of the proud and lofty; it enables the veriest dunderheads to go hand in hand, as "philosophical inquirers" (forsooth!) with men of the highest scientific repute!' The problem here was partly that mesmerism arrived in Britain tarred with the brush of being occult and foreign; it seemed to be similar to faith healing and other magical practices from which Victorian doctors were trying to distance themselves. The ranks of the 'proud and lofty' could never be sullied by such healers.

Finally, let's not forget the profit motive. Many affluent patients were attracted to mesmerism (and other medical 'heresies' such as homeopathy and hydropathy). Orthodox doctors therefore lost income – and counter-attacked by calling mesmerists unprincipled mercenaries.

Elliotson After 1838

In a reprise of what happened in Mesmer's Paris, Britain in the 1840s found that mesmerism could not be confined. It was certainly not eliminated, as Wakley and others wished, by the suppression of Elliotson. Nor was London, the capital city, so easily able to dictate to the provinces what they should and should not know. Mesmerism was spread through the country by itinerant lecturers and showmen. Despised by the authorities, it was easy for anyone to learn and understand; it was a small act of rebellion to espouse it, and it was taken up by sufficient numbers for it to return and take the metropolis by storm. Elliotson was emboldened to return to the fray with the founding of the *Zoist*, 'A Journal of Cerebral Physiology and Mesmerism, and Their Application to Human Welfare'. The journal ran from 1843 to 1856 and was one of the longest-lasting of the many attempts enthusiasts made to found such journals. It remains one of the most important sources of information and case histories.

The journal had a clear crusading purpose, which also gave Elliotson the opportunity to continue his attacks on his critics, past and present. In the first issue Elliotson looked forward to the time when the value of mesmerism would be universally recognized, and declared:

> The science of Mesmerism is a new physiological truth of *incalculable* value and importance; and, though sneered at by the pseudo-philosophers of the day, there is not the less certainty that it presents the only avenue through which is discernible a ray of hope that the more intricate phenomena of the nervous system, – of Life, – will ever be revealed to man. Already it has established its claim to be considered a most potent remedy in the cure of disease; already enabled the knife of the operator to traverse and divide the living fibre unfelt by the patient. If such are the results of its infancy, what may not its maturity bring forth?

Typically, the journal would publish long letters from correspondents who described in detail their successes with mesmerism on patients suffering ailments such as insanity, melancholy, epilepsy, or hydrophobia, after all other remedies such as cupping and bleeding, or drugs such as calomel, opium, musk and so on, had been extensively used but had failed to bring about any relief. Here is one of the shorter and less dramatic reports, by Elliotson himself:

> On June 16, 1838, a young gentleman, 16 years of age, was brought to me by his father-in-law from Wales, on account of epilepsy, under which he had laboured for a twelve-month; and he was none the better for medical treatment. The fits occurred once or twice a week, or once a fortnight; and consisted of sudden insensibility with violent convulsions, foaming at the mouth, frightful contorsions, suffusion of the face and eyes, the appearance of strangulation, biting the tongue, and at length a dead stupor. One half of the system, and generally the left, was not convulsed, but perfectly rigid, in the fit. The attacks originally occurred three or four times a day. It is not unusual for epileptic fits to occur much more frequently at first than when they are established. The first attack took place about half an hour after a javelin had fallen upon his head in a court of justice. He could now never attend a place of worship or other assemblage of persons without a fit. Even the tearing of a piece of cloth would bring one on, or any sudden noise. Neither he nor his friends, living remotely in Wales, knew anything of mesmerism. Instead of writing a prescription, I without saying anything began to make slow longitudinal passes before his face. He had not suffered an attack for a fortnight, so that the usual period for one was arrived. In a minute or two he looked strange, and a fit took place ... I mesmerised him, and in five minutes he was still, though insensible for some minutes longer, just as happened ordinarily with him. After the fit, he had no head-ache, but giddiness and dimness of sight. I applied my hands at the back and front of his head, and it began to ache. I then mesmerised him again for five minutes, when the pain ceased, and he said his giddiness and dimness of sight were much less than usual after a fit. I advised that the cure should be attempted with mesmerism, and mesmerism only, stating that medicines were not likely to be of any service ... The patient and his father-in-law at once consented, and I directed them to Mr. Symes of Hill Street, Berkeley Square, who,

knowing the truth and power of mesmerism, employs it in disease just like any other remedy. *From the day that I mesmerised him he never had another fit.* The following is a letter which I received from him at the end of nearly a twelvemonth . . .

And before turning to a detailed analysis of the effects produced on the boy by Symes's treatment, Elliotson says that now, five years after the original treatment, he is in perfect health.

Some of the reported cures are quite remarkable. In the volume for October 1848, Elliotson reported a cure of breast cancer. The patient presented with a large tumour, about five or six inches across, in her right breast, and with pains in the armpit (presumably the lymph nodes) too. She had considerable confidence in mesmerism, so Elliotson suggested using it. He meant that he would use it as a general anaesthetic during the operation, but she took him to mean that he would use it to cure the cancer. He allowed her to continue in this belief. At first, although mesmerism enabled her to sleep better at night, the tumour continued to grow. Six months later, although other doctors too had recommended surgery, the woman continued in her faith in mesmerism, especially as applied by Elliotson himself. To cut a long story short, as the months and then years rolled by, there was gradually remission of the tumour and of the related ailments from which the woman suffered, until the cancer had completely vanished.

Neither the medical establishment nor Elliotson had much time for psychological approaches. The value of post-hypnotic suggestion, for instance, was not fully appreciated until later in the century. George Barth's handbook, calling it 'the mesmeric promise', devotes only one short paragraph to it. Elliotson believed that mesmerism was physical, that it made use of a previously unrecognized force which was as natural as magnetism or electricity; but this quasi-scientific argument split the ranks of the mesmerists, some of whom rejected such reductionism in favour of mysticism, and so denounced, for instance, Elliotson's association of mesmerism with phrenology, which was seen as a hard science. But for Elliotson and his physicalist colleagues, their theories seemed to be corroborated by accounts of mesmerizing animals. Surely no imagination could be involved in such cases. Since it was generally agreed that a certain invisible and immaterial something passes from the operator to the subject, it came as no surprise to them to find that they could mesmerize inanimate objects such as glasses of water or chairs (which would then have a beneficial effect on a patient when sat upon).

Because of his physicalist views, Elliotson spent much of the rest of his life attempting to prove the validity of mesmerism against not only the narrow scientism of the medical establishment, but also the sensational spiritism of other mesmerists. The so-called 'higher phenomena' of hypnotism were a problem for physicalist theories; that is no doubt one reason why Elliotson was somewhat reserved about them. Perhaps a fluidist could explain the phenomena associated with sympathy between operator and subject, and, at a stretch, clairvoyance at close quarters; but they were hard put with clairvoyance at a distance. So, for instance, in the fifth edition of his textbook *Human Physiology* (1840) Elliotson vilified Mesmer as 'a very glutton in all that was marvellous', and although earlier he had believed that the O'Keys could prophesy the death or survival of patients in the hospital, he is at pains to distance himself from anything paranormal (though he would give some room to these 'higher' phenomena in the *Zoist*). At the same time, he insists:

> I have no hesitation in declaring my conviction that the facts of mesmerism which I admit, because they are not contrary to established morbid phenomena, result from a specific power. Even they are sometimes unreal and feigned, and, when real, are sometimes the result of emotion, – of imagination, to use common language; but, that they may be real and independent of all imagination, I have seen quite sufficient to convince me.

He then recounts such phenomena, noticeably omitting any of the O'Keys' more marvellous effects, except to admit that a patient may accurately diagnose her own ailments. But he says he's sceptical about whether they can do the same for others.

By 1843, no doubt as a result of his persecution, Elliotson was sounding more like a crusader. Not only did he start the *Zoist* in that year, but he also published a book with the confrontational title *Numerous Cases of Surgical Operations Without Pain in the Mesmeric State; with Remarks upon the Opposition of Many Members of the Royal Medical and Chirurgical Society and Others to the Reception of the*

Inestimable Blessings of Mesmerism. And in the context of the radicalism of the mesmerists, it is significant that Elliotson dedicated the book 'to those, however humble their rank, who prize truth above the favour of the ignorant or interested, and feel more satisfaction in promoting the comfort, the knowledge, the virtue, and therefore the happiness, of their fellow-men, than in promoting what is commonly called their own interest'.

This is a truly mind-boggling book (or pamphlet, since it is short). The first chapter describes in detail the 1842 amputation of a leg above the knee; the mesmerist was not Elliotson, but a barrister called W. Topham, while the surgeon was Mr Ward. The description is clinical. The patient, James Wombell, moaned a little, but remained still and asleep even while the surgeon was cutting the sciatic nerve. Afterwards he reported feeling no pain, although he did once hear the 'crunching' of the saw on his thigh bone. He not only survived the operation, but lived for another thirty years.

The second section of the chapter records the reaction of the Royal Medical and Chirurgical Society (the main body of the medical establishment at the time) on hearing the report of this operation. The first speaker declared that the patient had no doubt been trained not to express pain. Others reminded the audience that patients frequently underwent operations without being anaesthetized, and without expressing pain. (But not without *feeling* pain, Elliotson reminds us.) And so on and so forth. Elliotson sarcastically entitled this section 'Determination of the Royal Medical and Chirurgical Society of London, that this fact was not a fact'. The learned members one by one rose from their seats to pat one another smugly on the backs by denouncing the patient as an impostor. And at their next meeting they proposed to strike the record of the meeting from their minutes, which is rather similar to the way Trotsky was airbrushed out of Soviet photographs after his downfall and murder. Out of sight, out of mind!

Elliotson sensibly agrees with his critics that all the phenomena of mesmerism can occur naturally or under other circumstances, but points out that this does not detract from the value of mesmerism as a means of inducing somnambulism or 'sleep-waking' artificially. The second and final chapter describes a number of other cases of anaesthesia, mostly involving surgical or dental operations, from all over England, and ends with the famous case from Paris of Madame Plantin, which we looked at in Chapter 4.

One of the highlights of Elliotson's career came in 1846, when it was his turn to be invited to deliver the Harveian Oration before the Royal College of Physicians. There was a vigorous campaign of letter-writing to medical journals both before and afterwards by his enemies, deploring the fact, but there was nothing they could do about it. The College's protocol allowed the youngest member who has not previously had the privilege to deliver the Oration. They did, however, take the precaution of arranging a police presence on the premises, in case of any disturbance – an astonishing and unique sight in those august academic surroundings. Elliotson rose to the occasion and grasped the opportunity for a showcase piece of rhetoric. It is an extended plea for open-mindedness, showing how Harvey himself was at first ridiculed and despised for suggesting that the blood circulated around the body, how vaccination and inoculation met with considerable ridicule, and so on. 'Let us never forget these things: never allow authority, conceit, habit, or the fear of ridicule, to make us indifferent, much less to make us hostile, to truth.' His conclusion is particularly orotund:

> Never was it more necessary than at the present moment to bear all these things in mind. A body of facts is presented to us not only wonderful in physiology and pathology, but of the very highest importance in the prevention of suffering under the hands of the surgeon and in the cure of disease. The chief phenomena are indisputable: authors of all periods record them, and we all ourselves witness them, some rarely, some every day. The point to be determined is whether they may be produced artificially and subjected to our control: and it can be determined by experience only . . . It is the imperative, the solemn, duty of the profession, anxiously and dispassionately to determine these points by experiment, each man for himself. I have done so for ten years, and fearlessly declare that the phenomena, the prevention of pain under surgical operations, the production of repose and comfort in disease, and the cure of many diseases, even after the failure of all ordinary means, are true. In the name, therefore, of the love of truth, in the name of the dignity of our profession, in the name of the good

of all mankind, I implore you carefully to investigate this important subject.

Later in the 1840s, Elliotson was one of the driving forces behind the establishment of the London Mesmeric Infirmary, but circumstances were already making him a relic of a bygone age. Braid, whose work we will shortly turn to, had decisively moved hypnotism away from the kind of physicalist theories that Elliotson had espoused, and in so doing had sounded the death knell of animal magnetism. The jewel in mesmerism's crown, surgical anasthaesia, was made redundant by the introduction of chemical anaesthetics. Moreover, the spiritist craze swept through Britain in the 1850s as it had through the United States, and mesmerism became more or less forgotten in the rush. Elliotson's long campaign eventually wore him down and by the 1860s he was often suffering from depression, and appears to have contemplated suicide. Dickens and other friends remained loyal to him throughout.

Charles Dickens and the Banker's Wife

A reader of Dickens's novels would be forgiven for not guessing that Dickens had a passionate involvement with mesmerism. It finds little reflection in his books, apart from the occasional image of entrancement, as in *Oliver Twist* Fagin, perhaps, exerts some such hold over Oliver and the others in his lair. But Elliotson was his son Walter's godfather, his family doctor and a lifelong friend. Dickens's letters frequently allude to him or to the subject in general, and it was the occasional publication of these letters that informed his readers of his interest. On 27 January 1842, Dickens wrote to Robert Collyer in Boston:

> With regard to my opinion on the subject of mesmerism, I have no hesitation in saying that I have closely watched Dr Elliotson's experiments from the first – that he is one of my most intimate and valued friends – that I have the utmost reliance on his

honour, character, and ability, and would trust my life in his hands at any time – and that after what I have seen with my own eyes and observed with my own senses, I should be untrue both to him and myself, if I should shrink for a moment from saying that I am a believer, and that I became so against all my preconceived opinions.

This letter was widely reprinted in US papers and magazines, such as the Boston *Morning Post* (1 February 1842), the *New World* (12 February 1842) and the Baltimore *Patriot* (25 February 1842). Opinions were divided. The *Patriot* held that Dickens's belief in animal magnetism should be classed as one of the 'infirmities of genius', but the *New World* applauded the courage of a frank avowal which might detract from Dickens's popularity.

Dickens's first recorded contact with mesmerism took place in January 1838, when he and his illustrator, George Cruikshank, met Elliotson and watched him work with Elizabeth O'Key. The two became friends, and Dickens returned again and again to watch demonstrations by Elliotson and his associates at University College Hospital. Between 1839 and 1844 the two men met frequently, and Elliotson also introduced Dickens to Townshend in 1840. Dickens refused to be hypnotized himself, because he didn't want to lose control, but he was prepared to try his hand as a mesmerizer and first did so during a lecture tour of the States in 1842, in Pittsburgh. His subject was his wife Catherine (Kate):

> And speaking of magnetism, let me tell you that the other night at Pittsburgh, there being present only Mr Q. and the portrait-painter, Kate sat down, laughing, for me to try my hand upon her. I had been holding forth upon the subject rather luminously, and asserting that I thought I could exercise the influence, but had never tried. In six minutes, I magnetized her into hysterics, and then into the magnetic sleep. I tried again next night, and she fell into the slumber in little more than two minutes . . . I can wake her with perfect ease; but I confess (not being prepared for anything so sudden and complete), I was on the first occasion rather alarmed.

He pronounced it an 'extraordinary success', and on returning to London he practised on a wider circle of friends and relatives, chiefly

for display and entertainment, but also occasionally to calm someone's nerves and get them to relax.

In 1844–5 Dickens and his family were on an extended visit to
Italy. In Genoa they met and became close friends with the banker
Emile de la Rue and his family. Madame de la Rue (born Augusta
Granet) suffered from a range of symptoms typical of the hysterical
Victorian upper-class woman: she had a nervous tic, headaches,
insomnia, and occasional convulsions and catalepsy. Dickens recog-
nized the type from Elliotson's demonstrations and realized that her
symptoms were psychosomatic and could be helped by hypnotism.
He undertook to mesmerize her, and started treatment on 23
December 1844. While she was in a trance, he used to get her to talk
about her fears, fantasies and dreams through free association. To
the dismay of both Emile and Catherine, Dickens and Madame de la
Rue built up a very intense relationship, which was aided by the
undoubted improvement of Augusta's health. She was certainly
strongly dependent on Dickens, but Dickens was so absorbed that he
was just as dependent on her too. One of the main aspects he
enjoyed was the struggle with the Phantom, a projection of Augusta's
fears who frequently put in an appearance in their sessions and tried
to undermine Dickens's therapeutic work.

Dickens was never one to tackle anything half-heartedly, and his
confidence and energy were inexhaustible, while, for her part,
Augusta's needs were insatiable. The mutual dependency was such
that even when they were apart (Catherine, by now thoroughly
jealous, insisted on a tour of the rest of Italy), they had an
appointment at 11 o'clock each day, when Dickens undertook to
concentrate on her for an hour; she obligingly went into a trance at
that time, but tended to relapse while Dickens was away, until they
were reunited in Rome later in April and travelled together back to
Genoa. The whole business was undoubtedly one of the factors
leading to the breakdown of Dickens's marriage with Catherine.
Long before Freud gave it the name of 'transference', Victorian
amateur psychologists were aware of (and deeply concerned about)
the phenomenon of attraction between operator and subject, which
was a natural extension of a magnetic theory. They were at pains
to argue that it was like the love of a child for a parent, rather
than sexual attraction. It manifested (as in the case of Dickens and

Madame de la Rue) most commonly in the subject suffering from anxiety when she felt that the operator's attention was not focused on her.

After Dickens's return to London in June 1845, the bond between him and his patient was weakened, and although they met and corresponded occasionally over the subsequent years, the intensity was gone for ever. Madame de la Rue continued to be unwell. Dickens offered to restart the treatment, but she refused, because she knew he could not be her full-time doctor, and she preferred to suffer rather than have a merely temporary improvement followed by relapse. After this episode with the banker's wife, Dickens never again found the opportunity to mesmerize another person, but he retained a theoretical interest in the subject. Mesmerism had seemed to offer hope of true self-knowledge – that is, knowledge of the source of one's life-energy; but eventually he concluded that while it could reveal problems, it could not finally cure them. His interest in the subject remained strong, if somewhat extra-curricular; for instance, in 1850 he both stage-managed and took the leading role in a private showing of Mrs Inchbald's eighteenth-century farce *Animal Magnetism*, at Knebworth House, home of the Bulwer-Lyttons.

As I have already said, many British intellectuals in the nineteenth century dabbled or expressed some kind of interest in mesmerism. If Dickens took things further than, say, Charlotte Brontë (who allowed herself to be mesmerized once only), that is due to the intensity of his nature. Dickens told Catherine that his commitment to mesmerism, to exploring the nature of power, to asserting his will and his personality, to testing deeply the possibilities of all kinds of human relationships, was inseparable from his art and his life. 'The intense pursuit of any idea,' he said, 'that takes complete possession of me, is one of the qualities that makes me different – sometimes for good; sometimes I dare say for evil – from other men.'

The Affair of Harriet Martineau

The cause of mesmerism in Britain was enormously boosted by the famous illness and even more famous cure of Harriet Martineau, a social activist and popular writer who was at the centre of literary Britain in the early Victorian period. She shared with Dickens the kind of passionate nature that forced her to extremes of enthusiasm, but was far less reticent than he was about trumpeting her involvement with mesmerism to the public at large. Although mesmerism had acquired a word-of-mouth reputation for its medical efficacy, and under pressure from their patients doctors were beginning to make use of it, Martineau's fame guaranteed enormous exposure to the issues.

She suffered from severe abdominal pains and constipation, over-frequent menstruation accompanied by unusual discharges, and nervous pains which eventually prevented her from walking or standing up. Her gynaecological problems developed until there was a solid substance of some kind protruding from her vagina. (Did she have a prolapsed uterus? Uterine polypi? After her death, she was found to have a huge ovarian cyst.) Standard medical treatment, which involved the additional pain of regular applications of iodine to the affected part, proved to be no help, and this once active woman, who had travelled extensively in the United States, for instance, took to her bed in Tynemouth, in north-east England. She continued to write, when she could, and indeed was one of those writers who think that an account of her illness will be of interest to the general public. In this case it was, but chiefly because of her remarkable cure.

Medical science was baffled by her illness (which was perhaps psychosomatic, since she also suffered from bouts of self-doubt), and she was convinced it was incurable. Her friend, Sir Edward Bulwer-Lytton, the writer of occult mysteries, suggested that she consult a somnambule. By serendipity, several other friends wrote at much the same time (early in 1844) with the same suggestion, or at least drawing her attention to the increasingly popular phenomenon of mesmerism. Not that this was Harriet's first contact with the subject: she had met Elliotson in the 1830s in London, friends of hers had been mesmerized, one of her brothers-in-law had incorporated it into his medical practice, and as a dissenter she would have been attracted to their progressive radicalism. Anyway, she contacted Spencer Hall, the famous mesmeric showman and champion of the common people, and he brought her some relief, but she found him 'simple-minded' and turned first to her maid, who imitated the hand passes she had seen Hall performing. Finally, she ended up in the hands of Mrs Montague Wynyard, who became a kind of companion, and within a few weeks this formidable woman had cured Harriet of all her ills. Not only that, but she had also hypnotized Jane Arrowsmith, the nineteen-year-old niece of Harriet's landlady, who proved to be clairvoyant and a medium, and came through with spiritual doctrines of a high order. Since it seemed unthinkable to Harriet that such an uneducated girl could on her own have invented such stuff, she was more than ever convinced of the truth of mesmerism. When mesmerized she too occasionally felt herself to be transported to another realm.

Harriet was an enthusiastic convert, and being a writer, she decided that she had to write about it. She chose the popular magazine the *Athenaeum*, despite its sceptical editor (in September 1838 the magazine had covered the Wakley–Elliotson controversy and come down firmly on the side of Wakley, considering that he had killed mesmerism stone dead), because she wanted to reach as wide an audience as possible, and not just preach to the choir. Her six 'Letters on Mesmerism', published in November and December 1844, proved to be a great attraction, and boosted the fortunes not only of the magazine, but also of mesmerism in general, which became the most talked-about subject of the day. Even Prince Albert, the queen's beloved husband, remarked, on hearing of the controversy and the dismissal of mesmerism by the orthodox medical community, that medical men were conducting themselves improperly in refusing to investigate the topic. Martineau's letters were published in book form early in 1845, and in the preface she looked forward to a day, in the not-too-distant future, when mesmerists would cure half the illness in the land. The first edition of the book sold out in four days, and in the *Zoist* Elliotson crowed: 'The subject which the critic, a few months since, would not condescend to notice, has been elevated to a commanding position. It is the topic with which the daily papers and the weekly periodicals are filled . . . The immediate cause of all this activity is the publication of the case of Miss Martineau.'

There was a backlash. To Harriet's disgust the editor of the *Athenaeum* published a series of anonymous and highly critical letters; the *Lancet*, of course, renewed its attacks; Jane Carlyle took Harriet's devotion to mesmerism to be conclusive proof of her insanity; the reviewer of *Letters on Mesmerism* in the *Edinburgh Medical and Surgical Journal* treated it as yet another case of female weak-mindedness ('She becomes nervous, fanciful, feeble in body and imbecile in mind, – also common occurrences . . .'). But the genie was now well and truly out of the bottle.

James Esdaile and Mesmeric Surgery

One of the recurring topics in the pages of the *Zoist* was mesmeric anaesthesia, confirmed through numerous case histories; in particular, Elliotson gave plenty of space to the extraordinary work of a surgeon working in British India, James Esdaile (1808–59), originally from Scotland.

It would be hard to fit Esdaile into the mould of a modern hero: he was as liable to colonial prejudices as any European in India in the 1840s, and operated on his patients with little regard for the then unknown phenomenon of post-operative trauma. Witnesses were amazed at the nonchalance with which he might simply stab down into a tumour to see how deep it was. He tended to see his successes with native patients as helped by their animal-like passivity and awe of the European, and by their confusion of mesmerism with their own native mumbo-jumbo. Mesmerism was seen by him and others as another way of proving the superiority of European culture to native culture. But for all that, the work he performed was truly amazing.

In 1845 Esdaile was responsible for the Hooghly hospital near Calcutta, and he found himself dealing with a painful problem endemic to the region. Due to filiarisis transmitted by mosquitoes, many men suffered from hydroceles of the scrotum – tumours which grew enormous as bodily fluids accumulated in the scrotal sac. The operation to deal with this condition was so painful that patients put it off for years and years, so that Esdaile was faced with many severely enlarged tumours, one weighing as much as 103 lbs (over 46 kgs), which was more or less the natural body weight of the patient as well. I'm sure that any man reading this is by now cringing in sympathy. Esdaile needed to find a way to win his patients' confidence, so that they would allow the operation to take place. He turned to mesmerism, and immediately found it astonishingly effective. He was a meticulous recorder of his work and so we have good information about his procedures. Some of his descriptions of scrotal operations are not for the squeamish. Here is one from his 1846 book *Mesmerism in India*:

> Oct. 25 – Gooroochuan Shah, a shop-keeper, aged 40. He has got a 'monster tumour', which prevents him from moving; its great weight, and his having used it for a writing-desk for many years, has pressed it into its present shape. His pulse is weak, and his feet oedoematous, which will make it very hazardous to attempt its removal . . . He became insensible on the fourth day of mesmerizing . . . Two men held up the tumour in a sheet, pulling it forward at the same time, and, in the presence of Mr Bennet, I removed it by a circular incision, expedition being his only safety. The rush of venous blood was great, but fortunately soon arrested; and, after tying the last vessel, . . . he awoke. The loss of blood had been so great that he immediately fell into a fainting state . . . On recovering he said that he awoke while the mattress was being pulled back, and that nothing had disturbed him. The tumour weighed eighty pounds, and is probably the largest ever removed from the human body. I think it extremely likely that if the circulation had been hurried by pain and struggling, or if shock to the system had

been increased by bodily and mental anguish, the man would have bled to death, or never have rallied from the effects of the operation. But the sudden loss of blood was all he had to contend against; and, though in so weak a condition, he has surmounted this, and gone on very well.

Following his first successes, he turned the surgical side of his hospital into a kind of mesmeric factory. Since he found the process of mesmerizing patients very tiring and time-consuming, he turned that side over to trained native assistants, saving his energies for the actual operations. Over the next few years, the hospital performed, astonishingly, over 3,000 operations; just as importantly, Esdaile found that his post-operative death rate plummeted from 50 per cent (which was more or less normal for the time for serious operations) to 5 per cent. He explained this by arguing that a mesmerist passes vital energies on to the patient, and that these energies in turn mobilize the body's natural curative resources. More probably, it was due to the reduction in trauma consequent on the patients being for the first time genuinely anaesthetized.

Esdaile also devoted some of his time and energy to proselytizing. As well as using the Indian papers and journals to publicize his successes, he wrote a number of pamphlets and books. His work aroused some suspicion from the snobbish Anglo-Indian medical community, who thought that mesmerism smacked too much of native medicine. He was even accused of bribing his native patients: 'You know what a Bengalee will do for a few pice,' said one correspondent to the *Englishman and Military Chronicle* for 29 May 1846. Others suggested that the patients were all impostors or hysterics liable to spontaneous anaesthesia. Esdaile's response to this kind of criticism was properly impatient: 'Suffering humanity cannot afford to wait for the slow conviction of indolence and healthy indifference.' And so he asked the deputy governor, Sir Herbert Maddock, to convene a committee to assess his work.

The committee gave him a 70 per cent success rate after observing him at work on ten patients. They confirmed that in all these cases there was genuine trance (Esdaile employed some of the tricks of the showmen to prove trance), but were disturbed by cases where the patient writhed a bit, as if in pain. Esdaile dismissed these

as instinctive movements, but the committee wanted to see more
tests: would it work on Europeans, for instance, as well as on lower
forms of life? Was the post-operative death rate really as low as
Esdaile claimed? Would being mesmerized make patients liable to
nervous diseases later in life? Their hesitation seems to have been
prompted as much as anything by the dubious reputation of mesmerism in general, but they did raise some valid worries. For instance, it
took Esdaile so long to mesmerize some of his patients – he even
found on occasion that he had to warm them up for several days
beforehand – that the procedure was clearly useless for emergencies.
But Maddock overruled their doubts and ordered that a mesmeric
hospital be established in Calcutta for a trial year, starting in
November 1846. Here Esdaile was required to test mesmerism's
medical as well a surgical benefits, to find out whether race and class
made any difference, and to report on his findings.

As well as continuing with his surgical work, then, Esdaile began
to use hypnotherapy for a range of illnesses from deafness to epilepsy,
via rheumatism and neuralgia, and even to treat some cases that
were clearly psychological. He deliberately employed an open-door
policy, presumably in order to spread the word: anyone could
wander in off the streets and witness what was going on. His surgical
successes continued, but the extension of his practice beyond them
was regarded with suspicion; and it turned out to be impossible for
him to experiment much on different races and classes, because
neither the Indian upper castes nor the colonial British were prepared
to enter a hospital which was largely staffed by native Indians. But
he did manage successfully to treat a few Europeans there and at
other hospitals which adopted the practice through Esdaile's
influence.

The mesmeric hospital closed in January 1848, largely because
the new deputy governor, Lord Dalhousie, promoted Esdaile beyond
the sphere of hospital medicine, probably as a diplomatic way of
ridding the community of this renegade. A dingy wing of another
small hospital was turned over to mesmerism, but the practice soon
went into decline, as a result of the introduction of chemical
anaesthetics into India from Europe, and of continuing white doubts
about the close interaction required in mesmerism between natives
and themselves. Esdaile held an honorary position as the superintend-

ent of this reduced mesmeric hospital until he retired back to Scotland in 1851.

By the middle of the 1850s, mesmerism was on the decline, not so much because the conservatives had won the war, as because of fresh medical discoveries in the field of surgical anaesthesia, which appeared to do away with the necessity of mesmerism in this respect. Until then this had been the greatest boon the mesmerists could offer – insensibility during surgical procedures, and before the introduction of ether in 1846 and chloroform in 1847, literally hundreds of pain-free operations had been performed in Europe and India. Curiously, the anaesthetic properties of some chemicals, such as nitrous oxide, had been known for some time, but there was a marked reluctance to employ them. Apart from the difficulty of finding the right dose, it was not at all clear at the time that insensibility was a desirable state. It was close to death; it was what happened after ingesting too much alcohol or opium; it seemed to undermine a person's free will altogether; it might lay women open to the sexual desires of an unscrupulous doctor.

While the doctors dithered, other mesmerists – not just Esdaile – were performing astonishing feats. I have already summarized the amputation of James Wombell's leg, which was widely publicized in one of Elliotson's books. Many members of the medical profession, however, suggested that Wombell was faking – that he had been conscious throughout the operation, and had colluded with the surgeon and mesmerist in pretending otherwise. The mesmerists just could not defeat this kind of stubborn hostility. It was considered to be evidence of Wombell's collusion that his other leg had not jerked automatically as the amputation was being performed; when, two years later, a woman underwent a similar amputation and her other leg *did* jerk, this was taken to show that she was still feeling pain! In 1850 the eminent physiologist Marshall Hall told the Royal Medical and Chirurgical Society that Wombell had finally confessed to his cheating. Wombell denied it vehemently. Pressed for his evidence, Hall said that he had been told so by a person he trusted; this person in turn said that he had been told by an unimpeachable source. This hearsay was preferred over Wombell's denials.

By 1848 the Reverend George Sandby was able to count over 300 surgical operations performed painlessly in Britain alone under hypnosis – and still the medical profession refused to consider it an authentic method. In the 1850s the Royal College of Physicians reviewed a public amputation of a gangrenous limb while the patient was under hypnotic anaesthesia. They simply discounted the phenomenon altogether. The *Lancet* concluded that the patient was an impostor who had been trained not to show pain. Another reviewer decided that the patient was a 'hardened rogue', hired by for a fee by the surgeon. A remark in Elliotson's *Zoist*, addressed to the Council of Surgeons, says it all: you should blush, he said, for 'your bigoted, your stupid, your cruel opposition to the reception of a mighty and all-important fact . . . How long will you refuse to spare a single wretched patient the pain of your instruments?' Indeed, in retrospect it is very hard to understand the surgeons' resistance. Here was the only effective way to induce full anaesthesia, to stop patients feeling sometimes agonizing pain – and they would have nothing to do with it.

In fact, it was the benign influence of mesmeric anaesthesia that hastened the introduction of chemical techniques into the surgeon's arsenal, since the infliction of pain during surgery began to be seen as something avoidable, not a necessary evil. But medical science's efforts were hampered by the relative inefficiency of the chemical agents in their arsenal to bring about the desired insensibility. Nitrous oxide, for instance, could dull the pain, or distract the patient, but it could not bring about complete unconsciousness, except in doses large enough to be dangerous. But then in 1846 the anaesthetic properties of ether were discovered in Boston. 'Gentlemen,' said Robert Liston, the first British surgeon to make use of ether, on 21 December 1846, 'the Yankee trick beats the French one.' Picking up on this implicit reference to mesmerism, when the English medical press announced the discovery, it was expressly contrasted with the fraudulent claims of mesmerism. Doctors soon found reasons other than rhetoric to compare ether favourably with mesmerism. For a start, while mesmeric anaesthesia was hit and miss, ether worked on everyone; and a mesmerist might have to work on a patient for several days in order to make him receptive to a deep enough trance, but ether worked in seconds. These benefits were seen as outweigh-ing the fact that, in the beginning, ether killed a few patients, and that it needed practice and skill to administer it in just the right dose. Many patients were in a state close to drunkenness, rather than being unconscious. But, hastened by official hostility to mesmerism, before long chemical anaesthetics had taken over and had prised the jewel out of mesmerism's crown.

James Braid

One of the problems with the contempt in which the medical establishment held mesmerism after the Elliotson affair is that other work in the area became tarred with the same brush of fraud and eccentricity. This was particularly unfortunate in the case of the theories of James Braid (1795–1860), because he laid the foundations for a sane and scientific study of hypnotism, free of the grandiose metaphysical schemes of animal magnetism. But from his fellow doctors he received the usual snide treatment of rejected papers and of both overt and covert criticism.

Braid was a Scotsman, born in Fife, and with a medical degree from Edinburgh. On 13 November 1841, by which time he was living in Manchester, he took in a show by Charles de Lafontaine. He went out of simple curiosity, sure that he would find it a load of rubbish, and in fact was loud in his accusations of humbuggery after the show. Lafontaine invited him and his fellow critics from the medical community to examine his female somnambule, and Braid came away convinced that there was something worth researching. He was one of those provincial researchers who would not have his work dictated by the whims of the medical establishment in London. Scorned equally by both Elliotson (who stubbornly stuck to his magnetic, physicalist views and called Braid 'a most vain and swaggering mechanic') and Wakley of the *Lancet*, he used the pages of the *Medical Times* to announce his results. As a result of his experiments, he quickly found that he could reproduce many of the phenomena of mesmerism in his subjects simply by getting them to fix their gaze on an object. One of the first such objects he used was a cork with a shiny plated top in a wine bottle; usually he used his lancet case.

Magnetic mesmerism had survived the attacks and counter-evidence of Faria and Bertrand in France, but the *coup de grâce* came from Braid. Braid demonstrated time and again that mere fixation on a small, bright object could produce the state previously known as mesmeric somnambulism, but which Braid preferred to call 'hypnotism'. The hand passes of a mesmerist were quite unnecessary (though Braid himself occasionally used them to inspire confidence in a patient), nothing even closely resembling magnetic fluid was involved, and indeed anyone can hypnotize himself, Braid asserted, by staring at the kind of object he described. In his 1843 book *Neurypnology* he listed and described the cures he had effected through hypnosis, and they parallel the successes of mesmerism. Braid came to the realization that the mesmerists had accidentally stumbled on to something of supreme importance.

Why was Braid effective where Faria and Bertrand were not? Because he was meticulous, plainly a medical man not a showman, a lucid writer, sober, cautious and unconcerned with paranormal and exotic phenomena (which he either found no evidence for, or attributed to hyperaesthesia). Moreover (although in this respect I would hesitate to say he differed from Bertrand), he based his views on observation and experiment, rather than on preconceived theories. Indeed, he was somewhat inclined towards a form of mechanical materialism, and at first attributed the cures he achieved under hypnosis to changes brought about in the deeper trance state to the blood flow of the body. Later, however, he was prepared to acknowledge that concentrated attention and imagination played some part in the cures, as did the implanting of suggestions. He also exploded the myth that under hypnosis a subject could be made to break his or her moral code: if anyone had listened to him, female fears about rape would have been laid to rest. In any case, much of the taint of mesmerism was removed by Braid's development of it into hypnotism. In hypnotism, no close proximity with a mesmerist was required, the passes with their sexual overtones were no longer necessary, and the theory of emanations passing from one person to another by will power was made redundant.

Braid's later, more psychologically oriented writings prefigured much of the psychotherapeutic work of the later nineteenth century. All the various procedures for inducing a trance are designed, he saw, solely to promote the state of single-mindedness, with everything else passing into oblivion. In later years, he found that he could induce fixation simply by talking to his subjects, and could hypnotize blind people just as effectively as those with sight, and so he totally abandoned his earlier physiological theory, according to which it was fixation of the gaze affecting the blood flow from the eyes to the rest of the body that induced a kind of narcotic state.

Arguing that the hypnotized subject becomes occupied by a single idea to the exclusion of others – for which he coined the word 'monoideism' – he appreciated that it might be possible to treat certain cases of monomania and hysteria by replacing the idea on which sufferers were fixated with another, more life-affirming idea. This is what we nowadays call 'reframing'. The mind, Braid argued, obviously has an effect on the body. If we salivate at the mere thought of food, what else might we not be able to do?

> Since it cannot be doubted that the soul and the body can mutually act and react upon each other, it should follow, as a natural consequence, that if we can attain to any mode of intensifying the *mental* power, we should thus realise, in a corresponding degree, greater control over physical action. Now this is precisely what my processes do – they create no new faculties; but they give us greater control over the natural functions than we possess during the ordinary waking condition.

We can therefore occupy the mind with a healing suggestion to effect cures.

Braid was not the kind of person to stand still. Having moved already from a physiological theory of blood flow to a psychological theory of monoideism, in his latest work he was also prepared to abandon or modify monoideism. He distinguished the shallow and deep phases or layers of the trance state; the first he called 'sub-hypnotic' and claimed that it was this that the electro-biologists could produce; the second he called 'double consciousness', because he found his subjects to be dissociated (as we would now say) from their normal states. For instance, he got his subjects to learn a few sentences in a foreign language; when awake, they could no longer remember the sentences, but when hypnotized later they could again recall them.

Although some members of the medical profession found Braid's work more acceptable than they had Elliotson's, there was still far too much resistance for its importance to be widely appreciated. Animal magnetism or mesmerism had come to Britain from France and been transformed into hypnotism; but prophets are rarely welcomed or acknowledged in their home countries. In lingering dissatisfaction at the failure of his fellow physicians in Britain to recognize the importance of his discoveries, in 1860 Braid sent a paper to be read at the French Academy of Sciences. This galvanized a number of French psychologists, and it was once again France which led the field for many years.

Mesmerism and the Paranormal in Britain

The Victorian belief that hypnotized subjects had supernatural powers may be illustrated by an episode from the life of Sir Richard Burton, the traveller and diplomat (1821–90). Burton believed that he had a 'gipsy' soul, and that under hypnosis he could read people's minds. He was apparently a skilled mesmerizer, and claimed that he could hypnotize even at a distance, unless there was a stretch of water in between, which would presumably serve to absorb the magnetic rays between him and his subject. In particular, he used to mesmerize his wife, the aristocratic Isabel Arundell, and consult her about the future. On one occasion, in Brazil in the later 1860s, Burton was very ill, and there were no doctors available. Burton hypnotized Isabel to get a remedy from her while she was entranced.

> But instead of answering his question about his illness, she became very troubled and foretold (accurately, as it turned out) the murder by poison of their cook by a jealous rival in love, which occurred some weeks later. Then she warned him not to

trust 'the man that you are going to take with you, because he is a scoundrel'. Since Richard intended to travel alone they could not make sense of this.

As it happened, however, Burton did end up with a companion – a man calling himself Sir Roger Tichborne – and he *was* a scoundrel! He was a common English sailor, who knew that Tichborne had been drowned at sea and was trying to cash in on Tichborne's inheritance.

This story is as intriguing as many similar stories from the time. It is hard to dismiss them all as fraudulent, but at the same time it is hard to believe them, because they threaten the comfortable world views we have constructed for ourselves. In the vast majority of cases, we would like to hear more details, to be certain that there was no possibility of cheating at the time, or of embellishment after the facts.

Alongside mesmeric performers such as Spencer Hall there were others who specialized in the so-called 'higher' phenomena, which were supposed to be the privilege of trance subjects who could enter the deepest states. In these states, their souls were assumed to separate from their bodies, so that they could see things at a distance – at a small distance if they performed tricks such as reading a book while blindfolded, at a greater distance if they described events and people's homes elsewhere in the country, and at incredible distances if they reported on the geography and inhabitants of other planets.

The two most famous such performers in Britain in the 1840s were the French Didier brothers, Alexis and Adolphe. Alexis was already famous in France before the brothers came over to England in 1844 with their mesmerist, J.B. Marcillet. Accounts of their performances were written up in the *Zoist* (for instance, in the July 1844 and January 1845 issues). Their feats are astonishing, but it has to be said that there were never any properly controlled tests of their abilities. Here, for example, are a couple of instances where there is room for doubt. Once a sceptic in the audience in a private house produced a book and asked Alexis to tell him the title. He had covered the title page with doubled paper so that it could not be read. Nevertheless Alexis soon told him the title, after placing the book on his chest, and then on the back of his head. Could he have surreptitiously read the title on the spine as he was moving it from his chest to his head? In another experiment, following the successful blindfolded reading of sentences from a book, the blindfold was removed. The book was opened at random, and Alexis was asked to read from ten pages further on. He did so – but he had the 'habit' of idly flicking through the leaves of the book.

The sceptical comments on these feats by Alexis Didier are taken from an exposé by Sir John Forbes. Here, to give the other side of the picture, is an account of one of Alexis's feats from the January 1845 *Zoist*:

> His eyes were now open, and after a few minutes' delay a sealed envelope was given him by a gentleman who had brought it with him, and could not divulge to any one present what it contained; after examining it some time, he said there were two words, but they might also pass for one; that they were French; he said if the gentleman who wrote it, and who, he said, was so firm an unbeliever that his influence affected him, would go into the next room, and whisper it to the lady of the house, and she would come and give him her hand he would be able to write the word for her. This being done, he wrote the word *clairvoyance*; she said he was wrong. 'True,' said he, 'I ought to have written *clairvoyant*,' and so corrected it. On opening the envelope, the word was found to be correct, written on a sheet of note paper, folded up.

The history of parapsychology has been beset by the claim by sensitives that the 'vibes' of sceptics in the audience put them off. This has often been used to excuse poor performance under laboratory conditions. Just as in this report Alexis asked a sceptic to leave the room, so he often failed in the company of sceptics, but he encouraged them to attend his séances and be the ones who wrote the words down.

The reading of words from inside securely sealed envelopes or packages was a special trick of Alexis's. He was also occasionally a very successful travelling clairvoyant, giving accurate descriptions of people's houses and their contents, for instance. But we hear only the conclusions to these séances: how long did he take? How many questions did he ask the house-owner? In other words, how much opportunity did he have to witness their pupils dilating, or other involuntary gestures, which are the clues still used today by stage magicians for 'mind-reading' tricks. Other than this hypothesis, we have to accept that Alexis and Adolphe, his younger brother, did possess remarkable paranormal abilities. There were, as even the *Zoist* admitted, a lot of frauds in the field of clairvoyance, using plainly inadequate blindfolds, for instance; but the Didier brothers do come off better than most.

As a kind of footnote, I will add that Hippolyte Bernheim and J. Milne Bramwell, two of the most prolific hypnotizers of the later nineteenth century, hypnotized literally thousands of people, and never found evidence of paranormal feats. You can make of this what you will. Sceptics will take it to be evidence that it is all fraudulent; others, more charitably, may be inclined to deny that it proves or disproves anything, except that only maybe one person in a million is truly gifted with paranormal powers. Bernheim and Bramwell just didn't come across such a person, or didn't set up their experiments in such a way as to encourage the manifestation of the higher phenomena. Braid, for his part, tried to be meticulously fair – unless it is right to detect irony in his words. In remarking that he himself had never been able to produce any of the paranormal phenomena that his predecessors had, he says:

Now, I do not consider it fair or proper to impugn the statements of others in this matter, who are known to be men of talent and observation, and of undoubted credit in *other* matters, merely because *I* have not *personally* witnessed the phenomena, or been able to produce them myself, either by my own mode or theirs. With my present means of knowledge I am willing to admit that certain phenomena to which I refer *have* been induced by others, but still I think most of them may be explained in a different and more natural way than that of the mesmerizers. When I shall have personally had evidence of the special influence and its effects to which they lay claim, I shall not be backward in bearing testimony to the fact.

The *Zoist* was not alone in reporting the marvels performed by the Didier brothers and others; the whole country was fascinated by them and by others who could carry out similar feats. *The New*

Monthly Belle Assemblée of February 1849, for example, reported a case in which a lady had lost a brooch, which she last remembered having in August, it being now November. She suspected it had been stolen by one of her servants. She consulted a mesmerist, Dr Hands, whose patient Ellen Dawson was noted for her clairvoyance. Ellen described the lady's house in detail, and the bedroom where the brooch had been kept, described the servant who had stolen it, and told where it was now to be found, despite the fact that it had been pawned. The brooch was recovered.

Clairvoyance was just one of a range of peculiar phenomena associated with mesmerism. The Victorians were amazed by the alleged phenomenon of sympathy between the operator and subject, and believed that sensations and thoughts could be transferred mysteriously between the two. The subject might be in a totally analgesic condition: you could tickle the soles of his feet and he would not respond. But tickle the soles of the operator's feet, and the subject feels it too. Then there was 'traction', which involved the subject mirroring the operator's movements, even when they were invisible to each other, in separate rooms. Worrying as the apparent erasure of boundaries between two individuals might have been to some, far more were simply fascinated by the phenomenon.

There are plenty of unconfirmed reports of what today we might call 'telepathic hypnotism' – that is, hypnotism at a distance, by the operator simply focusing his will on the subject. Of course, the difficulty in these cases is to be sure that the subject really had no idea that she was supposed to go into a trance at such-and-such a time. Hypnotism at a distance was tested under proper conditions at the Medical School of the University and King's College, Aberdeen. H.E. Lewis, a black American electro-biologist who was on a sell-out tour of the country in 1851, was the chosen mesmerist. Students from the university were tested by Lewis for susceptibility, and then taken to a different room, where some committee members could watch over them and assess the results, while others remained with Lewis. The experiment was a total failure: not one of the students entered into a trance state.

The whole topic of parapsychology and paranormal phenomena immediately engages one at a very personal level. Do you believe in them or not? Believers are different kinds of people from non-believers. Most of us sit on the fence and refuse to commit ourselves either way; we like to be entertained by the phenomena, but don't go all the way into full belief. But even one's position on the fence is maintained by a kind of oscillation between inclining one way and inclining the other. Each of us will deal with this tension in his or her own way. Speaking for myself, it makes me somewhat angry that I cannot know for certain, at this distance, which, if any, of the mesmeric paranormalists of Victorian Britain were genuine.

Aftermath

The phrase 'mesmeric mania' was coined (by Edinburgh academic John Hughes Bennett) to refer to the year 1851 in particular, when on top of the Elliotson–Wakley controversy, Braid's stream of publications and the itinerant lecturers, electro-biology came over from the States and the tackier side of hypnotism took the country by storm. The electro-biologists could have dozens of people in a trance at a time, and soon other mesmerists were achieving the same results without the help of the electro-biologists' bimetallic discs. Polite society was frequently entertained by the sight of half a dozen young women swooning simultaneously under the impassive and assertive gaze of a mesmerist. Electro-biology was a short-lived craze, however – not because people saw sense, but because it was overtaken by the epidemic of table-turning and spiritism. The mes-meric mania of 1851 was the last twitching of a dying art. Although the electro-biologists' methods were similar to those of Braid, Braid's work had fallen on such deaf ears that no one made the connection which would have accelerated the acceptance of hypnotism by the scientific community.

Braid died in 1860, Elliotson in 1868, but interest in mesmerism in the UK had already died before that. By the 1880s, however, respectable medical scientists in France could take up, in effect, Braidian and Elliotsonian positions, and yet retain their reputations untarnished. This is part of the story of the next chapter, but it fed back into Britain. In 1891 the British Medical Association appointed a commission to investigate hypnotism. The subsequent report was cautiously favourable, but distanced itself from the controversy earlier in the century:

> The Committee have satisfied themselves of the genuineness of the hypnotic state. No phenomena which have come under their observation, however, lend support to the theory of 'animal magnetism' . . . The Committee are of the opinion that as a therapeutic agent hypnotism is frequently effective in relieving pain, procuring sleep, and alleviating many functional ailments . . . The Committee are of the opinion that when used for therapeutic purposes its employment should be confined to qualified medical men, and that under no circumstances should female patients be hypnotised, except in the presence of a relative or a person of their own sex . . . In conclusion, the Committee desire to express their strong disapprobation of public exhibitions of hypnotic phenomena, and hope that some legal restriction will be placed on them.

This report was merely 'received' by the BMA, rather than being endorsed, but it marked the beginning of the acceptance of hypnotism in Britain. In part this change of heart was due to the advances made by Braid over Elliotson and his peers; the wild speculations of the animal magnetists no longer sidetracked official attention from the reality of their results. In part it was due to the British medical community by now being more secure in itself, so that it could shed the blinkers which had blinded it to the value of mesmerism earlier in the century.

7

Murder, Rape and Debate in the Late Nineteenth Century

In 1891 a sensational trial gripped Paris. The defendants were a twenty-six-year-old woman, Gabrielle Bompard, and her lover and occasional pimp, a middle-aged lowlife called Michel Eyraud. The year before, finding themselves in need of cash, Gabrielle had lured a bailiff called Alexandre-Toussaint Gouffé to her room with the promise of sex. Under five feet in height, with her hair cut short, it was not difficult for the *gamin* slut to entice him over to her bed, where she sensually unwound from her waist the silk rope which acted as her belt, and provocatively placed it around the unfortunate Gouffé's neck as he kissed her throat. This was the signal for Eyraud to come out from behind the curtain where he had been waiting. He took hold of the other end of the rope and hung Gouffé, who died without a struggle, and remarkably quickly, considering the amateur set-up. To their dismay the lovers found only a few francs on Gouffé's person. They dumped his body in a trunk and disposed of it in a wood near Lyons before fleeing to America.

Months later, seeing her picture in a French newspaper, Gabrielle returned to France from California and gave herself up. The police now knew where Eyraud was, but he evaded capture for another six months, before finally being tracked down in Cuba and extradited. The gruesomeness of the murder, the paltriness of the killers' profit, and the year-long search for the culprits kept the Affair of Gouffé's Trunk in the headlines, and while the trunk was on display in the Paris morgue about 20,000 people are said to have come to see it.

Gabrielle's defence tactics were to claim that her participation in the crime had been the result of a post-hypnotic suggestion planted by her lover, and that therefore she could not be held responsible for the crime. A team of psychologists examined her and concluded that she was simply a depraved character, mildly 'hysterical', but perfectly aware of what she was doing. In her defence, however, a professor of law, Jules Liégeois, was brought in to testify, at tedious length, that under hypnosis an impressionable subject is nothing more than an automaton. Her lawyers also stressed the age and gender difference, and pointed to her respectable background as the daughter of a middle-class tradesman (although in fact she seems to have long lost any shred of middle-class respectability). In other words, they played on the popular view of hypnotism as a means of depriving impressionable (i.e. female and young) people of their well-brought-up moral wills, while the best that Eyraud's defence could do, in a kind of parody of the arguments produced by Gabrielle's lawyers, was to claim that he had been led astray by her youth and beauty. Gabrielle was given twenty years, while Eyraud was put to death. The difference in the sentences does not, however, reflect any weight given to Liégeois's testimony, which fell on deaf ears; he was not even allowed to make a psychological assessment of the woman. More relevant to the judges, who had already been convinced by the panel of Parisian doctors, was the fact that Gabrielle had returned to give herself up to the police. It may also be worth noting that Liégeois's arguments, taken to their logical extension, undermine the whole notion of legal responsibility, which can't have gone down well with the judges.

During the course of his testimony, the enthusiastic Liégeois did not confine himself just to the facts of the case at hand, but launched into a spirited but complex theoretical attack on the views of his rivals, which provoked more of the same from his opponents. One wonders how the judges viewed this psychological wrangling. They could see that the Paris doctors were laying exclusive claim to medical professionalism and were accusing Liégeois of supporting charlatans such as stage mesmerists, but some of the intricacies may have left them cold. As we find time and again in the history of hypnosis, there were social undertones as well. Close to the surface at several points during the trial was the accusation that Liégeois's arguments strengthened the kind of anarchic lower-class movements which threatened the stability of the Third Republic.

This seemly wrangling was part of an ongoing debate. What had spilled over into the courtroom was an argument between two rival schools of psychology. Liégeois was an associate of Hippolyte-Marie Bernheim (1837–1919), the doyen of the Nancy school, who was unable to attend the trial himself because of ill health, while the opposing expert witnesses were friends and associates of Jean-Martin Charcot (1825–93) of the Paris Salpêtrière school. While the death sentence was inevitable for Eyraud, in Gabrielle's case the issue became not just her guilt or innocence, but the topic of hypnosis and coercion, which struck at the heart of the theories of the rival schools.

Liébeault and the Nancy School

Players of Scrabble like the word 'od', but few are aware of its origins. In the 1840s and early 1850s many educated Europeans were caught up in a wave of enthusiasm for the theories of an Austrian chemist, Baron Karl von Reichenbach (1788–1869). Having previously discovered paraffin and creosote, von Reichenbach announced in 1845 the discovery of a new force, od, which pervaded the universe, and which magnetized and sensitive subjects could see emanating from magnets and crystals. James Braid wrote a stunning reply in his pamphlet *The Power of the Mind Over the Body* (1846), in which he displayed the results of his counter-experiments and argued that von Reichenbach's subjects were suggestible people who produced the results the baron himself wanted to see. (Oddly enough, something similar to Reichenbach phenomena were still being investigated in La Charité Hospital in Paris, with the help of hypnotized subjects, at the end of the century, by J.B. Luys and Colonel de Rochas, until debunked by the English writer Ernest Hart, among others.)

Hypnotism was indeed in the doldrums, and remained there for some time. The excesses of Elliotson in Britain had condemned even Braid's views to obscurity, tarred with the brush of occultism and eccentricity. No medical man worth his salt would bother to investigate the matter, lest his career suffer. The only people who kept it alive were the stage mesmerists, but they attracted popular audiences, not academic kudos. But there was a certain amount of interest on the Continent in Braidism. Dr Durand le Gros (who wrote under the English pseudonym Phillips) wrote a book on the subject in 1860, which was well received in limited circles, and he also lectured in Belgium and France. At much the same time Eugène Azam was looking after a young girl known to posterity simply as Félida X., a hysteric who turned out to have multiple personalities. He used Braidian hypnosis on her and reported the case in the prestigious *Archives de médecine* for 1860. Azam told his friend, the eminent doctor Paul Broca, about his work, and Broca tested it for himself by carrying out a hypnotic operation. The results were impressive, but out of date: by now chemical agents were in almost universal use for surgery.

This flurry of medical interest was compounded in 1860 when Braid, who was by then close to death, sent a paper to be read at the French Academy of Sciences. The consequences of this modest move by Braid were enormous. In effect it initiated the whole modern movement of hypnosis, but it would take quite a few years for the impact to become public. In the audience was a doctor called Ambroise-Auguste Liébeault (1823–1904). Intrigued, he went home to the village near Nancy where he had his practice, and quietly experimented on his patients, in a special clinic set up in the peaceful surroundings of his garden. He came to realize that it was all suggestion. No induction process was required beyond suggestion – no hand passes, nor even Braidian fixation – and he found that suggestion effected cures too, in a great many cases, whether the disorder was organic or otherwise. His method was simply to look into the patient's eyes and assure him that his symptoms were cured. He thought that hypnotic sleep was the same as natural sleep, except that it was induced by suggestion, which focuses the attention on the idea of sleep. His views were strongly influenced by Braid: the concentration of the mind on a single idea, the idea of sleep, induces relaxation, the isolation of the senses from the external world, the arrest of thought and a distinct trance state. But he did not dismiss magnetism as a theoretical possibility.

Liébeault was an unusual man. The twelfth child of a peasant family from Lorraine, he had made a name for himself in his home village and the surrounding district as a man of integrity and a skilled doctor, and so had won a place in the ranks of the French medical establishment, which was still almost entirely dominated by the upper classes. Short, talkative, and with a peasant's dark complexion, he displayed the opposite of Mesmer's greed. He found that he earned enough money from his practice to offer hypnotism for free. Not surprisingly, he soon had plenty of patients. After five years of research he wrote a book on his findings.

Liébeault's book surely holds the record as the least successful publication of all time. It sold precisely five copies in its first five years. He was regarded (if he was known at all) as a quack for his hypnotism and a fool for his lack of concern about money. Nevertheless, he persevered, and continued to make use of hypnotism in his practice. There is a saying that dripping water hollows a stone not by using force but by just going on dripping, slowly and surely, and in 1882 Liébeault's long, quiet isolation came to an end when he was approached by the professor of internal medicine of the nearby University of Nancy. In actual fact, though, Hippolyte Bernheim was sceptical: surely hypnotism was the province of charlatans and fools. He sent a recalcitrant patient to Liébeault, to test him out. The patient was suffering from chronic sciatica, and Bernheim had been unable to cure him. His intention was to expose Liébeault as a fraud, but the man was cured to Bernheim's satisfaction. Bernheim was converted. He struck up a friendship with Liébeault and subsequently invited him to work at the university, where he cured him of his tendency to be attracted towards magnetism, by proving that unmagnetized vials of water were just as successful in bringing about cures as magnetized ones.

Between them, these two men developed the influential Nancy approach to hypnotism, which is the foundation of modern hypnotism. The basis of this view is that hypnotism works through suggestion – that is, that the psychological force of suggestion can influence even physical disorders. They were the first to call what they did 'psychotherapy'. Psychologically speaking, hypnotism involved, according to the Nancy school, the concentration of attention, or the 'nervous force', in various organs of the body and the brain. Their technique was a combination of permissiveness, in that they liked to win the patient's confidence, especially by letting him view other hypnotic sessions, and authoritarianism, in that they would commonly tell the patient to 'sleep' in a commanding tone of voice, and even hold his eyelids down for a while. Later, however, Bernheim was to find that suggestion was almost as effective even when the patient was awake. Interestingly, in order to contradict the view, prevalent among their contemporaries, that hypnotizability was a form of weakness to which mainly women were liable, Bernheim practised largely on male subjects. He found that hypnosis was easier to induce in those who were used to obedience, like soldiers.

Bernheim, who was short in stature, with friendly blue eyes, a moustache, goatee and soft voice, defined hypnosis as a state of suggestibility induced by suggestion. The book he wrote in 1884 has the distinction after all this time of being a model of clarity and a mine of information. It altered the course of hypnosis research for ever. Within a few years he and Liébeault were the centre of what was effectively an international school, though there were differences of opinion among them. In France there were the lawyer Jules Liégeois and the forensic medical expert Henri-Etienne Beaunis, who were particularly interested in the impact of suggestion on criminal responsibility. Abroad there were Albert Moll and Baron Albert von Schrenck-Notzing in Germany; Richard von Krafft-Ebing in Austria; C. Lloyd Tuckey and J. Milne Bramwell in Britain; Boris Sidis and Morton Prince in the USA; Vladimir Bechterev in Russia; Otto Wetterstrand in Sweden; Cesare Lombroso and Enrico Morselli in Italy; August Forel in Switzerland; Joseph Delboeuf in Belgium; A.W. van Renterghem in Holland – and this is to mention only the most prominent researchers, the pioneers who brought hypnotism into the modern era.

At home or abroad, however, Bernheim did not meet with ready acceptance, for all the clarity of his thought. There were powerful forces ranged against him. The war between physiology and psychology is far from over even now – are schizophrenics deranged or suffering from a chemical imbalance in the brain? Should certain violent criminals be acquitted because of their extra Y chromosome or deficient serotonin? Bernheim was simply on the side of psychology in one phase of the drawn-out fighting.

Charcot and the Paris School

If Bernheim and Liébeault are the heroes of this chapter, their opponent, Jean-Martin Charcot, is hardly an unmitigated villain. He was the most famous medical man in the world, and it was his interest in hypnosis that finally established it as a legitimate subject of scientific enquiry.

In 1862 Charcot was appointed chief physician to the Salpêtrière, an immense 100-acre complex on the left bank of the Seine, comprising forty-five run-down buildings, almost a town in its own right, with streets, squares and gardens, housing about 5,000 destitute, or insane, or senile, or disturbed women (the neighbouring Bicêtre housed men), who were jumbled together with no real attempt to classify their disorders and put them in separate wards. This was a paradise for a budding neurologist such as Charcot, but until he made it famous and added laboratories, a museum, and research and teaching units, it was an inferno most doctors wanted to avoid. Within twenty years, as a result of his numerous publications, and of the eminence of many of his pupils, he had achieved international fame and founded the science of neurology. He identified multiple sclerosis, increased understanding of poliomyelitis, had a neurological disorder named after him and so on and so forth.

Charcot, physician to kings and princes, was a small, stout, vigorous man with a big head, a bull's neck and a low forehead. He somewhat resembled Napoléon and liked to cultivate the similarity; he had no objection to his nickname, 'the Napoléon of the Neuroses'. Artistic and learned, with a famed collection of old and rare books on witchcraft and demonic possession, he was a spellbinding teacher and an authoritarian figure who couldn't stand criticism at home or at work. By the 1880s, he was surrounded by what has wittily been called a 'charcoterie' of adoring students, and his already huge prestige was enhanced by an aura of mystery and a reputation for achieving 'miracle' cures. Not only did he often display an uncanny insight into patients' disorders, but if he recognized a case of hysterical paralysis, he simply commanded the patient to throw away his crutches and walk.

The range of problems classed in the nineteenth century as 'hysteria' became Charcot's special field. It was a protean disorder, used to label a variety of different ailments, both organic and neurotic. Anyone liable to hallucinations, fainting, non-organic paralyses, or fits was likely to be classified as a hysteric. (Nowadays, what used to be called 'hysteria' is covered by four diagnostic categories: post-traumatic stress disorder, Briquet's syndrome, conversion disorder and dissociative disorder.) In order to bring order to the chaos, Charcot defined grand hysteria as involving three phases: a fainting fit, convulsions and intense expression of some emotion. Sometimes there was a fourth phase, of delirium, lasting up to several days. Charcot believed that hysteria was an organic disorder, the sign of a diseased brain, but a less retrogressive aspect of his work was to point out that men were just as liable to hysterical complaints as women; previously (as the etymology of the word, from the Greek for 'womb', shows) it was thought that only women were afflicted by hysteria. An important subclass of hysterics were somnambulists and those who were liable to fugue states, in which they might forget for a while who they were and take on a different personality, with neither of the two personalities having much or any memory of the other.

Charcot cured hysterics effectively by a kind of faith healing. So great was his fame and prestige that he had only to win the patient's confidence and encourage her, and half the battle was won. The other half consisted of various forms of treatment, which may have had a physical component, even though, again, the psychological component was what did the healing. For instance, if a hysteric was suffering from paralysis of the arm, Charcot would get him to exercise the paralysed arm; but since there was no organic damage to the arm, this too was a form of psychological healing. He came to believe that hysterical symptoms were caused by autosuggestion. To take a simple example, suppose a man sustains a slight injury at work – an injury that could have been worse. It preys on his mind: 'If I'd been a few centimetres to the left, my whole arm would have been crushed.' As a result, although the slight injury heals perfectly, his arm develops hysterical paralysis.

Charcot's friend Charles Richet, the recipient in 1913 of the Nobel Prize for medicine, persuaded him to try hypnosis on his patients. Having forged a connection between hysteria and suggestibility, Charcot was inclined, when he turned to consider the nature of hypnosis, to find further connections. He found that his patients entered one or another of three states of hypnosis – lethargy, catalepsy, somnambulism. Lethargy is total inertia, like the fainting phase of hysteria, but if the subject's eyes were opened, it passes into catalepsy, where the limbs retain any position imposed on them by the operator. This catalepsy he compared to hysterical paralysis, and another similarity with hysteria was that if the limbs of one of his hypnotized subjects were put into an aggressive position, aggressive thoughts and actions followed. Somnambulism was also related to hysteria, in the manifestation of anaesthesia: anaesthesia of the hand ('glove anaesthesia') or of the arm ('sleeve anaesthesia') was not uncommon among hysterics. Charcot concluded that hypnosis was an artificially induced modification of the nervous system which could be achieved only in hysterical patients and which manifested itself in three distinct phases (as above). It was this scientistic talk above all which gave an aura of scientific credibility to the previously taboo subject of hypnotism.

Charcot's interest in hypnosis, which began in 1878, was triggered not only by Richet's researches, but by the 'metallotherapy' of Victor Burq (1822–84) who proposed, among other things, that metals and magnets could be used either to inhibit or to bring on a trance state. The researches of Charcot and his colleagues (especially J.B. Luys) into metallotherapy form a bizarre footnote to the story of hypnosis. They found not only that hysterical anaesthesias, spasms and paralyses could be removed if the appropriate part of the body were touched with magnets or various metals, but also that symptoms could be transferred from one side of the body to the other. Charcot's student Joseph Babinski even found that symptoms could be transferred from one patient to another. Luys then developed an incredible therapy.

He would transfer the real symptoms of a hysteric patient to a hypnotized patient by drawing a magnet along a limb of the ill person and on to the corresponding limb of the healthy but

hypnotized one. The latter would assume not only the symptoms but also the personality of the hysteric. Then the somnambule would be awakened, the symptoms would vanish from
everyone, and the hysteric would assume her own personality,
without the paralysis or whatever else afflicted her.

Bernheim argued, to the contrary, that all these results were due to
suggestion.

In 1882, having already held a variety of chairs, Charcot was
appointed to the Chair of Diseases of the Nervous System, which
was created by governmental decree especially for him. In a bold
move, when he was up for election to the Academy of Sciences
in 1883 – the Academy which had a pretty consistent history of
condemning mesmerism – he presented to them a paper on hypnosis.
Perhaps his assimilation of hypnosis to hysteria, and his belief that
hysteria was an organic disease, made it more respectable: he could
claim that he wasn't talking about the forbidden topic of animal
magnetism, but a brain disorder which mimicked hysteria, another
brain disorder. He was elected, the dam burst, and from then on
hypnosis was a viable subject for scientific research. Psychology
became an academic discipline in its own right, distinct for the first
time from philosophy.

Charcot's prestige and the semi-public nature of his lectures
(which were often attended by members of high society and reporters) also catapulted hypnosis into the popular press, which indulged in
vivid descriptions of cataleptic patients and, later, lurid stories, often
false, of clairvoyance and sexual seduction under hypnosis. Charcot
was so famous that stage hypnotists advertised their shows as 'in the
manner of Charcot at the Salpêtrière'. Among other discoveries
Charcot reached as a result of using hypnosis on his patients, he
proved that psychological factors alone could cause some paralyses,
by suggesting a paralysis to hypnotized patients and demonstrating
that their symptoms were identical to those of organic paralyses, and
he was able to distinguish 'dynamic amnesia' (in which memories
can be recovered) from 'organic amnesia' (in which memories are
irrecoverable).

Charcot didn't invent the assimilation of hypnosis to hysteria.
Not only had many hypnotists in the past remarked that hysterics

are deeply hypnotizable, but at least one had pre-empted Charcot in defining hypnosis as a morbid state. The Salpêtrière researchers felt that they were just confirming all these hypotheses by careful experiments. But, seeking clarity, they used only the best subjects – about a dozen in all, all female hysterics, inpatients of the hospital, who displayed the three phases Charcot was looking for more or less perfectly. And there's the rub: he was already looking for the three phases, and this is not a scientific way of going about research, using only subjects who confirm your preconceived notions. In fact, it is not impossible that they were trying to please him by going along with his suggestions. The Salpêtrière was crowded, intimate; doctors and patients jostled one another in the wards and corridors, and patients inevitably overheard what the doctors were talking about, and then gossiped to other patients. Patients knew, then, what was expected of them in experiments. It is even unclear how often Charcot himself practised hypnosis on patients, rather than getting his assistants to prepare them in advance for him; it is possible, then, that the patients were more or less told by these assistants what the great man would expect from them. Charcot thought that the three phases of hypnosis occurred spontaneously, but in all probability both patients and his assistants were showing him only what he expected to see. Certainly no independent researcher has been able to corroborate his results.

At this point, Charcot's eminence obviously had pernicious results. Although he had succeeded in making hypnosis respectable, his theory that hypnosis was a form of hysteria was patently limited and false, and yet his eminence guaranteed that it received serious consideration. It even followed from Charcot's theories that, despite Liébeault's and Bernheim's string of remarkable cures, hypnotherapy was downgraded, because according to Charcot hypnosis could be dangerous, in that it could arouse latent hysteria. In any book on hypnosis, Charcot is bound to receive a bad press; while his important work on neurology goes almost unmentioned, his belief in metallotherapy and his misleading views on hypnosis are given prominence. He was a great man, one of the giants of nineteenth-century science; but like all great men, he had blind spots.

The Rivalry Between the Schools

Battle was joined between the two schools, and the Parisians, at any rate, waded in with unscholarly rancour, denouncing the Nancy school as provincial cranks and Bernheim's book as unscientific. Bernheim, in response, proved that Charcot's three stages or phases of hypnotism were an illusion. Here is one of Bernheim's measured statements against Charcot:

> The hypnotic condition is not a neurosis, analogous to hysteria. No doubt, manifestations of hysteria may be created in hypnotized subjects; a real hypnotic neurosis may be developed which will be repeated each time sleep is induced. But these manifestations are not due to the hypnosis, – they are due to the operator's suggestion, or sometimes to the auto-suggestion of a particularly impossible subject whose imagination, impregnated with the ruling idea of magnetism, creates these functional disorders which can always be restrained by a quieting suggestion. The pretended physical phenomena of the hypnosis are only psychical phenomena. Catalepsy, transfer, contracture, etc., are the effects of suggestion. To prove that the very great majority of subjects are susceptible to suggestion is to eliminate the idea of a neurosis.

To this Charcot and his colleagues could only make the weak reply that it was nonsensical to think that most of us are hypnotizable. On the offensive, the Paris school widened the attack and took in those who still adhered to magnetic views. They accused the magnetizers of being money-grubbing charlatans, but since not a few of them were priests it was hard to make the image stick. For their part the magnetizers, divided though they were on other issues, were unanimous in decrying Charcot's positivistic approach and the reduction of hypnosis to hysteria, and his voyeuristic displays of hysterical patients at the Salpêtrière. They said he was inducing hysterical attacks in his patients, rather than proving that hypnosis was hysteria, and joined Bernheim in arguing that Charcot's patients were complying with his suggestions. And in due course, for the ultimate good of hypnosis, the views of Charcot and his pupils at the Salpêtrière were gradually defeated by the Nancy school. After Charcot's death in 1893, one by one his former students and colleagues recanted their views, until by 1903 Bramwell was able to write simply: 'The views of the mesmerists and those of the Salpêtrière school have ceased to interest scientific men.'

In the law courts, however, when the question of the coercion of hypnotized subjects arose, the tables are turned. Here it is Charcot who is the hero, and Bernheim who seems to have barked up the wrong tree. Since Bernheim believed in the absolute power of suggestion over a susceptible subject, then, as his colleague Liégeois argued at the Gouffé trial, a hypnotized person might as well be an automaton – a tool without a will, as the Swedish psychologist Fredrik Björnström, a follower of the Nancy school, would later put it. Not only can a hypnotized person be a victim of crime, but she can be made to act against her conscience. But Charcot's researches led him to believe that a hypnotized person still has a functioning conscience, and so can be held accountable for his actions. Only in extreme cases of mental illness, which do not include hysterics, is the capacity for willed action lost. Bramwell, though sympathetic to the Nancy school, found himself as a result of his own experiments 'forced to abandon all belief in the so-called "automatism", or better termed "helpless obedience", of the subject'.

Bernheim likened the state of hypnotized automatism to the automatism of reflex action. This is certainly an exaggeration of the degree to which a subject, even a deeply hypnotizable subject, loses control. One of the weaknesses of all experiments designed to get subjects to perform antisocial actions is that the subjects presumably know in advance, or guess, that the circumstances are artificial and that no real danger is involved to themselves or others. Relatedly, Bernheim seems to me to have ignored the extent to which hypnotized subjects are capable of and may actually enjoy role-playing. Many of his most crucial tests smack too strongly of role-playing to be secure evidence. For instance, here is a section of his work with a man known simply as 'C.', who is identified only as a forty-four-year-old photographer:

I provoked a truly dramatic scene one day with him, as I was anxious to see just how far the power of suggestion went with him. I showed him an imaginary person at the door and told him that he had been insulted by him. I gave him an imaginary dagger (a paper-cutter) and ordered him to kill the man. He hastened forward and ran the dagger resolutely into the door, and then stood staring with haggard eyes and trembling all over. 'What have you done, unhappy man?' I said. 'He is dead, he is bleeding, the police are coming.' He stood terrified. He was led before an imaginary magistrate (my intern). 'Why did you murder this man?' 'He insulted me.' 'We do not kill the man who insults us. You must be complained of to the police. Did any one tell you to kill him?' He answers, 'M. Bernheim did.' I say to him, 'You are to be taken before the justice. You killed this man. I said nothing to you, you acted as your own master.'

The poor man is then taken before an imaginary judge. On another occasion, Bernheim, sounding rather like a stage hypnotist, got the same subject in rapid succession to imagine that he was a young boy, a young girl, a military commander, a priest and a dog. Each time C. does his eager best to comply.

But Bernheim's work with criminal cases was not all misguided. His emphasis on suggestibility also led him to be the first to recognize and clearly state that alleged criminals could be induced to make false confessions, and witnesses give false reports, in order to please their interrogators, and to suggest guidelines to check that no such falsification is taking place.

On the criminal potential of hypnotism, Gilles de la Tourette was the spokesman for the Salpêtrière in response to Nancy: he argued that subjects are play-acting, that hypnotism does not alter character. A famous event at the Salpêtrière seems to prove de la Tourette's point:

On one occasion Charcot had invited a distinguished audience of jurists, magistrates, and specialists in forensic medicine to a demonstration in the lecture theatre at the Salpêtrière. Blanche [Blanche Wittmann, Charcot's subject], in a state of somnambulism, had obediently performed the most bloodthirsty tasks,

1. John Barrymore as Svengali in the 1932 film of that name. The character was created by George du Maurier in his 1894 novel *Trilby*, and heightened the fears of Victorian matrons and maidens about Jews and the dangers of hypnosis.

2. Here Balsamo (Cagliostro) mesmerizes Lorenza, from Alexandre Dumas's novel *Joseph Balsamo*. It was firmly believed for most of the nineteenth century that women were more susceptible to hypnosis than men. Note the authoritarian pose of the mesmerist, and the sinister lighting.

3. This trick – the human plank, or full-body catalepsy – used to be a favourite of stage hypnotists. However, it is said to be possible even for non-hypnotized subjects.

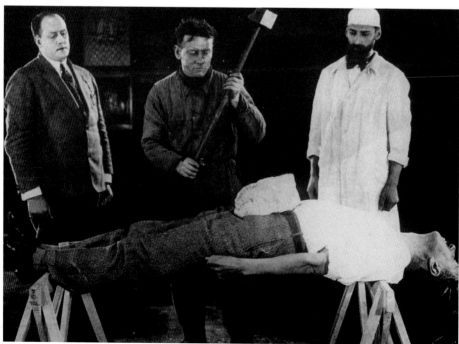

4. The remarkable ability of hypnosis to anaesthetize has been exploited by stage hypnotists as well as by doctors and surgeons.

5. Hallucination is a well-documented phenomenon of deep hypnosis. The hypnotist maintains the illusion that he is manipulating a material force, while the girl believes she is nursing a young man who believes he is a baby.

6. An American advertisement from the 1960s promises sexual conquest through hypnosis. In fact, though, it is impossible to make even a hypnotized subject go against her moral code.

7. Franz Anton Mesmer (1734–1815), the irascible and controversial prophet of 'animal magnetism' or 'mesmerism', and the forerunner of hypnosis.

8. The Marquis de Puységur (1751–1825) was at first a loyal disciple of Mesmer, but later developed his own techniques and theories, which became the bridge between mesmerism and hypnosis.

9. Orthodox mesmerists believed that the healing power of magnetism could be transmitted by purely mechanical means, as well as by a magnetist in person. Here patients surround a magnetized tub and apply the rods to the afflicted parts of their bodies. Note the lady on the left swooning in mesmeric crisis.

10. This engraving from a book published in 1790 clearly illustrates the belief that a mesmerist was passing a physical force to the patient he was trying to heal. Contemporary stage hypnotists still use hand passes, even though the theory of mesmerism has long been refuted.

11. In 1784 Benjamin Franklin headed a French commission which damned mesmerism as worthless. In this contemporary cartoon Franklin routs the mesmeric asses, demons, witches and lechers, whose tub (see illustration 9) lies broken in the centre.

12. At the height of the British 'mesmeric mania', it became a form of fashionable entertainment. Here an impassive mesmerist exerts control over young women and children, while men look on, and the rest of high society continues its social business.

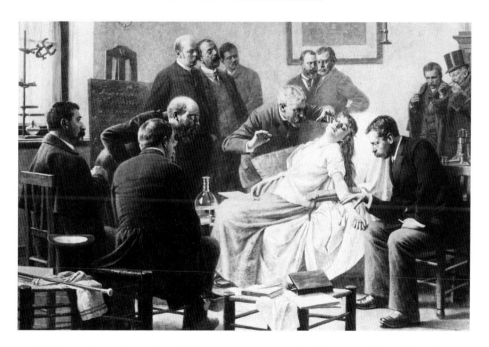

13. Fears about the vulnerability of a hypnotized subject manifested in subtle ways. This picture appears to show a group of Victorian scientists examining a hypnotized patient, but at second sight her posture and clothing are rather provocative, and at least one of the doctors is fascinated by her, while another caresses her arm, rather than taking her pulse.

14. John Elliotson (1791–1865) was a famous doctor who became the main champion of medical mesmerism in Britain. His excesses and stubbornness brought the whole topic into disrepute.

15. James Braid (1795–1860) showed beyond the shadow of a doubt that mesmeric theory was false, and thus ushered in the era of modern hypnotism.

16. Ambroise Liébeault (1823–1904, standing on the left), a French country doctor, was the first to apply Braidian methods extensively in a clinical context, and proved that suggestion alone can achieve all the cures and results that had previously been attributed to the physical force of magnetism.

17. Hippolyte Bernheim (1837–1919) was the academic from the University of Nancy who developed and corrected Liébeault's views. All modern hypnosis stems from his work.

18. Jean-Martin Charcot (1825–93), the 'Napoléon of the Neuroses', was the most famous medical scientist of his day. Although his theories about hypnosis were soon proved wrong, it was his influence above all which made hypnosis a respectable subject for academics to study.

19. Emile Coué (1857–1926) was the pioneer of autosuggestion as a means of attaining health and happiness. His most famous affirmation, 'Every day, in every way, I am getting better and better', is still very familiar.

20. Milton Erickson (1901–80) is the best-known hypnotherapist of the modern era. He aimed to bring out his patients' own unconscious resources for healing, and his methods are in wide use today in the hypnotherapeutic community throughout the world. Here he is shown with his younger colleague Ernest Rossi.

21. Theodore Barber is the contemporary American academic who has most vociferously attempted to demonstrate that there is no such thing as hypnosis or the hypnotic trance. He and his colleagues believe that subjects are merely strongly motivated to comply with the hypnotists' instructions.

22. Ernest Hilgard of Stanford University (here with his wife). His experiments have gone a long way towards proving that hypnotized subjects enter a special trance state which gives them some unusual abilities and faculties. But the issues will not finally be resolved until unique neurophysiological correlates are found for the hypnotic trance.

'shooting', 'stabbing', and 'poisoning'. The notables withdrew from a room littered with fictive corpses. The medical students who remained, being very like medical students in all times and places, then told Blanche (still in a state of somnambulism) that she was alone in the hall and should undress and take a bath. But Blanche, who had waded through blood without turning a hair, found this suggestion too infamous and came abruptly out of hypnosis.

It is certainly hard to see how Bernheim would account for this. It is clear, as I have had occasion to remark before now in this book, that even a deeply hypnotized subject is not wholly unconscious, and can resist the suggestions of the hypnotist if they are too outrageous or transgress the subject's ingrained moral code.

Hypnosis and Coercion

The question of the influence (for good or ill) that a hypnotist could have over his subject was not new. It had been simmering since the early days of mesmerism, when the Marquis de Puységur discovered the close rapport that is built up between operator and subject. Was the subject any more than a tool wielded by the magnetist? the mystic marquis wondered, and this of course immediately raised the spectre of sexual and criminal possibilities. Sexual energy also reared its head in the form of the attachment – transference, as Freudians would say – the subject might come to feel for her healer, and possibly the other way round too, as Dickens seems to have become attached to Augusta de la Rue. Opinion was divided even in the early days. D'Eslon believed that it would be possible for a magnetist to take advantage of a woman who had reached the crisis state (which, remember, was often orgasmic in nature anyway); de Puységur asked several of his somnambulists how far they would go, but they all said that while he could make them do something silly, such as hitting him with a fly-swat, he could not make them take off their clothes. The debate continued throughout the nineteenth century without resolving the issue.

Nineteenth-century fascination with mesmerism and hypnotism was tinged with fear, and novelists and stage hypnotists titillated that fear. Stage hypnotists made great play with phrases like 'You are totally under my control.' But if this was literally true, then anything could happen. A chaste Victorian maiden could be made to yield her virginity; a man could be turned into an assassin. These were precisely the scenarios hinted at or made explicit in fiction, in a series of books culminating in du Maurier's *Trilby* and Ambrose Bierce's short story 'The Hypnotist'. Class and racial considerations muddied the waters: the lower classes were supposed to have larger sexual appetites than the bourgeoisie, and so were more liable to want to take advantage of middle-class women, and Jews were supposed to make better mesmerizers. In 1878 a Jewish dentist in Rouen called Paul Lévy only made matters worse when he was sentenced to ten years for the unlikely crime of having raped one of his patients in his dentist's chair with her mother present in the room. But this was not a clear case of anti-Semitism: it seems that he did have sex with the daughter, while the mother was asleep, having persuaded them both that in order to help with the daughter's chronic dental problems he had first to find out whether Berthe, the daughter, was a virgin. This seduction was classified as rape because of his supposed hypnotic powers.

Once the phenomenon of post-hypnotic suggestion was recognized, the possibilities were doubled. Not only could a novelist have someone kill while actually hypnotized, but also while fully awake, as a result of a suggestion implanted earlier in his mind by an evil mesmerist. These were the fears that spilled over from the pages of novels and smoky theatres into the courts in the Gouffé affair, and at least one other notorious trial some years earlier – a case which, to the modern ear, sounds even less plausible than Gabrielle Bompard's defence.

In 1865 Timothée Castellan was an ugly, club-footed tramp who had been invalided out of his occupation as a cork-cutter and now roamed the countryside of southern France, near Toulon, as a vagabond healer. One evening he turned up at a house in the village of Guiols where a man lived with his fifteen-year-old son and twenty-six-year-old daughter, Josephine. Although Josephine was disgusted by the man's appearance, her father took pity on him and invited him to share the family supper and to sleep in the hayloft that night. During the evening several neighbours dropped by, attracted by Timothée's reputation as a magician. Actually, the man seems to have had delusions of grandeur, since he wrote on a scrap of paper that he was the Son of God. He was using sign language and writing to communicate, because he was pretending to be deaf and dumb.

In the morning Josephine's father and brother left for work, and Timothée too went on his way. But before long he returned and made himself at home again. Once more, some neighbours dropped in, and one of them observed the tramp making strange signs behind Josephine's back. According to Josephine's later report, after lunch Timothée hypnotized her, carried her into the back room and raped her. In the evening, much to the astonishment of the neighbours, Josephine left with Timothée, apparently to join him in his vagabond life. Over the next few days the odd couple were seen in the district, and Timothée boastfully displayed his power over the young woman by making her walk on all fours like a dog, laugh hysterically, and things like that. Her attitude towards him was a strange mixture of alternate affection and loathing. After a few days she escaped and returned home, where in due course she recovered from her fright. Timothée was arrested and at the trial respectable doctors testified that it was possible for one person to control another person as completely as Timothée appeared to have done Josephine. In a version of the normal nineteenth-century attitude towards women as the weaker, more hysterical, less rational gender, they made much of the fact that she was female and he was male. Timothée was found guilty and sentenced to twelve years of hard labour.

More recent experimental work has tended to show, however, that you cannot force a person under hypnosis to do something against his or her will. This is not surprising, given that you can't even hypnotize a person without her consent. What happens if you try to get her to act against her conscience is that she either wakes up or goes to sleep – but in either case she is refusing to cooperate. There appears to be some kind of internal monitor or sentinel which is never put to sleep and which finds a way not to obey commands which transgress the person's moral code. Perhaps it is the same psychological function as the 'hidden observer', which we met in Chapter 1. You might ask: 'Why, then, do people make fools of themselves in hypnotic stage shows?' The answer is that their inhibitions are lowered, and they feel that it is all just a bit of fun. But more extreme scenarios, in which a criminal hypnotizes a bank manager, let's say, to open a safe, are nonsense.

I may not be able simply to hypnotize you and get you to kill Mr Smith, but suppose that, using the common phenomenon of hypnotic hallucination, I redescribe Mr Smith to you, and make you see him as a chainsaw-wielding maniac who is threatening your loved ones, and . . . oh, look! You just happen to have a pistol in your hand . . . Or suppose (more remotely) that through hypnosis I can create a second personality in you, a hate-filled murderous personality.

Oddly enough, even this would not necessarily make it possible for me to get you to kill Mr Smith. Hypnosis may lower inhibitions, but it does not make you oblivious, and it does not rob you entirely of your critical faculties. Some part of you would still recognize that Mr Smith was just sitting peacefully in his study smoking a pipe, with not a chainsaw in view. But what about the fact that under experimental conditions hypnotized people have been persuaded to pick up dangerous snakes, throw acid at others, reveal fake military secrets, shout obscenities at others, mutilate the Bible, expose themselves, and steal examination papers? Here is a dramatic report from one of the main researchers in this area, American psychologist John Watkins. Watkins hypnotized a soldier during the Second World War and told him that when he opened his eyes he would be in a kill-or-be-killed situation with a 'dirty Jap soldier'. In actual fact, the person in front of him was a senior officer of the US army.

> The subject opened his eyes. He then slanted them and began to creep cautiously forward. Sudddenly in a flying tackle he dove at the Lieutenant Colonel, knocking him against the wall, and with both of his hands (he was a powerful, husky lad) began strangling the man . . . It took the instantaneous assistance of three others to break the soldier's grip, pull him off the officer, and hold him until the experimenter could quiet him back into a sleep condition.

On another occasion, when Watkins tried the same experiment with another subject, the man had a knife in his pocket, which he produced and tried – or pretended – to use against the 'Jap'. These experiments and all others like them are flawed, however. The participants know that they are involved in psychological experiments, and may be presumed to believe that the testers are responsible enough not really to be asking them to commit murder or whatever. Notice that in the experiment described above there were other people standing around, acting as reminders to the subject or some part of his mind that this was only an experiment. Other experimenters have made use of a glass barrier, protecting the 'victim' against thrown 'acid' and the subject from really handling venomous snakes. But in addition to the factor already mentioned, it is quite possible that the subject could see the glass – remember that a common effect of hypnosis is hyperaesthesia, the ability to perceive things which are normally hard to see. In any case, psychologist Martin Orne found that the same people who were prepared to endanger themselves and others under hypnosis were also prepared to perform identical actions while not hypnotized. Hypnosis adds nothing for criminals, then.

The most notorious and often alleged crime against a hypnotized victim is rape. (In the USA an advertisement used to run in magazines headed 'How to Get Girls Through Hypnotism', and offering a course in the subject. To make its point, the advertisement showed a voluptuous woman unbuttoning her clothes. In our more fetishistic era, things have turned around: the Web now offers videos showing 'dominant women' using hypnosis on happy, helpless men.) The topic of rape under hypnosis is tricky, because it is so easy to offend people – especially the victims, if you suggest that they might not be entirely innocent. Nevertheless, that is pretty much what I'm going to suggest; the evidence compels this conclusion.

Ever since the beginnings of hypnosis, in the days of animal magnetism, there have been rumours of hypnotists taking advantage of their patients. In Britain, just to bring things more up to date, there were the cases of Michael Gill in Wales in 1988, and of Nelson Nelson in north Devon in 1991; both of them set themselves up as hypnotherapists and had sex with a number of their patients. Gill's case was more or less dropped because of the difficulty of deciding whether the three women involved had consented at all. Nelson's case is particularly distressing, since his crimes were spread over a number of years and locations – he was fifty-seven when he was convicted in 1991 and had already fled to this country from South Africa, where he was known as Nelson Lintott – and involved possibly as many as 200 victims, some of whom were under age, since he had a distinct preference for teenagers. As the manager of a health club or a swimming pool, he would offer himself as a hypnotherapist for minor problems such as nail-biting or nicotine addiction, and pursue things from there.

Now, I've been claiming throughout this book that a hypnotized person does not lose control, so what is going on in these rape cases? Clearly, the victims were conscious, otherwise they would not be able to report the rape afterwards. They claim afterwards to have been conscious, but in a state of such profound lethargy that they could not be bothered to resist, and some scientists have theorized that in some deeply hypnotizable subjects hypnosis can cause muscular inhibition to such an extent that a person might be unable to fight back, even if she wanted to (I shall use 'she' and 'her' for the victim throughout this discussion of rape, although there have been cases of male-on-male rape too). Let's look at a particular report, with apologies for the graphic nature of the woman's words. In a previous session, the therapist had caressed her breasts. Nevertheless, she went back again:

> I felt heavy, like the other time. He told me that I would like to unbutton my blouse and pants. I didn't do it, but then he said that I would like to prove and show that the first treatment sessions really had helped me [she had gone to him with sexual problems]. He caressed my breasts again and after a while pulled down my pants and panties and he even put his hand in my vagina. I heard him say, 'You will go deeper and deeper and become more excited.' I just said yes to everything. He kept on going and wanted me to take his genitals in my hands. I said no, I would rather not, I'm scared. I was very scared. After a while I held his penis, he caressed me and rubbed his lower body against the inside of my legs.

In Chapter 1 I spoke of the double-edged feeling most subjects of hypnosis experience. One part of you knows you need not go along with the hypnotist's suggestions, and another part of you simply can't be bothered to resist. It seems clear that this woman was in exactly that state. But you *can* snap out of it if you want to; your will to do so may be lowered, but it is not removed.

Let's look at things from another angle too. The hypnotherapists presumably knew enough about hypnosis to know that it doesn't cause oblivion, and so that their patients would know they were being sexually interfered with. In that case, for the hypnotherapists to proceed with rape, they must be deeply stupid people, although some of them do rather ineptly try to induce post-hypnotic amnesia. No doubt some are that stupid, or desperate, but again it does look as though there might have been a degree of consent given by the victim. I'm not trying to justify these cases of rape, but to understand them. And the whole emotive issue needs to be put in the context of some impersonal statistics. In anonymous surveys, up to 5 per cent of all doctors admit to having had sex with a patient, and up to 10 per cent to having got as far as kissing and cuddling. There is something about the doctor–patient relationship which makes a patient vulnerable to her doctor's charms. Suppose, then, that roughly the same number of sexual acts go on in a hypnotherapist's office as in a regular doctor's office. A proportion of these cases are then reported to the police because, looking back, the victim felt abused because of her lethargy. Because of the reputation of hypnosis, she probably expected her will to be undermined, and it is clear that the therapists involved encouraged that belief.

The notion that the victim is not always as unwilling as she later makes out is borne out by the best-documented cases. There is invariably a high degree of ambiguity about the reports alleged hypnotic rape victims give. Why did she go back for a second or third session? Why did she say no but do nothing about it? Why did she take so long before going to the police? Real-life situations are emotionally complex, and this makes it extremely difficult to come to any conclusions about coercion (sexual or otherwise) under hypnotism from experimental evidence, because it is virtually impossible to reproduce real-life conditions in the laboratory. But the majority of the evidence accumulated by recent researchers suggests that the only sensible conclusion to draw is that while it is impossible to get an innocent person to commit murder or submit to sex, it is possible to lower someone's inhibitions, so that if she was inclined towards murder or sex anyway, she might go along with it. Like any doctors who have had sex with their patients, the hypnotherapists involved in these cases are guilty of abuse of trust and abuse of authority; but it is not clear that they are guilty of rape, if that means forcibly having sex with an entirely unwilling victim.

This conclusion is in line not just with contemporary research, but with an important study published in the *Archiv für Criminal-Anthropologie und Criminalistik* for 1900 by von Schrenck-Notzing. As well as discounting the possibility of hypnotic murder, he found the same ambiguities in the grey area of hypnotic rape. To cite just one of his cases:

> A certain patient writes in his autobiography that he rendered a young woman, who was tied to a decrepit old man, deeply somnambulic, and commanded her during this condition to perform certain onaninstic manipulations with his genital organs. This she did, but did not remember anything about it after awakening. The sexual intercourse was continued for three months, and was not discovered. The lady, however, possessed a passionate disposition, and loved her seducer. He would in all probability have been able to possess her in the waking condition as well. He chose this peculiar hypnotic way, as he feared detection.

Contemporary arguments about whether it is possible to get a hypnotized subject to commit antisocial acts under coercion echo nineteenth-century debate, though generally with more sophistication and the backing of more experimental data. Bernheim and other members of the Nancy school – notably Liégeois and Forel – conducted numerous experiments designed to show that a hypnotized subject could commit crimes. With the sense of melodrama that seems to characterize the reports of many such researchers, including Watkins, Liégeois once began one of his reports: 'I am to blame for having tried to have my friend, M.P., killed – and as if that was not serious enough, I did so in front of the commissary general of Nancy.' But whether old or new, the discussion can only reach an impasse, since how you read the evidence depends on your predisposition. If a hypnotized subject commits an antisocial act, this may be taken only to prove that he was the kind of person to do so anyway; if a hypnotized subject fails to commit an antisocial act, this may be taken only to prove that he was a poor hypnotic subject, or that the hypnotist was incompetent. In other words, whichever position you want to argue for, you can come up with a conclusive argument.

Obedience to Authority

Although I am inclined, then, to dismiss such fears about hypnotism, they do raise a particularly interesting issue. It is a frightening fact that most of us are prepared to go considerably further than we would like to think in obedience to an authority figure – as the German people discovered in the Second World War. In his famous, disturbing book *Obedience to Authority* Stanley Milgram describes a series of experiments he conducted in the psychology department of Yale University in the 1960s. Of two people, one plays the role of 'teacher', the other of 'learner'; they have been told that they are taking part in a study of memory and learning. The teacher asks the learner questions, and is told by the psychologist, an authority figure, to administer an electric shock when the learner gets an answer wrong. The voltage is increased every time a wrong answer is given. The teacher is encouraged to believe that this will help the learner correct his mistakes, and the psychologist gradually becomes more insistent that the punishment is applied. In actual fact, though, the learner is an actor, and the impressive electrical machine, with complex dials and switches, delivers no shocks. But the teacher doesn't know this, and Milgram found that many people – over 60 per cent – were quite prepared to administer dangerous doses of electricity in obedience to the psychologist's demands, and so to ignore their own conflict at the belief that the learner was suffering. Milgram played with variables, such as the visibility or invisibility (and inaudibility) of the learner and his increasingly agonized shrieks and pleas for the experiment to stop. An even higher proportion, about 90 per cent, were prepared to go all the way when it was not they themselves, but a third party who was manipulating the dial that was supposed to administer the shocks: they could more easily console themselves that they were not responsible. About 65 per cent went all the way even when they believed that the learner had a weak heart. When the authority figure of the experimenter was removed, or two experimenters gave contradictory orders, no subject administered a potentially dangerous level of shock, even if the learner insisted on it. The subjects of these experiments were not monsters; they were ordinary people, you and me.

But even this should not raise the hopes of a would-be hypnotizing criminal. Note, first, that it ruins a great many fictional scenes – the kind in which a stranger on a train hypnotizes an innocent young woman and . . . just then the train enters a tunnel and draws a discreet veil of darkness over what happens next. This kind of instantaneous overcoming of moral barriers just cannot happen. It takes time and patience, or at least conformity with established patterns, even to try to establish oneself as a valid authority figure. In the second place, it is not at all likely that the criminal would succeed in investing himself with the right kind of authority.

There are a number of variables, above all the following: how suggestible the subject is; how deeply hypnotizable the subject is; how good a hypnotist the operator is; how deeply embedded the criminal suggestions are; the usual character and tendencies of the subject (that is, does she already have criminal tendencies?); the temporary condition of the subject. Only if all these variables fell into line would hypnotized crime be possible – and note that even then it would not be involuntary criminal action, since by one of the conditions the subject must already have criminal tendencies.

In short, hypnosis would be a very erratic tool of crime. There is no guarantee of success. The same goes, by the way, for hypnotic amnesia, which one could imagine might also be useful in criminal circumstances. It is true that a hypnotist can plant a suggestion that his subject will not remember something later, but success is not assured, and in any case another hypnotist (working for the police, perhaps) could come along and recover the memory.

Not all thrillers, simply *qua* thrillers, make sensationalist and inaccurate use of hypnosis. Ian Rankin's *Knots and Crosses* breaks the mould by simply having a hypnotist unlock the suppressed memories of a traumatized policeman, enabling him to solve the case. But *The Mesmerist*, by Felice Picano, is a thriller which exploits every single cliché about hypnotism. Set in the early years of this century in a small town in Nebraska, the mesmerist of the title, Dinsmore, has the ability to make men and women his puppets for life. He uses his skills for the purposes of sexual domination and to gain political control; he can drive people to suicide and murder; he can hypnotize them in an instant merely by reflecting the sun off his cufflinks into their eyes. They often suffer from negative after-effects. At one point, towards the end of the book, he hypnotizes a whole crowd of 300 people, including a man previously found to be unhypnotizable, by glinting the sun off the manacles binding his hands. Such clichés are finally condemned by their own unreality, for if there ever had been a Dinsmore, he would by now control the whole world.

In addition to the question whether a hypnotized person could be made to commit a crime, there is also the question whether a hypnotist could use his powers to commit a crime against the subject, for instance by getting him to commit suicide. This is more plausible. A hypnotist could tell a subject to drink a glass of water which was really poison (but he could do that anyway, without hypnosis), and in a more extreme scenario might even be able to get him to self-induce a heart attack. This, as far as I can see, is the only possible criminal use of hypnosis – but it is pretty implausible. The hypnotist would have to have taken time to build up a relationship of trust with his subject, which would involve either disguising his hostility (even against hyper-sensitivity) or being a supposed friend in the first place. I know of no such cases ever having come to light.

'Hypnotized' Criminals in the Twentieth Century

In the nineteenth century, fears about hypnotism were such that it was occasionally invoked successfully as a defence in court cases. In 1879, for instance, a young man, who was a patient of a hypnotherapist, exposed himself in a public lavatory. When his case came to court, in France in the early 1880s, he was held to have suffered an attack of spontaneous somnambulism and amnesia, and was acquitted. Times have changed.

Two of the most notorious serial killers of recent times, Kenny Bianchi and Angelo Buono, worked as a pair and were known as the Hillside Stranglers. In the late 1970s they terrorized Los Angeles, until their capture in 1979. Now, the late 1970s were also characterized by a higher degree of sympathy towards alleged 'multiples' (people with MPD, multiple personality disorder), and this had even been success-fully used as a defence, as a form of insanity. Bianchi and his lawyers seized on this. Bianchi did his homework by reading *The Three Faces of Eve* and seeing the movie *Sybil*. He was examined by a psychologist who was professionally sympathetic towards the genuineness of MPD, and hypnotized. Under hypnosis he duly produced an alternate personality. The prosecution lawyers, however, were convinced that Bianchi was faking. They brought in Dr Martin Orne, director of the Unit for Experimental Psychiatry in Philadelphia, a world-renowned expert on hypnosis. He watched the videotape and decided Bianchi did not know enough about hypnosis to fake it successfully. He tested Bianchi under hypnosis – and Bianchi failed the tests. For instance, when asked to hallucinate his lawyer sitting in the chair next to him, he loudly expressed surprise when it was pointed out to him that his lawyer was actually standing at the back of the room. Hypnotized people do not do this; one of the standard features of the hypnotic trance is what is called 'trance logic', the ability to accept anomalous situations. In another test, Bianchi was hypnotized and told that a particular area of his hand, within a drawn circle, was anaesthetized, while the rest of the hand was not. With eyes closed, he was asked to say 'Yes' when he was touched outside the circle, and 'No' when he was touched within the circle. This was a trap, because anyone who was genuinely anaesthetized would say nothing when he was touched in the numb area, since he couldn't feel it. But Bianchi duly said 'No'. He failed other tests too – and both he and his cousin Buono were subsequently sentenced to life imprisonment without the possibility of parole. Courts are no longer quite so gullible about hypnosis as they were in the nineteenth century.

In the 1966 trial of Dr Carmelo Coppolino in New Jersey on the charge of murdering Colonel Farber, his lover, the colonel's wife, claimed to have been hypnotized by the good doctor and instructed to kill her husband. The court rejected this argument on the grounds that she could not be made to kill her husband against her will, and in any case what she was calling hypnotism was probably no more than strong sexual attraction. Coppolino was acquitted, by the way – but later found guilty in Florida of killing his own wife.

In the 1981 *United States* v. *Phillips* the defendant was charged with having shot and almost killed two US marshals in an attempt to help her husband escape as he was being brought into a federal courthouse. She claimed that she had been hypnotized by her husband, and her husband admitted having hypnotized her many times for a number of years. This defence did Ms Phillips no good, and she was found guilty.

One of the most amusing cases occurred in 1959 when two escaped prisoners were caught. One of them, Thomas Marsh, claimed to have been hypnotized by the other, whose name was Jack Cox. Cox claimed that the escapes were all the result of a bungled hypnotic experiment. In an attempt at age-regression, he had told Marsh to go back to where he was happy. Marsh had taken the instructions literally and walked out of prison! Realizing what he had done, Cox had followed him to explain the mistake and persuade him to return to prison before he got into trouble. This cunning defence was rejected by the court.

In a somewhat similar case, from Copenhagen in the 1950s, the court's verdict was rather more ambiguous. One criminal, who is referred to only as H in the transcript of the case, met another, N, in prison. They shared a cell and H came completely under N's influence. N hypnotized H repeatedly, and continued doing so after they left prison. N got H to rob a bank, and during the robbery two bank officials were shot. When the case came to trial (in a state of disorientation, H had allowed himself to be caught), N was sent to prison, but on the grounds that he was insane, or in a state comparable to insanity, H was committed to a lunatic asylum. This was hardly an acquittal, though, as might have happened in the nineteenth century.

Hypnotism is not a truth serum: it cannot make you unwittingly reveal all the skeletons in your cupboard, your deepest and darkest sexual fantasies, your youthful dreams and misdemeanours. You can even lie when hypnotized, either deliberately or unconsciously, in the sense that you might be recovering pseudo-memories. Some of the fears surrounding hypnotism are justified, but only to this limited extent: hypnotism cannot make you do things that are utterly contrary to your nature, but it can lower your inhibitions to the extent that you might do things you would otherwise have stopped yourself doing.

8

Psychic Powers and Recovered Memories

This chapter is going to seem a little strange to some readers, but no history of hypnotism would be complete without covering, in even more detail, the topic of the paranormal abilities which have been claimed, ever since Mesmer's time, to be awoken in certain hypnotized subjects. The theory underlying the supposed connection between hypnosis and paranormal feats is not in itself implausible. In hypnosis the subject's attention is withdrawn from all the distractions of the outside world and allowed to focus on fewer stimuli. Perhaps this withdrawal from the outside world allows it to uncover reaches of the mind which are not normally in play, because we are normally too distracted by sensory data and so on. It is at any rate clear that our sensory apparatus and ego systems are designed as much as anything as filters, to limit the amount of material getting through. What might happen if those filters are removed? This is the kind of question the occult mesmerists were asking themselves from early in the nineteenth century.

Not that the belief that hypnosis can trigger or develop occult powers is confined to the nineteenth century. In the twentieth century, we find perhaps the most dramatic and well-known instance of this belief realized in the person of Edgar Cayce, the most famous clairvoyant, prophet and healer of the century. In 1898, at the age of twenty-one, Cayce was suffering from a gradual paralysis of his throat muscles and had nearly lost his voice. A travelling hypnotist was called in to treat the young man. Under hypnosis, Cayce manifested a quite different personality, and began to exhibit the powers that he went on to use for the next forty-three years, until his death, starting with clairvoyant self-diagnosis and diagnosis of others. And the idea that there is a connection between hypnotism and psychic powers has been perpetuated by bestselling authors such as Jane Roberts, who channels an entity called Seth, and is recognized to be one of the more sober and sane channellers. Two chapters of her first book, *How to Develop Your ESP Power* (1966), are devoted to the use of hypnotic trances to achieve heightened states of awareness and to uncover the deeper reaches of the human psyche.

Two related claims are made for hypnosis in the context of psychic abilities: it can bring out such abilities in anyone, and it can greatly increase the abilities of someone who is already naturally psychic. The first claim is the one that has dominated the minds of researchers; the second has only occasionally been explored in the West, but more in pre-glasnost days in Russia and Czechoslovakia, as reported in the bestselling book *Psi: Psychic Discoveries Behind the Iron Curtain*, by Sheila Ostrander and Lynn Schroeder. However, the modern pioneer of parapsychology, J.B. Rhine, of Duke University, eventually found that hypnosis did not significantly increase ESP performance (ESP stands for 'extra-sensory perception'), and most recent works on parapsychology tend to ignore hypnosis more or less completely. The only qualification that needs to be made is the one I made before: there does seem to be a correlation between increased ESP performance and a slightly unfocused, relaxed mental state. If, as seems likely, hypnosis could help a subject reach and maintain that state of mind, then there could be a significant link between hypnosis and ESP.

Although I could write this chapter from the standpoint of an objective reporter, I feel inclined to begin by confessing my own position. Like any healthy-minded investigator, I adopt the simplest explanation for things. Paranormal faculties are very often *not* the simplest explanation. Let's go back to John Elliotson and the O'Key sisters in the middle of the nineteenth century. When handed half a dozen lumps of metal in a random order, they could tell which one had been magnetized by Elliotson. Were they psychic? It would be hard to prove it on the basis of this test. It is more likely that the 'magnetized' piece of metal retained more warmth from Elliotson's hands than the other pieces, since he had to hold it to magnetize it, and the O'Keys responded on the basis of this perceived warmth.

Or again, at several times in the history of hypnotism a prize has been offered for any hypnotist who could successfully prove to a scientific committee that his subject possessed clairvoyant powers. Not a single one of these prizes has been claimed, and contestants who came forward sometimes proved their charlatanism by refusing to let the committee use their own blindfolds. In all such cases, it blunts Occam's razor not to suppose that these 'clairvoyants' were mere conjurers, peeping out from slight cracks around their blindfolds.

It is important to be clear what is at issue here. The question is this: does the hypnotic state involve nothing more than an imagined fantasy on the part of the subject, which, however compelling, has no reality outside his or her imagination? Or does the hypnotized subject have the ability to transcend the imagination – indeed, to transcend all normal states of mind – and touch on some higher level of reality? All professional academic psychologists today would react straight away by claiming that this is a non-issue – that there is no question of such transcendence, only of vivid fantasy.

I maintain that inexplicable things happen in everyone's lives. One of the most hard-boiled people I know is in fact one of the most psychic people I know. We have all experienced telepathy, or psychometry (picking up 'vibes' from a room), or something. Most often such experiences are brushed under the carpet, because they are immensely threatening to the world in which we normally live. They are threatening because, if such things are possible, what else might be possible? The safe, tidy world view we have constructed over the years seems to blur and crumble at the edges. For most of us, such experiences are rare; for the few they may be more common. It is the same in the history of hypnosis. For all the obvious charlatans, there are cases that cannot easily be rationalized, and enough of them to make anyone with an open mind pause before dismissing the whole domain as fantasy and rubbish.

A Historical Survey of the Main Paranormal Abilities

Although Mesmer himself largely refrained from commenting on the apparent mystical effects of magnetism, his disciples and successors, starting with the Marquis de Puységur, were not so modest, and made enormous and often far-fetched claims about the arousal of paranormal abilities in their mesmerized subjects. These abilities ranged from the ability to see through closed eyelids, via self-diagnosis of ailments, to clairvoyance, telepathy and spiritist contact with the dead. This occult or mystical tendency was fed by the mystical movements current at the time (the ideas of, especially, Swedenborg, the German mystic Jacob Boehme and Saint-Martin), by the Romantic revolt against the Industrial Revolution, the 'dark satanic mills', and by von Schelling's nature-philosophy. These thinkers boosted the mystical strand of mesmerism by giving it a voice and grounding it in respectability.

The mystical mesmerists relied heavily on the publication of case histories to prove their point, most of which involve the mesmerized individual (usually a young woman) clairvoyantly seeing something that was happening a long way off in space, but simultaneous in time. These visions could be either spontaneous, or sought for in an experimental manner. Some of them concern events elsewhere in France, say, but there are also bizarre reports of journeys to the moon and elsewhere, and descriptions of beings and civilizations there. There are also spiritist reports of contact with the dead. Typical is the work of the magnetist Justinus Kerner with the famous Seeress of Prevorst, covered in Chapter 4. As happened with others, the Seeress's remarkable gifts were triggered by magnetism, which was initially employed in an attempt to alleviate her pitiful and chronic physical ailments.

In France the mystical mesmerists added to the German repertoire a variety of parlour tricks, including playing card games while blindfolded, and reporting on the personal history of the owner of a random object handed to them. But French somnambulists had their more serious side too, and there are reports of dramatic clairvoyant solutions to crimes. Madame Morel was a famous hypnotic clairvoyant in the 1910s. She helped police locate missing persons, sometimes describing their whereabouts in minute detail. Once, on being given a book by a third party, she gave an accurate account of the owner, and how he had died in battle. The French could also on occasion rise to the spiritist and bizarre heights of their German counterparts. The closest parallel to the Seeress of Prevorst is the remarkable Adèle Maginot, who on one occasion 'travelled' to Mexico, complained how hot the sun was, and was found on her 'return' to have one side of her face tanned as if by the sun. Never mind the uncritical researchers of the Puységurian era – even sober academics later in the century were not immune to the lure of clairvoyance. Pierre Janet hypnotized a supposedly clairvoyant subject, Léonie B., and asked her to travel from Le Havre, where they were, to Paris, and to visit the laboratories of his friend Charles Richet. She cried out: 'It's burning. It's burning.' This was true: there had been a fire in Richet's laboratory on that very day.

Psychometry is the psychic reading of the 'vibrations' or whatever given off by objects. The word was coined by the American writer on mesmerism Joseph Rodes Buchanan (1814–99), the founder of the remarkable-sounding Eclectic Medical Institute of Covington, Kentucky. The Mexican seeress known in the annals of the American Society for Psychical Research only as Señora Reyes de Z. was one of the most famous psychometrists. Once, in a controlled experiment, she was hypnotized and handed four pieces of pumice stone, cut from the same lump, which had been subjected to different treatments in the prior weeks. The first had been soaked in a tincture of gentian and asafoetida; the second had been put inside a clock; the third had been rolled in sugar and saccharine; the fourth had been heated by burning sulphur. When presented with these four pieces of pumice, she reported that the first gave her an impression of taste, the second of rhythmic sounds, the third of sweetness, and the fourth of heat and sulphur dioxide. She was just as accurate with objects which were inside closed boxes.

It's often hard to distinguish telepathy – the inexplicable communication of two minds – from clairvoyance or psychometry. Consider again the case of Señora Reyes de Z. Was she 'reading' the stones, or picking up from the minds of those around her what they knew of the recent history of the stones? What we would now call 'telepathy' (the word was coined in the late nineteenth century by Frederic Myers) is part of what was in earlier times called 'sympathy'. Sympathy was one of the most popular phenomena of Victorian times, as we have seen. It is the phenomenon whereby, even though the subject may be desensitized himself, he still responds to stimuli applied to the operator: if the operator's arm is raised, the subject's arm is raised; if the operator's sole is tickled, the subject giggles. All this, of course, goes on behind the subject's back.

In his book *Psychical Research*, published in 1911, Sir William Barrett reports an experiment in which he played a part in 1870. A child was hypnotized and given instructions to respond to no one else who was in the room other than Barrett. Once this rapport was established between Barrett and the child, Barrett took a number of different substances and put them in his mouth – salt, sugar, ginger, pepper and so on. The child accurately sensed each of the tastes in her own mouth. Perhaps the child could see what was going on; we have no record of how far apart the two of them were. But in later experiments Barrett tested other subjects' ability to 'see' playing cards that he was seeing. One subject had a 100 per cent success rate even when the two of them were in different rooms. In another experiment, a blindfolded hypnotized boy could tell which parts of Barrett's body were being pricked by a pin, to an astonishingly high degree of accuracy. In France Pierre Janet was conducting similar experiments, and in Germany Dr Albert von Notzing (later von Schrenk-Notzing) conducted experiments for paranormal faculties in a hypnotized subject, Lina, which caused such controversy that the police threatened to dissolve the Society for Scientific Psychology (Gesellschaft für wissenschaftliche Psychologie) under whose auspices he was working. Von Notzing's experiments were truly remarkable: Lina felt the pain of others being pricked behind her back with a pin, in the exact places where they were being pricked; she reproduced drawings made behind her back; she received precise telepathic communications, such as the instruction to go to the bookshelves and open a particular book at a particular page.

Peculiarly, much the same sympathy sometimes obtained between a hypnotized subject and an inanimate object. The subject held a glass of water (or an apple or something) and was told to drain all the feeling from her arm into the water. When the water was pierced by a needle, she reacted, but when her own arm was pricked by the needle she felt no pain. In this experiment, good results were obtained even when the glass was taken into another room, out of sight of the subject, in case she could see through or around her blindfold.

Telepathic hypnotism – the ability to hypnotize someone from a distance, even when she doesn't know that the experiment is taking place – was taken very seriously in the nineteenth century, though far less work was done on it in the last century. At the end of the nineteenth century, in the era of more reliable experiments, even mainstream scientists such as Janet and Bernheim were doing research into this area. Janet claimed that it had worked for him, though not with perfect consistency, while Bernheim regretted that it hadn't for him. Janet experimented with telepathic hypnotism over various distances, from near by to a mile away, and achieved a high degree of success.

Ostrander and Schroeder report that certain Russian and Bulgarian scientists were experimenting with telepathic hypnotism from the 1920s to the 1960s, and achieved successes at distances of up to 1,000 miles. It's hard to know what controls there were on these experiments. For instance, in one experiment, the subject was lowered into a kind of lead casket, and the experimenter, Professor Leonid Vasiliev, found that he could still entrance him; but with all this elaborate preparation, the subject must have known what was going on, and have been prepared to go under. More impressive – astonishing, in fact – are reports of telepathic hypnotism where the subject was completely unaware that she was the subject of any such experiment, but still fell into a trance. But (even assuming these reports are valid) the scientists acknowledge that very few of us are susceptible to telepathic hypnotism, so there is little cause for alarm: you are not going to be prevailed upon in this way by an unknown assailant!

One subject in Czechoslovakia apparently gained such telekinetic abilities that he could kill birds at a distance by focusing his will upon them. This particular story is unsubstantiated, at the level of hearsay and rumour, but personally I have no doubt that this kind of thing can happen. Once, years ago, at the only time of my life when I was experiencing various psychic phenomena, I was distracted from deep meditation by the buzzing of a large fly. I willed it to go away – or perhaps I cursed it, though no actual words were involved, out loud or in my mind. There was a 'plop' beside me on the cushion, and I opened my eyes to find a dead bluebottle.

Channelling is the modern term for what in the past would have been called acting as a medium, or contacting spirits. The late-Victorian craze for spiritism grew naturally out of the mid-Victorian mania for mesmerism, because so many hypnotized subjects appeared to be acting as mediums. It was only when table-rapping and other spiritist phenomena that did not require a hypnotized subject became popular that the two fields became separated, and interest in spiritism waxed and the other waned. I have to confess that this is the area about which I feel most sceptical, because I do not believe that the dead survive in a form that allows them to be contacted, because it is impossible to set up objective experiments to prove or disprove that so-and-so was in touch with Aunty Ada (deceased), and because the whole domain has been riddled by charlatanism and wishful thinking since its beginnings. By 'wishful thinking' I mean that it is obvious to most people that most mediums are in touch with nothing more than a secondary personality of their own.

The Society for Psychical Research

By the end of the nineteenth century, largely thanks to mesmerism and hypnotism, there was enormous interest in paranormal phenomena, the so-called 'higher' phenomena of hypnotism. But the whole domain was, of course, saturated with cranks and charlatans. Nevertheless, a number of more respectable thinkers were interested, and wanted to put the subject on a more professional, respectable and academic footing. In Britain, in 1882, chiefly thanks to the initiative of the classicist Frederic Myers (1843–1901), the justly world-famous

Society for Psychical Research (SPR) was established. This was followed two years later by the foundation, instigated by the eminent Harvard psychologist and philosopher William James (1842–1910), of the American Society for Psychical Research (ASPR).

Right from the outset hypnotism was central to their concerns, and the first twelve or so volumes of the British Society's *Proceedings* contain a number of important articles on mesmerism and hypnosis, not just as they impinge on paranormal phenomena, but in the domain of what would now be recognized as straight psychology. Myers's posthumously published enormous work *Human Personality and Its Survival of Bodily Death* (1903) shows what the impetus was behind their research on hypnotism. More aware than most of the vast potential of the human mind, Myers argues that the subliminal mind (whose reality he was one of the first to establish) borders not only on our normal consciousness, but on a larger world where contact with other minds is possible, and where extraordinary faculties reside. The clairvoyant abilities of hypnotized subjects seemed to him to compel such a conclusion.

The SPR very soon formed a committee of highly respected and respectable academics for the 'study of hypnotism, and the forms of so-called mesmeric trance, with its alleged insensibility to pain, clairvoyance and other allied phenomena'. The task they set themselves was to see whether the phenomena could be adequately explained in purely psychological terms (i.e. as hypnotism), or whether some physical force such as magnetism was involved. They experimented above all with a hypnotist called George Albert Smith and his subject, Fred Wells. In their initial three reports, published in the first two volumes of the Society's *Proceedings*, they came to the conclusion that it was 'almost impossible to doubt the reality of some sort of special force or virtue, passing from one organism to the other, in the process of mesmerisation'. Braid no doubt turned in his grave, since this was a plain reversion to the old days of animal magnetism. Indeed, in their first report they stated that they had tried Braidian hypnotism, but with little success, and attributed the unfortunate contempt in which mesmerism was currently held to the 'partial truth' discovered by Braid.

The main test they used – or at least the one they found most convincing – was the famous 'finger experiment'. In this experiment, the subject spread out his ten fingers on a table, with his hands projecting through a blanket or screen which stopped him seeing what was happening on the other side. He was also blindfolded, just to be sure. Smith very gently (so as to avoid air currents and contact) magnetized two fingers chosen at random by a member of the committee, so that just these two fingers became anaesthetized and rigid. 'The points of a sharp carving fork gently applied to one of the other fingers evoked the sort of start and protest that might have been expected; the same points might be plunged deep into the chosen two without producing a sign or a murmur.' Fortunately for the peace of Braid's repose, however, the committee members soon recanted. Further tests suggested that thought-transference rather than anything material was at work. If a material force was being transferred, then the operator would not need to know which fingers he was working on, but it was found that if he didn't know which fingers he was operating on, the experiment didn't work. They concluded, therefore, that thought-transference was involved.

The sympathy between Smith and Wells seemed astonishing. When Smith pointed at the chosen finger, there were nineteen successes and six failures; when he pointed with the screen in place, there were eighteen successes and three failures; with Smith in the same room, not pointing, and standing between 2½ and 12 feet away, nineteen successes, two partial successes, sixteen failures; with Smith in another room across the passage, with both doors open, three successes, three failures; with doors closed, twelve failures, two partial successes; with Smith pointing but willing that no effect should follow, four successes and no failures.

But some doubts remain. Others could not reduplicate the success of these experiments, and Smith himself was not at all successful with other subjects: could it be because they had no opportunity to work in collusion? Smith was involved in discussions about how to set up the experiments, so could have talked in advance to Wells. These doubts resurfaced with a vengeance some years after the finger experiments. In 1908 the magazine *John Bull* published a sensational piece called 'Confessions of a Famous Medium' by Douglas Blackburn, who had worked with Smith after Wells's death. Blackburn said that the demonstrations of thought-transference which he and Smith had performed in front of members of the SPR (and which had been taken by the SPR to be genuine) were fraudulent and had been achieved through a series of complex codes.

Here is a simple example of the kind of code that is still used by stage performers. The supposed mind-reader turns his back to the audience, guaranteeing that he cannot see what is going on. His assistant circulates among the members of the audience. They keep up a patter between the two of them. The conjurer is to guess, let's say, the material and colour of lady's dress. The assistant's patter at that point consists of five sentences. The first starts with 'r' ('I see the colour red,' says the mind-reader), the next with 's', the next with 'i', the next with 'l', and the last one with 'k'. This kind of code is impossible to detect unless you are looking out for it – and even then you have to be quick.

Blackburn went on to claim that when the test conditions set by the SPR were too stringent for success, Smith and he made excuses for their failure – there were too many sceptics around, they were too tired, whatever. At one point the SPR measured magnetic currents emanating from Smith – but he was holding a metallic nib under his tongue. In response to all these allegations, Smith simply assured the shocked SPR that Blackburn was lying. The allegations were repeated in an article by Blackburn in the London *Daily News* for 1 September 1911 (and spread across the Atlantic into a long article on the subject in the New York *Evening Sun* for 13 September). The pot was still simmering six years later, when in the *Sunday Times* for 16 September 1917 Blackburn said that the experiments only 'worked' because certain eminent members of the SPR were so incredibly gullible. The SPR continued to support Smith and to denounce Blackburn.

But by then the SPR's focus had shifted away from hypnosis. As William James said in his retiring address (he was president of the SPR for two years from 1894 to 1896): 'I should say first that we started with high hopes that the hypnotic field would yield an important harvest, and that these hopes have subsided with the general subsidence of what may be called the hypnotic wave.' They thought that hypnosis would reveal the whole map of the transcendent realms of the universe, but found that at best it could do no more than prove telepathy, and only then if they trusted someone like Smith not to be cheating. Other experiments in telepathy were failures: the hypnotized subjects tried to guess cards randomly drawn from a pack, but the number of correct guesses fell below the number one would have expected just from the laws of chance. Hypnosis was perhaps not the royal road to the paranormal after all.

Past-life Regression

'You are five years old . . . two years . . . less than one year. You are experiencing your own birth . . . Now you are going back, further back than your own birth and the time you spent in your mother's womb. Back, further back. Suddenly you find yourself in a particular location at a particular time. Please tell me what you see . . .'

It is common practice for a psychotherapist, whether or not she is using hypnosis, to regress her patient. Regression – or, in full, age-regression – is the practice of taking the patient back through the years to a period of his childhood. This is a useful tool because, given the psychoanalytic assumption that most of our psychological problems and complexes are formed in childhood, the therapist can get her patient to explore the roots of his problems. There are two forms of regression, indirect and direct. In indirect regression, the client acts like a witness of his childhood past, as if he were watching a movie or a dream; in direct regression, the client seems actually to relive the past, and speaks, writes and thinks in the manner appropriate to the age to which he has been regressed.

The extent of the genuineness of direct regression is disputed, and the evidence is ambiguous. Some researchers insist that a regressed subject can display the Babinski reflex. Up until the age of about seven months, the toes of an infant whose foot is tickled on the sole will turn upward ('dorsiflexion'); after that, they turn downward ('flexion'). This is a reflex, which is to say that it is an instinctive matter, not subject to conscious control. If subjects who are regressed to infancy back beyond six months or so display dorsi-flexion, while those who are not regressed this far display flexion, it would be convincing evidence of the genuineness of regression. Unfortunately, the experiment does not always work. And despite anecdotal rumours to the contrary (especially about work in the former Soviet Union), there is no evidence that subjects regressed to childhood display the brainwave patterns of a child rather than those of an adult.

Or again, psychologist Martin Orne once got hold of some pictures drawn by a student when he was six. The student had not seen them since the age of six, and Professor Orne was sent them by the student's parents. He was delighted to find that the parents had lovingly written the exact date of their son's sketches: 23 October 1937. He regressed the young man back to that exact date, and asked him to draw exactly the same objects: a house, a tree and so on. In repeated tests, the two sets of pictures showed little correlation, until after the student had been shown the original 1937 drawings. Sceptically, one might say that until then he was drawing as an adult imagined a six-year-old might draw; more charitably, that he was simply drawing like a different six-year-old. On another occasion, Orne asked someone regressed back to age six to write 'I am conducting an experiment which will assess my psychological capabilities.' Slowly and laboriously, as a six-year-old might, the subject printed the sentence – but there was no problem with the spelling.

In any case, someone some time got the idea of regressing one of his clients back even further, back beyond birth. It is said to have been either Dr Mortis Stark in 1906 or Colonel Albert de Rochas a little earlier, though there had already been cases of spontaneous regression under hypnosis to past lives. Perhaps the most famous such medium was Mrs Smith, whose recollections were written up in 1900 by the Swiss psychiatrist Théodore Flournoy.

One of the most tireless workers in the field of past-life regression in recent years has been Helen Wambach, who has regressed thousands of subjects, often in groups. Her approach is different, because she is an academic researcher, not a therapist. So, for instance, she guides more than a therapist would, directing her subjects to particular eras in time. Early in her research she seems to have realized that it was going to be impossible to find a historically verifiable past life, uncontaminated by her subjects' buried memories from this lifetime, so instead she has focused on statistics. She finds it significant, for instance, that the percentage of her subjects who find themselves female or male in a past life is statistically accurate; that the same goes for the percentage of upper-, middle- and lower-class lives; that the kinds of clothing, footwear, foodstuffs, etc., seem to check out. But despite her academic credentials, her work is characterized by a high degree of gullibility. If one of her groups displays the same proportion of men and women as in the century to which they were regressed, that hardly proves they were actually remembering events from that century.

Bridey Murphy

There are by now a huge number of past-life regressions on record, but probably the single most famous case is the one published in the bestselling 1956 book *The Search for Bridey Murphy*, by Morey Bernstein, which was the first to alert the public to the phenomenon. It makes sense to focus on this case, old enough for the facts to have been checked, rather than on more recent cases such as those described by Joe Keeton in *The Power of the Mind*. Bridey Murphy is also one of the better cases, in the sense that a lot of so-called past-life memories do not stand the slightest investigation.

Bernstein was a skilled amateur hypnotist who found that 'Ruth Simmons' (actually Virginia Burns Tighe), the wife of a friend, was a good hypnotic subject. Having become interested in the possibility of reincarnation, in 1952 and 1953 he regressed Ruth back past what she could remember of the childhood of her present life, and she began to reveal details of a previous life, from Ireland early in the nineteenth century. And there are plenty of these details: nearly 100 pages of Bernstein's book are transcripts from taped sessions, which were always conducted in the presence of witnesses. Ruth's description of her life as Bridey impresses by its consistency (her ability to repeat the same facts during separation sessions, although Bernstein sometimes leads her in this respect), and its ordinariness. She also spoke in an Irish accent, which was more marked at some times than at others, and displayed a vivacious character. After one session, in which she said that as Bridey she had been good at dancing a particular jig, Bernstein planted the suggestion that after she came to she would dance it for them, and with a certain amount of reluctance she did.

As Bridey she also reported how, after dying in 1864 at the age of sixty-six, she lingered around her married home in Belfast, and returned to Cork, where she had been born, to watch over her brother Duncan. Then she lived in the spirit world, before being reborn in 1923 in Iowa as 'Ruth Mills'. She gave some details of life in the spirit or astral world. She also vaguely remembered an even earlier life in New Amsterdam (the place that later became New York), but seemed reluctant to talk about it.

Although a great deal of what Bridey said about Ireland was trite and predictable (for instance, that it is a beautiful country), or at the level of common knowledge (for instance, that the currency was pounds, shillings and pence, or that there is a legend of gigantic Cúchulain), she did also come up with some more obscure facts. Bernstein and his friends checked up on several of the details of Bridey's life – a newspaper and a book she remembered, for instance – and found that they existed. Most interesting was her mention of a place called Baylings Crossing. This was not on any map, nor had the British or Irish embassies heard of it, nor the relevant railway company. But people who had visited the area (as 'Ruth' had not) knew of it; it was just too small to be widely known. Later, once a book contract had been signed, the publisher arranged for a legal firm in Ireland to run some more checks. Remarkably, a couple of the Belfast shops Bridey mentioned did actually exist; she was accurate on stories, customs and legends current in Ireland at the time; she seemed again (as in the case of Baylings Crossing) to have peculiar local knowledge, in that she said that tobacco was grown around Cork, and indeed it was at the time, though in such small quantities as to escape the record books.

But there were also a number of details for which corroboration should have been easy, but was not forthcoming. For instance, to mention just a few of the oddities, Bridey claimed that her husband Sean Brian Joseph MacCarthy taught law at Queen's University, Belfast, and she named a couple of his colleagues there. She also said that her husband published letters in the Belfast *News-Letter*. Not all the names of Belfast shops she mentioned have been found, nor has the church at which she worshipped, nor the Dooley Road on which the church was located. She failed to recognize the names of some well-known shops and people from Belfast at the time. She gave her birthday as 20 December 1798, and yet on another occasion claimed to have died aged sixty-six in 1864, leaving her only eleven days of 1864 in which she could have died. There were no wooden houses in Cork, and no lyres in Ireland.

The case was headline news, so all this evidence and counter-evidence has been thoroughly sifted and worked over. Each piece of evidence that seemed to support or refute the book became news throughout 1956, with the Hearst group of newspapers leading the attack. The reaction of the scientists and professional hypnotists may be gauged by the fact that within only two or three months the collection of responses edited by Milton Kline as *A Scientific Report on 'The Search for Bridey Murphy'*, a book which combines hard-headed and hard-hitting analysis with the occasional sly innuendo, had been rushed into print. Meanwhile newspaper reporters took up the investigation and amateur hypnotists around the world began to regress their subjects back to past lives. Even the recordings of Bernstein's sessions with Mrs Tighe went on sale. Reincarnation was the topic of the day. The publishers must have been delighted.

But there are both theoretical and factual grounds for concern. There is little doubt, as we have seen, that Bridey came up with 'facts' that have not been confirmed by research, but other possible concrete pieces of evidence proved more elusive, especially because over-eager newspaper reporters muddied the waters. Hearst reporters claimed that an Irish woman named Bridie Murphy Corkell had once lived across the street from Mrs Tighe when she lived in Chicago, and that the two had been friends; and that Mrs Tighe also had an Irish aunt who had regaled her with stories in her childhood. But neither of these 'facts' is unassailable. A reporter from a rival newspaper found that although the aunt was Irish in origin, she had been born in New York, and didn't meet Virginia until the girl was in her late teens. It is not even certain that Mrs Corkell's middle name was Murphy. By the time this news was published, how-ever, the damage was done, and other newspapers got carried away, claiming falsely that either or both of Bernstein and Virginia Tighe had confessed to a deliberate deception.

The theoretical grounds for concern are a little more complex, and a couple of parallel cases will help first, by way of illustration. A hypnotized patient in America in the early 1950s suddenly began to speak a few words in an unknown language. Since the therapists could not understand a word he was saying, they got him to write it out. It looked like this: *Usurs inim malaks nistrus Pakiu Kluvatui Valamais pulukui antkadum damia.* Was this gibberish? A language from outer space? Or what?

A very similar case, also involving xenoglossy (speaking a foreign language), is a little more recent. In the 1960s psychiatrist Reima Kampman from the University of Oulu in Finland hypnotized a number of teenage schoolchildren, several of whom seemed to remember past lives. Perhaps the most amazing was 'Niki', who revealed a whole sequence of past lives, stretching back 2,000 years. One of them was as 'Dorothy', an innkeeper's daughter in thirteenth-century England. When regressed to this life, Niki began to sing the old English song which begins 'Sumer is icumen in, Lhude sing cuccu! Groweth sed and bloweth med, And springeth the wude nu.' Actually, though, she sang it in a modernized version of the words. How on earth did a teenage Finnish girl know this song?

In a way, the explanation for both these cases is just as remarkable as reincarnation. The apparent gibberish coming from the mouth of the American patient turned out to be a curse in old Oscan, an Italian language, from the third century BCE. The patient denied any knowledge of Oscan. Is this, then, not proof of reincarnation? From where did he learn Oscan if not from a previous life, either as a scholar or even in ancient Italy? If the therapists had been inclined to believe this, they could have pursued the fantasy, and the patient would have constructed for himself a past life as coherent as that of Bridey Murphy. Or if they had failed to identify the language as Oscan, all the parties involved might have assumed reincarnation from another planet, and become caught up in a fantasy along those lines. In actual fact, though, this is what they found:

We discovered that one afternoon he had seated himself at a table in the Library of the University of Pennsylvania in order to prepare for an examination in Economics that was scheduled for the following day, but that instead he began to daydream about his girl friend, who had just broken a date with him, while looking not at the text he was supposedly outlining but at another book which was on the table and which was opened at page 243. This was Buck's *Grammar of Oscan and Umbrian* (Ginn & Company, Boston, 1904). In the middle of the page, in English, was the phrase: 'the Curse of Vibia'. 'Vibia' looked like his girl friend's nickname. Without being aware of the fact that he was looking at this book, he nevertheless photographically imprinted on his memory the Oscan Curse printed immediately below the English title.

And the case of the Finnish schoolgirl is exactly the same. When questioned under hypnosis, the girl explained that she was once sitting in a library and happened to be flicking through a book in which the English song was printed. It was (in Finnish) *Musiikin Vaiheet* (*The Phases of Music*), by Benjamin Britten and Imogen Holst. She gave Kampman exact details of whereabouts in the book the song was to be found, and Kampman found these to be true. Both these subjects were affected by what has been called 'source amnesia': they had an accurate memory for information, but could not remember where the information had been acquired.

Whatever one thinks about reincarnation, is it not remarkable – *and just as remarkable in its way as the possibility of reincarnation* – that the human mind is capable of absorbing and retaining apparently meaningless information with such precision, for such a long time, when that information was so casually come by? What does this tell us about the powers of the mind? They are obviously far greater than is normally assumed. In another famous pseudo-reincarnation case, the subject spoke fairly fluent German, when she hardly knew it at all in her waking state.

Now add to this extraordinary capacity another equally remarkable mental ability. We all know far more than we are consciously aware of knowing. An everyday example of this is that we can all recognize many more words than we use in our personal vocabularies. We have taken in and stored all kinds of odd pieces of information. But that on its own is not the remarkable ability I'm getting at. We can also put all these odd pieces of information together and create a vivid and coherent story. We do it every night in our dreams. In my dreams I have composed symphonies and spoken foreign languages with fluency – neither of which are daytime abilities. The mind is astonishingly creative. Vividness is no guarantee of a genuine reincarnation experience, though it is often taken to be. The most convincing factors of the many supposed reincarnation cases I have read are their vividness and consistency, but if I was able to relive one of my vivid dreams out loud it would have the same qualities. In short, I believe that past-life regression is not genuine, but an instance of the mind's imaginative capabilities.

Films like the star-studded *Dead Again* (1992) have helped to perpetuate the idea that we can access past lives through hypnosis, and in *On a Clear Day You Can See Forever* Barbra Streisand doesn't just regress to a past life, but progresses to a future life too. Though nowhere near as common as past-life progression, there have been cases of future-life progression under hypnosis (recently popularized by Chet Snow in *Dreams of the Future*). Since the early days of hypnotism subjects have imagined the future. In the nineteenth century mesmerized 'clairvoyants' would describe life in the 1920s; they have since all been proved wrong. There is no reason to think that hypnotized subjects today who describe life in the 2020s, or on other planets, are any less wrong. There is every reason to think that they are creating a story in exactly the same way that others do when regressed to supposed past lives. The pictures they paint of the future are obviously built up from current concepts of the future, which shows that imagination and not objective reality is at work.

Anyway, to return to the Bridey Murphy case, the point is that in a sense Bernstein was just as entranced as Ruth Simmons. Because he wanted to believe in reincarnation, he shelved all other possible interpretations in favour of just this one, and joined her in a *folie à deux*. If the transcripts are read in this light, it is easy to see that Ruth was responding to his eagerness, and when she cannot answer one of his questions she resorts to vague replies such as 'I don't know: that's not for a woman.' The phenomenon of cryptomnesia (apparently lost memories which are actually capable of being recalled in dreams or under hypnosis) was well known and documented by the early 1950s, but Bernstein, not being a professional, did not take it into account as a possible explanation. A couple of times I have read the Bridey Murphy case described as a 'hoax'. This seems unfair, since a hoax is a deliberate attempt to deceive. It would take considerable cynicism to describe Bernstein or Virginia Tighe as anything other than innocent and well meaning. Bernstein made mistakes, that's all.

But this is one of those areas of psychiatry where errors should not be allowed, and amateurs therefore should be excluded. Imagine a man who 'remembers' having committed a murder in a past life. What would be the emotional effect on him? On the other hand, even if past-life regression is false, it can still be useful therapy, and a number of therapists make use of it while claiming to be sceptical about the reality of their clients' fantasies. Precisely because the client is emotionally involved in the fantasy, it can cause an abreaction – an emotional release which is therapeutic. Suppose a client has arthritis in the elbow, and the therapist guesses that there is a neurotic component to the ailment. The therapist might regress her patient to a past life and ask when the elbow first started to hurt. The patient might come up with a 'past life' in which he broke his elbow while fighting in the Battle of Trafalgar. If his involvement in the battle scenario has the appropriate emotional quality, abreaction might follow, and the pain might be relieved. The most important recent Russian researcher into this area, Dr Vladimir Raikov, has found that past-life regression helps people develop a critical attitude towards their behaviour, and so has been an aid in the rehabilitation of criminals and, especially, recovery from alcoholism. To sum up, then, past-life regression is an uncertain practice, and should only be used, if at all, by professionals.

Confabulation

At one point in her book *Hypnotism Made Easy* (which, despite the title, is fiction), French novelist Marie Nimier says: 'One can inject basically any event, shaped appropriately, into the memory of a well-disposed individual, as long as it isn't against his principles.' Once such a memory has been installed, it becomes as real, subjectively, as any true memory. This is the phenomenon of confabulation – the trap into which I have just accused Morey Bernstein and Virginia Tighe of falling. Confabulation is when two people unwittingly conspire to create a scenario; they implant a false memory into the subject's mind, and then make it concrete. Suppose a subject has fragmentary memories (true or false) of an event; in confabulation the gaps between these memories are filled in with a seemingly coherent story, which then takes on the appearance of a series of true memories.

The phenomena of confabulation and the creation of false memories ('retroactive hallucination', as Bernheim accurately called it) were well known in the nineteenth century. If only they had been known 200 years earlier, when, during the notorious Salem witch trials of the 1690s, it is clear with hindsight that the children involved named many of the accused in order to please their questioners and put an end to the hours of interrogation to which they had been subjected. Nineteenth-century researchers also recognized the importance of the feeling of certainty to one's impression of the accuracy of a memory, and the legal repercussions of these phenomena were discussed. Nevertheless, despite this background of nineteenth-century knowledge, there have been too many distressing cases since then, and especially in the 1980s and 1990s.

As Debbie Nathan and Michael Snedeker reveal in *Satan's Silence: Ritual Abuse and the Making of a Modern American Witch Hunt*, the interview techniques used on children in recent alleged sexual abuse cases are frequently, even invariably, leading. For example, in order to encourage the children to talk about what might have happened, anatomically correct dolls were used. Having got a child involved in imaginative play, the questioner would bring on these dolls and sometimes almost force the child to accuse whoever it might be of performing obscene acts. If the child said that nothing happened, this was taken to be shyness or reluctance, and the questioner, in her enthusiasm for her cause (an enthusiasm often fuelled by feminism or Christian fundamentalism, or both in an unlikely alliance), would continue to press the child to make accusations, and praise the child once he or she had made the accusations. Although a number of these cases have since been overturned, there are undoubtedly people in prison today who should not be; and even apart from their torment, one wonders what the long-term effect of these forms of questioning might be on the children.

Here is a fragment of an interrogation (not involving the use of dolls) of a five-year-old boy:

> ADULT: Did she put a fork in your butt? Yes or no?
> CHILD: I don't know, I forgot.
> ADULT: . . . Oh, come on, if you just answer that you can go.
> CHILD: I hate you.
> ADULT: No, you don't.
> CHILD: Yes, I do.
> ADULT: You love me, I can tell. Is that all she did to you? What did she do to your hiney?
> SECOND ADULT: What did she do to your hiney? Then you can go.
> CHILD: I forgot.
> SECOND ADULT: Tell me what Kelly did to your hiney, and then you can go. If you tell me what she did to your hiney, we'll let you go.
> CHILD: No.
> ADULT: Please.
> CHILD: Okay, okay, okay.
> ADULT: Tell me now: what did Kelly do to your hiney?
> CHILD: I'll try to remember.
> ADULT: What did she put in your hiney?
> CHILD: The fork.

The case against Kelly Michaels, it should be added, was thrown out, partly as a result of this kind of interrogation technique – but not before she had spent some years in jail. Perhaps the most astonishing aspect to the whole hysterical business is that the children's accounts were accepted as more authoritative than common sense and good evidence. Even if a day-care worker had been in plain view of other responsible adults, and of dozens of children, all the time, it could still become accepted that he was abusing the children in his care.

Confabulation is not always as crude as this, however; it is subtle and hard to guard against. Consider these two questions: 'How fast were the cars going when they smashed into each other?' 'How fast were the cars going when they collided?' The first question seems only to use an innocent colloquialism for 'collision', but in fact when put that way the question elicits responses which exaggerate the speed of the cars. Or again, the question 'Didn't you see a gun?' encourages respondents to answer yes more than 'Did you see a gun?'

As an appendix, I cannot resist adding the little-known fact that the modern mass hysteria about sexual abuse of children was played out, on a small scale, in the analysis rooms of Freud. In the early years of his work, he found that almost all the 'hysterical' women coming to see him had a history of sexual abuse, often of a perverted kind, by their fathers. However, it was gradually borne in on him that hardly any of this was true. For Freud, this was a crisis point; he nearly threw up the whole enterprise of analysis in disgust. If he, the analyst, could be taken in so thoroughly for so long, and if his patients could come up with lies as if they were truth, how could progress be made by means of psychoanalysis? Nevertheless, he persevered – for better or for worse.

Cryptomnesia, Hypermnesia and Forensic Hypnosis

Cryptomnesia means 'buried memory'. We all have them. Sometimes we have buried a memory because it is too distressing to face (though this is rarer than Freudians would have us believe); sometimes an event was just too trivial to be fully registered at the time in our conscious minds, though it was taken in unconsciously. Hypermnesia is the ability to recall, under hypnosis, such forgotten memories.

There is no doubt that hypnosis can significantly enhance memory recall. I argued (in Chapter 1) that it is hit and miss, but when it scores a hit it can be very dramatic, and has been used in criminal cases. In 1976, for instance, a school bus was hijacked at Chowchilla near San Francisco and held to ransom. In the course of the adventure, the driver and the children were shoved into the back of closed vans. Under hypnosis the bus driver was able to recall enough of the number plate of one of the vans to allow the police later to arrest the gang. He caught only the merest glimpse of the number plate, and was unable to remember its details by conscious recall. Actually, he 'recalled' two numbers, only one of which was right – perfectly illustrating the hit-and-miss nature of hypnotically refreshed memory.

In 1973 a terrorist bomb exploded on an Israeli bus. By great good fortune, the bus had just pulled in at the main station in Haifa and unloaded its passengers, so although there were injuries, there were no fatalities. The bus had been packed; it was a normal busy day for the driver, and he could not be expected to remember all the passengers who had come and gone. But he agreed to be hypnotized by the police, and then he remembered that there was something odd about one of the passengers: he had been sweating profusely, as if in fear. The hypnotist asked him whether he could also remember details of his features, glimpsed for maybe a couple of seconds. A police artist sketched the driver's description not only of the passenger but of a companion who had not boarded the bus – and the police were able successfully to pick up one of the terrorists and chase the other out of the country.

In the 1980s a woman was found wandering in the dark, confused and amnesic, somewhere in North America (the precise place has been suppressed in my source). She had been beaten and sexually assaulted. Under hypnosis she was able to recover quite a few details of the man, the car he had driven (including the make of a can of beer that had been shoved down between the front seats) and the location. She told the police, among other things, that the car had crashed and dented its front wing during the abduction. The police went round repair garages and eventually found one that had fixed a car that fitted the description. They went to the man's house and found, inside the car, not only the squashed can of beer, but also the woman's small purse, which had ended up on the floor of the back seat, covered by some old clothes. The man was tried and convicted.

American psychotherapist Milton Kline once had to deal with a patient who had inexplicably started to have anxiety attacks. It turned out that these had begun four weeks earlier, the night after she had been invited to a party at her neighbour's; she had refused the invitation, but had lent him her steak knives. Under hypnosis she remembered having heard cries and the sound of a struggle in the next-door apartment. Police broke down the door to find a four-week-old corpse, apparently killed with one of the steak knives.

Hypnosis has been used to recover memories even in such high-profile cases as the Florida *State* v. *Bundy* – Ted Bundy being better known as the charming, good-looking sex killer of at least twenty-two women in Washington, Oregon and Florida in the early 1970s. Or through hypnosis an innocent person might come to remember details establishing her alibi. More surprisingly, hypnosis has also been used to elicit or confirm confessions from suspects, as in the famous Boston Strangler case in 1962, when under hypnosis Albert DeSalvo willingly revealed details of the series of sex killings which only the perpetrator could have known.

What most impresses about these cases is their matter-of-factness: hypnotism simply seems to work well under these circumstances and can be used by open-minded police forces without fuss or bother. It may help and, with the proper legal guidelines and awareness of its hit-and-miss nature, it cannot hinder. It is a fact that memory can be refreshed under hypnotism in many cases, provided the operator suggests it – memory is not automatically enhanced by hypnosis – and the subject wants to remember. The technique is a form of age-regression: the subject is regressed back to the event details of which he or she is to remember. The hypnotist is either a professional brought in by the police, or, increasingly, a trained police officer. The Los Angeles Police Department (LAPD) pioneered the training of its own people, starting in the 1970s.

It goes without saying that checks and controls are needed. Only experienced hypnotists should be used, not policemen fresh from a four-day course on the topic – this has actually happened, and led to abuse: two suspects to a crime were identified and even arrested before it was found out that the victim was making the whole thing up. And whenever hypnotic testimony is given in court, it needs to be clearly stated that this testimony was gained under hypnosis, so that judge and jurors can look at it in that light. For, as we will see, although hypnosis can refresh memory, our memories are far from accurate.

Up until about the 1970s courts in the English-speaking world tended to rule that information gained under hypnosis was inadmissible. They did so for a variety of reasons, both good (such as worries that the hypnotist may have asked leading questions) and bad (such as ignorance about hypnotism). But one of the basic reasons was the equal inadmissibility of the evidence of a lie-detector test. Both methods of arriving at the 'truth' were felt to offer useful corroborative evidence out of court, but to be too unreliable for the degree of certainty courts aspire to attain. Only gradually did courts come to see that hypnosis could be a valuable tool where, for instance, a defendant had a complete blank in his memory due to alcoholic stupor, perhaps. And even now courts chop and change. In the 1959 Californian case of *Cornell* v. *Superior Court* it was clearly stated that the defendant had a right to be hypnotized to help him recall forgotten facts, but in the 1982 *People* v. *Donald Lee Shirley* it was equally clearly stated that the testimony of witnesses who had been hypnotized to aid their memories 'should not be admitted in the courts of California'. Similar rulings have been passed in other American States (such as *State* v. *Mack* (1980) in Minnesota). British and French courts don't accept testimony which has been elicited under hypnosis, although like most other courts around the world they are prepared to give it a guarded hearing, provided it has been confirmed by proper police investigation. In America, although hypnotic testimony can be viewed with some suspicion, courts are reluctant to outlaw it altogether, because that would restrict the right, under the 14th amendment, to due process, and the right, under the 6th amendment, to call witnesses.

The landmark case in the States was *State of New Jersey* v. *Hurd* in 1981, which outlined conditions for the use of hypnosis on a witness. The most important of these conditions are that a trained medical doctor should be used, not an amateur hypnotist; that the witness should have given his or her testimony in the first place *before* being hypnotized, so that there is a point of comparison in case the hypnotized version of the story differs; and that the witness should be hypnotized by the expert with no one else present, to prevent any undue pressure.

Before these sensible guidelines were in place, there were some extraordinary cases. Perhaps the most outrageous happened entirely within the court, in Columbus, Ohio, in 1962. The defendant was Arthur Nebb, who, in front of witnesses, had broken into the home of his estranged wife and shot both her and her lover, the latter fatally. It seemed an open-and-shut case, with only the quirk that Nebb had or claimed to have no memory of the events. At the defence lawyer's request, the judge allowed Nebb to be hypnotized *in court* to enable him to recall the fatal evening's events. Although members of the public were allowed to stay, the jury was temporarily removed from the court while induction went on, and were then brought back in to hear the hypnotized man's testimony. His account of the events differed crucially from that of the witnesses; he claimed, for instance, that it was during a struggle with his wife that the gun had first gone off, as opposed to the prosecution's claim that he had calmly walked into the room and opened up. Nebb's account of the events obviously won the day, because he was found guilty only of second-degree murder, and imprisoned for a term of one to twenty years, which would make him liable for parole in a mere eight months.

A similarly bizarre scene was enacted a few years later in a court in Canada, so that hypnosis in court entered the British system too. In 1967 Gladys Pitt was charged with the attempted murder of her husband. She had battered him around the head with a hammer because of his insistence that she have sex with a friend of his, who was there in the bedroom with them. She had no memory of what happened, but under hypnosis recalled that the hammer had been lying on a bookcase in the bedroom, so that she did not have to leave the room and fetch it, which would have been a premeditated act. She was eventually found guilty only of assault, and sentenced to a year in prison.

At the other extreme US courts have more than once thrown a case out because when the defendant confessed to the crime he was deemed to have been hypnotized by the questioner, and such a confession was held to have been not freely extracted. In one such case a man, Camilo Leyra, was released after several years on death row in Sing Sing prison; another, involving a teenage boy, was made into a TV movie called *Murder or Memory?*. These kinds of cases have led the relevant agencies, such as the FBI and the LAPD, to tighten up their procedures, and so some courts have become more open to evidence gained by pre-trial hypnosis. However, it is still a ploy for the opposing lawyers to cast doubt on the testimony by challenging the scientific credibility of hypnotism, and the validity of such refreshed memories: 'Did you remember this on your own, or only when hypnotized?' This may lead to an expert witness being called in to give complex evidence as to what hypnotism can and cannot achieve, and to citing a raft of precedents from prior trials, and so the whole case becomes less straightforward.

In the States, the admissibility of scientific evidence in court has traditionally been based on a criterion of 'general acceptability within the relevant scientific community' (*Frye* v. *United States*, 1923). In my opinion (and in the opinion of a lot of people more qualified than me), this should still be the guideline. Provided proper safeguards are in place, as outlined above, there is no good reason to exclude hypnotically induced testimony. The 'relevant scientific community', psychotherapists and psychologists, are aware of the limitations and can allow for them.

Are Recovered Memories Accurate?

The assumption in the Nebb and Pitt cases was that memories recovered under hypnosis are accurate, and writers on forensic hypnosis have sometimes claimed that this is the whole justification for eliciting testimony under hypnosis. But there are serious grounds for doubt. First, there is the general question whether our memories are ever as accurate as they seem to us to be; second, there is the question whether faculties such as self-protection and self-deceit are so thoroughly bypassed by hypnosis that it is, in effect, a truth serum; third, there is the possibility of confabulation.

Repeated tests have shown that, however much we like to think that our memories are reliable, they simply are not. American university students who filled in a questionnaire on 29 January 1986, the day after the Challenger space shuttle exploded, on the circumstances of their hearing the news, were given the same questionnaire just three years later. Only three out of the forty-four students involved gave the same answers, while as many as eleven – fully 25 per cent – scored zero, in the sense that their answers in 1989 were in all details different from what they had said in 1986. But many of the students also reported that they were confident in the accuracy of their memories. It is this confidence that makes hypnotically refreshed testimony in court dangerous, because the witness's very confidence can make what he says carry conviction. There is good experimental evidence to show that under hypnosis, as in sleep and other ASCs, we are strongly inclined to accept the reality of subjective experience, without critically evaluating it. In other words, in trusting a recovered memory, we may make an honest mistake. In the stage show *Gigi* the well-known song 'I Remember It Well' cleverly shows how two people can have completely different memories of the same event.

Children's memories are even more malleable. Some school-children were questioned a few weeks after a sniper attack on their school, and most of their accounts of what happened had been infected by fantasy and wish-fulfilment. Although many of us like to believe that every event we have ever experienced is lodged somewhere in our minds, capable of recall, there is actually little or no evidence for this. The vast majority of researchers nowadays would claim that memory is inaccurate and selective, and that it is reconstructive, not merely reproductive, especially where autobiographical memories are concerned. Memories are not imprinted, as it were on some wax-block within the mind, once and for all; we play with them, embellish them, alter them. We may have camcorders in our minds, but they are not switched on all the time, and we edit the material. Moreover, memory is not an isolated mental phenomenon: it is affected above all by mood and imagination.

In short, contemporary researchers and thinkers on memory maintain that the accuracy of a memory is not guaranteed by the amount of detail recalled, nor by the richness of the detail, nor by the vividness of the memory, nor by the emotional involvement of the rememberer, nor by the consistency of the memory over time, nor by the confidence of the rememberer, nor by the honesty of the person, nor by the fact that on the whole he has a good memory. There is no way to test the accuracy of a memory except by independent physical corroboration.

What is important here, and what interests me, as earlier in this chapter, is that the human mind is capable of these feats of imagination. There is a famous case of an American chaplain who under hypnosis came up with vivid memories of his experiences as a prisoner of war in Vietnam. There was just one snag: he never went to Vietnam. If the Vietnamese War had taken place centuries ago, enthusiasts would have taken this to be a case of past-life recall, but in fact it is recent history, and within the lifetime of the subject in question. As it happens, I have a pseudo-memory. For all my teenage years, I knew for an absolute fact that as a child, some time between the ages of four and seven, I had once been taken to a doctor's office, had electrodes fitted to my head, and been wired up to some machine or other. This was as vivid as any memory – more vivid than most, in fact – and I was completely persuaded of its authenticity. Aged about twenty, I asked my parents what I was being tested for – only to be met with their denial that the event had ever taken place. Now, my mother happens to keep meticulous appointment diaries, and at that time also hung on to them for years. I pored through about six or seven years of diaries, and failed to find any reference to any relevant doctor's appointment. I now accept, without any feeling of loss, that this was a pseudo-memory. The question is: how does one distinguish memory from imagination?

There is plenty of evidence that therapy *creates* a narrative by the technique of free association, despite the fact that patients and therapists alike may mistake this narrative for historical truth. I am not denying that the narrative may have therapeutic value, but that doesn't make it true. In a therapeutic context, meaning is more important than history – but that is not the case in a forensic context. Its therapeutic value comes from the fact that it can provide the patient with emotional release, and the images constructed may point towards significant factors in the subject's psychological make-up.

It is also clear that the therapist's own preconceptions are often dominant in giving meaning to a narrative. For instance, therapists may assume that a symptom (such as low self-esteem) is indicative of a memory of childhood abuse, and then steer the therapy along the lines of this assumption. We all know how unreliable dreams are, and yet in a therapeutic context dreams are frequently taken to be memories. Once the therapist confides her suspicion about these 'memories' to her client, the two of them work together to fit pieces into place and recreate the situation, now taken to be historical, that these jigsaw pieces make up. The close bond between therapist and client, or the dependence of the latter on the former, only help to make the narrative all the more convincing. They both invest in the belief that it is true. This happens not just in cases of childhood abuse, but also in many cases of MPD: the pattern of therapeutic indoctrination is remarkably similar. Most MPD victims do not display any symptoms before they begin therapy; it is only after therapy has been going a while that they start to flip from babyish behaviour to devilish behaviour, from male to female, from old to young. A therapist committed to the reality of MPD will claim that in actual fact his patient did display the symptoms before therapy, but that, since 'alters' (alternate personalities) tend not to remember what other alters do, he simply didn't remember the symptoms. An alternative explanation, however, is that therapy actually creates MPD.

As if all this were not enough to cast doubt on the use of hypnosis to recover memories, tests have also shown that it is possible for hypnotized subjects to lie, to tell deliberate falsehoods. A minority view of this, however, is that in all cases where the subject tells lies, he was not properly or fully hypnotized. It is notoriously hard to tell whether someone is fully hypnotized. The 1987 Miranda Downes case in Australia shot to fame when Ernest Knibb, the main suspect (who was later convicted of the murder), appeared on TV and described how, if he had been Downes's killer, he would have gone about it. The TV programme also arranged for him to be hypnotized. Throughout the hypnotic session, Knibb continued to lie, pretending that he saw other possible suspects on the beach where Downes had been run down by a four-wheel-drive car, raped and drowned. Whether or not Knibb was fully hypnotized, the basic point is that self-defence mechanisms are not necessarily undermined in a hypnotic session.

Hypnosis is often assumed to be a royal road to accurate recovery of memory, an idea which ignores the fact that memory can be enhanced without hypnosis. The assumption is that (as Herbert Lom puts it in the film *The Seventh Veil*) under hypnosis a patient lets down all his guards, including everything that might be hindering one from remembering something. Unfortunately, there is no real reason to assume that accurate recovery of memory is certain even under hypnosis. In fact, pseudo-memories may be created even more effectively under hypnosis, because of the increased suggestibility of the subject. Sensitive to the slightest nuances of the hypnotist's questions, he eagerly responds in a way that will satisfy the implicit demands of the hypnotist. His confidence in his memories increases when he is hypnotized, but confidence does not mean reliability. This is where the whole fallacy of reincarnation recall comes in: a subject's confidence in the images infects the hypnotist, and between them they concoct a reincarnation narrative.

Now, all this must cast doubt on the use of hypnosis as an aid in legal situations, at any rate in the interrogation of suspects rather than victims or witnesses. In fact, these days hypnotism is rarely used to interrogate suspects, for precisely the reasons just outlined. After all, presumably one of the main reasons for the statute of limitations in America is that memories from long ago are recognized to be inaccurate. There may be extreme cases, however, when hypnosis is called for in a legal situation. Suppose a defendant's grasp on reality is so impaired (as a result of mental retardation or emotional disturbance, perhaps) that he is incapable of mounting a defence on his own; perhaps evidence gained from hypnosis should then be taken into consideration. Another kind of situation when hypnosis may legitimately be used to refresh memory is when the benefits outweigh the possible adverse effects of memory distortion, or when human life is threatened, as in a kidnapping case. But even so, it should be taken with a pinch of salt. It should guide the police into a channel of investigation, rather than being taken to be gospel; the 'facts' need double checking. And in order to avoid confabulation, the hypnotist should know as little as possible about the alleged crime – just enough for him to be able to conduct a meaningful session.

A Dramatic and Ambiguous Case

Perhaps some readers will have read one of the several books on the case of George Franklin, or seen the TV movie. As we will see, hypnosis may or may not have been involved, but it is still a case that well illustrates the dangers of memory in a forensic situation.

In September 1969 eight-year-old Susan Nason vanished while running a domestic errand in Foster City, California. Three months later her decomposed body was discovered by accident. The police investigation was enormous and thorough, but no suspects were ever found or charged.

Twenty years later, in November 1989, Eileen Franklin Lipster walked into a police station and said that she had suddenly remembered, after all this time, that her father, George Franklin, had murdered her friend Susan Nason. She said that she remembered being in his Volkswagen minibus with Susan and her father, that her father performed a sex act with Susan, and then beat her to death with a rock. Police soon found that her father did have violent and paedophiliac tendencies, which had been indulged with his family and, for instance, with babysitters. He had an extensive collection of child pornography. Indeed, family members had often wondered aloud whether he might not be the killer.

George Franklin was brought to trial, and the case received huge media attention. It was an astonishing trial, in that the evidence of psychologists and psychiatrists played as big a part in it as the evidence of the supposed witnesses (as in the Gouffé case in nineteenth-century France). The main psychological issue was whether it is possible to forget such an event. It is easy to forget things for twenty years, and then suddenly to recall them, but they tend to be trivial things, like the colour of the curtains in a childhood bedroom. But in cases of extreme dissociation, it is possible to forget major traumatic events. Perhaps this is what happened in Eileen's case.

But traumatic events are generally repressed when they are repeated – say, constant abuse by a close relative – rather than a one-off event such as Eileen's witnessing the murder. So Eileen's repression of the memory would be unusual, but not impossible. However, such repressed memories usually have an effect on behaviour, yet Eileen remained on good terms with her father, and even travelled in the same minibus with him on other occasions without feeling any aversion. Further doubts may be cast by the fact that she was not a very truthful witness. In particular she kept changing the story of the circumstances in which she had suddenly remembered the events of twenty years previously. At first she said that she had been hypnotized by the therapist she was seeing at the time; later she denied that hypnosis was involved. Did she now want revenge on her father for his drunken, sexually abusive treatment of her as a child, and had she been warned that hypnotic evidence was not allowed in a Californian court? Finally, it is worth mentioning that she didn't produce any new evidence: her story consisted of nothing she could not have read in newspapers.

Nevertheless, she was a good witness in court, the jury believed her, and her father was convicted of first-degree murder. The appeal court also upheld the conviction. But there is, of course, room for doubt. Was Eileen lying? Or was she an 'honest liar' – that is, someone who genuinely believes in the accuracy of her memory, despite the fact that it is a construct? There is no doubt that George Franklin was an unsavoury character; he may even have been the killer, for all we know – but there are reasons to doubt Eileen's testimony.

Hypnosis and Alien Abduction

I was intrigued to read in the personal finance section of the *Sunday Telegraph* for 25 June 2000 that at least one London-based insurance company has already made a few million pounds offering insurance against alien abduction. No one has yet made a claim – and indeed, if the abduction is really successful, it's hard to see how they would.

After the last few pages, the reader will find it easy to guess what my position will be on the topic of alien abduction – polite scepticism. In the last quarter of the twentieth century there was something of a craze for the idea of alien abduction. This was kick-started in 1966 by a book by John Fuller called *The Interrupted Journey*, about the experiences of Barney and Betty Hill. Then the craze died down somewhat, until Whitley Strieber (who until then had been a not-too-successful fiction writer) published *Communion* in 1987. In this book (and in the follow-up, *Transformation*), Strieber recounts how ever since childhood he has been abducted for brief periods by aliens – the grey, child-sized, almond-eyed, insectoid figures who are now pretty familiar, largely as a result of Strieber's bestseller, as inflatable dolls and cartoon characters – who invade his home, stick needles in his head, take him up to their ship, and do further experiments on him, including buggering him with something penis-like and making him get an erection. A sexual component is common in such abduction experiences: men are masturbated by machines, woman are made pregnant by implants and then have the foetus removed later. But these are just the most striking of the 'experiments' that are carried out on people, which regularly seem to involve instruments being stuck into their noses or ears.

Aliens are supposed to have the power to make those they abduct forget all about it afterwards, or the trauma of the abduction is so great that they bury the memory. Experiencers commonly find that they have covered up the memory of the abduction with a screen memory of seeing some kind of magical creature, such as an owl or a deer, under unusual circumstances. And that is where hypnosis comes in. Since hypnosis has, or is assumed to have, a good track record in recovering repressed memories, hypnotists get their subjects to remember details of their abductions. Strieber says: 'Because of the evident presence of fear-induced memory lapses and even possible amnesia, this therapist [the ideal therapist he was looking for] would have to be a skilled hypnotist as well.' In other words, Strieber's working hypothesis, despite his recognition elsewhere that it is possible to lie under hypnosis, is that memories recovered under hypnosis are infallible. It is true that in his case no leading questions were involved, so that there was little or no confabulation between him and the therapist, but that is not the only possible source of error: there is also fantasy, the excitation of the imagination, the creation of false memories. In hypnosis one is put into a sleepy, dream-like state, but we don't take all our dreams to be true; the imagination can become just as active in hypnosis too, and the mere vividness of the experience convinces subjects (and often their therapists as well) that it is recall. This was identified as a source of error in hypnotic experiments in the middle of the nineteenth century by James Braid, but it is still overlooked. There is also often a strong element of wish-fulfilment, as the aliens tell abductees that they have been specially chosen, and sometimes promise to save the planet from ecological disaster or something like that. Abductees are often aware of the weakness of their reliance on hypnosis, because nearly all cases of abduction emerge or emerge in detail only under hypnosis. But they defend themselves only against the charge of confabulation, as if that were the only possible source of error.

The standard psychological explanation for these experiences runs parallel to that for supposed memories of past lives. They consist of fragmentary memories of other experiences, and of things read and seen on TV, embedded within a fantasized narrative. But in this case it may be worth floating an alternative view, even though this might seem to explain one oddity by another. The reason for looking for an alternative view, however, is that, astonishingly, the evidence for alien abduction is stronger than one might think. It is based mainly on the striking similarities between the abduction accounts of 'experiencers' from all over the world who have had no chance to talk to one another. But we still don't need to talk about literal abduction. Suppose that we understand the act of seeing not just as seeing something that is objectively 'out there'. Suppose that the act of seeing always, to a greater or lesser extent, involves the imagination. If I look out of my window I seem to see rooftops and leaves; actually, all I see are colours and shapes, and I interpret those, on the basis of past experience, as rooftops and leaves. Vision is never unmediated by the mind. In that case, it is easier to understand how some people might see things which are not there for other people, even for the majority of people. This is essentially the thesis well argued for and illustrated in Patrick Harpur's important book *Daimonic Reality*. In the context of alien-abduction scenarios, it means that it is plausible to think of them as a modern myth, neither true nor false, but a bit of both, mediated by the archetypes of the collective unconscious (such as the evil scientist experimenting on and manipulating human beings for his own obscure purposes) and the imagination. Under hypnosis, the imagination is stimulated to embroider the myth and make it a personal experience. The case of Candy Jones, outlined in Chapter 12, shows that exactly the same kind of narrative can crop up in different circumstances: the parallels between her case and alien abduction make it all the more plausible to talk of archetypes.

One of the interesting offshoots of recent research into hypnosis has been the discovery that a proportion of the population, perhaps as many as 20 per cent, have what is now known as 'fantasy-prone personalities' (which is very similar to what other psychologists have called 'imaginative involvement' or just 'absorption'). Such people spend a great deal of their life fantasizing. I know a woman – a skilled musician – who often imagines, as she plays the piano, a scenario such as that she is a gifted gipsy princess who has just been discovered by some royal court and asked to give a concert. Secondly, these people have the ability to hallucinate what they fantasize as really real; this may give them, among other things, the enviable ability to reach an orgasm without physical stimulation! Thirdly, they are prone to psychic and out-of-body experiences. They do sometimes find it difficult to differentiate fantasized from real events and persons, but being sensitive to social norms, they keep their fantasy lives very private. You may know many such people, but unless you are in their confidence, you might not guess at the

richness of their inner worlds. These are the people who under hypnosis will concoct strange ideas about past lives and alien abductions.

Paranormal and Supernormal

Speaking for myself, I certainly do not rule out the possibility that
some people are psychically gifted. As I have said, I have had certain
extraordinary experiences myself, and so it is impossible for me to
rule it out. And who knows what results future scholarly experiments
may bring? Nineteenth-century researchers, who waxed enthusiastic
about their paranormal findings, resemble the amateur archaeologists
of the same era. These people plunged in, dug trenches and tunnels,
and took out the artefacts, all in the space of a few weeks. Today's
archaeologists work at a snail's pace, carefully sifting, methodically
searching every square centimetre, looking for minute variations in
soil colour as much as gold and silver and foundations. Modern
psychologists are like that too: it is slow, painstaking work. But some
freaky results have come up already. Think of surgical memory,
discussed in Chapter 1. Or here's another instance. I have already
mentioned that researchers might use automatic writing to tap into
a subject's unconscious. Of course, often what is written down
comes out as an illegible scrawl, incomprehensible even to the
awoken subject, let alone to the operator. But another hypnotized
person can often decipher the scribbles.

   Even if the evidence for *para*normal phenomena is slight, nevertheless the mind does have *super*normal abilities. Hypnosis is an
excellent means of discovering amazing facts about the mind and
our capacities. Without going into the realms of the supernatural,
evidence gleaned from hypnosis does constantly have the ability to
make us go 'Wow! We are capable of *that*?', and to make us realize
that there is far more to being a human being than is commonly
supposed. To start with psycho-physical phenomena, hypnotized
subjects can, for instance: reproduce on the surface of their skin
tissue injuries sustained at some previous point in their lives; not just

ignore the pain of, say, a lighted cigarette being held to the palm of their hand, but not even blister either (or conversely to blister when told that they are being touched by something hot, which is actually cool); produce something akin to stigmata; localize the anaesthetic effect to particular areas of their bodies, as in 'glove anaesthesia'; and, of course, they can undergo surgery, even painful surgery, while under hypnosis. At the mental level, there is the possibility of superlearning and the phenomenon known as 'transcendence of normal volitional capacities' – a state where the subject's thoughts have remarkable clarity, creativity and meaningfulness. The Russian Dr Raikov has achieved significant results in bringing out latent artistic talents in hypnotized subjects. And even at the physical level work on athletes has demonstrated an increased ability to perform.

In the last fifty years or so, there have been consistent and well-argued attempts to prove that these supernormal phenomena are not necessarily the product of hypnosis – that there is no special state, the hypnotic trance, which enables us to perform these super-feats. This debate will be the subject of a later chapter. At present all I need to point out is that even if these feats are achievable by other means, nevertheless they can be economically and easily achieved by hypnosis; and the fact remains that, however they are produced, they teach us an awful lot about what we are capable of, and point the way forward for future research.

Let's focus on the case of a hypnotized subject anomalously either producing or failing to produce blisters. I've seen this on TV, and just in case anyone thinks that might have been faked, let me add that scientists just take the phenomenon for granted. Milton Kline, for instance, in cataloguing the subjective experiences of a hypnotized person, wrote: 'Similarly, if the hypnotist says, "I am going to touch you with a hot branding iron," and then touches the subject with a piece of simple cloth, the subject will experience pain, will feel burned, and will develop a real blister from this burn.' Now, Kline casually tries to assimilate this to a case where a subject blunders about in a well-lit room because he has been told that it is dark. But are the two cases really the same? Blundering about a lighted room as if it were dark is a purely mental phenomenon, but the case of producing or not producing blisters on a false stimulus involves the interaction of mind and body.

The point I'm getting at is this. Blistering from a burn, one would naturally suppose, is a purely automatic phenomenon. The hand is burnt; the spot reacts with a blister. But now it turns out that either it is not a purely automatic phenomenon – that we also have to *believe* that the spot will blister in order for it to blister – or at any rate that the mind is so powerful that it can override the purely instinctive functions of the body. This is quite astonishing. And anyone can do it. We all have supernormal powers locked up inside our minds; we are all capable of miracles.

9

Freud and Other Alienists

Oddly enough, a considerable boost was given to the scientific study of hypnotism by the rash of stage hypnotists who trekked around Europe in the later nineteenth century. Two in particular were contacted and studied by academic psychologists – a Dane from Odense called Carl Hansen (1833–97) and a Belgian who called himself Donato (real name A.E. d'Hont, 1845–1900). Their shows reveal all the stock-in-trade of the modern TV hypnotist: the human plank, inability to move or speak, acting (often in a demeaning manner) under the influence of hallucinations and so on. Donato would ask his subjects to place their hands, stretched out, on his, which were resting flat on a table, and then to press down as hard as they could. By these simple means he could induce a trance state – remember that focused attention and the exclusion of distracting data are essential to trance induction. Followers of the Nancy school, especially Enrico Morselli in Italy, were certainly influenced by Donato's methods. Meanwhile, Liégeois himself took lessons from Hansen, who was one of the greatest evangelists for hypnotism. Hansen travelled to Sweden, Finland, Germany, Austria, France, Britain and Russia, and received good press coverage wherever he went. He asked his subjects to focus their attention on a shiny piece of glass, while he made a few passes over their faces, lightly closed their eyes and mouth, and gently stroked their cheeks.

Not that the mesmeric performances which swept Europe in the 1880s and 1890s were without their detractors. Rumours spread of how a stage hypnotist had induced his whole audience to believe that the theatre was on fire, causing a panic in which several women and children were trampled underfoot. Another story had a mesmerized young woman walk into the lions' cage at a circus where she was savaged. Professors and medical men argued that hypnotism was like poison, and should be restricted to respectable and capable hands. Shows, they said, which degraded both their subjects and the powerful tool of hypnotism should be banned. Donato responded with equal rhetoric, arguing that freedom of thought and democratic concern for patients whatever the weight of their purses existed in the lay hypnotherapeutic community rather than the professional medical community. The same argument resonates in America and Europe today.

The very success of reputable stage hypnotists like Donato and Hansen led to intense study in Europe, by academics such as Rudolf Heidenhain, the Professor of Physiology at the University of Breslau. How, scientists wanted to know, could subjects be made to drink ink in the belief that it was beer? Inhale ammonia fumes with smiles on their faces? Imagine they were singing like the most glorious diva? Research, especially in German universities, led to a refinement of hypnotic techniques and a variety of sensible theories about what was going on.

The last twenty or so years of the nineteenth century were the high point for hypnosis – not in terms of the number of people practising it and its prevalence on the streets: we would have to go back to the middle of the century for that. But the researches of Charcot and Bernheim and their respective schools had brought hypnosis into the centre of psychology, which was at that time a booming and exciting field of study. Genuine new ground was being broken, and the stage was set for hypnosis to occupy a central position in the discovery of the deep operations of the mind. But in our day hypnosis is again a marginalized subject. What went wrong? In this chapter I will show how hypnosis assisted in the discovery of some fundamental psychological concepts and therapies, and explain how the heyday of academic hypnosis was brought to an end largely by the influence of a single man – by far the most important figure in modern psychology, Sigmund Freud (1856–1939).

The Discovery of Double Consciousness

It was a natural assumption that if through hypnotism or animal magnetism a person reached the deepest somnambulic state, this was only an artificial way of inducing what occasionally happened naturally. Researchers adduced sleepwalking, sleep-talking and other related naturally occurring phenomena to show that the two states of 'sleep' were essentially the same. Psychologists tended to recognize only two states of consciousness: sleep and waking, off and on. But in many of these cases, both spontaneous and artificial, it was as though the person had two consciousnesses – his normal one and a somnambulistic one. It was soon discovered that when hypnotized a person would invariably switch to his alternate personality, with its set of characteristics and memories, and be amnesic for his normal self. The link between memory-set and personality was such that psychologists could trigger the alternate personality just by plugging it into the appropriate memory-set. In other words, memory is (as we would say today) 'state-dependent': we all remember certain things only when we are in the same or a similar state to when the event to be remembered was first experienced. So hypnotized subjects might, when awoken, be completely unaware of anything they had said or done while hypnotized, but when hypnotized again be capable of remembering it all. This, of course, immediately tended to undermine the simple on–off theory of consciousness, because there seemed to be an extra state which was brought about in hypnosis. Then it was found that this extra state can also happen naturally, not just in somnambulism, but in the strange condition known to psychologists as 'fugue'.

Although by this stage of the book the reader may have become inured to weird events and states of mind, fugue is really pretty strange. The Latin root of the word implies 'running away' – fleeing from reality – and the running in most cases is a real occurrence. In *Principles of Psychology* (1890) William James made famous the case of Ansel Bourne, an elderly itinerant preacher, who disappeared from

Rhode Island and reappeared as A.J. Brown, running a store in Norristown, Pennsylvania, with no memory of his previous life until he came to himself after six weeks. Having come to, he could not figure out what he was doing in Pennsylvania rather than Rhode Island: Brown had no memory of being Bourne, nor did Bourne of Brown. Only under hypnosis was he able to remember what he had done as A.J. Brown. Quite a few similar cases have been documented. One man lived an alternate life for almost two years; another turned up in Switzerland after disappearing from Australia.

Fugue is puzzling. If you think of consciousness as either on (waking) or off (sleeping), what is happening in fugue? On the one hand, consciousness is clearly not off, because A.J. Brown can function perfectly well in the world; on the other hand, it is not quite on, either, since Ansel Bourne is unconscious throughout the whole period.

But fugue is just an extreme form of what became known as 'double consciousness' – the fact that in either the natural or the artificial state a subject might display different characteristics from those he showed when awake, as de Puységur's Victor did. In extreme cases the characteristics displayed might be so radically different that the single person might appear to be in effect two or more different people. Nowadays, in its pathological manifestations, we call this multiple personality disorder, or MPD. But the notoriety of the extreme manifestation conceals a very simple psychological truth: that two (or more) streams of consciousness can take place within a single individual at the same time, and that this is not a phenomenon merely of abnormal psychology.

Here is what John Elliotson had to say about his famous subjects, the O'Key sisters:

> These sisters exhibit perfect specimens of double consciousness; the most remarkable perhaps on record. In their ecstatic delirium, they know nothing of what has occurred in their natural state: they know not who they are, nor their ages, nor any thing which they learnt in their healthy state: and in their natural state they are perfectly ignorant of all that has passed in their delirium. Their memory in their delirium reaches back only to the moment when each first woke from mesmeric sleep

into the delirium. They would then, indeed, speak: but their minds were nearly blank: they knew nobody, nor the names, nature, nor use of any thing: they had to learn everything afresh.

Double consciousness was also used in some quarters as an explanation of table-tipping, the spiritist fad of the 1850s. If this was not to be dismissed as fraud or delusion, and if one was disinclined to accept the spiritist interpretation, another view had to be found, and some psychologists speculated that the unconscious mental activity of the participants in the séance was producing the phenomena. It was pointed out that the temperament or beliefs of the sitters were invariably reflected in the messages received. Personally, I find this idea attractive. Once, many years ago now, two friends and I decided to hold a séance. We used the technique of an upturned wine glass on a table with the letters of the alphabet around the perimeter of the table, and at one point – the only coherent message we received – the glass was flashing around the letters 's', 'e' and 'x'. This is perhaps not surprising for three teenage boys! What was surprising, however, was the speed with which the glass moved, which was far too fast for our conscious control.

The Unconscious

Many people think that Freud 'discovered' the unconscious. This is not so. He was simply the first to chart the region systematically, and so to confirm the idea, which had already occurred to others, that it is a feature of normal human beings, not a pathological state. He proved that we have only one consciousness, and that everything else is unconscious, as opposed to the earlier view that we have different centres of consciousness – as it were, different minds within us. What consciousness does, in the Freudian view, is cast light on different areas of the unconscious at different times.

People have always been aware of the unconscious, as long as they have been aware of dreaming, of alternate personalities, of trance and psychosis. Apart from dreaming, consider Shakespeare's portrait of Lady Macbeth reliving her crime while sleepwalking at night, and the phenomenon of lucid possession, in which one is aware of the struggle within oneself of a good spirit and a bad spirit. In the thirteenth century Thomas Aquinas said that there were processes going on in the soul of which we are not immediately aware. In the eighteenth, Rousseau recognized that the true motivations for his actions were often unclear to himself. Early in the nineteenth century the German philosopher Johann Herbart said: 'Arrested ideas are obscured and disappear from consciousness, and these unconscious ideas continue to exert their pressures against consciousness.'

Then along came hypnosis, an excellent tool for the exploration of the mind. One of the most important aspects of the history of hypnosis is that it allowed a new paradigm for unconscious activities to emerge. Instead of attributing all these phenomena to the intrusion of gods or demons, or to some organic disturbance, thinkers in the nineteenth century began to think in terms of an alternate stream of consciousness, below the threshold of normal consciousness. And it was this new paradigm that led to Freud's great enterprise. In other words, the background of the man who has revolutionized the way we think about ourselves more than anyone else in recent times was formed by hypnosis.

The recognition of double consciousness led directly to the modern psychological theory of the unconscious. It was already known that the secondary personality was co-conscious – that it existed alongside our normal consciousness. All that remained was to see that the second personality had a purposeful, intelligent agenda of its own, and that it lasted longer than the period of hypnosis. For, logically, the second self that researchers were noticing might have been a phenomenon specifically associated with hypnotism: it might appear in a hypnotized subject, and then disappear afterwards. But evidence was being amassed that, to the contrary, the second self persisted, even when it was not apparent and the first self was not aware of it. One of the most important pieces of evidence came from post-hypnotic suggestion. If I can plant a suggestion in your hypnotized self which you then carry out afterwards by means of your normal self, that shows that the alternate self persists at a subliminal level and can influence your conscious actions and behaviour.

Nowadays, this is scarcely a startling truth; but when it was first studied in a scientific manner, and documented, by Pierre Janet (1859–1947), a shy, bespectacled academic, it took the medical world by storm. Particularly through inducing automatic writing in his Salpêtrière subjects, Janet demonstrated the constant presence of what he called the subconscious. He then proposed that in hypnosis there occurred a dissociation, or splitting of the conscious from the subconscious parts of the psyche. As the conscious mind was gradually suppressed through the phases of the hypnotic induction, so the unconscious mind gradually surfaced until in deep hypnosis it took over completely, so that, in effect, the subconscious became the conscious. He also held that much the same process went on in hysterical and nervous disorders (in fact, like Charcot, he believed that the hypnotic state was a form of hysteria), and therefore anticipated Freud in developing a theory not just of the unconscious, but also of repression and of the therapeutic effects of abreaction (the discharge – e.g. by weeping or screaming or vomiting – of the energy bound up in childhood traumas). Because the true meaning of our nervous problems was often too painful to be faced, it was pushed back into the subconscious where it festered, formed what he called 'a subconscious fixed idea', and became responsible for all sorts of problems.

Other experimental psychologists were also working at much the same time along similar lines. All of them drew on the findings of hypnosis to support their theories. For Max Dessoir (1867–1947) the 'underconsciousness' was not, as it was for Janet, merely a pathological entity, but a feature of the mental structure of all ordinary human beings. Then there was the indefatigable work of early members of the SPR and ASPR, especially Frederic Myers and Edmund Gurney. Myers even went so far as to suggest that 'storms' or disturbances in the subliminal self were responsible for disturbances in the supraliminal or everyday self. The main contribution of hypnotism to psychology in this context is admirably explained by some comments of William James on the researches of Edmund Gurney:

Gurney's most important contribution to our knowledge of hypnotism was his series of experiments on the automatic writing of subjects who had received post-hypnotic suggestions. For example, a subject during trance is told that he will poke the fire in six minutes after waking. On being waked he has no memory of the order, but while he is engaged in conversation his hand is placed on a planchette, which immediately writes the sentence, 'P., you will poke the fire in six minutes.' Experiments like this, which were repeated in great variety, seem to prove that below the upper consciousness the hypnotic consciousness persists, engrossed with the suggestion and able to express itself through the involuntarily moving hand.

Gurney shares, therefore, with Janet and [Alfred] Binet, the credit of demonstrating the simultaneous existence of two different strata of consciousness, ignorant of each other, in the same person. The 'extra-consciousness', as one may call it, can be kept on tap, as it were, by the method of automatic writing. This discovery marks a new era in experimental psychology, and it is impossible to overrate its importance.

Another important forerunner (and colleague) of Freud, in the context of a history of hypnotism, was Josef Breuer. He elaborated Janet's view that hysteria was due to earlier traumatic experiences. In his work with one of his patients, known as Anna O. (real name Bertha von Pappenheim), he regressed her back to the start of her problems to achieve a cure. His assumption, clearly, was that early traumas, long repressed into the unconscious mind, could still have an effect on us today. The case of Anna O. was written up in *Studies on Hysteria* (1895), which was co-authored by Freud.

Multiple Personality Disorder

Let's go back to fugue for a moment. If this odd thing happens only once in a lifetime, it is called 'fugue'. But what if it recurs? What if Bourne had not become Brown just once, but time and again, for longer and shorter periods, with exactly the same combination of amnesia and state-dependent memory? From late in the eighteenth century, psychologists began to note that the phenomenon of double consciousness could occur spontaneously and in what we would now call a more pathological form in which an individual could oscillate between a number of personalities, all of which have plausible and coherent lives, and none of which is seen as an intrusion in the sense that they all equally belong in the same body. Add to this state-dependent memory and amnesia, and you have the condition we now call MPD.

Oddly, there are no reported cases of MPD until after de Puységur's discovery of double consciousness. This might lead some to doubt the reality of the syndrome. But Adam Crabtree, a therapist and one of the better writers on human psychology, has some important remarks on this:

I believe that the discovery of magnetic sleep and the appearance of multiple personality disorder are directly related. It seems to me that in non-organic mental disturbance there are two elements: the disturbance itself and the phenomenological expression of that disturbance, the symptom language of the illness. The symptoms are a message to others telling them what is going on inside the individual. That is, the symptoms are the language of the inner disturbance. How clearly that inner disturbance will be expressed depends on the adequacy of the language available, and that in turn depends on what categories for understanding humans and the world are current in society.

Until the emergence of the alternate-consciousness paradigm the only category available to express the inner experience of an alien consciousness was possession, intrusion from the outside. With the rise of awareness of a second consciousness intrinsic to the human mind, a new symptom language became possible. Now the disordered person could express (and society could understand) the experience in a new way: it was the second consciousness acting at odds with the normal self.

This means that when Puységur discovered magnetic sleep, he contributed significantly to the form in which mental disturbance could manifest itself from then on. For he helped make possible a symptom language through which the experience of an interior alienation of consciousness could be expressed without resorting to the notion of intrusion from the outside – in other words, without experiencing that condition as possession.

In short, there *were* cases of MPD prior to the late eighteenth century, but they were not recognized as MPD: they were seen as possession by spirits.

MPD cases tend to be oddly similar, so I shall recount just one or two famous early ones. The first ever occurred in 1789, when Eberhard Gmelin in Stuttgart had a patient calling herself Caroline Brune who alternated between two personalities, one of whom spoke French and was more vivacious, while the other was German and more modest. The most famous early case is undoubtedly that of Mary Reynolds, a quiet, shy woman who in 1811, aged thirty-six, had a fit. When she came to herself, she found she was blind and deaf, and she remained that way for some weeks before recovering her senses. Later she fell into a comatose sleep, and when she woke up, after twenty hours, she had a quite different personality – vivacious, attractive, outgoing. But she was like a young child: she could not even speak, let alone remember people, things and skills. She had to learn everything all over again. Five weeks later she woke up one morning back in her original personality. She was very upset to discover what had been going on for the previous weeks, none of which she remembered. A few weeks later she again fell into a prolonged sleep and returned, on waking up, to Mary-2, the outgoing version, which she picked up where she had left it before in terms of language skills and so on. This switching to and fro between the two states went on until 1829, when she changed permanently to Mary-2 until her death in 1854.

One of the forefathers of MPD research was Pierre Janet. Two of his female hysterical patients – Lucie and Léonie – proved to have multiple personalities. In both cases, through hypnosis, Janet found that the original cause was a childhood shock. It was precisely this kind of work that enabled him to develop the concept of 'subconscious fixed ideas' and to show that they continue to exert an influence on conscious life too. Janet was the first to achieve cures by integrating the repressed memories into the consciousness of his patients. Just the mere voicing of these lost memories by patients can lead straight away to the cure of a symptom. Breuer's Anna O. (who was also, incidentally, a 'multiple', as MPD sufferers are colloquially called) could not drink water, until she remembered and described an occasion when she was shocked that a friend let her dog drink out of her glass; after that, she could drink again.

Janet, as we have seen, classified MPD as a form of hysteria, and it is true that MPD is often accompanied by some of the appalling 'conversion symptoms', such as bleeding, headaches, spasms, paralysis and local anaesthesias, which are one of the characteristics of hysteria. Louis Vivé (born in 1863) suffered from paralysis and lack of feeling on his right side, and found it difficult to speak; Félida X., the famous patient of Azam, suffered from hyperaesthesia of the skin, haemorrhages and poor circulation.

In a long and famous book, *The Dissociation of a Personality* (1905), Boston psychiatrist Morton Prince (1854–1929) described his work with a patient known by the pseudonym 'Miss Beauchamp'. Prince, Boris Sidis (1867–1923) and William James were the main researchers keeping hypnosis alive in the States in the early years of the twentieth century. Christine Beauchamp (real name Clara Fowler) was a modest girl who was occasionally taken over by a mischievous personality whom she called 'Sally'. Actually, Christine had four personalities in all: what Prince called B1, the person who came to his office with headaches and insomnia; B2 was simply B1 hypnotized; B3 was Sally, and B4 was a short-tempered personality. Although at first Prince decided to try to make B4 the dominant personality, effectively eliminating B1, he eventually chose to amalgamate B1 and B4, squeezing out B3-Sally. This process of amalgamation or integration has been the therapy of choice in all MPD cases since the time of Janet and Prince.

I should stress, before going any further, that MPD is rare. Only a few hundred cases have been documented, though there is anecdotal evidence of many more. It is only psychologists such as Eugene Bliss who are heavily committed to the existence of MPD who speculate that about 10 per cent of the population may be multiples. Most people, including professional psychologists involved in the field, would regard this as a huge exaggeration – and that is assuming that they believe in the reality of MPD in the first place.

Three Famous Recent Cases of MPD

The book that really brought MPD to people's awareness in modern times was *The Three Faces of Eve*, published in 1957. It tells the story of the psychiatric treatment, by two American doctors, of a woman known as 'Eve White'. Her real name, Christine Sizemore, was revealed in the autobiographical sequel *I'm Eve* (1977), which also shows how incomplete her earlier treatment had been, in the sense that nineteen more personalities had appeared since the end of her treatment. A further autobiographical sequel, *A Mind of My Own*, published in 1989, tells of her eventual triumph over MPD. Anyway, in *The Three Faces of Eve* she was a mousy, timid, conventional person who spontaneously manifested another personality, 'Eve Black', who was flirtatious, coarse and mischievous – exactly the same character differences as were exhibited by Caroline Brune, Mary Reynolds and Christine Beauchamp (and by a number of other MPD victims too). Prince had used hypnosis to bring Miss Beauchamp's other personalities into existence, but Eve Black did not appear through hypnosis, although hypnosis had already been used on Eve White in the course of the therapy, and it was subsequently used as an easy way to summon Eve Black. Later, Eve Black's appearances became so normal that hypnosis was no longer necessary to summon her. At a late stage of the therapy, a third personality appeared, called 'Jane', a mature, calm and intelligent person, who seemed to the therapists to offer hope for the future, if Jane could become the dominant personality. This in fact happened, and the new, more integrated person is called Evelyn White in the book.

Each personality had different handwriting, different brainwave patterns, different profiles arising from various psychological tests, but above all such different personalities, body languages, facial gestures and so on that it was easy for the therapists to tell which personality was in the room with them at any time. Eve White exhibited fugue states and state-dependent memory. She could remember nothing that Eve Black or Jane did, but Eve Black could remember what Eve White did, and Jane could remember all three states.

Speaking as a layman, I have some worries about this – and my worries coincide with those of a number of professional psychologists. My basic worry is that it's all too neat. Eve White had originally entered therapy with marital problems and inexplicable headaches. Once Eve Black has emerged, *every* misdemeanour, right back to childhood, is blamed by Eve White and her husband on Eve Black, leaving Eve White lily-white. But no one is so one-dimensional; everyone does wrong sometimes, or makes mistakes. It looks as though Ms White was simply objectifying a different side of her nature into a separate personality. The fugue condition is odd: it is this that really characterizes MPD. If it were not for the amnesia and the state-dependent memory, we would clearly be faced with no more than different sides of a person's character. But perhaps it is possible for someone to be so neurotic or hysterical, or so prone to fantasies, or under such stress, that she can reify separate sides of herself successfully enough to bring about such amnesia. It has been known at least since the time of Breuer that hysterical people perform a kind of self-hypnosis on themselves, in which they can (among other things) induce amnesia for certain events. And it isn't really surprising to find amnesia in connection with the kind of radical dissociation that characterizes MPD; after all, we have known about state-dependent memory for ages.

So perhaps MPD sufferers are no more than hysterics who have chosen to blank out some parts of their lives, which then seem to be the work of a different personality, resident in the same body. This is the kind of explanation I would prefer to full-fledged MPD. I remember a difficult interview I had with my father in my early teens, after he had found a confessional notebook I had written and had confronted me with some of the material from it. I just kept saying, as an implausible defence: 'It wasn't me. Daddy, it wasn't me', as if that would make it go away. Perhaps if I was a more neurotic type, and had kept this up, the 'I' that had misbehaved would have begun to seem a different personality.

Another worry about MPD is that too often the alternate personalities start to appear only *after* psychotherapy begins. If there were clear evidence in a number of well-documented cases that alternate personalities had been active in someone's life before therapy, that would be different; but such evidence is conspicuously lacking. I'm not suggesting that patients deceive their therapists, or that they are merely role-playing. With dry wit British psychologist Alan Gauld says, about Morton Prince's Miss Beauchamp: 'The hypothesis of deceit . . . has therefore little to recommend it except the fact that it would make psychological science simpler if it were true.' But I am suggesting that it is possible in the therapeutic situation for a hysterical or over-imaginative patient to objectify what are no more than sides of his character, and for therapists to encourage such objectification and to ignore the possibility of spontaneous self-hypnosis.

Perhaps better known than *The Three Faces of Eve*, and certainly better written, is Flora Rheta Schreiber's *Sybil*, which was also made into a successful film. But here things seem to get really out of hand. The protagonist, named 'Sybil Dorsett' in the book, is said to have no fewer than sixteen personalities before finally, as in the case of Eve's fourth, a seventeenth emerges to combine and reconcile the rest. The book contains dramatic descriptions of the fugue states between personalities, and the distress and isolation Sybil feels when this happens.

Or are things out of hand? If my complaint before about one-dimensionality has any force, then sixteen personalities add up to a more rounded human being. And remember that nineteen more personalities later appeared in Eve. Sybil just expresses more of herself than Eve originally did, on this sceptical hypothesis. Psychologists who believe in MPD talk of the secondary selves 'depleting' the primary personality – depriving it of emotions and motivations; but this is just another way of describing what common sense calls the one-dimensionality of each personality. Talk of 'depletion' is a redescription, not an explanation, as often happens when scientists try to explain away something bizarre. Consider this paragraph from *Sybil* in which the personality called 'Mary', a practical homebody, is explaining why she has to come out:

> Well, Dr Wilbur, right now, it's a practical matter. You probably know that Sybil and Teddy Reeves – a friend from Whittier Hall – have just taken an apartment together on Morningside Drive. You know what a new apartment involves. At 8:45 yesterday morning I had to come out to receive the workmen who are putting in new windows. I had to come out again at

7:15 p.m. because I didn't want Sybil to put up the new drapes.
I feel it's up to me to keep the home going.

Surely it makes sense to think of 'Mary' simply as a projection of
Sybil's practical self. Those who are committed to the reality of MPD
talk of the 'autonomy' of the separate personalities, by which they
mean that 'Mary', for instance, can function in the world just as well
as Sybil could. But when I am exhibiting the generous side of my
nature, I am functioning in the world just as well as when I am
exhibiting the mean side. If my scepticism is right, Sybil and her kind
are merely suffering from a severe case of dissociation.

Dissociation may be defined as a division of consciousness into
two or more simultaneous streams of mental activity, especially
when one of these streams influences experiences, thought and action
outside phenomenal awareness and voluntary control. It's quite easy
to explain the concept of dissociation, because most readers will have
experienced it. When you're a little bit drunk, in the state we call
'being less inhibited', what you've done, in effect, is given another
side of your character permission to come out and play. This is a
mild form of dissociation. When you're stoned on marijuana, it's
even easier to see that this is a dissociated state, because one of the
effects of the drug is a certain clarity of observation of oneself. When
you're extremely drunk, you can enter the quasi-amnesic condition
in which (perhaps thankfully) you don't remember the next morning
what you did. In this case, the dissociation is far more extreme, but
no one thinks that a drunk is an MPD sufferer. Or again, many
children have an imaginary playmate: this is a case of quite extreme
dissociation. Such a playmate may even speak in a different voice
and be heard, as if externally, by the child. I suggest that Sybil and
her kind choose at some point to fragment themselves so thoroughly
that they experience a combination of amnesia and objectification of
sides of their character.

Although it's not clear from *The Three Faces of Eve* what originally
made Eve retreat into MPD, in the subsequent *I'm Eve* Christine
explains how it was early shocks relating to violent death that caused
her first dissociations. In Sybil's case it was the awful, cruel and
sexually perverse tortures inflicted on her by a schizophrenic mother,
and the terrors of the rigid fundamentalism with which she was

brought up. Recent studies of MPD have been closely connected with the scare, especially in the States, over childhood sexual abuse, since many apparent multiples reported such abuse as the source of the amnesia and the consequent separation of personalities. I take it that this scare has now been more or less laid to rest. It was a form of mass hysteria, compounded by confabulation between therapists and patients. Of course, incest and sexual abuse of children occur, and may even be more common than we like to think; but at the height of the scare it seemed as though some 50 per cent of people had been abused, and that is too much.

Sybil gradually learnt to recover the other personalities' memories for herself, and to integrate a more complete human being, a new Sybil. Hypnosis was not used at first, but the breakthrough came using a drug, sodium pentothal, which was administered for many months. When Sybil showed signs of becoming dependent on the drug, it was withdrawn, and hypnosis was used instead. In the first place, because some of the personalities were stuck in childhood, it was used to progress them all to the same age, Sybil's age, to aid integration. Then it was used to visualize integration and make it real. But none of this was instantaneous; it took several more years (Sybil had 2,354 sessions with her analyst in all, spread over eleven years). As integration began to happen, hypnosis was used only for the purposes of analysis – to bring about temporary dissociation of the separate selves to enable the therapist to communicate with them. Finally, hypnosis was used to check that Sybil could recall everything the other selves recalled. There were no gaps: Sybil was integrated.

Though hypnosis played less of a part, it is also worth mentioning the remarkable case of Billy Milligan, a young criminal who terrorized the women of Ohio State University for a while in 1977 as a rapist and burglar. Cornelia Wilbur, Sybil's therapist, was again called in, because someone suspected that he might be suffering from MPD. In the event he was found to have no fewer than twenty-four separate personalities – but what is most astonishing is that he was acquitted of his crimes, found not guilty by reason of insanity. Instead of being sent to prison, he was put in the charge of a therapist at a medical centre. Not that MPD is really a form of insanity, in the sense that each of the various personalities may be perfectly sane and capable of functioning in the world, without hallucinating or whatever, but this was the nearest category in the judicial world that the judge could find to acquit him. Among Billy's main personalities was Arthur, who spoke with an English accent, was a scientist, and was fluent in Arabic; Ragen Vadascovinich, a vicious Yugoslavian; and Adlana, a female personality who was a lesbian and was responsible for the rapes. (I should say that multiples often have alters who are children, while they are grown up, and others that are the opposite gender.) His doctor worked towards the integration of the separate personalities under a new, responsible personality – as worked, more or less, in other MPD cases – and progress was being made when Billy was accused (with uncertain justice) of the rape of a woman at the medical centre. Billy regressed, and was eventually sent to prison.

So, is there such a thing as MPD? I am not qualified to give a definite answer to the question, but I have raised certain doubts that occur to me as a lay wielder of common sense. I suppose I feel about it pretty much as Margaret Atwood does, in her novel *Alias Grace*, in which she alludes to the phenomenon. The 'Grace' of the title is Grace Marks, a historical figure notorious in Canada in the 1840s for having allegedly assisted in the double murder of her employer and his housekeeper, and having helped her lover dump their corpses in the cellar of the house where she was a servant. At one point in the novel, which takes place after Marks has been in prison for sixteen years already, Atwood has Marks hypnotized and she reveals a separate personality, that of Mary Whitney, who had been a friend of Grace. While possessed by Mary, it seems as though she could have carried out the murders. But, cleverly, on reading this episode, you're not sure that it's not all a hoax, designed to get Grace off the hook, since the hypnotist, Jerome DuPont, is actually an old friend of Grace's in disguise, and we know from earlier in the book that the brand of stage hypnotism he practises is largely fraud.

MPD has had a chequered history. Once, with the help of hypnosis, it was the searchlight that cast its beam on the road that led to the discovery of the workings of the unconscious. Once it was the flagship in the fleet of pathologies, but now it has fallen victim to the cutbacks of modern scepticism. The bottom line is that nowadays many psychologists think that sufferers from MPD are simply making it all up, exaggerating a tendency we all have. Believers in MPD often point to research indicating that different personalities exhibit different brainwave patterns on an electroencephalograph (EEG). But this is neither here nor there: we all exhibit different brainwave patterns when we are in different states, and no one denies that each personality is a different state. For instance, suppose a deeply angry person has (for whatever reasons) forbidden herself to express her anger. That anger will burst out from time to time as an 'alternate personality' – an angry person within the apparently calm person. I would not be at all surprised if the angry person displayed different EEG readings. Even actors playing different roles have been found to display different EEG readings. It is also disturbing that while the number of multiples multiply in North America, the disorder is virtually unknown elsewhere in the world; and that 90 per cent of the sufferers are middle-class women. It begins to look as though MPD is simply, as the philosopher Ian Hacking said, 'a new way to be an unhappy person'.

Freud and Hypnosis

One day around the middle of the 1870s, while a medical student of Vienna University, Sigmund Freud happened to buy a ticket to see the Danish stage hypnotist Hansen do his tricks. He was impressed:

> While I was still a student I had attended a public exhibition given by the 'magnetist' Hansen and had noticed that one of the persons experimented upon had become deathly pale at the onset of cataleptic rigidity and had remained so as long as that condition lasted. This firmly convinced me of the genuineness of the phenomenon of hypnosis. Scientific support was soon afterwards given to this view by Heidenhain; but that did not restrain the professors of psychiatry from declaring for a long time to come that hypnosis was not only fraudulent but dangerous and from regarding hypnotists with contempt. In

Paris I had seen hypnosis used freely as a method for producing symptoms in patients and then removing them again. And now the news reached us that a school had arisen in Nancy which made an extensive and remarkably successful use of suggestion, with or without hypnosis, for therapeutic purposes. It thus came about, as a matter of course, that in the first years of my activity as a physician my principal instrument of work, apart from haphazard and unsystematic psycho-therapeutic methods, was hypnotic suggestion.

Freud graduated as a doctor in 1881, and the following year his friend and colleague Josef Breuer introduced him to hypnotherapy. In June 1885 Freud worked as a locum at Heinrich Obersteiner's private clinic near Vienna, where hypnosis was practised. In October he went to Paris to study neurology under Charcot. He stayed in Paris until February 1886, and during this time he frequently attended hypnotherapy sessions at the Salpêtrière. He also visited Bernheim in Nancy, where he became convinced (by the phenomena of amnesia and post-hypnotic suggestion) that there could be powerful mental processes in people that were hidden from our normal everyday consciousness. This conviction stayed with him for the rest of his life, of course, and from time to time he acknowledged the importance of hypnotism in making this clear to him.

In the 1880s he was a passionate spokesman for hypnosis, in the face of the usual incredulous suspicions of the establishment, as revelatory of the psychological processes not just of hysterics, but of everyone. Back in Vienna he established his own practice, gave lectures on hypnotism to several learned societies, translated books by both Bernheim and Charcot, and wrote a number of studies on the subject. He attended the pioneering First International Congress for Experimental and Therapeutic Hypnotism in Paris in 1889, incorporated hypnosis into his own practice in the form of direct suggestion, sometimes accompanied by pressing his hands on the patient's head, and used it continuously from 1887 to 1892. The 'small but significant successes' he achieved – the phrase comes from a letter to his friend Wilhelm Fliess – gave him confidence and removed the feeling of helplessness that had dogged his first attempts at psychotherapy. In later years he confessed that it was flattering to be regarded by those he hypnotized as something of a miracle-worker. But by the middle of the 1890s he had more or less given hypnosis up, and on one occasion he condemned it as 'a senseless and worthless proceeding'.

What were his reasons for abandoning hypnosis? This is an important question to answer, because if I had to pinpoint a single reason for the marginalization of hypnosis as a psychotherapeutic tool these days, I would have to pick Freud's abandonment of the practice. Every analyst knows that he made use of it early in his career; every analyst also knows that he had abandoned it by 1896 in favour of free association – the 'talking cure', as Breuer's Anna O. called it. Nearly every analyst makes the assumption that he did so because he was unsatisfied with it and, therefore, out of an understandable desire not to re-invent the wheel and out of awe of Freud, they don't bother to investigate further or consider hypnosis a viable therapeutic option. But in fact, as we will see, Freud's reasons for giving up hypnosis are more complex than this simple picture assumes, and certainly don't imply that he found it useless. On the contrary, in one respect he found it too powerful.

Freud's reasons for abandoning hypnosis are both personal and objective. First, we should not discount his personal enthusiasm at having discovered the importance of dreams and of free association, initially relating to dream themes: he wanted to explore the possibilities of this method, and this meant that other techniques were relegated to a dusty corner of his therapeutic arsenal. Second, he simply found that he himself was not a very good hypnotist. Third, it made him feel uncomfortable, in two respects: since the method he used had him making passes over the patient's head and upper body, Freud found himself stared at by his patients for hours every day, and he didn't enjoy it; also, he didn't understand how it worked, since he had been convinced by the theories of neither Charcot nor Bernheim. Fourth, he found that the phenomenon of transference was enhanced under hypnosis, so that the patient's affection for the therapist could increase beyond desirable limits. This is the respect in which hypnosis was too powerful a tool for Freud: the hypno-therapist has to be careful to prevent too intense a relationship developing between himself and his clients, as they go on a journey of exploration together. In hypnosis the patient becomes very aware of the hypnotist's feelings and motives. This, in Freud's view, is a limitation: it obviously arouses the possibility of the client doing and saying things to please the therapist rather than out of any deeper impulse. On one occasion a hypnotized female patient flung her arms around Freud, to his embarrassment. The entry of a servant into the room interrupted the ensuing painful discussion. He found hypnosis too hot to handle.

These are respects in which Freud personally found hypnosis unsatisfactory, but he also sometimes stated more objective, clinical grounds. First, he found that suggestion fails to produce lasting therapeutic results: 'I gave up the suggestion technique, and with it hypnosis, so early in my practice because I despaired of making suggestion powerful and enduring enough to effect permanent cures. In all severe cases I saw the suggestions which had been applied crumble away again, and then the disease or some substitute for it returned.' Others too have complained about the erratic nature of hypnosis: it is not always possible to induce trance in a patient or to guarantee that a cure induced by post-hypnotic suggestion will last. Freud's most famous pupil, Carl Gustav Jung (1875–1961), also gave it up before long, although it had been a book by Janet on hypnotism which got him interested in psychology in the first place. But, as he recalls in his famous autobiography *Memories, Dreams, Reflections*, as well as finding it unreliable, Jung was frightened when one of his subjects proved difficult to wake up, and he found it too authoritarian (as indeed it was, as invariably practised in those days); he was more interested in listening to his patients than in telling them what to do.

Freud's second clinical reason for giving up hypnosis was that it can obscure what he called the patient's 'resistance'. This needs a word or two of explanation. Resistance is when, in the course of analysis, a patient determinedly ignores certain memories and ideas. Having noticed how regularly this happens, Freud was led to further insights into repression. He saw that its function was to weaken emotionally powerful ideas, in order to protect the patient from the painful experience of the emotion. However, despite the fact that hypnosis had led Janet to discover the fact that patients tend to suppress certain memories, Freud came to believe that hypnosis masked the patient's resistance.

Third, he found there was too great a contrast between the grim truth of patients' problems and the rosy-tinted suggestions he felt as a hypnotherapist that he had to make.

Before discussing these objections, another Freudian concept which needs mentioning is that of 'transference'. This is the evocation by the analyst from the patient, during analysis, of an intense emotional attitude, which could be either sexual, affectionate or hostile in form, and the attachment of these feelings to the analyst. The whole theory of psychoanalysis, according to Freud, was no more than an attempt to explain the two observed facts of resistance and transference, which occur whenever an attempt is made to trace the symptoms of a neurosis back to their source in the past. Freud's mature thoughts on hypnosis led him to define it in terms of transference, as a kind of loving relationship between patient and therapist. It was precisely this that led, at a theoretical level, to his dissatisfaction with hypnotism as a therapeutic technique. It carried with it the danger that its benefits would end as soon as the patient's emotional ties to the therapist ended. Nevertheless, despite his abandonment of hypnosis as a therapeutic technique, throughout his life Freud continued to recommend it as a short-cut procedure in some cases, especially to enable the benefits of analysis to reach the more general lay public.

The first point to notice about these objections by Freud is that he seems to be assuming that hypnosis is the *only* method a therapist would use. On that basis, few psychotherapists would disagree with him – but why make that assumption? Hypnosis may be just one weapon in the therapist's arsenal, in which case Freud's reasons for abandoning it evaporate into mist. Moreover, and more specifically, research since Freud's time has undermined all his reasons for being wary of hypnosis: suggestion *can* bring about permanent cures, and it has proved a very useful tool in the exploration of mental forces, including resistance. It is also worth remembering that the patient can become very attuned to the hypnotist's mind; if Freud was uncertain about hypnosis, that may have communicated itself to the patient, locking Freud into a self-fulfilling cycle within which hypnosis was not as productive as it might have been. The only conclusion possible, considering both Freud's personal and impersonal reasons for abandoning hypnosis, is that he simply wasn't very good at it: his interests lay elsewhere, so he never explored its potential to its fullest.

Freud's dissatisfaction with hypnosis is not unrelated to the fact that he was employing a nineteenth-century authoritarian approach: 'I held my finger before her and called out "Sleep!", and she sank down with an expression of stuporification and confusion.' Elsewhere, in his 1921 book *Group Psychology and the Analysis of the Ego*, he talks about the 'humble subjection' of the subject before the operator, winning compliance from him, but not consensual compliance. Because he was looking for this abject compliance, and because hypnosis fails reliably to produce it, his dissatisfaction increased. But it is precisely when the hypnotist takes on this role, denying the creative participation of the patient in the remedial process, that hypnotherapy is least effective. As a simple example, if a subject is told in a commanding fashion that his body temperature will fall, he may experience the subjective sensations of cold, but nothing objective happens; but if he is allowed to participate – perhaps to create a fantasy of rolling in a snow drift – his body temperature may actually fall.

Freud's reasons for abandoning hypnosis were limited both by his own personality and by the kind of hypnosis that was practised at the time. They do not constitute good reasons for contemporary Freudians and post-Freudians to despise hypnosis and condemn it to the margins of psychotherapeutic techniques. Some Freudians do now combine hypnosis and psychoanalysis as 'hypnoanalysis', having also found that Freud's original objections are no longer valid. One of the earliest to do so was Lewis Wolberg, whose 1945 book *Hypnoanalysis* is still worth reading. The basic point is this: hypnoanalysis is essentially the same process as psychoanalysis, but hypnosis enables aspects of the unconscious to be expressed and seen by both patient and analyst more quickly than in regular analysis.

Hypnosis in Decline

There was a sharp decline in interest in hypnotism, in the circles of experimental psychology, at any rate, after the First World War. Freud must take some of the credit (or blame) for this, as his psychoanalytic methods and theories swept the world clear of everything that had gone before it, and seemed to herald not just a fresh start for psychology, but a fresh impetus for the whole of humanity. Many of the lay hypnotherapists who continued working felt rather out of harmony with the prevalent Freudianism anyway, because whereas Freud stressed the negative aspects of the unconscious, such therapists tended to get their patients to heal themselves out of the great positive power of the unconscious. They held that the patient wanted to be cured, and had the internal resources to cure himself, and that their job was simply to bring their patients to the point where they could harness those resources.

There were other factors causing the decline of hypnosis as well. In the first place, there was the great influence of those, like Bernheim in his later years, who said that there was nothing special about hypnosis – that most of the so-called phenomena of hypnosis, and many of its therapeutic benefits, could be gained through suggestion alone, in subjects who are in a state of ordinary wakefulness and have not been put through a hypnotic induction procedure. The obvious response, that even if this is the case, still the state of hypnotic somnambulism is *more* effective than the waking state, since it is characterized by an increase in suggestibility, was not enough to convince pragmatic working clinicians: suggestion could be used on a wakeful or at least hypnoidal patient without all the bother of trying to see whether she was susceptible to hypnotism, and without all the induction procedures.

In the second place, the supposed dangers of hypnotism were much in the air. The focus in the 1900s and 1910s was less on the question of its possible use for criminal ends, as on whether hypnosis weakened the will of the subject, and made her a kind of slave to the hypnotist. Despite the obvious falsity of this notion, and the fact that any attempt to prove it met with swift rebuttal, the idea did attain a certain popular credence, as in the fictional version of hypnotism in which the hypnotist intones: 'You are my slave. You will obey my every whim.'

And finally, these were the years when, while Freud was king in the offices of American psychotherapists, behaviourism ruled the roost in the universities. Behaviourism reduces everything to stimulus and response: a poem is merely a patterned set of words, designed to achieve the goal of a lover's kiss; the mind is no more than a series of programmed reactions. There was no room here for hypnosis, which seemed to show that the mind had a will of its own.

10

State or No State:
The Modern Controversy

The period between about 1915 and 1945 saw flat years for hypnotism, both in the popular domain and in the groves of academe. There was little knowledge or practice of hypnosis, and even less research into it. Janet lived long enough to see this decline, and he remarked in a book published in 1919 that hypnotism was almost defunct, but would rise again. Once more, it was up to the stage hypnotists to fill the breach – to act as a kind of underground stream until hypnosis should be revived and put to more constructive uses. An index of the decline is that when Robert Lindner wrote his famous 1944 book *Rebel Without a Cause* (on which the 1955 film of the same name starring James Dean and Natalie Wood was loosely based) he felt the need to write an introductory chapter defending hypnoanalysis both in itself and as a tool in the particular case he was writing about – the treatment of a young psychopath.

The only real shaft of light in the otherwise dull climate was Clark Hull's 1933 book *Hypnosis and Suggestibility*. The importance of this book is that it applied recent advances in experimental psychology to hypnosis, and so made hypnosis a suitable study for laboratory experiments. Previously research had been carried out almost entirely by therapists on their patients, with all the consequent dangers of bias. I mean, what conclusions might Charcot have reached about hypnosis if he had not made hysterical women his subjects? Or if he had used a proper control group against which to check his results? But from Hull's time onward it has become more usual to make your research subjects normal people – if the university students who constitute the main pool of subjects can be said to be normal! Hull also gave impetus to the later desire among many psychologists to deny the existence of a special state which may be called the 'hypnotic trance'; he was in favour of trying to explain hypnotic phenomena by reference to more normal psychological mechanisms, especially suggestibility.

Since about 1960, however, there has been such academic interest in hypnosis that Gauld considers it a 'golden age'. The USA is the main centre of research, helped by a number of thriving societies and their journals, and by good university departments and research laboratories. Especially worth mentioning are the Society for Clinical and Experimental Hypnosis, the American Society of Clinical Hypnosis, the International Society of Hypnosis, and Division 30 of the American Psychological Association. Since gold is a heavy metal, the epithet is appropriate in view of the weight of the material written on the subject, mostly designed to bewilder the unwary researcher. Hundreds of learned papers and books have been published, many to support, basically, one of two different views. The proponents of one view proclaim that a hypnotized person is in a distinct state, an altered state of consciousness, while the others stridently assert that there is no such thing as hypnosis, no special state, and that the word ought properly to be put in scare quotes to indicate this.

The debate is important, and not least because the debunking view is commonly reflected at a popular level: 'Hypnosis? A load of superstitious mumbo-jumbo, isn't it?' But before we get into the details of this controversy, I must introduce a man, once a student of Clark Hull, who fits neither in time nor in character into the neat parcels a non-fiction writer likes to use to order his book.

Milton Erickson and Conversational Hypnosis

In his time, Milton Erickson (1901–80) was the most respected and famous hypnotherapist in the world, and since his death a great many books and articles have been written about him, his techniques and their applications. His influence has been enormous, and in some quarters there has been a tendency almost to deify the man. But he had to battle against the odds to win his reputation. In his late teens he was badly affected by polio, so that he was more or less a cripple, and by the end of his life he was confined to a wheelchair. In his middle age, he was so mistrusted for his apparently miraculous cures and his unorthodox methods that the American Medical Association tried to revoke his medical licence. This was the paranoid 1950s and they simply didn't understand him.

Erickson was a superlative therapist with or without hypnosis. He liked to be extremely flexible in his approach – whether he chose to use hypnosis, whether the sessions were long or short, whether they met at his office in Phoenix, Arizona, or somewhere else. He could be aggressive or gentle, direct or indirect. Once, in a highly dramatic instance, he cured a man who had been paralysed for a whole year after a stroke, unable to move or speak, by insulting him so drastically that he forced him to respond, first verbally, and then by getting up and leaving the room so that he didn't have to hear any more. This is typical of his therapeutic methods, in the sense that he would never leave a symptom alone, but would bring about a change in it – a change of intensity, of frequency, of location, anything. He used to say that it takes a lot less effort to channel a river in a new direction than it does to dam it up.

He was often unconventional; for instance, he cured a young man of terrible acne by having his mother take him on holiday and ensure that there were no mirrors around for the whole two weeks. Where hypnotic induction is concerned, he found that imaginary devices were more effective than real objects. Rather than getting his clients to stare into a real crystal ball, for instance, he got them to stare into an imaginary one. This is because it was always Erickson's purpose to get to his client's unconscious, which he believed contained the resources and knowledge needed for a cure. Harnessing the imagination is a quick way to the unconscious.

Believing that everyone is hypnotizable, and that a failure to induce hypnosis reflects the inabilities of the hypnotist rather than those of the subject, he adapted his techniques of induction to the patient, rather than following a limited repertoire. And it is indeed arguable that those researchers who claim that a certain percentage of people are not hypnotizable have used more or less the same technique on their experimental subjects, rather than drawing on the kind of flexibility for which Erickson was famous. Erickson's colleague Ernest Rossi would add that a hypnotist should be sensitive to his subject's natural rhythms of energy and rest, and that his chances of hypnotizing the subject are greatly increased if he times the induction to coincide with the resting period of her cycle.

Erickson was such a skilled hypnotist that he raises again the question whether it is possible to hypnotize a person against her wishes. But his life and practices cannot give us an answer. He was seeing patients who knew that he was a hypnotist, and so they had, at some level, already given their assent. I still maintain what I said in an earlier chapter, that a person cannot be hypnotized against his will, and cannot be made to do things he would not otherwise do.

A lot of Erickson's techniques involved the distraction of the subject's conscious attention and barriers. So, for instance, the 'my-friend-John' method had Erickson imagining that there was another person, John, in the room with him and his subject. Erickson would describe what a good hypnotic subject John was, and go through all the phases and stages of a fictional past trance induction with John – until the subject himself or herself was in a trance. Whereas this and most other techniques used nowadays involve the use of words, Erickson could put someone into a trance merely by means of actions. In fact, he defined hypnosis as a cooperative experience dependent on the communication of ideas by whatever means are available. Rapport with the subject – with the subject's unconscious especially – was crucial. So on a couple of occasions, as a demonstration, he hypnotized subjects who spoke no English simply by pantomiming the gradual induction of a trance.

One of his well-known methods is the 'confusional technique': by confusing tenses and bringing in non sequiturs and small talk, a sense of frustration builds up in the subject until he is actually looking forward to clear suggestions to which he can respond; at that point Erickson would introduce a clear suggestion for entering or deepening the trance. The patient escapes from confusion into trance. A similar method for engaging the subject's curiosity was his use of pauses and hesitation to build up the subject's expectancy and undermine his alertness. A non-verbal parallel is the interrupted handshake: by holding out his hand as if for a handshake, but then stopping and doing various ambiguous things with his hand instead, he was able to induce arm catalepsy in a subject, who thereby showed that he had gone into a trance.

Nobody appreciated the importance of trust better than Erickson. One of his most common induction techniques was simply to begin by telling his client truths, as a method of induction. 'You are sitting comfortably in the armchair' – quite right, nothing to resist there. 'Your hands are resting on the arms of the chair' – undeniable, Dr Erickson. 'You can feel your feet on the floor and the weight of your seat in the chair'. And so on. After half a dozen of these truths, Erickson would reach the point of saying: 'Your eyelids are feeling heavy' or whatever, and the patient was prepared to accept it because Erickson had won his trust by telling him truths for so long. Not only had he won credibility; by pointing out things which were true but unconscious until he drew attention to them, Erickson had accustomed the client to altering his state of consciousness, and so prepared him for the shift into hypnotic trance. Erickson understood that winning trust is more than half the battle; if you trust a person in authority, his suggestions carry weight. One of the main non-verbal methods Erickson used for gaining trust was subtly mirroring his patients' body language, rate of breathing, intonations and so on.

Erickson could win over even a patient who was determined to resist, either out of stubbornness or anxiety. In fact, this was his specialty, and he devised a number of techniques (called 'techniques of utilization', because they make use of whatever behaviour the subject presents to the operator) to overcome resistance without appearing to do so. In all his therapeutic strategies, he was concerned to intervene, but to do so subtly, in order to enhance the healing with empowerment of the autonomy of the individual. He was directive and manipulative in dealing with his patients' symptoms, but left the choice of how to live after those symptoms were resolved entirely up to each individual.

Here is a description of one of Erickson's most famous coups, involving a typical technique to overcome resistance, the 'double bind':

A resistant subject once said to Milton Erickson, 'You may be able to hypnotize other people but you can't hypnotize me!'

Erickson invited the subject to the lecture platform, asked him to sit down, and then said to him, 'I want you to stay awake, wider and wider awake, wider and wider awake.' The subject promptly went into a deep trance. The subject was faced with a double-level message: 'Come up here and go into a trance,' and 'Stay awake.' He knew that if he followed Erickson's suggestions, he would go into a trance. Therefore he was determined not to follow his suggestions. Yet if he refused to follow the suggestion to stay awake, he would go into a trance.

Erickson got his way, but it was a self-chosen act; he undermined the patient's resistance while preserving his autonomy.

He also developed a simple but powerful way of overcoming resistance to therapeutic suggestions. He would intersperse therapeutic suggestions between suggestions for trance maintenance. In this way, before the subject could begin to contradict the therapeutic suggestion, his attention was diverted on to maintaining the trance. Likewise, if Erickson saw that for therapeutic purposes it was important for a patient to do something he would not want to do, he would not ask him directly to do that thing. Instead, he asked him to do something else, something which the patient would be even more reluctant to do. In that way, the patient would freely choose to do the thing which Erickson wanted him to do in the first place.

If you go to a hypnotist today, she will talk a lot – gently, persuasively. It was Erickson above all who perfected this conversational technique of hypnotic induction. Erickson's use of language was probably natural and instinctive, but by now it has been extensively analysed. It would take too long to cover all the nuances, but here are a few samples of the art of conversation according to Erickson and his followers.

Certain key words occur time and again – 'and', for instance. By connecting even logically unconnected statements with 'and', Erickson could take a client deeper into the hypnotic state. 'You are sitting on the chair *and* your arms are resting on the arms of the chair [two undeniable truths] *and* your eyelids are getting heavy *and* you are feeling sleepy *and* now you can hardly keep them open . . .' Another technique is to ask questions that require the answer 'yes', so that the patient assents to the process of hypnotic induction. 'It's nice to be calm and relaxed, isn't it?' 'You'd like all your problems to dissolve, wouldn't you?' Assent and trust are, to repeat, critical. Questions are often more powerful than direct statements anyway, because they seem to leave the decision up to the client: 'Can you tell me what it's like to go into deep sleep?' encourages sleep without seeming to be a command. 'Did that surprise you?' opens the patient's mind to surprise and the possibility of change. Disguised questions may also be used: 'I don't know how deeply you want to go into hypnosis.' Commands might also be hidden, embedded in a seemingly innocuous statement: 'I don't want you to *become more relaxed* as you listen to my voice.' By subtly emphasizing the italicized words with a change of tone or pitch, they become a suggestion, aimed at the unconscious.

Once this degree of trust and lethargy have been reached, the Ericksonian hypnotist might introduce some forcing words – 'must', 'impossible', 'can'. 'As you go deeper and deeper into the trance state, you will not be able to open your eyes. No matter how hard you try, it is impossible to open your eyes. You are so relaxed, so very relaxed [repetition is another good Ericksonian technique], that you find you must sleep ... You cannot raise your arms ...' A similar technique is to use attention-grabbing words such as 'now' and 'obviously', perhaps with a slightly more emphatic tone of voice: 'Now you are feeling sleepy; you obviously know how to relax; you can begin to go deeper into hypnosis now.' John Grinder and Richard Bandler explain the thinking behind whether the Ericksonian therapist uses forcing words or something rather vaguer:

The guideline I use is this: I don't want anyone that I do hypnosis with ever to fail at anything. If I'm making a suggestion about something that can be verified easily, I will probably use words such as 'could' or 'might' – what we call 'modal operators of possibility'. 'Your arm *may* begin to rise ...' That way, if what I've asked for doesn't occur, the person won't have 'failed'. If I'm making a suggestion about something that is completely unverifiable, I'm more likely to use words that imply causation: 'This *makes* you sink deeper into trance' or 'That *causes* you to become more relaxed.' Since the suggestion is unverifiable, he won't be able to conclude that he's failed.

Emotional words – sometimes called 'anchors' – are important. Having found out enough about his client to tell which words were likely to trigger emotional responses, either positive or negative, Erickson would pepper his talk with these words in order to harness the emotional energy for therapeutic purposes.

But the technique for which Erickson is most famous is his use of analogies and metaphorical stories, for which he apparently had an astonishing gift. I'm sure some of the stories were prepared and polished, but others were spontaneous: Erickson could think in this metaphorical mode as swiftly and clearly as he could in normal associative mode. The tales are very often personal, details of Erickson's own life which he tailors to suit the moment, with the purpose of reframing the patient's problems. Most of the stories are too long to quote, but here's a short one designed to communicate the point that the unconscious mind can be trusted to do the right thing at the right time:

> A lot of people were worried because I was four years old and didn't talk, and I had a sister two years younger than me who talked, and she is still talking but she hasn't said anything. And many people got distressed because I was a 4-year-old boy who couldn't talk. My mother said, comfortably, 'When the time arrives, then he will talk.'

Simple and to the point. And the point of the stories was always the same: 'First you model the patient's world, then you role-model the patient's world.' Stories and metaphors engage the imagination and pleasant emotions of the client; Erickson also used jokes, puns and riddles to the same effect. They relax the client and make him open to their metaphorical content, for they are in fact parables for his own problem and the way out of it. They can contain hidden action commands. One famous example involved a case of chronic bed-wetting in a twelve-year-old boy. The parents had tried every-thing, from patience to bribery and punishment. Erickson found out that the boy loved baseball, so he talked to the child about the muscle control needed to play expert baseball. In order to catch the ball, he said, the muscles have to all clamp down at just the right moment; in order to release the ball, the muscles have to let go at just the right time, or the ball doesn't go where you want it to go. If you get it right, Erickson concluded, it's great – a real achievement. The boy stopped wetting his bed.

Or again, and perhaps with rather less subtlety, in dealing with a married couple who had sexual difficulties, he might get them to talk instead about food, a common metaphor for sex. He would get the woman to agree that she enjoyed lingering over the starters, while the husband liked to plunge straight into the main course. If the clients began to see what Erickson was driving at, he would change the subject, but re-introduce it from time to time. And he would end by suggesting, apparently just as a general piece of advice, that they find an evening when they could have a pleasant dinner together – hoping that a fulfilling dinner would lead to fulfilling sex.

This example is taken from a case where no hypnosis was involved. But most of Erickson's stories were told to hypnotized patients, because Erickson believed that in a trance state we instinctively understand the point of the story, without consciously realizing that we do. As the Ericksonian therapist Lee Wallas puts it, they are stories for 'the third ear'. The point of the story is absorbed and acted on unconsciously. Moreover, being in a receptive state, the point is seeded deep within our psyches. But the point of the story is only half its therapeutic purpose; a good story leaves a good feeling – the kind of good feeling you have on leaving the cinema after a great movie. Creating that good feeling is also part of the therapy of Ericksonian story-telling, and so his stories were invariably life-enhancing, positive, supportive of growth and of taking charge of one's own life. They talk of achievements, of breaking barriers, of new horizons.

From a theoretical perspective, Erickson is most interesting as marking a clear break with the Freudian assumption that regression is the way to get at most problems, which have been caused in the past. Erickson worked, Zen-like, with patients here and now, believing that we each have within us the resources for complete health, and that we should focus on improving ourselves rather than correcting past mistakes. Moreover, since he thought that 'Your conscious mind is very intelligent, but your unconscious is a lot smarter', the therapeutic process did not necessarily require 'insight' – the bringing into consciousness of whatever was required. He believed that we have the resources from our past to overcome any obstacle. If you have solved a problem in the past, you can do so again. So he would talk his patient through how she solved some problem in the past, and then recreate those conditions in the hypnotized patient's mind for the present.

Milton Erickson died over twenty years ago, but it is safe to say that almost any hypnotherapist you might visit today has been influenced by his work, and will be practising several of his techniques. I would describe Erickson as a kind of poet. There is a difference between hypnotic or 'trance-inductive' poetry and the kind of poetry that appeals mainly to the intellect. The main features of hypnotic poetry are that it has a regular, soothing rhythm; it is repetitive; it uses vague imagery; and it contains obscurities which tire the mind. All of these features are present in Erickson's methods. He was an artist.

The Professional Doubters

The question is: is there such a thing as hypnosis? Are people who are said to be hypnotized in a special state, distinct from other states of consciousness, or not? Can all the feats attributed to hypnotized subjects be performed equally well by people who have not undergone any kind of hypnotic induction? The literature on the debate is enormous, and the best that can be said for the controversy is that it has generated a huge volume of significant research. In what follows I have stuck to the heart of the issues. Although it is arguable that in hypnosis a number of different altered states of consciousness are involved, depending on the depth of the trance, it makes life simpler if I use the singular and just talk in terms of a single state.

In brief, state theorists argue that: (1) there is a special state of awareness called the hypnotic trance; (2) this state is marked by increased suggestibility, and enhancement of imagery and imagination, including past visual memories; (3) the state involves a decrease in the planning function, a reduction in reality testing and a number of reality distortions such as false memories, amnesias and hallucinations; (4) the state involves involuntary behaviour – the subject has temporarily lost conscious control of his behaviour. They also predict, while admitting that there is as yet no conclusive proof in this regard, (5) that EEG results will one day demonstrate a unique physiology for this supposed hypnotic state.

Non-state theorists deny all these points: (1) concepts such as 'trance' or 'dissociation', taken from abnormal psychology, are misleading, in the sense that responsiveness to suggestion is a normal psychological reaction; (2) differences in response to hypnotic suggestions are not due to any special state of consciousness, but rather to the individual's attitudes, motivations and expectancies, or to his imaginative involvement in the task; (3) all the phenomena associated with hypnotic suggestions are within normal human abilities; (4) the apparent involuntary behaviours of subjects can be explained otherwise, without bringing in a special hypnotic trance; (5) they predict that no such physiological proof will ever be found, because there is no such state. In short, looking for the hypnotic state is like looking for the emperor's new clothes.

There is an interesting and fundamental difficulty in researching hypnosis, which goes some way towards undermining the work of both schools. It has been known since the time of Mesmer that in order to be successful a hypnotist must exude a certain confidence and assurance in the outcome of a given suggestion. A scientific researcher, however, is supposed to maintain a sceptical distance from both his subject and the hoped-for outcome. It is hardly surprising, then, that those researchers who have erred on the side of distance and aloof objectivity have often failed to find that hypnosis produces any results, while those who have gone too far in the other direction have suggested that there is no such thing as hypnosis, only rapport and suggestibility.

The chief proponent of the anti-state view since the 1950s has been Theodore Barber. I cannot resist telling an anecdote about Barber. There is a rumour, apparently started by Ernest Hilgard, that the reason Barber was so convinced of the non-existence of hypnosis as a separate state was that he was very highly hypnotizable himself

– so much so that he could never see what all the fuss was about, and so he denied the existence of hypnosis. Anyway, Barber argues (repeatedly) that the concept of hypnotism is meaningless. Hypnotism is defined as an induced state of increased suggestibility, and yet it is the fact that a person is hypnotized that is supposed to produce the phenomenon of increased suggestibility. Thus the argument is circular, or so Barber claims (and he has been echoed by many others). But this argument is not as strong as it seems. We can reject his premiss by not defining hypnotism merely in terms of suggestibility, and by claiming instead that suggestibility is just one of the phenomena of the hypnotic state.

But in any case, Barber adds, the supposed phenomena of hypnosis can be explained more simply by reference to the subject's attitudes, motivations and expectancies. In an enormous number of papers, Barber has tried to show that certain hypnotic phenomena (especially amnesia, enhanced muscular performance and arm levitation) can equally well be obtained with unhypnotized subjects who have been led by the researchers (i.e. himself and his colleagues) to have a positive attitude towards the outcome of the task they have been set, to be motivated to perform well, and to expect that they will be able to perform the task. As for the more extreme or exotic phenomena, such as hallucinations, age-regression, hypermnesia and hypnotic blistering, Barber has tried either to dismiss them or to claim that in reality they do not occur in dramatic ways and that therefore unhypnotized subjects have little difficulty in displaying them too.

Once, at a meeting of the American Psychological Association in the early 1970s, Barber was banging on as usual about how it was easy to bring about analgesia in people without hypnotic induction. Among other eminent psychologists on the stage with Barber was Martin Orne. Orne flicked open his cigarette lighter and held his palm over the flame. Fine: this seemed to confirm Barber's point. But those who knew Orne chuckled because they knew that he was also making a further point – that Barber's views did not advance our understanding of hypnosis at all.

There are further serious difficulties with Barber's view. Suppose he finds that both hypnotized and task-motivated people are equally capable of task X. He then infers that the hypnotized people are actually task-motivated rather than hypnotized, and that there is no such thing as hypnosis. This is a blatant fallacy. If A produces X and B produces X, it does not follow that A and B are identical; they may simply have the same effect. What is true in Barber's position is nothing new, but has been known since the time of Bernheim – that suggestions given to susceptible or fantasy-prone individuals in the waking state (and especially when relaxed) can often produce the same effect as suggestions given to hypnotized subjects. Barber's list of suggested responses includes: colour blindness, deafness, various emotions, improvement of short sight, hallucinations of taste and sight, and allergic reactions. But, again, this does not disprove the existence of a special state which we can call the hypnotic trance.

In his later work Barber began to move towards the view that so-called hypnosis, as well as being a product of task-motivation, is also an act of the imagination. This is called the 'cognitive-behavioural' approach, and its main proponents, apart from Barber, are psychologists Nicholas Spanos and John Chaves. They claim that being 'hypnotized' is like reading a book or watching a film: 'The responsive hypnotic subject . . . has intense and vivid experiences that are produced by the words or communications he is receiving.' Elsewhere, Spanos claims that so-called 'hypnosis' is just 'goal-directed fantasy': the subject imagines a situation which, if it actually occurred, would produce the results which the suggestions imply. Thus, as with Barber's early views, hypnosis is reduced to *behaviour* rather than a *state*.

Apart from the emphasis on imagination, the views expressed in the book Barber co-authored with Spanos and Chaves read pretty much like early Barber. The supposed hypnotic induction procedure serves only to produce positive attitudes, motivations and expectancies in the subject. Hence subjects show a high level of responsiveness to test suggestions (e.g. you cannot raise your right arm) and a 'hypnotic' appearance (e.g. relaxed, eyes closed, drowsy, etc.), and report that they were hypnotized. Perceptual and physiological effects, age-regression, trance logic and visual hallucinations are not best explained by reference to 'hypnotic trance' because unhypnotized control subjects are also capable of manifesting the same phenomena. Hypnotic surgery is explicable because most parts of the body are actually rather insensitive to the surgeon's scalpel. Also, pain is reduced when patients have low levels of anxiety and fear, and positive expectations. Some cases of alleged hypnotic analgesia may actually be cases of post-'hypnotic' amnesia – the patient has simply forgotten that she suffered pain. Stage hypnotism works partly by fraud, and partly because the atmosphere makes for suggestibility and obedience.

Where the cognitive-behavioural emphasis on imagination is involved, it should be said that this has turned out to be a double-edged sword, working against them just as effectively as it does for them. They argue that the subjects' imaginative involvement in the task is what creates or helps to create the phenomena. State theorists have turned this on its head. They agree that imagination is an important factor – but a factor that enables a person to reach a trance state, in which the phenomena will be produced.

I don't want to get into all the experimental evidence that supports the non-state theorists, or tends to disprove their position, because it is obvious to the unbiased reader that experiments can be made to prove or disprove all sorts of things, depending on what you want to read into them. In reading accounts of the often ingenious experiments psychologists have set up in order to test one or another alleged phenomenon of hypnotism, it is clear that the results are frequently ambiguous, and that the researcher's own philosophical preconceptions invariably guide how the results are interpreted. For instance, in a classic experiment a psychologist called Seymour Fisher showed that subjects responded to post-hypnotic cues only when they thought the experiment was still ongoing; if they thought the experiment had ended, they stopped scratching their ears in response to the trigger-word 'psychology' (which was the post-hypnotic suggestion that had been implanted in them). This experiment was meat and drink to the non-state theorists, since it cast doubt on the validity of hypnotic phenomena. But actually it is arguable that, the way the experiment was set up, Fisher had implicitly asked his subjects to respond to the cue only as long as the experiment was in progress, in which case it is not surprising that he got the results he did. This is a subtle point, but it goes to show that experimental results are not as hard and fast as they seem to be.

In task-motivational experiments the subjects are under strong pressure to report in a way that pleases the experimenter, regardless of what they actually felt, whereas subjects in hypnotic experiments are rarely under such pressure. When an honest report is insisted upon, the results are far less striking, far less supportive of the task-motivational theory, whereas the same demand on hypnotized subjects makes little or no difference to their reports. Task-motivational instructions can alter reports but not experiences. So, to return for the moment to the vital issue of resistance to pain, and those who report in Barber's experiments that they feel no pain: 'Common sense suggests that the subjects really did experience the pain but dared not admit it. The negative report . . . might well be due to Barber's telling them that they would not feel pain if they really tried, and that if they did they were making his experiment a failure, wasting time and making their professor look silly! Most of us will tell a convenient lie if we are under sufficient moral pressure.'

It also seems possible to me that for a light trance the social-psychological model might be correct – that so-called hypnosis is 'strategic social behavior' – while for a deep trance, the state theorists might be correct. This would explain why the cognitive behaviourists get the results they do, and others get results which tend in the opposite direction. For instance, Barber and his colleagues have frequently found in their experiments that non-hypnotized subjects display the same phenomena as supposedly hypnotized subjects; others, however, have found that hypnotized subjects can produce, for instance, a far greater variation of skin temperature than non-hypnotized subjects. Perhaps, as the Victorians found, the deeper the level of trance, the more striking the phenomena that are produced. Erickson once defined a deep trance as 'that level of hypnosis that permits the subject to function adequately and directly at an unconscious level of awareness without interference by the conscious mind'. The social-psychological model can only deal with a quite different level of the mind, and denies any functioning on the part of a hypnotized subject at an unconscious level.

Another prominent sceptical and behaviourist position on hypnosis is that of Theodore Sarbin and William Coe. They claim that hypnosis is just role-playing (or compliance, as British psychologist Graham Wagstaff puts it). The subject wants to please the operator, and plays out the role expected of him; he may even feel under some kind of pressure to comply. Now, there is an element of truth in this. Anyone who has been hypnotized knows that there is a point (in a light trance, at any rate) where he chooses to go along with the hypnotist's suggestions, and so may be said to be playing a role; this has been a recognized aspect of hypnosis since the nineteenth century. But that is not a reason to deny that there is such a special state as the hypnotic trance: you could say that part of the definition of the hypnotic trance is precisely that it involves this mental ambiguity – the parallel-awareness feeling of 'Shall I or shan't I go along with this?' In any case, I go back to Esdaile's surgical operations. Speaking as a man, there is no way that I'm going to play a role while someone is probing my testicles with a scalpel. I'm going to have to be in a deep enough trance to be analgesic in the relevant area.

Nicholas Spanos has a slightly more sophisticated take on analgesia. He argues that the phenomena attributed to hypnosis are what he calls 'social behavior'. Subjects are so motivated to respond in keeping with their expected role that they develop 'cognitive strategies' to do things such as overcoming pain. In this view, to say that they are playing a role is not to say that they are faking it: they make use of 'cognitive strategies' such as imagery, self-distraction and verbalizations that help to convince them that the pain is not so bad, and these strategies do genuinely raise pain thresholds. So-called 'hypnotizability', according to Spanos, is a learnable skill, as subjects learn to deploy their cognitive strategies more successfully. Graham Wagstaff agrees with this view, and adds that only if the cognitive strategies fail to work will a subject resort to mere behavioural compliance – that is, faking it. And Wagstaff should know, since in 1970, while a university student, he was 'hypnotized' on stage by the magician Kreskin, and put through some of the usual tricks of a stage hypnotist.

The pain-relieving effect of hypnosis has, however, been proved time and again to be real. In one experiment, for instance, outside assessors could not distinguish simulators from genuinely hypnotized subjects by their responses, or lack of responses, to electric shocks. After the experiment, however, the simulators said that they felt the shocks and had to suppress their response, while the hypnotized subjects said that they felt nothing. Contrary experiments which are supposed to show that task-motivated or compliant subjects gain as much relief from pain have often been poorly designed. The idea is not to hypnotize subjects, but just to persuade them by suggestion and relaxation not to feel so much pain. The problem with these experiments is that any of the subjects who are susceptible to hypnosis will drift into a hypnotic state as a result of relaxing and listening to the suggestions, and so at least some of the subjects are gaining relief from pain through hypnosis, after all. It is as hard to prove that someone is *not* hypnotized as it is to prove that she is.

While it has generally been my role in this book to report rather than to comment, I feel impelled to offset the vociferousness of these non-state theorists, who basically rule the roost at the moment and are in danger of carrying the day by the sheer weight of their publications. Although there are certain minor differences between their views, they are similar enough for Spanos and Barber to have spoken, prematurely, of a 'convergence' in academics' opinions about hypnosis, as if the state theory had been laid to rest once and for all. So let me say that there are five kinds of phenomena which, as far as I can see, still present obstacles to their view. These are: first, state-dependent memory; second, resistance to pain; third, the ability not to blister and other remarkable effects showing control of organic processes; fourth, the phenomenon of post-hypnotic suggestion; fifth, the phenomenon of trance logic.

State-dependent Memory: We have met this facet of memory before. In an interesting experiment much earlier this century, the Swiss psychologist Edouard Claparède (1873–1940) read his subjects ten bizarre words when they were deeply hypnotized, and ten equally unfamiliar words while they were awake. These twenty words were then jumbled together with a number of other words. The subjects, after being dehypnotized, were then asked which words they recognized. They always recognized only the ten they had heard while awake, and never the ten they had heard while hypnotized. Unhypnotized people can only *pretend* not to recognize the words. Post-hypnotic amnesia is a genuine, state-dependent phenomenon, which makes it look as though the hypnotic state is genuine too.

Resistance to Pain: It is not just that hypnotized subjects can resist pain. Experiments have shown that unhypnotized subjects can also resist pain, either under conditions of distraction, or because they are suitably motivated and so on. There are of course subjective elements to the sensation of pain: everyone knows that some people have a higher pain threshold than others, and surveys show that soldiers resist the pain of wounds better because for them a wound is a good thing (it allows them to go home with honour), whereas for a civilian a wound is usually a bad thing, and so he feels it more acutely. Part of the problem here is that Barber and his colleagues rely heavily on experimental evidence and tend to ignore the down-and-dirty evidence of hypnotists who have performed surgical operations. But some of the surgical operations performed under hypnotism are extremely painful, and extremely protracted. Even if people had higher pain thresholds in Esdaile's day, it is still unthinkable that an eight-hour operation could be performed under hypnosis, that patients would lie still for amputations, the removal of breast cancers, scrotal growths and so on. Not all of them did, but a good 50 per cent did. Esdaile had the definitive response to the doubters, and it still rings absolutely true:

> I have *every month* more operations of this kind than take place in the native hospital in Calcutta a year, and more than I had for the six years previous. There must be some reason for this, and I can only see two ways of accounting for it: my patients, on returning home, either say to their friends similarly afflicted: 'Wah! brother, what a soft man the doctor Sahib is! He cut me to pieces for twenty minutes, and I made him believe that I did not feel it. Isn't it a capital joke? Do go and play him the same trick.' . . . Or they say to their brother sufferers, – 'Look at me; I have got rid of my burthen (of 20, 30, 40, 50, 60, or 80 lbs., as it may be), am restored to the use of my body, and can again work for my bread: this, I assure you, the doctor Sahib did when I was asleep, and I knew nothing about it; – you will be equally lucky, I dare say; and I advise you to go try; you need not be cut if you feel it.' Which of these hypotheses best explains the facts my readers will decide for themselves.

Or consider this case. Once a worker in an aluminium plant slipped and immersed his leg up to the knee in molten aluminium, with a temperature of 950° C. Under the hypnotic suggestion that his leg would not be inflamed and would be cool and comfortable, the man needed nothing more than a relatively mild painkiller, and he was discharged from hospital after only nineteen days, with new skin already growing well over the injury. If this is role-playing, or imaginative involvement, or response to social cues of any kind, it is quite remarkable. Whereas the non-state theorists frequently claim that they are the ones wielding Occam's razor, in this kind of case it seems more economical to think that a special state is involved, one which activates the naturally remarkable powers of the mind.

Remarkable Effects: Going back to some of the supernormal capacities detailed in an earlier chapter, what is remarkable is not just the ability to defy pain, but the ability of the body of a hypnotized person not to bleed when pierced, or not to blister when scalded and so on. Or again, there was an experiment in which the hypnotized subjects were told they would not be able to hear, out of the whole range of sounds, a tone with a particular frequency (575 cycles per second). When this sound was played loudly in their ears, they showed no measurable physiological reactions. I challenge any unhypnotized person to do any of these things, or a whole host of other strange feats. I certainly don't know of any experiments that have shown that any of these effects are possible under non-hypnotic conditions.

Post-hypnotic Suggestion: If a subject will display behavioural changes after the hypnotic session, when the hypnotist is no longer present and the subject has no knowledge that his or her behaviour is being monitored, how can hypnosis be compliance, role-playing, or the desire to please?

Trance Logic: In repeated experiments using unhypnotized control subjects ('simulators') as well as fully hypnotized subjects ('reals'), a distinctly dreamlike form of mentation was displayed by the reals, but not by the others, even if they were instructed to do their best to simulate a trance state. For instance, everyone is told to hallucinate a figure sitting on a given chair in the room. They do so, and they all describe the figure with equal vividness. But then they are asked to describe the back of the chair; the simulators say that they cannot see the back of the chair, since there is someone sitting in it, but a fair proportion of the reals have no difficulty in seeing the back of the chair. Non-state theorists try to explain this difference by saying that the reals, but not the simulators, were imaginatively involved in the task they had been set, but this smacks to me of a weak response – a plea born of desperation, like others among their arguments. For instance, in one experiment state theorists proved that some subjects remained amnesic after hypnosis despite explicit instructions to remember everything; non-state theorists tried to blunt the force of this experiment by arguing that it was just that the subjects did not want to lose face, since they believed that good hypnotic subjects would be amnesic.

The Hilgards wrote in 1975:

> In summary, hypnotic phenomena appear to have a rather robust quality; they survive repeated attacks upon them and upon the manner in which they are conceptualized. Continuing controversy is valuable in that it demands ever better proof to replace conventional lore. The study of hypnosis is strengthened as it survives attacks by its critics and makes advances through critical, systematic research free from prior commitments to one or another position on controversial issues.

I can only agree.

All sceptical and positivist positions seem to me to be liable to the same logical objection that I raised earlier. The fact that some people can reproduce the effects of hypnotic phenomena without being hypnotized, by the use of their imagination or whatever, does not disprove the reality of hypnotism at all; it just proves that the same or similar phenomena can be produced by other means as well (though, as I said before, I think they should distinguish between deep and light trances). In 1844 Edgar Allan Poe wrote, at the beginning of his short story 'Mesmeric Revelation': 'Whatever doubt may still envelop the *rationale* of mesmerism, its startling *facts* are now almost universally admitted. Of these latter, those who doubt are your mere doubters by profession – an unprofitable and disreputable tribe.' Nothing has changed.

But I feel that I have given the doubters short shrift in this section. Their arguments are too many, and too scientifically sophisticated, to be reproduced in this book or easily summarized. They often appear to have reason on their side: 'The view expressed in this chapter is not that all hypnotic behaviours are "faked", that hypnosis does not "work" or that hypnotherapy is useless. It is rather that the processes responsible for hypnotic effects are more readily explicable by reference to familiar psychological processes than to a unique hypnotic process [i.e. a trance state].' There is indeed a great deal of ambiguity in trying to decide whether there is such a thing as a hypnotic trance, or whether 'familiar psychological processes' such as compliance, role-playing and so on are enough to explain all the phenomena. But let me repeat what I see as the central point: this ambiguity is precisely a reflection of the ambiguity sensed by the hypnotized subject himself, and referred to in Chapter 1 as 'parallel awareness'. I feel that the definition of the hypnotic trance should include a reference to this feeling. Both the doubters and the state theorists are right.

Ernest Hilgard and Neodissociationism

Since Erickson, the most prominent spokesman in North America who has resisted this broad alliance of doubters is Ernest Hilgard. Hilgard regards hypnotic phenomena as being linked in a way which may fall short of being an actual, distinct ASC, but certainly makes up a 'domain' of a particular kind, or a 'special process'. Neodissociationism, the theory he has developed to account for hypnotic phenomena (among others), is quite a mouthful of a word, but quite easy to understand, at least at a basic level. (There are, though, certain differences of opinion between even those scientists who call themselves neodissociationists, which I will have to more or less ignore here.) Neodissociationism, then, 'postulates a hierarchy of control systems operating at any one time in a given individual, and sees hypnosis as modifying the hierarchical arrangement of these controls, so that some become segregated (dissociated) from others'.

We all have the ability to function in our lives in an infinite number of ways, large and small. The kinds of example Hilgard gives range from trivial responses such as brushing a fly off the face, to longer-lasting tasks such as writing a letter, to more complex and open-ended activities such as raising a family and holding down a job. At any given moment, some of these abilities, which he calls 'subsystems', will be active, others latent, and a 'central control structure' is needed to monitor and marshal the hierarchy of subsystems. Dissociation is the separation of subsystems from one another, or from the central control system. This is no big deal. We all (except for President Jimmy Carter in the famous joke) have the ability to do more than one thing at the same time. Hypnotic induction prepares us for dissociation by making it seem as though one part of us is acting beyond the control of another: our eyes, for instance, seem to close 'by themselves'. Then we pass over 'executive function' to the hypnotist. So hypnotic induction brings about such dissociation, leading to lethargy, submission to the hypnotist's suggestions, involuntary behaviours and all the other phenomena of hypnotism.

We have already met Hilgard earlier in the book as the proposer of the important and interesting theory that we have a hidden observer inside us which monitors our activities and can register pain, for instance, even in a hypnotically anaesthetized arm. We can now see how this fits in with his broader views. The hidden observer is precisely the central control system of the human mind. It observes all the various neurological subsystems. Hypnotic analgesia is to be explained as the hidden observer diverting the pain behind an 'amnesia-like barrier' before it reaches consciousness; it is still accessible to the hidden observer itself, but not to the conscious awareness of the subject. In simpler terms, normally conscious experiences are concealed, but not lost – and so they are still noticeable by the hidden observer.

An easy way to understand the contrast between Hilgard's views and those of the doubters is this. According to the anti-state theorists, 'hypnosis' is *distraction*: you do really feel the pain, but you distract your attention away from it and so are able to cope with it. According to Hilgard, however, hypnosis is *disattention*: the act of focusing attention which constitutes hypnotic induction creates dissociation or a new source of attention.

Now, it is clear even to a layman that a great deal of this is highly speculative, and needs a lot of extra work before it can be regarded as certain. Hilgard himself is now too old to undertake such work (he was born in 1904, but is still alive as I write), and so it will have to wait for future generations of psychologists and neurologists. His opponents gleefully pounce on the fact that in order to study the hidden observer, Hilgard has to suggest to his subjects that there is such a thing monitoring the pain or whatever. In other words, they say, the hidden observer is only elicited by such a suggestion, and doesn't exist in its own right. They have, of course, pinpointed a weakness in Hilgard's experimental methods, but they do not have it all their own way. In the first place, Hilgard finds that only about 50 per cent of his subjects respond with hidden-observer phenomena; since hypnotized subjects are supposed to obey the suggestions of the hypnotist, why don't all of them come up with a hidden observer? Secondly, there are other kinds of experiments which point towards the hidden observer, experiments which do not rely on the operator eliciting the phenomenon. In one experiment, for instance, it was found that hypnotized subjects who negatively hallucinate that a chair isn't there still avoid bumping into it. In other words they do still see it – even though they don't see it! In another experiment subjects were found to have the appropriate physiological responses to an electrical shock, even though they didn't feel anything. One subject even reported, about herself: 'I don't feel anything, but *she* seems uncomfortable.' Whatever it is that enables a hypnotized subject to avoid a chair and think of herself in the third person might as well be called the hidden observer.

Hilgard himself has famously pointed out that from the experimental point of view it makes little difference whether or not there is such a thing as the hypnotic state: there are certain behaviours that are typically manifested by those who are hypnotizable and not by those who are unhypnotizable. He chooses to call this set of behaviours the 'domain of hypnosis' rather than a state, but this makes little practical difference. If the kind of dissociation he is talking about cannot be described as an altered state of consciousness, I don't know what can.

The writer Aldous Huxley (1894–1963) had an intense interest in ASCs. A number of his novels show this, but most readers will probably be more aware of his experiments with the hallucinogenic drug mescalin, written up in *The Doors of Perception* (1954). He used to spend hours in a self-induced trance state he called Deep Reflection. In this state, he could function in the world, but was perfectly amnesic afterwards for the things he had said and done. At a famous meeting in 1950 with Milton Erickson in Huxley's home in Los Angeles, Erickson hypnotized him and he displayed all the usual features of a deep trance state, which was in fact identical to his Deep Reflective state. He was not task-motivated: he had nothing to prove. He was not play-acting: why would he have done so? There is no reason not to think he was in a distinct state of consciousness we can call the hypnotic trance – and therefore there is no reason not to think that others can go there too.

The Neurophysiology of Hypnosis

So far I have argued, on philosophical grounds (so to speak), that there is more evidence in favour of there being a special state of hypnosis, and that the doubters are on shaky ground. The arguments on both sides had to be philosophical, because there were no objective reasons for preferring a state theory to a non-state theory. This is no longer the case. Neurophysiological research, starting especially in the 1980s and gaining momentum all the time, has come up with objective evidence that something is going on inside the brains of hypnotized subjects which does not happen to non-hypnotized subjects.

The technology involved is amazingly complex. Gone are the days of simple EEG scans, which were notoriously a blunt instrument. For instance, it is possible for someone under the influence of LSD to register a normal EEG. As anyone knows who has ever taken LSD in a sufficiently high dosage, you are definitely not in a normal state of mind. Researchers now study event-related potentials (ERPs). When the brain is stimulated – say, by seeing a tree – a train of electrical responses can be registered in the appropriate part of the

brain, showing not only the brain's initial reception of the stimulus
(the first glimpse of the tree), but also its continued attention to the
stimulus. In addition, there are sophisticated machines called positron
emission tomography (PET) scanners, which employ gamma rays to
monitor brain activity, by tracing the movement of a radioactive
tracer substance injected into the bloodstream. It may sound grue-
some, but it works. It shows how much energy is being used by
various parts of the brain in a given situation. Using this modern
technology, researchers have been able to pinpoint brain activity
more precisely than the old EEG technology, and they have come
up with some remarkable results.

An experimenter hypnotizes a dozen people, and has a control
group of another dozen unhypnotized subjects. He sets them all the
same task. Let's say that he tells them to imagine that there is a chair
in the room, when there is no such chair. All twenty-four subjects
equally report that they can see a chair, but the part of the brain that
governs sight is not activated in the unhypnotized subjects, while it
is in the hypnotized ones. Conversely, the task they are set involves
a negative hallucination: they are not to see a chair, because they
imagine a screen between themselves and it. The relevant part of
the brains of the hypnotized subjects, but not those who remain
unhypnotized, shows a decrease in activity.

In another experiment, the colour areas of the brain were
activated when hypnotized subjects were asked to perceive colour
both when the colour was really there and when it wasn't. And these
areas showed reduced activity when they were asked to see mere
grey both when it was there and when there were more vivid
colours there. In yet another experiment, the relevant brain activity
increased and decreased depending on whether the hypnotized
subjects were told to feel or to block the feeling of pain. Or again,
high susceptibles show the neurophysiological correlates of habitua-
tion to a task, and focused attention, far more and more quickly than
subjects who are either merely relaxed or hardly susceptible to
hypnosis.

If the brains of hypnotized subjects show such activation, while
those of unhypnotized subjects do not, it looks as though there is
something real going on. The role-players, complying with the
operator's instructions but without being hypnotized, can simulate

the experience verbally, but their brains cannot lie. Doubters, the anti-state theorists, suggest that these neurophysiological results are no more than the traces of the cognitive strategies subjects come up with which enable them to comply with the operator's instructions (to see a chair, or whatever). But this response is looking increasingly implausible. Both the reals and the simulators were responding to the same set of instructions, yet the neurophysiology of only the reals showed the appropriate response. It very much looks as though there is a real ASC which is hypnosis. The Holy Grail of identifiable brain activities which are *unique* to the hypnotic trance still remains elusive, but they're getting closer to it.

If there is such a thing as the hypnotic trance, what kind of a state is it? Milton Erickson's definition, penned for the 1954 *Encyclopedia Britannica*, seems admirable. It is

> a special psychological state with certain physiological attributes, resembling sleep only superficially, and characterized by a functioning of the individual at a level of awareness other than the ordinary state, a level of awareness termed, for convenience in conceptualization, unconscious or subconscious awareness.

The ASC which is the hypnotic trance is not a state that *makes* anything happen; it is a state *in which* certain things happen – chiefly absorption, dissociation and suggestibility. These phenomena allow direct access to the wisdom (as Erickson would put it) of the unconscious mind.

I have nailed my colours to the mast in this chapter. The evidence compels me to believe that there is a special state, an altered state of consciousness (ASC), that deserves to be called the hypnotic trance. There is so much that is strange and currently inexplicable about the phenomena of hypnosis that it seems more economical to think in terms of an ASC than to try to account for them all in different ways. Perhaps the most remarkable phenomenon of all is the ability of hypnosis to relieve pain and to enhance healing, and that is the topic to which we must now turn.

11

Hypnotherapy: Mind and Body

The controversy which occupied our attention in the last chapter rages between experimental psychologists – those who work in university departments, away from the realities of trying to cure physical and psychological ailments. It is not too surprising, then, to find that the debate has had hardly any effect on working hypno- therapists. Whether or not there is such a thing as hypnosis, or the hypnotic trance, they have a tool which works over a wide range of disorders, so they just get on with it.

There are very many articles and books describing cases of hypnotherapy, assessing the successes or failures, giving recommen- dations for methods, suggesting for what conditions hypnosis should not be used, and so on. There is no point in my repeating the substance of works which are designed for clinicians. What I want to do in this chapter is give some idea of the range of disorders for which hypnosis may be effective, show how hypnosis works in practice in the case of a few of these disorders, and then go on to related questions which will bring us back to one of the main themes of this book: the potential of the human mind.

Hypnosis Works

When I first heard about her problem, I was not optimistic that I could be of any help. The patient, a 40-year-old woman, had literally dozens of open sores the size of silver dollars all over her body. They were extremely tender and sensitive when touched – and it was impossible for all of them to remain untouched at the same time ... The patient had suffered this malady for more than 20 years and had received the attention of some of the most competent medical authorities on the continent. They had virtually guaranteed the patient that a very expensive operation to remove all the sores would not prevent their return ... The patient was desperate, but she had also become convinced that hypnosis could be of help.

As a clinical psychologist who had worked with hypnosis both in treatment and in research contexts, I was willing to try to help her ... As it happens, the patient was an excellent hypnotic subject, who readily behaved and experienced in accordance with suggestions. We met more or less regularly for about three months, with one prolonged interruption necessitated by the patient's hospitalization.

During the course of treatment, I administered repeated suggestions for the patient to imagine herself being sprayed by or swimming in shimmering, sunlit liquids that would purify and cleanse her skin. I also told her to become aware of her skin and to experience it as warm and cold, as prickly and smooth and so on – suggestions that constituted lessons in skin awareness and control, so to speak. She was instructed to practice these exercises by herself and, especially, to imagine her skin as smooth and unblemished.

At the end of treatment, the patient was virtually free of sores. The tendency for pustules to form remained, but, instead of progressing to monstrous open wounds, they retreated promptly and soon disappeared. Her dermatologist was amazed, and, frankly, so was I. A recent two-year follow-up revealed that the problem was still under control.

This is one modern story among many – very many. Healing through hypnosis is not just something that happened in the last century and then went out of fashion when more stringent clinical methods came into practice. Even in those times when hypnosis was out of fashion, there was always a quiet underground continuing to make use of its remarkable properties. Of course, it is not a panacea. If you had a broken leg, you wouldn't go to a hypnotherapist (unless you wanted help with pain). But it is one of a number of complementary treatments which are effective over a surprisingly wide range of disorders, and which should therefore be brought into the mainstream. This is especially so in the case of hypnosis, because it is far more gentle and non-invasive than the alternatives. We live in a materialistic age: faced with something that can be prodded by a scalpel, doctors assume that a scalpel is what they had better use. But times are changing, and the shallowness of this assumption is fast being exposed.

At the moment, hypnotherapy is recognized by the public as the treatment of choice for a small range of problems, such as nicotine addiction, but it is usually a last resort (as it has been throughout its history). But the cumulative weight of the success stories from anecdotal evidence and clinical trials is now so enormous that it is time for this situation to change, and for hypnotherapy to be less meekly acknowledged by the medical authorities as a genuine and useful tool. It should be stressed, however, that cases where hypnosis has an *automatic* effect are rare; when I say something like 'Hypnosis has cured or alleviated an enormous range of illnesses and ailments', I mean that it does so by means of the suggestions of cure or alleviation proposed by the therapist and accepted by the patient.

Hypnosis has cured or alleviated an enormous range of illnesses and ailments. Even a partial list is astonishing – and too long and full of technical terms to bother with in a book of this kind. But any such list can be broken down into categories, and that is more useful. First, hypnosis is excellent for the alleviation of pain; hence its use as an anaesthetic, on victims of burns, on terminal cancer patients, in childbirth, and for arthritis, rheumatism and so on. Second, hypnosis boosts the immune system. This is helpful in the case of allergies (which often have a psychosomatic element anyway) and arthritis, and in the fight against cancer, because cancer cells are always there in the body, just waiting for the right conditions (which include a depressed immune system) to multiply. Third, hypnosis acts on the body's nervous systems, and this enables it to deal with all kinds of post-traumatic inflammations, a wide range of skin conditions (acne, eczema, urticaria and so on), gastro-intestinal problems, tics, cramps and certain speech disorders. Fourth, relaxation dilates the blood vessels, and so hypnosis can cause changes in skin temperature, control bleeding in haemophiliacs and menstrual problems, cut off the blood supply to warts (and perhaps this is how it might deal with tumours too), cure migraine, and even enlarge breast size. Finally, hypnosis is an extremely powerful tool in all stress-related and obviously psychological ailments, such as various addictions, obesity, bed-wetting, eating disorders, learning disabilities, phobias, stage fright, stammering, post-traumatic stress disorder, depression, fugue states, psychosexual problems, asthma and insomnia. Since all major illnesses cause stress, which both aggravates the illness and increases the patient's suffering, hypnosis is a useful weapon in the doctor's arsenal across the board. A surprising number of disorders have a psychosomatic component anyway – even haemophilia and asthma – and these are all helped by hypnosis. In short, the body and mind have huge resources for self-healing, and hypnosis can unlock them.

Hypnosis in the Treatment of Pain

The evidence for the effectiveness of hypnosis in dealing with pain is overwhelming. On top of anecdotal evidence, and even if the clinical trials of people like Esdaile in the nineteenth century should be taken with a pinch of salt, since we cannot be there to review their techniques and results, there is also a great deal of watertight modern clinical and experimental research. For instance, to take just one example, thirty burn patients were due to have their burns debrided – an excruciating process in which dead or infected tissue is scraped from the burn site. The patients were assigned randomly to three groups. One group was genuinely hypnotized, the second group was told to relax, as placebo hypnosis, and the third group was left to its own devices. Only the genuinely hypnotized patients had genuine pain relief. Of course, opioid drugs remain the mainstay in the management of burns, but experiments like this one just show the power of hypnosis.

Then there is the use of hypnosis in surgery. Cancerous tumours have been cut out; cardiac and brain surgery have been performed; haemorrhoids ('piles') have been excised; vaginal hysterectomies have been carried out; appendixes have been removed; eye cataracts have had done to them whatever it is that eye cataracts need; and so on. In theory, any surgical procedure can be carried out on a hypnotized patient.

The source of pain we are all probably most familiar with is a visit to the dentist. Hypnosis had been used for dental operations since 1837, but it was the Second World War which really brought its benefits to the attention of modern dentists. In the prisoner-of-war camps, few or no anaesthetics were available, and so interned dentists had to do without when operating on their fellow prisoners. They discovered – or rediscovered – the use of hypnosis. As usual, hypnosis helps not just with the actual pain of extracting a tooth or filling a cavity, but also with the pre-operational apprehension that most people feel. Some people have such a phobia of dentists that the dentist has had to practise a bit of psychotherapy – regressing the patient to discover the source of the phobia and cure it. Other dental problems, such as control of bleeding or of tooth-grinding, can also be helped by hypnosis.

I'm not a woman, but it seems obvious to me that chemical intervention at childbirth is undesirable if it can be avoided. Hypnosis has an excellent, proven track record in alleviating the pains of labour and of obstetric surgery (if needed), and in helping the new mother cope with any anxieties or depression that may arise after the birth. If there is a problem with lactation, hypnosis can even help with that too. A hypnotherapist will give the expectant mother lessons in self-hypnosis that she can practise during labour. Reports say that the pain of even a difficult labour is reduced to a 'light tingling'.

> I feel relaxed – no tensions, no fears, no anxieties . . . I know the pain perception should be pretty rough at this point . . . but I am comfortable . . . very comfortable . . . just a dull pain . . . like having a period and yet I normally have a low pain tolerance . . . I should be perceiving pain, but I'm not . . . I almost feel like a 3+ drunk, relaxed, lethargic, but my brain is functioning so clearly, only a tight band about my abdomen occasionally.

Once, visiting my daughter in hospital, I met and chatted to children with sickle cell disease, a genetic disorder that afflicts many children of African heritage and causes a great deal of pain. So far, it has resisted attempts to find a cure, and the main recourse is management of the pain it causes these children. Hypnosis has proved effective in reducing their pain. Hypnosis is a good thing. We can relieve these children's pain without having recourse to drugs, with all their complications. They already have to take enough drugs.

A large number of clinical trials have demonstrated that hypnosis helps to relieve pain for cancer patients and after all kinds of surgery. For any condition involving pain, hypnosis has a three-pronged benefit. First, relaxation takes the edge off the pain; second, the compression of time that occurs in any trance state makes the pain seem to pass more quickly; third, the anxiety that naturally accompanies pain is reduced. On the issue of the ability of hypnosis to control pain, I can only echo Robert Temple's indignation:

> Hypnosis has the wonderful advantage that when it can be used against pain, it carries no side effects. Unlike morphine, it does not cloud the mind. Terminal cancer patients are amongst the most urgent cases needing hypnosis. There is no need for the hypnotizable terminal cancer patient to be doped up and to die in a haze of confusion ... With hypnosis, he or she can die in dignity with a clear head up to the last moments of life, free from agony and enjoying the company of loved ones. It is an outrage that this possibility has been denied to all but a fraction of those terminal cancer patients who have died in the past century or so.

There are three strategies in hypnosis to decrease pain, over and above the natural effect of relaxation. First, the operator might make a direct suggestion that the subject cannot feel the pain; alternatively, he might, in the case of diffuse pain, concentrate it to a small area and then relocate it to somewhere else in the body where it is more tolerable; or, thirdly, he might turn the subject's attention away from the pain.

How does it work? At first, with the discovery in the 1970s that the brain releases endorphins to dampen pain, it was assumed that hypnosis triggered their release. Recent research, however, suggests that this is wrong. Suppose I have chronic back pain, and I use hypnosis to inhibit the pain. If endorphins were released into my bloodstream, the inhibition of the pain would last quite a while – as long as the endorphins were effective. But what we find with hypnosis is this: on the suggestion that the pain is less, the pain grows immediately less; on the suggestion that the pain returns, the pain immediately returns. It all happens too quickly for endorphins to be involved. It is more likely, then, that there is some neural process which inhibits pain, and which is switched on and off by hypnosis. Inhibition of pain stems from the frontal and limbic areas of the brain, and is associated especially with the presence of theta brainwaves. As we have seen, theta brainwaves are produced in deep hypnosis. But this is not to say that 'lows' – people who are not deeply hypnotizable – cannot gain relief from pain through hypnosis. A number of studies show that if 'lows' are motivated to gain relief, they will do so, and also that through biofeedback they can learn to do better. In other words, astonishing though it may sound, we can train the relevant neural triggers and pathways.

This training also accounts for another puzzling aspect of the way that hypnotism relieves pain. Suppose we follow Ernest Hilgard and say that during hypnosis the pain is hidden behind an amnesia-like barrier, and that this is why we don't feel it. This only explains why we don't feel it *during hypnosis*. What factors ensure that we don't feel it afterwards? Basically, these are the suggestions put to us during hypnosis by the therapist, and the suggestions triggered afterwards. But pain is a real thing, so in order for the pain not to be noticed afterwards, we have to be affecting the neural pathways even then.

Close to the beginning of this book I said that 'highs' are those who are good at deploying attention. This is important because it means that they are also good at deploying *dis*attention. Suppose you have a young child who is screaming at the prospect of having a splinter of wood removed from his hand. There are two ways you might go about a painless removal of the splinter. First, you could have someone create a diversion, and while the child's attention is distracted you try to remove the splinter. Second, if the child was amenable to reason, you could ask him to turn away and think of something pleasant instead. The first method is distraction, the second is disattention – the deliberate deployment of attention away from something, in this case pain. There is evidence that disattention from pain stimulates the neural pathways that block pain, and so this would explain why 'highs' are instinctively good at overcoming pain in hypnosis.

But whatever explanation scientists eventually come up with for the effectiveness of hypnosis in lowering pain, the empirical fact remains that it works. The alleviation of pain is the single most important product of hypnosis in a therapeutic context.

Hypnosis in the Treatment of Psychological Problems

Hypnosis is particularly good at treating problems stemming from or involving anxiety – and there are a lot of these. Not a lot of people know that asthma and over-eating, for instance, are anxiety-related problems: they are at least aggravated by anxiety. Let's take a look at asthma, since it's so widespread these days. An asthmatic attack may be precipitated by taking exercise, by an infection, by an allergy, or by emotions. Studies have found that many emotions can precipitate an attack of asthma: anxiety, the anticipation of pleasure, frustration, anger, resentment, humiliation, depression, laughter, feelings of guilt, and joy. Hypnosis can help with the allergic aspect of asthma, and with the emotions. It cannot cure an attack, but it can prevent one; the patient is taught self-hypnosis to practise at the onset of an attack.

Tinnitus – which is far more widely spread than many people imagine – is another disorder which, like asthma, may have a physiological basis, but is certainly aggravated by psychological factors such as anxiety. Obviously, phobias, psychosexual difficulties, stammering and so on are psychological problems, and so are a range of childhood problems such as bed-wetting, shyness and learning difficulties. Anxiety is also a factor before and after operations, during cancer treatment, when someone has heart disease and so on. Hypnosis can help with all of these, because hypnosis can manage stress.

I am told that King George VI of Great Britain used to suffer from terrible stage fright and stammering – a distinct drawback in a king and emperor who had to make a lot of public speeches and appearances – and that he was cured by hypnotism. The same therapist treated the writer W. Somerset Maugham for his terrible stammer. The treatment would probably have focused first on getting them to relax at a muscular level, to decrease their fear at the prospect of speaking. Once that was well established, they might have been given a visualization of a calming scene, to induce feelings of inner tranquillity. The hypnotist would have given them suggestions and post-hypnotic suggestions to help remove the anxiety. They would have been taught self-hypnosis, so that they could call up the calming visualization whenever they needed it, and relaxation techniques. Finally, if necessary, the therapist might have used visualizations to boost their self-image. Royalty and bestselling authors aside, just to bring matters down to a homely level, on 29 April 1999 *The Times* reported, under the headline 'Hypnosis Beats Exam Stress', how a school in Cheshire had brought in a hypnotherapist to help students to relax and improve their revision before exams.

Sergei Rachmaninoff, the brilliant Russian composer, suffered from total composer's block after the failure of his First Symphony in 1897. He continued to find acclaim as a concert pianist, but he could not write a note. He sought out the hypnotist Nikolai Dahl, who taught him, in three months of daily sessions, to relax, and instilled in him the suggestion that he would be able to continue composing. The immediate result was Rachmaninoff's Second Piano Concerto, reckoned to be one of his best pieces, which was first performed in Moscow on 9 November 1901. In gratitude, Rachmaninoff dedicated the concerto to Dahl.

It is odd that the reputation hypnotherapy has for the public is that it is good with addictions. Overall, tests have shown that it is *less* effective for self-initiated behaviours (e.g. obesity, addictions) than for other kinds of disorders. Quite a large proportion of smokers treated by hypnosis do not permanently give up. The method adopted by therapists with addictions is usually a form of aversion, to put the smoker off cigarettes (or whatever it may be) in the future. But an 88 per cent success rate (higher than usual) was achieved by a radical alternative therapy, in which smokers were brought to a state of appreciating the kind of gratification they got from cigarettes, and then hypnosis and follow-up self-hypnosis were used to induce precisely the same gratification in the subjects. They had found an alternative way to gain the same gratification.

Although the use of hypnotherapy as a cure for addictions is well known, hypnotist Frank Genco puts it to the opposite use. Rather than cure people of their addiction to gambling, the one-legged marathon-runner Genco teaches self-hypnosis as a means for people to shed their 'loser's image' and win. Everyone who has played poker knows how mood seems to have an effect on the run of the cards.

Genco's use of hypnosis is a small example of its ability to uncover or unlock potential, which is one of its most familiar aspects – familiar from its use in fiction, since it is the basic role that hypnotism plays in, say, both George du Maurier's *Trilby* (where Trilby's talent as a singer is revealed by Svengali) and Henry James's *The Bostonians* (where Verena's talent as an inspirational lecturer is unlocked by her father). We've all heard stories of people who have performed a physical feat well beyond their usual capabilities – a mother, perhaps, whose child is trapped under a car and who has lifted the car on her own to free the child. These stories show that our unused physical potential can be unlocked by the right motivation.

Sports hypnosis is a way to unlock that potential for athletes, and to deal with other problems that can slow them down that vital fraction of a second, such as pre-competition nerves, lack of self-esteem, or some more general anxiety. A surprising number of athletes have used hypnosis or similar techniques (especially visualizations) to improve their performance. It was used to instil the 'killer instinct' in Ingmar Johansson in 1959 so that he could win the world heavyweight boxing championship against the formidable Floyd Patterson by a knockout in the third round. Fourteen years later Ken Norton used self-hypnosis before the astonishing match in which he beat Mohammed Ali, and broke his jaw in the process. Mike Brearley, England's cricket captain in the late 1970s, was plagued (as many England captains have been) by low scores; he attributes an improvement to his consultation of a hypnotherapist. Early isolated uses such as these paved the way. In 1962 the Olympic Committee considered that hypnosis should be banned, along with a range of drugs, as giving athletes an unfair advantage. They soon changed their mind, obviously because they realized that hypnosis cannot make a sportsman gain powers he would not otherwise have, just unlock his abilities. Only one motivational psychologist accompanied the US Olympic team in 1988, but a mere eight years later there were 100. Nowadays, it is perfectly normal for top athletes, whether their sport is tennis or sumo wrestling, to have their own motivational psychologist on their staff, or to check in from time to time at a centre offering to fine-tune skills through such means. Hypnosis works brilliantly with motivational encouragement – as long as nothing goes wrong. In an episode of the popular satirical cartoon *The Simpsons* a sports hypnotist who, in a monotonous voice, is encouraging his team to 'give 110 per cent' accidentally makes a member of the team behave like a chicken and gets out of trouble in the end only by hypnotizing the boss into thinking he did a good job.

Sports psychologists use hypnosis along with affirmations and visualizations to encourage the sportsmen and women under their charge. As I write, the Oxford University boat crew has just beaten Cambridge for the first time in many years, and against the odds. Before the race it was reported on the front page of *The Times* for 25 March 2000 that Oxford had employed a motivational psychologist, a former rower herself, Dr Kirsten Barnes, whose methods of visualization and affirmation she herself describes as 'verging on hypnosis'.

In short, hypnosis can change the way you feel about yourself, and apart from the obvious psychological benefits of that, there are physical results as well. We will soon see why.

Hypnosis and Blood Flow

Hypnosis has a good track record with the cure of warts. Sceptics often point out that warts come and go rather mysteriously on their own, as a result of psychological conditions that are still obscure to medical science, and so that the hypnotic cure of warts really proves nothing. But this leaves them rather stuck to explain the following test. A group of wart-infested patients were hypnotized and told that the warts on one side of their bodies alone would clear up. And that is exactly what happened. But since warts are also commonly treated by placebos and various forms of faith healing (in remote parts of Britain, one can still come across 'wise women' who can cure warts), it seems that hypnosis itself is not a necessary factor. Suggestion alone will get rid of the nasty little things. Hypnosis is good in situations like this because it increases our responsiveness to suggestions.

In the 1932 film *Rasputin and the Empress*, the Mad Monk of Russia hypnotizes the czar's haemophiliac son in order to stop his bleeding. This is not too far removed from the truth: hypnosis has been shown to be good at controlling blood flow, and to do so even in haemophiliacs. In fact, it is possible that this is how hypnosis gets rid of warts, since starving them of blood seems to do the trick. Somerset Maugham's 1944 novel *The Razor's Edge* contains one of the few sensible fictional treatments of hypnosis. In one episode Larry cures someone's migraine after a straightforward induction. Maugham was probably unaware of the mechanism, which again has to do with blood flow, since migraines are accompanied or caused by dilation of blood vessels in the head. Perhaps we could also use the success of hypnosis with blood flow to explain how quite a few women have been able through a combination of hypnosis and visualizations to enlarge their breasts by up to 1½ inches. The visualizations, by the way, were along the following lines: 'Imagine that the sun is shining on your breasts and feel the heat flowing through them. Imagine your breasts growing as they did in puberty, and feel the tenderness and tautness of the skin over the breasts. Imagine that your breasts are becoming warm, tingling, pulsating and sensitive, and that they are growing.'

Who can doubt that hypnotherapy can be effective for things like rashes when there is good evidence that through suggestion or autosuggestion alone inflammation, blisters and bleeding can be produced? A hypnotist called H. Bourru in nineteenth-century France traced a patient's name on his arms with a blunt instrument and told him, when he was deeply entranced, that in the afternoon his arms would bleed along the lines he had traced. They did just that, showing red and oozing drops of blood. A number of similar cases were reported in the nineteenth century, until scientists felt the need to give a name to the phenomenon: rather cutely, they called it 'autographic skin'. The willed production of blisters has been tested in modern laboratories; it is a genuinely recognized phenomenon of hypnotism.

One of the most extraordinary products of mind–body interaction is the appearance of stigmata, the apparently miraculous manifestation of bleeding wounds corresponding to Christ's wounds on the cross. Since scientists have been able to cause spontaneous bleeding in certain subjects by suggestion alone, we can be pretty sure now that this phenomenon is not miraculous but comprehensible – in so far as the powerful effect the mind can exert on the body is yet comprehensible. Nor is this a new-fangled theory; the psychosomatic origin of stigmata was first proposed in 1855 by the French physician Alfred Maury. More recently, researchers have found a background of psychological trauma; stigmatists are often hysterical, masochistic, depressive, frigid and dependent, and suffer from nervous anxiety. Add a good pinch of religious fervour to such a personality, and you may well get a stigmatic, someone who by autosuggestion can produce all or some of the marks on her skin. But I must immediately add that not all stigmatics fit this profile: Padre Pio (1887–1968), whose stigmata made him an international celebrity and his monastery in Italy a place of pilgrimage, seems to have been a hearty and robust person, fond of his beer and wine.

I sincerely hope that this paragraph will not offend some people. In the first place, I hope they can accept that at least some 'miracles' (even those of Jesus) may become explicable as time goes on; clinging to an explanation in terms of divine miracles in such cases is not religion but superstition, and the distinction some writers make between hysterical and religious stigmata is hard to maintain. In the second place, one of the main points I am trying to make in this book, and especially in this chapter, is that however close science might come to explaining mind–body interaction, some of the phenomena and abilities of the mind are truly remarkable. It is astonishing – perhaps even miraculous – how much bigger we are than we think we are. If we could realize and remember that, each of us would live in a larger, more meaningful world, which it is one of the purposes of religion to promote. As Jesus said: 'That they might have life and have it more abundantly' (John 10:10).

The most famous stigmatist was St Francis of Assisi, who developed the marks on 14 September 1213, and kept them until his death in 1215. He was the first, and since then there have been several hundred cases, mostly women. In a typical case of mass suggestion, another thirty cases were known by the end of the thirteenth century. Other famous stigmatics are Anne Catherine Emmerich (born 1774), Gemma Galgani (1878–1903) and Marie-July Jahenny (late nineteenth century). But scientists and medical men were able to study two in particular: Louise Lateau and Therese Neumann. Louise Lateau was a Belgian peasant girl, born in 1850, who showed more than 800 stigmata in her short lifetime (she died in 1883), which started when she was eighteen. She would go into a trance state after receiving Communion in church, and then start bleeding, typically from her hands, feet and under her left breast (where, remember, Christ was wounded by the Roman soldier's spear). Generally, the appearance of the stigmata was preceded by head-aches; she was anorexic and often bedridden. Therese Neumann was a very similar case – a peasant girl filled with religious fervour. Born in 1898, she suffered from hysterical paralysis, blindness and false appendicitis, until in 1926 she began to show stigmata, which bled very freely. She too would go into a kind of trance before the bleeding started. Her stigmata continued until her death in 1962.

There is a very good reason why I have concluded this survey with the effect of hypnosis on blood flow, and have lingered a little over the phenomenon of stigmata. It is common knowledge that hypnosis is a mental treatment which can have only mental or psychological effects, or at any rate deal with only mentally caused illnesses. *But this common knowledge is wrong!* The remarkable truth is that hypnosis and autosuggestion can have organic, physiological effects. Just ask the women who have increased their breast sizes. This is not to say that hypnosis can cure cancer (though as we have seen it can help in certain respects), but it is the case that it is not limited to the mind, but works on the body via the mind. Research in the last forty years has demonstrated beyond the slightest doubt that the mind can bring about organic changes in the body. I will go into this in more depth shortly.

After-effects

While we're on the subject of hypnotherapy, I should lay to rest the idea that hypnosis has harmful after-effects (or 'sequelae', as doctors will insist on calling them).

In 1897 in New York State a seventeen-year-old boy called Spurgeon Young died. For six months prior to his death he had been a practising hypnotic clairvoyant. The court investigating his death asked a panel of medical experts whether the fact that he had been repeatedly hypnotized contributed to his death, since it was widely believed at the time that hypnosis had a deleterious effect on the nervous system. The experts concluded that his 'nervous organism' had been 'shattered', and that, if he had not died, he would have at least been driven insane or imbecilic.

Times have changed. Nowadays, everyone is agreed that the after-effects of being hypnotized are minimal and are classifiable as complications rather than as dangers. The trance *per se* is benign, and any complications that arise come from the induction procedure or something other than the trance itself. There is certainly no evidence that you will fail to wake fully from the trance, or that you will be liable to unwanted trance flashbacks later, or that your will is weakened. As for waking up, it is true that a very few individuals are hard to dehypnotize, but if they were left alone they would either gently wake up of their own accord, or would fall asleep.

Some irresponsible or thoughtless commentators have occasion-ally accused hypnosis of bringing on severe disorders such as schizo-phrenia, but this is rubbish; there is no evidence that the subject would not have suffered from schizophrenia anyway. Being hypno-tized can be a significant event in someone's life, and that significance can shift the person towards a potential so far dormant, but it is not the hypnosis in itself that causes the shift. In other words, what dangers there are are *coincidental* dangers.

Complications are likely to arise more from stage shows than hypnotherapy, basically because some showmen are less responsible.

Imagine a performer suggesting to a person that she is walking on a tightrope, without first checking whether she has a fear of heights. This sort of thing has actually happened. In September 1993 a twenty-four-year-old woman, Sharron Tabarn, died hours after taking part in a show at a Lancashire pub. The hypnotist concluded his show by suggesting that the audience would feel a 10,000-volt electric shock in their seats, and that this would wake them up from the trance. Sharron felt dizzy, went home, vomited in her sleep, and choked to death. It was later discovered that she had a fear of electricity. In Israel in the 1970s a particularly dim-witted hypnotist regressed a middle-aged member of the audience back to her childhood – back to the time when she and her sister had been hidden in a house in Paris for the duration of the Nazi occupation, and triggered a psychosis that lasted for many years before being resolved. The Tabarn case received a good deal of attention, and a British government committee was convened to investigate the death; they concluded that hypnosis was not responsible.

These are very rare occurrences. The vast majority of people who go to see a stage hypnotist experience nothing but pleasure. In Britain these days no one under the age of sixteen is allowed on stage to take part in a hypnotic show, and certain tricks are banned, such as eating an onion as if it were an apple, and smelling ammonia as if it were the sweetest perfume. But the point is that not being in a one-to-one situation, the stage hypnotist may not have taken the time and trouble to screen his subjects and build up a psychological profile, as of course any reputable therapist would have. And since they generally pack up their bags and leave town for their next gig elsewhere, they are not available for consultation afterwards should they be needed. It follows from all this that stage performers should err on the side of extreme caution. A well-meaning Federation of Ethical Stage Hypnotists was set up in Britain in the early 1980s, but it had no means of seeing that the code of practice it drew up reached the statute books. Among its conclusions were that stage hypnotists should never be allowed to induce catalepsy or rigidity in subjects, or put them through age-regression, or suggest that they have eaten or drunk anything unpleasant; and that all post-hypnotic suggestions should be removed not only from the people who had actually been hypnotized up on stage, but also from all members of the audience. Stage hypnotism is now banned in several states of the USA, in parts of Australia and Canada, and in Norway, Sweden and Israel. In many other countries, as in Britain, performers have to be granted a licence by the local authority before they can put on a show. It would be a shame if the irresponsibility of some stage hypnotists deprived the rest of a good living and the audience of a lot of fun.

Hypnotic induction is hard to direct. A hypnotist might be carrying out an induction on Miss Smith, only to find that Mr Jones, an innocent member of the audience, has gone under, as well as or even instead of Miss Smith. In 1946 the BBC prohibited any experiments in mass hypnosis over television, because a discreet experiment in their studios showed that it worked. This is of course not the same as banning the screening of stage hypnotism; but the televising of a hypnotic induction is still banned, in case an irresponsible person hypnotizes the viewing population of Britain. Myself, I doubt there's too much danger, because the TV is a distancing device; otherwise we'd get frightened watching the violence of the lions on nature programmes.

The only consequence of hypnotherapy that can be severe is symptom substitution. This is when an apparent cure has dealt only with a symptom of an underlying disorder, which then makes its presence felt in some other way. For instance, a man comes for treatment for alcoholism. After a course of treatment he no longer drinks – but whatever it was that made him drink in the first place has not been cured, and may manifest as another addiction, or in some other way. I know this from my own experience: a long time ago I tried self-hypnosis to quit smoking. It worked: I didn't smoke for nine months. But I suffered from recurrent bouts of increasingly violent flu for the whole of those nine months, and they went away only when I took up smoking again. It was only many years later that I was able to give up smoking without suffering any side effects. Once in a blue moon, removing a symptom can have more disastrous consequences. Physician Bernard Raginsky tells a harrowing tale of a man in a psychiatric ward who was suffering from hysterical paralysis of the arm. A doctor hypnotized him and easily freed up the arm, much to the amusement of the other patients in the ward – but that night the patient committed suicide, arguably because 'his method of defense against some inner conflict had been taken away and he was left vulnerable and exposed to the ridicule of the patients about him'.

A very few people complain of headaches after hypnosis, but these were probably brought on by the focused concentration required, rather than from anything intrinsic to hypnotism. Another occasional complaint is a stiff neck or shoulder, but that too is almost certainly a result of sitting in one position for a long time rather than of hypnotism itself. Insomnia, a feeling of being 'spaced out', and other such after-effects are of equally short duration. Since college students are generally the guinea pigs for experiments in hypnosis, someone once had the bright idea of assessing the after-effects of hypnosis against the after-effects of college life in general. Hypnosis came out as rather more benign.

In fact, the main dangers are to the hypnotist rather than his subject, since there is a possibility of the hypnotist being accused of all kinds of things after the event. That is why these days responsible stage hypnotists tape all their shows and tell their subjects afterwards what they had them do. Otherwise, a patient may suffer from partial amnesia, and accuse the hypnotist of indecent assault during the amnesic period, for instance. A few years ago the most famous stage hypnotist in the world, Paul McKenna, was sued by a man who claimed that he developed schizophrenia as a result of being hypno- tized by him. McKenna won the case, but it was a Pyrrhic victory, in that (I have been told) he had to pay out-of-court costs rumoured to be as high as a million pounds.

Studies have shown that adverse effects of hypnosis in a clinical setting generally occur only as a result of inadequate dehypnosis, debriefing or follow-up, and that these become problems chiefly when the hypnotist has departed from his usual area of competence. So, for instance, a dental hypnotist who then agrees to help a patient with her nicotine addiction is more likely to see negative after-effects than if he had stuck to dental analgesia. He might find his patient experiencing unexpected amnesia, and not know how to cope with it. He might find that his patient has transferred affection or hostility towards him, or that she was a dependent type who develops over- dependency on hypnosis. If the hypnotist has adequately screened his subject, ensures that she has been fully disengaged from the trance, and throughout the procedure respects his client's integrity, there is

no more need to worry about hypnotherapy than there is about any
other psychotherapeutic relationship.

In short, the advantages of hypnotherapy hugely outweigh the
disadvantages. Speaking for myself, I would far rather face the minimal disadvantages of hypnotherapy than the unpleasant side effects of
a lot of drugs. The dangers can be reduced even further by improved
and expanded programmes of research and education, greater clarifi-
cation of standards for the clinical employment of hypnosis and legal
sanctions against quacks.

Mind and Body

It's obvious that in thinking about how hypnotherapy works, we
need to understand more about the relation between the mind and
the body.

> Genetic, environmental, social and other factors are increasingly
> recognized as having roles in the history of illnesses. Therefore
> it is no longer acceptable to ascribe a single cause to an illness
> and the term 'psychosomatic', intended to be helpful in healing
> the rift between mind and body of Cartesian dualism, now
> seems almost derogatory when used in the causative sense, 'It's
> all in your mind.' What is acceptable to the hypnotherapist is
> the psychosomatic approach, the assumption that amongst the
> many factors influencing the efficiency of a person's response to
> the situation in which he finds himself are his level of arousal,
> his thoughts about the situation, and his assumptions about
> himself. These assumptions include his level of self-esteem, his
> degree of trust in his conscious and unconscious mechanisms
> to see him through to a perceived, optimistic outcome. The
> modification of all these responses is within the scope of hyp-
> nosis.

In order to see how something as immaterial as your self-esteem
can have a physical effect, we should look, first, at the various

nervous systems of the body. The most important nervous system is the central nervous system (CNS), located chiefly in the brain and spinal column. Every part of the body is connected directly or indirectly to the CNS, and the psychological aspect of the CNS is an individual's personality, emotional life and so on. It is easy to see that emotions affect bodily functions: I weep in grief or joy, laugh with pleasure, blush in pride or embarrassment, find that my heart rate and breathing change with anger. In most of us, these emotions and the physical changes come and go. But what about neurotic patients, whose whole lives are given over to emotions? It was found that they developed chronic physical responses – say, paralysis of an arm. The idea that all illnesses had an organic cause had to go, and the concept of a 'functional' disturbance, one in which the mind as well as the body was involved, began to creep into medicine.

It is also easy to see that a functional disorder can lead to an organic disorder. Here is a simple example. Suppose someone is suffering from neurotic paralysis of his arm. This is a functional disorder, but it will soon cause an organic problem, as the arm's muscles and joints begin to degenerate. But appreciating *that* there was such a thing as psychosomatic illness was one thing; understanding *how* it happened was another. The picture is still far from complete, but scientists now understand that the CNS (especially the limbic-hypothalamic part of the brain) has an effect not only on the nerve impulses, but on the endocrine glands (which govern health by regulating the transportation of chemicals all around the body in the bloodstream), and on the immune system (which governs our susceptibility to and speed of recovery from illnesses).

> Those two realms [the brain and the immune system] were once thought to be fairly separate – your immune system kills bacteria, makes antibodies, hunts for tumors; your brain thinks up poetry, invents the wheel, has favorite TV shows. Yet the dogma of the separation of the immune and nervous systems has fallen by the wayside. The autonomic nervous system sends nerves into the tissues that form or store the cells of the immune system that wind up in the circulation. Furthermore, tissue of the immune system turns out to be sensitive to (that is, it has receptors for) all the interesting hormones released

by the pituitary under the control of the brain. The result is that the brain has a vast potential for sticking its nose into the immune system's business.

The branch of science which studies the interaction between the mind and the endocrine and immune systems is called psycho-neuroimmunology (PNI). Although PNI is as complex a science as its name, it is now perfectly clear that, for instance, stress depresses the immune system, delaying the production of antibodies and making us more liable to viral infections and slower to throw them off; that a secure, warm childhood increases one's immunity; and that bereavement and, perhaps above all, the feeling of helplessness in the face of the difficulties of modern life, lower your resistance to illness. As long as you have control, or think you have control, you have considerably less chance of a stress-related disease. Viewing life as a challenge and being committed to your own health are also important factors; if you don't think so, just read the autobiographical section of psychiatrist Viktor Frankl's *Man's Search for Meaning*, in which he illuminates the factors that allowed him and others to survive the horrors and degradations of Nazi death camps. Finding life meaningful – as in having religious faith – also helps hugely. When you think that even some forms of cancer are viral, you can begin to see the potential importance of these discoveries. Laughter, as Shakespeare knew long ago, is the best medicine:

> Your honour's players, hearing your amendment,
> Are come to play a pleasant comedy,
> For so your doctors hold it very meet,
> Seeing too much sadness hath congealed your blood,
> And melancholy is the nurse of frenzy.
> Therefore they thought it good you hear a play
> And frame your mind to mirth and merriment,
> Which bars a thousand harms and lengthens life.

Laughter, of course, should be taken as a cure only in conjunction with proper medical prescriptions from your doctor – but then even your doctor's attitude can influence whether or not you give in to an illness. The mind may or may not be able to move mountains, but it can certainly move molecules.

A particularly clear demonstration that the body and mind are intertwined came with the development of biofeedback technology. Suppose you are shooting a rifle at a target. You see that your first shot goes left of centre, and so you adjust your sights. That seeing and adjustment is feedback. Biofeedback is just feedback related to the body. By hooking people up to complex instruments which show them what they are doing with their bodies, they can be trained, with surprising ease and rapidity, to change things, even in parts of the body previously thought to be beyond conscious control. Blushers need not blush, warts can be dissolved, migraines vanish and so on. The instruments teach people to see what is going on in their bodies, and to make the appropriate adjustments.

The mind can affect the body in three ways. It can affect our voluntary behaviour: we anticipate meeting an attractive member of the opposite sex at a party and choose to dress accordingly. It can affect what are called our 'expressive innervations': blushing, weeping, laughing and so on. But it can also affect our vegetative responses, the working of our internal organs. To take an extreme example, there are reports that certain yoga masters can raise the rate at which their hearts beat from 80 to 300 beats a minute. This kind of ability – obviously less extreme in most of us – came as a surprise because these functions were supposed to be involuntary. This (in a hugely simplified version) is how it happens.

The nervous system as a whole has the job of maintaining the body in a state at which our oxygen, temperature and so on are at optimum levels. This state is called 'homeostasis', though physicians also talk about 'allostasis', which refers to the fact that under different conditions what counts as an optimum level is different. The nervous system is constantly trying to restore equilibrium, although things impinge on our bodies and our minds to disrupt it. The things that impinge and disrupt homeostasis are 'stressors', and the 'stress-response' is the body's attempt to restore equilibrium.

The nervous system achieves this goal by giving different parts of itself different specific jobs. The CNS regulates our relations with the external world, while the autonomic nervous system (ANS) looks after the internal vegetative processes. The ANS in turn has two parts. The parasympathetic division is concerned with the conserva-tion of the body: it does things like stimulating digestion so that we

absorb food and excrete waste matter, or like checking the level of
sugar in the liver. The sympathetic part of the ANS is responsible for
the functioning of the internal organs in emergency situations; it
shuts down things like your digestive system (which is unnecessary
in the circumstances, and is handled by the parasympathetic system)
and focuses only on fight-or-flight responses. You could say that the
parasympathetic nervous system slows down the functioning of
the body, while the sympathetic nervous system speeds it up.

The division of the ANS into sympathetic and parasympathetic
parts has important consequences for understanding how psychosomatic illnesses work, and how, just as certain pathological
micro-organisms have a special affinity for certain organs, so certain
emotional conflicts afflict certain organs too. Anger is an emotional
response to an emergency situation, a perceived threat; it affects the
internal organs in such a way as to get the body ready to fight. Now,
suppose we repress that anger, as we commonly do in civilized
societies: the body has been got ready to fight, but no fight has taken
place. Fine – or at least fine for most of us, since we don't spend all
that much time in a state of anger. But what about those who suffer
chronically from repressed anger? In the due course of time, just as
we saw above with the example of the paralysed arm, the effect of
more-or-less constant anger on the internal organs may well create
organic disturbances. It won't *necessarily* create organic disorders,
because nothing in this new medicine is straightforwardly mechanical; other factors, such as diet, or having hobbies or a supportive
family environment, can offset the risk.

Doctors now have to look at personality types, and at lifestyles
and how they might be changed to assist healing. Ayurvedic medicine
in India has always known this, but now even arch-rationalists among
the Western medical community are, at least to this extent, holistic.
Even cultural factors play a part in some disorders: anorexia nervosa
is predominantly found among middle-class teenage girls; Jews of an
eastern European origin suffer more from nervous disorders than
others. Typically, a person who affects his neuroendocrine systems
by means of the sympathetic nervous system will suffer from things
like migraine, hypertension, hyperthyroidism, cardiac neuroses and
arthritis, while a person who does so by means of the parasympathetic nervous system will find himself suffering from things like peptic

ulcers, constipation or diarrhoea, colitis, fatigue and asthma. This is not to say that all ailments and illnesses are 'psychogenic' (caused by the mind), but it is to say that a number are, and that certain personality types are more liable to certain illnesses than others. This is a controversial area: some doctors think that there is, for instance, a cancer-prone personality and an arthritis-prone personality; others are more cautious and speak only in a more general fashion of the type of personality – basically one which is subject to all kinds of stresses – which is liable to have an adverse effect on the immune system, and of another type which is stress-resistant.

Of course, many diseases are caused by particular micro-organisms, and there are powerful medicines available to destroy those organisms. But the psychogenic origin of some human illnesses has long been known, and so have the psychological benefits of a healthy attitude. In medieval times both illnesses and cures might be attributed to the imagination, and in the nineteenth and twentieth centuries the remarkable cures achieved by hypnotists brought the point home forcefully. We've long known that moving house, getting married (or divorced) and so on are stressful and likely to cause an illness; we've long spoken of emotions in physical terms – 'cold feet', 'butterflies in the stomach' – and known that people can die of a broken heart. You look around at your family members and see that it's the cheerful one who doesn't get the cold everyone else is suffering from. You've heard of 'phantom limbs' – of how a person whose leg has been amputated can still feel pain in the missing leg.

But understanding the whys and wherefores only really began in the 1930s, with research accelerating since the 1960s. Until recently, then, as the name implies, the *autonomic* nervous system was thought to be out of reach. Liébeault and Bernheim, ahead in this respect as in so many others, suggested that it was not as independent as it might seem; but they lived decades before this idea could be proved. So did the respectable English doctor Hack Tuke, who in 1872 published his *Illustrations of the Influence of the Mind upon the Body in Health and Disease*. But now psychosomatic medicine is a fast-developing area of research. In the seventeenth century the French philosopher René Descartes tried to separate the mind from the body, but that is no longer possible. We are each a unit of mind and body, and changes in one system result in changes in the other. In a nice turn of phrase, PNI specialists talk of 'the biology of hope' and 'the biology of belief'. PET scans have shown that remembering a visual event activates the same parts of the brain as the original seeing; in other words, the supposedly 'purely mental' activity of remembering has the same physiological result as the supposedly 'purely physical' activity of using the senses.

We all knew most of this anyway, but it is nice to have it confirmed by the men and women in white coats. But the point is this: if the mind can help to *cause* illness, can it also help to *cure* it? This is where hypnotherapy comes in. It can help, obviously, with psychosomatic illnesses; and it can help, psychosomatically, even with illnesses that were not psychogenic in origin. But how does it do so? The problem is, in a sense, one of communication. If I know only English and you speak only Urdu, we need a translator before we can communicate. Similarly, you could say that the body speaks one language and the mind another. Yet it is clear that they do communicate. Discovering the biology of how they do so is the job of PNI, but hypnosis research, especially by Ernest Rossi, an associate of Milton Erickson, has come up with some interesting results too, to suggest just how hypnosis acts on the brain's structures and chemistry to facilitate that communication process and aid healing. In brief, Rossi believes that hypnosis acts on the limbic-hypothalamic part of the brain, which coordinates and can alter mind-body interactions, and that it achieves this coordination and these alterations by normalizing the body's ultradian rhythms, disruption of which is a major cause of stress-related diseases. Our bodies are subject to a rhythmic cycle of roughly 90–150 minutes, from a peak of high energy down to a trough of low energy and back again. If we go along with these cycles (by, for example, resting from strenuous mental or physical activity when we're in the trough), we avoid stress. Hypnosis, according to Rossi, puts us back in tune with our natural rhythms.

Psychosomatic research is, as I've said, fairly new. There is still a lot of misunderstanding around, not only among us laymen, but also in the medical community:

> There remains a tendency to pigeon-hole people as suffering from one kind of disorder or another. Cancer is generally a

physical disease requiring medical attention. Anxiety is a psycho-logical problem for which a psychologist or psychiatrist may be consulted. Doubts about the goodness of God are usually labelled a spiritual problem needing pastoral care. How con-venient! How simple! How misleading!

As for the general public, I suspect that many people, faced with the idea that their illness is psychosomatic, might feel rather offended. They take this to mean that they have somehow caused the disease themselves, almost as if they wanted it to gain attention or something. There is an element of truth in this, but rather than giving offence, I hope readers can see it as exciting, and proof of the size and importance of the mind. Research has shown that people tend to get ill after rather than before important occasions; even mortality rates drop during major religious holidays. In other words, to say that an illness is psychosomatic, and caused by your uncon-scious, actually points to the fact that to say that something is unconscious is not entirely to say that you are not responsible for it. If you are or should be responsible for every product of your own mind, that extends even to psychosomatic illnesses, because – again – your mind is so much bigger than it is normally taken to be.

In this section I've focused on how the mind affects the body, because that is most relevant to a book on hypnosis. But the body and the mind are a unit, and the influence can run the other way too. In fact, some psychologists think that it's not so much that a stimulus causes an emotion (say, sadness) which then causes in its turn a physical reaction (tears), as that a stimulus causes the tears, which then cause the emotion. I have a friend who has a sure-fire method of cheering people up. He says: 'Robin, lift one corner of your mouth . . . Now lift the other.' And so you find you're smiling, and you suddenly feel better. But anyway, the basic message of this section is this: the body and the mind are such a unity that the one can affect the other. There are no longer a limited range of illnesses that can be called 'psychosomatic': every illness is psychosomatic, because every illness involves the body–mind unit. The body is not a mechanical automaton, nor is the mind a disembodied 'ghost in the machine'.

Placebos and Hypnosis

Psychosomatic medicine tends to be rather gloomy: psychosocial factors cause stress which causes illness. Fewer studies look at things the other way around and consider how the brain can influence the body for health. But one of the most fascinating ways in which it can clearly be seen that the mind affects the body for good is through the use of placebos. Positive expectations create health.

In 1625 the Prince of Orange was besieged inside the city of Breda by the Spanish general Ambrogio Spinola. The siege dragged on for months, and conditions inside the city grew desperate. As if he didn't have problems enough, the Dutch soldiers were being ravaged by scurvy, and there was little or no fresh fruit and vegetables available to supply the required vitamin C. Nor was there any medicine. And so the Prince devised a cunning plan. With the connivance of the city doctors, he prepared some phials containing a decoction of camomile, wormwood and camphor. This 'medicine' was no earthly use at all in itself, but the Prince surrounded it with a story of how it had been procured with great danger from the mysterious East, and how it was so effective that just two or three drops in a gallon of water would clear the disease up. And so it did.

The placebo effect was well known in medieval and Renaissance times, before the mind and the body were separated by Descartes; scholars used it to explain the efficacy of charms and talismans. In the nineteenth century, John Elliotson, the protagonist of an earlier chapter, who as a materialist is often accused of ignoring the power of suggestion, occasionally prescribed pills made of bread to his patients, telling them they were opium or calomel. I am reminded of how in the UK some time ago – perhaps in the 1970s – the manufacturers of the analgesic Anadin came up with a slogan for their product: 'Nothing works faster than Anadin.' Before long the muttered response from many on hearing this line was: 'So take nothing.'

This halfway decent joke has a serious underlying point. To see the point we need to know something about placebos. Placebo means, literally, 'I will please' in Latin – that is, it pleases a patient, rather than offering her anything effective. A placebo is any medical treatment that is not specific for the disorder being treated; thus a placebo may be a totally inert substance, or it may be something that is specific, but not for the ailment in question. As I've said, the effect has been known throughout human history, but serious research on the subject began only in the last century. To researchers' amazement, they found that dummy treatments not only cured or relieved a vast range of ailments, but also produced toxic side effects and the appropriate changes in mood and behaviour. A drug designed to induce nausea cured upset stomachs when the patients were told it would. Evidence is building, to the confusion of conventional medicine, that even some forms of placebo surgery may be effective.

The conclusion to be drawn from this is that we all possess enormous capacities for mental self-healing, if only we could find some way to unlock that potential. In fact, if you buy into the myth of scientific progress, and believe that almost all medicines up to about 1900 were chemically ineffective, it follows that you believe that almost all cures brought about by these medicines were the result of the placebo effect. Patients got better in spite of the treatment they received, not because of it. It has even been said that

> The great lesson of medical history is that the placebo has always been the norm of medical practice, that it was only occasionally and at great intervals that anything really service-able, such as the cure of scurvy by fresh fruits, was introduced into medical practice . . . [The skill of doctors in the past] was a skill in dealing with the emotions of men. They themselves were the therapeutic agents by which cures were effected.

A certain wave pattern is also noticeable in the history of medicine: a drug comes into fashion, works well for a while, but then ceases to be so effective. Along comes the next drug to take its place. As early as 1833 the French physician Armand Trousseau was urging his colleagues to hurry and use new drugs while they worked. This too suggests that psychological factors, such as belief in the medicine's potency, are as important as pharmacological ones in curing disease. From this it follows that *all* cures have a placebo component.

In order for the placebo to work, the patient, obviously, must be unaware of the deceit. (There was an amusing sketch on the British television comedy show *Smack the Pony* in April 2000 in which an inept doctor told her savvy patient that she was prescribing a placebo.) But more abstruse conditions have also been found to help. For instance, a coloured medicine works better than a colourless one, and a flavoured one (especially if bitter) better than a tasteless one. These conditions seem to satisfy patients' expectations about medicines. Also, injection works better than oral intake, perhaps because of the presence of the doctor or nurse, and capsules work better than tablets. Different-coloured capsules or tablets are assumed to have different properties: lavender for a hallucinogenic, yellow or orange for a mood manipulator, white for analgesics, grey or dark red for sedatives. It also helps if the person administering the 'drug' is female, presumably due to a perception that a woman is more sympathetic. The larger the group of people taking the medicine (fake or real), the better its chances of success, because of the power of suggestion: 'If it works for them, it must work for me.' If the doctor himself doesn't know that the 'drug' is a placebo, the effectiveness of the 'drug' goes up even further: we subtly pick up on his confidence or its lack. If an authority figure says something like 'Our tests show that this should work well for you', the effectiveness of the placebo improves.

If all this smacks of deception and quackery, the other side of the coin is that placebos already have a proven track record for physiological ailments such as angina, arthritis, asthma, high blood pressure, headaches, migraine, constipation, impotence, hay fever, cold sores and warts, and for psychological or behavioural conditions such as anxiety, depression, insomnia and obesity. If placebos are lies, they are lies that heal, and you could argue on both financial and other grounds that doctors should be giving their patients placebos for these ailments rather than active drugs. Or at least that they should once they had identified a patient as a placebo reactor. It so far defies explanation, but not everyone is a placebo reactor. Estimates vary and the evidence from experiments is ambiguous, but possibly as many as half the population (with intelligence, gender, age, race, social class and ethnic or religious background being irrelevant) are not reactors. In terms of the brain's functioning, it looks as though placebo reactors are operating with the right, holistic part of the brain, rather than with the left, logical side. If there is a reactor profile, you could say that they tend to be acquiescent and, at the time of presenting for therapy, anxious about their illness. Negatively, one could say that they were gullible; positively, that they have faith, whereas the rest are sceptics. And so we are back to the topic of faith healing, already discussed in Chapters 3 and 5. It seems to me that we can all be placebo reactors in the right circumstances, and the inability to be one is not a constant throughout one's life.

If the public think of hypnosis as a magical therapy, then might it not work as a kind of placebo itself? Some people do indeed think that hypnosis is a kind of placebo. These are the people whose views I summarized in the last chapter – the doubters, the non-state theorists, who believe that there is no such thing as hypnosis. For if their views are right, there should be no cures specifically attributable to hypnosis: all the cures attributed to hypnosis should be explained by other factors, such as the effect of mere relaxation. So it worries them that hypnosis does seem to be inexplicably effective in things like the treatment of chronic pain, warts and asthma. They therefore suppose 'that when hypnotic induction appears to "add" something to therapy, it is a placebo effect; i.e. what it "adds" is a ritual that culminates in some patients *believing* that the treatments will be effective'. However, experiments have shown that whereas hypnosis might act as a placebo for low hypnotizables, its effect on reducing pain in high hypnotizables is far higher than one might expect from a placebo. The same set of hypnotizable subjects in an experiment were hypnotized for relief from pain and given a placebo that they believed to be an analgesic drug; they gained more relief from hypnosis than from the placebo, whereas non-hypnotizable subjects gained roughly the same amount of relief from the hypnotic sugges-tion to relax as they did from the placebo. It would be rash to generalize either way: hypnosis is not entirely a placebo, nor are its effects entirely independent of the placebo effect. Every successful cure has a placebo component: that is one of the important lessons we have been taught by placebo research. Hence the effectiveness of hypnosis has a placebo component – but it is not entirely a placebo. And so we return to the message of this chapter: hypnosis works.

I am often asked, 'Can hypnosis be used for (fill-in-the-blank)?' My response is to promote the idea that hypnosis can be used as a tool in the treatment of *any* human condition in which a person's attitude is a factor. Wherever there is involvement of the person's mind in a particular problem, which is *everywhere* to one degree or another as far as I can tell, there is some potential gain to be made through the application of hypnotic patterns.

12

Mind Control

In the 1967 song 'The Red Telephone', performed by the West Coast psychedelic band Love on their seminal album *Forever Changes*, songwriter Arthur Lee uses the concept of hypnosis as a social metaphor. The hypnotism that disempowers us in the song is meant to be a product of society as a whole. Society has many ways of lulling us to sleep, entrancing us and closing our eyes against the things it doesn't want us to see. Taken to an extreme this is the paranoid view that the TV is a tool of the establishment, whose malignant purpose it is to control our minds.

Oddly, at this point the substrate of popular usage coincides with the most refined studies of the academics. The non-state theorists whose ideas we looked at in Chapter 10 also license the extended use of the term 'hypnotism'. In denying that there is such a thing, so that it should always be surrounded by scare quotes, they often digress into the claim that we are always or invariably in some kind of trance anyway. When our sensory awareness is restricted and focused on the TV, we are in a TV trance; when we listen to one conversation in a crowded room to the exclusion of the rest, we are in a party trance, which has perhaps been deepened by a glass or three of wine; when we play solitaire on the computer, we are in a solitaire trance. State theorists, on the other hand, restrict the use of the term to a specific psychological state, and to that state alone. They acknowledge that all trance states share certain features, but they also point to the differences.

By this stage of the book my position is clear, since I have declared myself in Chapter 10 on the side of the state theorists, and have already on one or two occasions taken to task the people I call 'hypnotic imperialists', who use the term 'hypnosis' to refer loosely to almost any kind of trance whatsoever. Of course selective attention is going on all the while – in fact, our sensory apparatus is designed to filter, not to take in without discrimination – but that does not mean that we are hypnotized. Nevertheless, in this chapter I will consider a number of topics which are more or less closely related to hypnosis, but which all centre around the issue of whether we can be persuaded against our wills, and whether hypnosis might be of help to someone who wanted to try to persuade us against our wills. In America in the 1950s and 1960s, certain government agencies certainly thought it could be, and they poured money into often farcical research to try to create a super-spy. But before turning to this embarrassing episode of American history, we can look at some less extraordinary cases of attempted mind control.

Consensus Trance and Advertising

In his 1986 book *Waking Up: Overcoming the Obstacles to Human Potential* California psychologist Charles Tart coined the phrase 'consensus trance', and claimed that this trance state is our normal state of consciousness, since we are all hypnotized by our cultures. This book by Tart is a largely successful attempt to update the ideas of the influential Russian mystic George Ivanovitch Gurdjieff (1866–1949), who trenchantly declared that we are each 'a rather uninteresting example of an animated automaton'. The point of both Gurdjieff's practical teaching, and indeed arguably of all mystical teaching, is to wake us up out of this state of quasi-sleep. An automaton has no free will, no real choice, and cannot really be said to do anything. It doesn't act, but just reacts to incoming stimuli. In this state we are less than fully human.

The idea of cultural hypnotism – of the hypnoidal unreality of so-called real life – is well conveyed in Lars von Trier's 1991 film *Europa*. The film begins with a hypnotic voice saying: 'When you hear my voice, you will go deeper into Europa. I will count to ten, and at ten you will be in Europa.' A standard relaxation technique follows, in which parts of the body are progressively relaxed, and this is accompanied by the monotonous sight of a railway track speeding endlessly on under one's gaze. The monotonous voice recurs at several points in the film. 'Europa' turns out to be Germany just after the Second World War – a time of treachery and uncertainty, ripe for the accusation of unreality which von Trier uses the framing device of hypnotism to achieve. The use of black-and-white photography, except at moments where some intensity of emotion is reached by the hero of the film, adds to the sense of unreality.

While I am wholly sympathetic to Gurdjieff's ideas and to the pressing need to wake up, I am not at all sympathetic to Tart's saying that we are in a permanent hypnotic trance. If we are in a hypnotic trance now, then what are we in when someone hypnotizes us? Is that state no different from our everyday state? Tart himself would be the first to acknowledge that the hypnotic trance is different, and he points out some of the differences, including the temporary nature of the hypnotic trance, and the fact that it is entered into voluntarily, whereas consensus trance is more or less forced on us as we become attuned to our culture during our formative years. Nevertheless, he thinks that there are enough similarities to warrant his calling the consensus trance a form of hypnosis.

Leaving this controversy aside, since if pursued it may well turn out to be no more than a quibble about words, I want to focus on the central point of Tart's describing us as in a permanent trance. This is that we have been and constantly are in a passive state of being manipulated by the authorities around us. We feel in control of our lives, but in many respects we aren't. Newspapers tell us what to think; canned laughter on TV prompts our laughter. Radio announcers appeal to the lowest common denominator and encourage us to belong to the herd. Propaganda of all kinds bombards us, especially in times of war: someone once said that in war the first victim was truth. Nowadays politicians employ spin doctors and make extensive use of TV and other media to present themselves and their policies in a favourable light. States and Churches use various forms of indoctrination to perpetuate what seems to them at any given time to be the correct set of views. One of the main ways in which we lack control is our subservience to advertising. Countless tests have shown that advertising works, and in America alone $200 billion a year is spent on it. When we walk into a shop we are not quite free agents: we buy the products the advertisers and packagers want us to buy.

What all these techniques – propaganda, advertising and so on – have in common is that they appeal to our emotions. We like to think we are rational creatures who weigh up issues and come to a considered opinion. Advertisers are well aware that this is an illusion. Louis Cheskin, the head of a Chicago research firm in the 1950s which carried out studies for merchandisers, said:

> Motivation research is the type of research that seeks to learn what motivates people in making choices. It employs techniques designed to reach the unconscious or subconscious mind because preferences generally are determined by factors of which the individual is not conscious. Actually in the buying situation the consumer generally acts emotionally and compulsively, unconsciously reacting to the images and designs which in the subconscious are associated with the product.

What Cheskin is saying is that advertising is not just about remembering the brand name. An advertiser would put nothing more than a brand name on a poster or screen, without any imagery or other peripheral effects, only if he was trying to appeal to an educated sector of society who would say to themselves: 'We don't need all that hype.' This pleasant feeling of self-importance would then become associated with the product. So even this kind of advertising uses the same technique of appealing to our unconscious motivations. We want to feel sophisticated and witty, and we are led to believe that drinking a certain brand of coffee will help us to do so. This same brand of coffee is advertised with background music dating from the halcyon days of our youth. And so on: it is obvious how it goes, but its obviousness does not stop it from being a potent force, just as a lightly hypnotized subject is in the ambiguous position of seeing through the operator's suggestions, but going along with them anyway.

Advertisers well know how to tweak our subconscious motivations, our vulnerabilities and hidden insecurities, to get us to buy their clients' products. Even children are regarded as 'consumer trainees', and therefore as legitimate targets of advertising campaigns. They have to aim for the subconscious, because surveys show time and again that we don't know our conscious minds, or even that we lie. For instance, a brewery asked consumers which of their products they preferred, the light beer or the regular beer. The reply was overwhelming support for the light beer – despite the fact that the brewery sold nine times as much of the regular beer. In another survey, people were asked whether they liked kippers, and most people said that they didn't – but then it turned out that over a third of the people in the survey had never tasted a kipper.

A practical reason why manufacturers from the 1950s onwards had to find more powerful ways of advertising was simply that they had the means, with increasing automation, of massive over-production. They therefore had to generate what euphemistically came to be called 'psychological obsolescence', which is to say that they had to persuade the public that last year's product was not what they really wanted, as compared with this year's, whether or not last year's was in fact ready for the dustbin. But we are not so stupid. At a conscious level we would protest this Machiavellian manoeuvre. So advertisers bypass our conscious thinking.

Another reason was increasing standardization. Advertisers have to try to make their product stand out, because otherwise it wouldn't. In the old days, when every shopkeeper made his own goods or foodstuffs, there were presumably noticeable differences in quality and character. Nowadays, there is hardly any difference between buying the product of one manufacturer or another, except presentation and packaging. And so advertisers have to work hard to make such a difference in our minds. That the difference doesn't exist in reality is clear. Blindfold people and ask them to tell which is the brand of cigarettes or soft drink they always ask for in the shops, and they fail miserably. But if the shopkeeper is out of their particular brand, they get upset. Clearly, advertising has touched some emotional point inside them. Modern marketers such as Scott Bedbury talk of 'emotional leverage': 'Nike, for example, is leveraging the deep emotional connection that people have with sports and fitness. With Starbucks, we see how coffee has woven itself into the fabric of people's lives, and that's our opportunity for emotional leverage.'

Repetition has been a feature of advertisements since their inception in a recognizably modern form in the nineteenth century.

It is a proven way of bypassing our critical faculties and appealing to the emotions. There are other methods, such as an appeal to authority (remember the men in white coats looking serious in a toothpaste laboratory?), or making us feel that we are not in with the in-crowd if we don't drink a particular drink, but repetition is simple and effective. But at a deeper level all advertising – probably all propaganda – follows the same threefold pattern. First, you have to gain someone's interest ('Wow! She's gorgeous!'). Then you have to make an emotional appeal ('I'd like to belong to the kind of group where such gorgeous women hang out'). Finally, you have to offer some way for the victim to resolve the conflict ('If I drink that brand of cocktail, I'll belong to the group').

From every point of view, then, it looks as though advertisers employ subliminal manipulation. They do not target our conscious minds, but our unconscious minds.

Subliminal Messaging

The most notorious attempt by advertisers to manipulate an audience was the use of subliminal messaging. Here is how bestselling author Vance Packard blew the lid off that particular game:

> The London *Sunday Times* front-paged a report in mid-1956 that certain United States advertisers were experimenting with 'subthreshold effects' in seeking to insinuate sales messages to people past their conscious guard. It cited the case of a cinema in New Jersey that it said was flashing ice-cream ads onto the screen during regular showings of film. These flashes of message were split-second, too short for people in the audience to recognize them consciously but still long enough to be absorbed unconsciously.
>
> A result, it reported, was a clear and otherwise unaccountable boost in ice-cream sales. 'Subthreshold effects, both in vision and sound, have been known for some years to experimental psychologists,' the paper explained. It speculated that

political indoctrination might be possible without the subject being conscious of any influence being brought to bear on him.

It should be added that this was a carefully controlled experiment. On some evenings, the subliminal messages were not flashed on the screen, and on those evenings ice-cream sales did not go up. At much the same time as these experiments in advertising, it was reported that *Playboy* magazine had been conducting its own experiments in subliminal messaging, by printing the word 'sex' too small for the eye consciously to detect, to stimulate sales.

Not all subliminal messaging is as provocative as the Gilbey's Gin advertisement with which Wilson Bryan Key begins his book *Subliminal Seduction*, which provided, on analysis, about a dozen clues suggesting relaxation after a sex orgy, starting with the word 'sex' half visible on ice cubes in the glass of gin. Nor is all of it as obvious, even when analysed and pointed out; in fact, you might think that Key and his like at times read too much into things, like the story of the man who tells a suggestive joke, and when his audience sniggers accuses them of having the dirty minds, not him. Admen themselves have had a laugh at Key's expense: Absolut Vodka's 1990 campaign displayed a glass of vodka on the rocks with the word 'Absolut' on the ice cubes. But there is no doubt in my mind that advertisers do employ subliminal techniques – that for all the scandal about subliminal advertising that followed the publication of Packard's book *The Hidden Persuaders* in 1957, we are still constantly being bombarded by such messages, especially by advertisers.

In the 1950s, as we will see before long, fear of brainwashing was in everyone's minds. This fear became attached to subliminal messaging, as if we could be compelled to act on a subliminally received suggestion without knowing why and even against our wills. But there is no evidence that we are *compelled* to act on a subliminal suggestion. It may, of course, incline us in a certain direction, as all advertising does; but it doesn't compel. And that, essentially, is why the advertising industry stopped making use of subliminal messaging: the public found it offensive, and it was no more effective than other, less offensive methods. A lot of people think that subliminal messaging was banned by legislation, but that is not true. The advertising industry made a decision not to use such crude forms of subliminal messaging. It hasn't stopped them using more subtle methods, however.

A good example of subliminal perception is body language. You can meet a man, and on the surface he might be perfectly polite and charming, yet you come away from the meeting certain that he doesn't like you. In all probability you unconsciously or subliminally (below the threshold of consciousness) took in the message his body language was giving you. He may have tilted his body slightly away from you, crossed his legs with the upper foot pointing away from you – that kind of thing. Instinctively, you picked up his aversion.

In other words, there is more to subliminal perception than receiving messages flashed on to a screen. Most of it is obvious and well known: a glamorous couple use a product in an advertisement, suggesting that we will be invested with glamour if we use the product, or that we will find love, sex and other forms of fulfilment. But the fact that it is obvious doesn't make it any the less effective. And in any case, not all of it is obvious: the next time you watch TV adverts, try not to focus on the main characters and the action, which is where the director wants you to direct your conscious attention. Try to see what is happening in the background, which is what we take in unconsciously. Where is that character's gaze directed? (At her breasts.) Why is the scene set in a party? (Because the advertiser wants to appeal to your desire to belong.) Wilson Bryan Key makes the basic point:

> In advertising recall studies, for example, advertisements are rarely or never recalled by the conscious mind. Any ad that can be recalled by a significant number of readers is of doubtful value. The conscious mind values, differentiates, and makes judgements. Conscious ad recall can subject an ad to critical judgement – the last thing to which any advertiser wants to expose his product. Ads are designed to implant themselves within the unconscious where they will lie dormant uncriticized, unevaluated, and unknown to the individual until the time a purchase decision is required. The buried information then surfaces as a favorable attitudinal predisposition.

As long as the snobbery and feelings of inferiority to which advertisers appeal are unconscious (as of course they are, until pointed out), advertising is working subliminally. Magazine ads and roadside hoardings (except those at busy crossroads) are designed to make an impact in no more than one or two seconds, as you flick idly through the pages or roar past at speed, probably in a hypnoidal state; there is no time for conscious evaluation.

Advertising is clearly not the same as hypnosis, but it works on some of the same features of the human constitution as hypnosis, above all our suggestibility. 'Media has the proven, completely established ability to program human behavior much in the same way as hypnosis,' says Key. Many writers on the subject use hypnosis as their model to express their fears about how subliminal manipulation might work: it is like someone who has been hypnotized acting on a post-hypnotic suggestion. And to a certain extent the analogy is true: advertising is a form of mind control. As with hypnosis, you can resist it, but since you are passive, in a state of mental lethargy, you are less inclined to resist it. Advertising is in a sense more pernicious than hypnosis because we choose to enter a hypnotic situation, but we have little choice in the advertisements we see and hear.

Hypnotic Sales Techniques

If you're worried about hypnosis, here is something that will make you pause before letting a salesman get his foot in your door. In Chapter 10 I outlined some of the hypnotic methods of Milton Erickson. They are subtle; they find ways around people's resistance. They have been a boon to salespeople.

There are books which claim that all successful salespeople use 'gentle forms of conversational hypnosis'. Since everyone agrees that a hypnotized person is in an increased state of suggestibility, the idea is that through 'conversational hypnosis' – talking to the target person in a particular way – you play on his suggestibility. The technique is roughly as follows. You set up expectations ('You're going to love what this washing powder can do!'); enthusiasm and genuine sincerity are helpful at this stage. It's not just mechanical: you are establishing what in the nineteenth century used to be called rapport or trust with your 'prospect' (as salespeople call a potential customer). Mirroring his body language is said to help at this stage. Discreetly emphasizing certain words (e.g. 'love' in the example above) embeds them in the customer's unconscious and guides his thinking. Indirect suggestions help: rather than suggesting straight out that he buy the product, you ask him whether he's satisfied with the whiteness of his current wash. The result is that the customer ends up thinking: 'I wasn't sold this product. It was my idea.'

Other selling techniques are also closely related to hypnosis. They include visualization (getting the customer to picture himself at the wheel of that new car, perhaps with a beautiful blonde sitting next to him), suggesting that he cannot remember details of the opposition's product and so inducing a kind of amnesia, and manip- ulating his emotions, for example by making him feel guilt for missed opportunities in the past so that he doesn't want to miss this golden opportunity you're offering him. They even go so far as to plant the equivalent of post-hypnotic suggestions: 'I'm sure that tonight, as you lie in bed, you're going to think about how nice it would be to have a new BMW.'

All these techniques and more are claimed to be effective and probably are. Nor does there seem to be any good reason to deny them the name of hypnosis. It is just an application of Ericksonian techniques to selling. Salespeople learn the techniques and sprinkle key words and tones of voice and body language into their pitch, until the 'prospect' is effectively in a light trance. They use stories to win the customer's confidence, name-dropping like mad because famous names help to win confidence. They ask all the right questions, direct the conversations with hidden commands and so on – whatever it takes to sell the product and pocket the commission. They find the indirect, Ericksonian approach far better than hard selling: 'Most people find that our product is the best . . . Have you ever wanted freedom from annoying paperwork? Now is the time to improve your working life.' Keep it vague, leave it up to the prospect to imagine exactly how his life will improve.

Ericksonian hypnotherapy empowers the patient by making the choice to get well effectively up to him. Pseudo-Ericksonian selling parodies this by having the customer think the choice is up to him. But don't worry. One of the themes of this book is that even in full-fledged hypnosis you can't be made to do anything you don't really want to do. So no salesman using quasi-hypnotic techniques is going to dupe you into spending vast amounts of money when you don't want to. The choice really is up to you.

The Charisma of Tyrants

One of the less tangible results of the Second World War was a widespread fear of charisma. Hitler had entranced an entire nation. This fear lasted a long time. I have long held a private theory that John F. Kennedy and Martin Luther King, the two most charismatic speakers of the post-war decades, were assassinated, in the broad view, because the American people were not yet ready for the re-emergence of charisma. And one of the rebellions of the next generation of young people was to attach themselves in large quantities to charismatic icons, and ultimately to gurus wielding mystical power and often leading new cults.

How do such leaders entrance us? One of the best analyses of tyrannical power came from the pen of Austrian novelist Hermann Broch (1886–1951), who was imprisoned by the Nazis until influential friends such as James Joyce and Thomas Mann obtained his release. For all the brilliance of his work, he died in poverty. In his book *The Spell* Marius Tatti is a true tyrant – that is, he is convinced he knows what's best for others. Marius is a Luddite, opposed to radios, threshing machines and so on; he is also a fake earth and nature-mother mystic, as opposed in the book to the true mysticism and insight of Mother Gisson. The village in which he arrives as a crippled Italian vagabond is a microcosm of Germany in the 1930s under Hitler. He gradually convinces the villagers, or a large proportion of them, that he has come to redeem them. Wentzel, another wanderer who becomes his chief sidekick, says at one point: 'He only speaks out loud what the others are thinking.' That is the secret of his success: he makes it seem as though he is not imposing anything on anyone, but only allowing them to express their essential selves and beliefs. His power comes from his eloquence and from the fact that, although he is crazy, he believes totally in himself and his insane ideas. His power is expressly likened to mesmerism: there is a scene in which Irmgard, an innocent village girl, is so entranced by Marius (with whom she believes herself to be in love) that she allows herself to be set up by him as a sacrifice to the earth spirits of the mountain which looms over the village and colours all their thinking. Tragically, this sacrifice later literally takes place, once Marius has whipped up the villagers by the power of dance and ritual theatre into a state of mass hypnosis.

One of the clever aspects of Broch's portrait of Marius Tatti is the idea that he allows people to think he is only expressing their own convictions. Similarly, as we have just seen in the section on hypnotic sales techniques, a clever salesman makes it seem as though his customers are doing the choosing, with no compulsion from him. If, as I suggested in Chapter 1, all hypnosis can really be seen as self-hypnosis, because you choose at some point to go along with it, so all entrancement is self-entrancement. As well as being one of the outstanding orators of the twentieth century, Hitler was a cynical exploiter of the power of rhetoric. He once said to one of his sidekicks: 'What you say to the people collectively in that receptive state of fanatical abandonment remains in their mind like an order given to someone under hypnosis, which cannot be wiped out and resists all logical argument.' Since rhetoric is not irresistible, even when combined with the suggestibility of crowds, it is clear that Hitler received the consent of the mass of the German people. Even crowds and nations cannot be hypnotized against their will.

Hitler is an interesting case in relation to hypnosis. Many of the reports of people who actually met him face to face, when asked what their chief memory is of the man, mention the power of his eyes. He seemed to look right inside them, to be focused entirely on them to the exclusion of everyone else. This is certainly part of the technique of hypnotism. In his classic book *The Mass Psychology of Fascism*, maverick psychologist Wilhelm Reich attributes the attraction of fascism to middle-class Germans to the sexual repression found in their authoritarian, patriarchal family structure. Hitler's rhetoric appealed to their sense of sin and salvation, with his pseudo-mystical emphases on the holy trinity of blood, soil and state, on the racial soul, mother Germany, the will of the people, national history and honour, discipline and so on. Such slogans bypass the rational mind and stir the emotions. As we have seen in the context of advertising, this is exactly the way to get people to do something you want them to do.

Part of Hitler's charisma was undoubtedly his identification of himself with the German nation. For instance, in his famous speech delivered at the Berlin Sportspalast on 26 September 1938, in which he attempted to justify on historical grounds the imminent invasion of Czechoslovakia, he portrayed the coming conflict as a personal confrontation between himself and Eduard Beneš, the Czech leader, and famously said: 'My patience is now at an end!' This was more than a monstrous piece of personal vanity; it was as if Hitler felt that he had transcended his individuality – that his soul was the soul of the nation. This seeming transcendence, this identification with something larger than themselves, is an important element in the attraction of leaders, both secular and religious.

The Charisma of Gurus

I once saw a TV documentary about the notorious guru Bhagwan Rajneesh. He had a marvellous speaking voice, and was incredibly erudite, but that was only part of his charm. He would hold out a piece of fruit and say: 'You see, truth is like an orange.' What on earth is that supposed to mean? If Rajneesh spelled it out at all, it was only in the vaguest terms. In other words, he gave his followers a lot of space for personal commitment or surrender to himself and his views – a lot of rope to hang themselves with. As we have seen in other instances of mind control, from selling to political tyranny, you have to allow the 'prospect' to convince himself.

Paradoxically, though, at other times Rajneesh and all other gurus and tyrants come up with well-defined views. If a tyrant is by definition someone who thinks he knows better than you what is good for you, and seeks to impose this good on you, to convince you of the correctness of his views, then this definition also fits gurus. Are all gurus tyrants, then? There must be a borderline, which some cross and deserve to be called tyrants, while others remain safely on the near side. Perhaps the border is the degree to which they try to impose their views on you, and the amount of repayment they require in terms of either money or devotion. A tyrant in any sphere – political, religious or domestic – manipulates a system of rewards and punishments, dispensing guilt, shame and forgiveness. By these means, he demands and gains surrender of the will. The deeper the surrender, the greater the emotional investment in seeing the guru or tyrant as perfect, whatever the indications to the contrary.

Surrender of the will is another way in which the profile of a typical guru coincides with that of a hypnotist, since there must be what I have called 'inequality of will' in the hypnotic relationship. Here are some of psychologist Anthony Storr's conclusions about gurus:

> Gurus tend to be élitist and anti-democratic, even if they pay lip-service to democracy. How could it be otherwise? Conviction of a special revelation must imply that the guru is a superior person who is not as other men are. Gurus attract disciples without acquiring friends. Once established, gurus must exercise authority, which again precludes making friends on equal terms ... A guru's conviction of his own worth depends upon impressing people rather than on being loved. Gurus seldom discuss their ideas; they only impose them.

A range of similar ideas are presented in a novelistic fashion in John Updike's marvellous satirical *S.*, published in 1988 and clearly based on Rajneesh.

It so happens that in my life I have met many charismatic people, and it is clear to me that, as Storr says, charisma is, at least in part, a product of conviction (and note that again Broch got his portrait of Tatti right). It is only when someone is absolutely certain that he *knows*, that he has or is conveying the truth, that he can be charismatic. Also, what that person knows or conveys has to be something larger than himself. Thus a politician or a religious fanatic is more likely to be charismatic than the world's greatest expert in earthworms, because the politician or the religious fanatic is or appears to be acting as a channel for a message of broad, even universal importance. Compared with conviction, eloquence pales into relative insignificance. Gurdjieff was never fluent in either Russian or English, but he succeeded in charming followers in both languages; I have met Japanese and Tibetan religious teachers whose attraction was enormous, despite the fact that some of them could hardly string two words together in English (apart from, perhaps, 'Come: follow me!'). For all their linguistic difficulties, they exuded authority.

Charisma is not only a characteristic of tyrants and fringe religious leaders. Some people are charismatic because of their personal integrity. Basil Hume (1923–99), leader of the Roman Catholic Church in England and Wales, was such a man. What made him charismatic was not just his conviction, his faith, but also his personal humility and honesty. But anyone who watches footage of one of Hitler's speeches in front of a mass audience, even if he knows little or no German, can feel the charisma exuding from the man, so that he could hold in his hand not just the immediate audience, but an entire nation. The difference is that Hume was not attempting to impose himself on anyone else; he was charismatic in spite of himself, so to speak. But any leader who uses his charisma to acquire personal power, and to bolster his self-assurance by the adulation of disciples, is a person to avoid.

In the fields of entertainment and politics charisma is channelled into legitimate paths. The same may happen in religion too, as in the case of Basil Hume, but if the person's thinking is at all unusual or unorthodox, if he challenges the existing order, then he gathers followers and forms a sect. The motto of the establishment is: Trust in the order, not the individual. This is why charismatics often pose a challenge, and they and their followers become marginalized as a sect or cult. A good definition of a cult is given by authors Joel Kramer and Diana Alstad: cults are 'groups with an authoritarian structure where the leader's power is not constrained by scripture, tradition or any "higher" authority . . . In a cult, absolute authority lies in a leader who has few if any external constraints.' But it is important to note that all or most of the world's major religions began as sects.

There is a great deal of fear about the religious cults that proliferated in the West especially in the 1970s, and there are organizations all over the world to provide information and even 'deprogramming' services to anxious parents. People enter cults of their own choice: they are not turned into zombies. But the presence of apparently free choice is not enough in itself to disprove the charge of mind control. After all, we *choose* to buy the advertised brand of coffee over the unadvertised one. And it is quite clear that in the early days of a person's membership of a cult his sense of self is broken down, and his fear of isolation played on, in ways that constitute a form of reprogramming. The fear of isolation or exile is very potent in all of us, and plays a part not just in minor sects, but in all mass meetings, religious and political, mainstream or marginal. Experiments have shown that individuals in crowds enter a kind of hypnoidal state, with increased and contagious suggestibility. Again, this falls short of (or, in a sense, exceeds) hypnotism proper – but again it is a culturally acceptable form of similar techniques. The state of an individual in a mob has best been described in a classic book by the nineteenth-century French social psychologist Gustave Le Bon:

> He is no longer conscious of his acts. In his case, as in the case of the hypnotized subject, at the same time that certain faculties are destroyed, others may be brought to a high degree of exaltation. Under the influence of a suggestion, he will undertake the accomplishment of certain acts with irresistible impetuosity. This impetuosity is the more irresistible in the case of crowds than in that of the hypnotized subject, from the fact that, the suggestion being the same for all the individuals of the crowd, it gains in strength by reciprocity.

So precisely the same features that make tyrants attractive also constitute the charisma of gurus. They have conviction, they allow their followers to entrance themselves, they channel something larger than themselves, they are sure they know what's best for us, they are committed to the cause themselves, but if they lapse at all that only adds to their charm, making them suddenly human. They have sexual magnetism. It helps if they are good speakers; it helps if they are different from their followers (as many gurus in the West are Asian, and as Marius Tatti was an Italian in Austria). They manipulate the emotions, and perhaps especially the desire to belong, to be part of the crowd, and the wish to escape a humdrum existence. These are the elements of mind control, as employed by advertisers, salespeople, tyrants and gurus.

The CIA and Brainwashing

The Background

In 1959 Richard Condon published his famous thriller *The Manchurian Candidate*. The plot of the book has an American soldier, Raymond Shaw, hypnotized by a Chinese psychologist during the Korean War so that he becomes a communist assassin. His reconditioning goes so deep that US psychologists are unable to unlock it. The trigger for him to become a covert assassin is that he is told to play a game of solitaire; when the queen of diamonds comes up during the game, he goes into a passive state and receives his instructions. Needless to say, afterwards he remembers nothing about his conditioning, and nothing about the murders he carries out. His chief controller, the communist agent in charge of him in the States, is said at one point to know that 'Raymond had to do what he was told to do, that he could have no sense of right or wrong about it, nor suspect any possibility of the consciousness of guilt.' That would indeed be powerful control.

Actually (and not surprisingly, since it is a good plot), Condon's was not the first thriller along these lines. In 1945 Colgate University professor of psychology George Estabrooks, perhaps irritated by the military's refusal to allow him to help them create a hypnotized super-spy or assassin, created one in fiction instead, in his co-authored book *Death in the Mind*. In this novel the cunning Germans have hypnotized American servicemen to turn against their side, so that,

for instance, a submarine commander sinks an Allied battleship. The
suave, gung-ho hero, Johnny Evans, realizes that this is a powerful
weapon, and decides to turn it against the Germans themselves. The
book is appallingly dated now, but it does raise a halfway interesting
dilemma: since you can't hypnotize someone without their consent,
how can you hypnotize someone to commit treason? They must
already have given their consent to you, which is to say that they
believe your ideology, and there is therefore no need for them to be
hypnotized to commit treason. This dilemma flummoxes Johnny
Evans for a good half of the book, which is surprising, given his
apparent intelligence on other occasions, because the solution is
obvious: they can be hypnotized by you provided you convince
them that you are on their side. But in real life, as I've said before,
that would be extremely difficult.

Outside the pages of fiction, the Germans did experiment during
the Second World War with a combination of hypnotism and drugs
(especially mescalin), but found it of limited use in controlling
someone's mind. When the same idea occurred to Stanley Lovell,
the head of the Office of Strategic Services (OSS) Research and
Development department during the war, he approached several US
psychologists, but they told him that hypnotism could not make
people do things they would not normally do, and so he dropped
the idea. Estabrooks disagreed. He had notoriously claimed in his
1943 non-fiction book *Hypnotism* that in all probability hypnotism had
a number of military uses, including getting someone to commit
treason against his country. In this book he paints fanciful scenarios
of the damage a team of hypnotized spies, or a singly highly placed
individual, could wreak on US defence systems – precisely the
scenario he could later create only in fiction. Less melodramatically,
he claims that by the use of a 'disguised technique' you can hypnotize
someone – say, an enemy agent you have captured – against his will.
You pretend you are taking his blood pressure, perhaps, and tell him
that as part of the procedure you need to get him to relax – and
then you take him through a standard induction until he is hypnotized. I cannot see that this would work. Nothing blocks induction
better than suspicion, and a captured agent would naturally be highly
suspicious of anyone attempting to take his blood pressure or
whatever.

Still, during and shortly after the Second World War, there was a certain amount of official interest in the potential of hypnotism. There were tests to see if soldiers could remember complex secret codes better when hypnotized than when normal, and in 1947 US army psychologist John Watkins got a soldier to hallucinate that a US officer was Japanese, and then persuaded the soldier to attack the officer (see p. 228). The soldier would presumably not under ordinary circumstances have attacked a superior officer, so Watkins was attempting to demonstrate Estabrooks's belief that the idea that no one will do anything under hypnosis that he would not do when awake is rubbish. On another occasion Watkins got a WAC to believe that she had learnt a number of military secrets, all of which she was persuaded to reveal under hypnosis. But when other psychologists attempted to reduplicate these and similar scenarios, they failed. It is quite likely that factors other than hypnosis were at work in Watkins's experiments. The subjects might well have been willing to comply with Watkins's suggestions, knowing that it was just an experiment. Moreover, they had been selected specifically for their ability to enter a deep trance state; the chances of getting just anyone to perform these acts of betrayal would be considerably less.

Nevertheless, these army experiments were found impressive. A government-sponsored think tank, the Rand Corporation, concluded in 1949 that the possibility of communist governments employing hypnotism against the United States was a real threat. The report pointed in particular to experiments in inducing antisocial or abnormal behaviour in hypnotized subjects by Professor Alexandr Luria in Russia, and stressed that to outside observation a hypnotized person may well behave no differently from an unhypnotized person. It also suggested that the use of drugs such as sodium pentothal could speed up the process or deepen the trance. The seeds of paranoia were sown in the fertile soil of US government agencies, and they were reinforced by the show trial in Hungary, later that same year, of Cardinal Josef Mindszenty, and then by the behaviour of US prisoners during the Korean War (1951–3). Mindszenty was shown dazedly confessing to crimes he obviously did not commit; American servicemen were shown admitting US aggression and praising communism. Was it drugs? Was it hypnosis? Just as in the later 'space race', US officials felt that the commies were ahead of the game, and they were eager to catch up and overtake. It was all part of what American journalist and author John Marks has called 'the ancient desire to control enemies through magical spells and potions'.

The CIA Gets Involved

A senior CIA official, Morse Allen, was the first to take up the challenge. In 1951 he spent a total of four days in New York studying hypnotism with a stage hypnotist, who had impressed him with his boasts to be able to use hypnotism to get women into bed. Allen put his new skills to use by persuading CIA secretaries to steal classified files and hand them on to total strangers, or to fall asleep in a stranger's bedroom. By early 1954 he was ready for the ultimate experiment, in which he persuaded one hypnotized secretary to fire a gun at another, who was asleep. The gun, of course, was not loaded. The 'assassin' claimed amnesia afterwards, and protested that she would never shoot anyone. Had Allen succeeded in creating a hypno-assassin? As he himself was the first to admit, these experiments were more or less worthless as analogies for what might be possible in the field. 'All he felt he had proved was that an impressionable young volunteer would accept a command from a legitimate authority figure to take an action she may have sensed would not end in tragedy. She presumably trusted the CIA enough as an institution, and Morse Allen as an individual, to believe he would not let her do anything wrong.' Allen knew that it would take months of preparation and careful work to get an unwilling and hostile subject into any such condition. Later in 1954, this kind of research was moved away from Allen and his 'Operation Artichoke' team to Sidney Gottlieb, from M-K-Ultra, the well-funded department within the CIA which remained for many years central to research into brainwashing and mind control in general.

The term 'brainwashing' was first used in public in the *Miami News* in September 1950. A new word entered the English language and a new fear the popular imagination. At this stage of US history, the era of Senator Joseph McCarthy's witch-hunts, the belief was widespread that communism was pure evil. Since it was unbelievable that so many millions of people could knowingly be taken in by pure evil, the idea was that they had been indoctrinated from birth. This was brainwashing – supposedly a translation of the Chinese words *hsia nao*, meaning 'to cleanse the mind'. The term came into common parlance during the Korean War, and in a way guaranteed to fuel American paranoia. Over 5,000 US prisoners of war were deemed to have been brainwashed during the war, far more both numerically and proportionally than other Allied prisoners. In fact, for some US prisoners it was not enough to go on record denouncing US aggression and praising communism; on returning home, they took to handing out pro-communist leaflets. The uproar was understandable, but that was public reaction. In private, the secret services simply stepped up their search for an equivalent tool.

However, there is a twist in this tale. It is extremely likely that hardly any of the American POWs who denounced their country had been brainwashed to do so, since they had explicit instructions from their superiors to cooperate with the enemy if they were captured, in order to make their lives as prisoners less arduous. In so far as the communists were successful in converting prisoners, the main factor was low American morale rather than any special techniques, and in any case the only successful converts were the misfits or those who were already inclined towards communism. Others paid only lip service to communism. Prisoners in Korea were subjected to heavy-handed indoctrination, but no special Pavlovian techniques describable as brainwashing. US officials must have known all this, and therefore have allowed the brainwashing scare to remain in place for propaganda purposes, to perpetuate fear of communism.

The brainwashing scare was resurrected in May 1960 when Francis Gary Powers was shot down in his spy plane over the Soviet Union, and subsequently appeared on TV apologizing to the Soviets for the actions of his government. However, Powers himself, who was returned to the United States in 1962 in an exchange for the communist spy Rudolf Abel and later wrote a book about his experiences, denied that he had ever been subjected to hypnosis or any reconditioning methods. He said that he was simply playing it safe.

Nevertheless, brainwashing remained a theoretical possibility, in the minds of the CIA and other US agencies, and so the research programme continued. This was the era of subliminal advertising and other attempts at mass mind control, when psychologists spoke of 'human engineering' and never read Aldous Huxley's *Brave New World* as satire, when the leading behaviourist B.F. Skinner wrote his 1948 novel *Walden Two*, in which children were programmed to be happy, and when the picture admen had of people was so mechanical they were convinced they could just tweak our neuroses to increase sales. Vance Packard's book, largely about this psychological approach to advertising, concludes in all seriousness, as if there were a real danger: 'The most serious offense many of the depth manipulators commit, it seems to me, is that they try to invade the privacy of our minds. It is this right to privacy in our minds . . . that I believe we must strive to protect.'

But brainwashing is an extreme and rare occurrence, and the term should not be used as lightly as the tabloid press often does. It certainly does not apply to any and every conversion, nor to every person who joins a sect or New Religious Movement. It is characterized by a complete change of personality, which unless reinforced may be only temporary. It is important to distinguish between indoctrination and brainwashing. We are all indoctrinated, but few if any of us have had our beliefs, memories and so on systematically broken down and replaced with an alternate set. Few of us have the capacity for executive control over our thoughts, feelings and actions undermined.

The theoretical mechanism of brainwashing has been well known since the time of Pavlov's famous experiments with dogs. The brain has to be stimulated until it can no longer tolerate the stresses imposed, at which point protective inhibition kicks in. This is the point of crisis or breakdown. After breakdown, the behaviour of the subject (be it canine or human) begins to differ from the normal behaviour one would expect of its type; previous behaviour patterns can be suppressed, what had been positive conditioned responses can become negative, and vice versa. In less complex terms, if you put someone under emotional stress, they become more suggestible and move towards the crisis point. In a religious context, if you assault a person's emotions by convincing her that she is in a state of sin, or is flawed in some way, that alone will increase her suggestibility to the next part of your message, which is presumably that you have the means to cleanse her of sin, or heal the flaw, or at least can teach her to do it herself.

Interestingly, in cases of sudden conversion the crisis often resembles the breakdown of victims of shell-shock in war: weeping, sweating, quaking (the phenomenon which marked out the earliest Quakers), change of character, physical collapse – all symptoms which are familiar from Bible-belt evangelical healing meetings. Rhythmic drumming, chanting and drugs also help to bring on a rapid crisis; and the presence of others, inducing mass hysteria, is a great boon to the would-be converter. British psychologist William Sargant's fascinating book *Battle for the Mind* shows how deliberately these techniques have been used by hellfire Christian preachers and modern evangelists for conversion and, in a political context, for indoctrination. The trouble with sudden conversion, of course, is that it can suddenly disappear too; this is the point at which you should invite your new convert to group meetings, where she can receive positive feedback from others in your group, and generally make her the focus of your attention in some way, to reinforce the idea that she is now in a state of religious or political grace, and to give her the sense of belonging that we all crave.

Who is vulnerable? In theory, you are, unless you are technically insane and so are following the beat of a totally different drum. The more 'ordinary' or conventional a person is, the better a candidate he is for hypnotism or brainwashing. This seems like a paradox, but look at it from this point of view. We measure ordinariness precisely by the extent to which a person has accepted society's norms – which is to say, by the extent to which a person has been conditioned, or has accepted external suggestions imposed on him by parents, school, peers, etc. In other words, ordinary people are suggestible people. They are the ones who are likely to join a cult; they are the ones stage hypnotists prefer as their subjects.

Intellectual ability is no guarantee of protection, because the techniques involved in brainwashing work at an emotional level. In an appendix to *The Devils of Loudun* Aldous Huxley imagines the following amusing scenario:

> It would be interesting to take a group of the most eminent philosophers from the best universities, shut them up in a hot

room with Moroccan dervishes or Haitian Voodooists and measure, with a stop-watch, the strength of their psychological resistance to the effects of rhythmic sound. Would the Logical Positivists be able to hold out longer than the Subjective Idealists? Would the Marxists prove tougher than the Thomists or the Vedantists? What a fascinating, what a fruitful field for experiment! Meanwhile, all we can safely predict is that, if exposed long enough to the tom-toms and the singing, every one of our philosophers would end by capering and howling with the savages.

Hypnosis actually played little part in US mind-control experiments, although the secret services were always interested in financing and hearing about the tests carried out by some clinical psychologists they knew. On the whole, the methods used were cruder: denial of sleep, large doses of drugs, repeated electric shocks, sensory deprivation – *Clockwork Orange* rather than *The Manchurian Candidate*. The US research programme included: attempting to monopolize the world supply of LSD, to prevent it getting into communist hands; dosing unwitting psychiatric patients in Canada with large quantities of LSD (two of them later successfully sued the CIA); experiments with the legendary drug BZ, said to be ten times as powerful as LSD and to induce an 80-hour trip with amnesic after-effects; treating Viet Cong prisoners of war, often lethally, with electroshocks; and the CIA running a brothel in San Francisco in the hope that it would gain them insights into men's natures and sexual drives. Many of these tests were at best irresponsible and unethical, and at worst illegal, but the men and women involved felt that they were at war against communism, and that this justified their actions. Ironically, it is undoubtedly true, as John Marks claims, that it was CIA release of LSD to psychology departments and psychiatric hospitals around the country that kick-started the hippie revolution. LSD was finally made illegal in the States on 6 October 1966.

In 1975, after CIA experimentation with drugs (and implication in the drug trade in several countries) became public knowledge, some astonishing statistics also came to light. In the previous twenty years they had tested LSD on some 7,000 subjects, 20 per cent of whom were not told in advance that they were to be given the drug. The statistics from the army and the prison service were just as alarming. In a few cases, the poor victims of these tests killed themselves. Dr Frank Olson, a scientist attached to the secret services by his work on biological warfare, was given LSD without his knowledge, though he was told after he had started tripping; he began to display agitated and erratic behaviour, and a few days later he hurled himself through the window of the hotel where he was staying and fell twelve floors to his death.

The Real Manchurian Candidate

The basic purpose of all this drug research was to find interrogation tools, not to create super-spies. Sometimes drugs alone were used for this, sometimes a combination of drugs and hypnosis. An internal CIA memo of 14 July 1952 reported the successful use of such a combination when interrogating two suspected Russian agents in America. Hypnosis was used not only to aid the actual interrogation process, but also to induce post-hypnotic forgetfulness that the interrogation had ever taken place. An alleged double agent in Germany, codenamed 'Explosive', was successfully interrogated in the same year by US agents using similar techniques. The CIA and US army also experimented with hypnosis as a means of training couriers to remember complex coded messages. They would then forget the message until triggered into recall by a cue given by another agent. The advantages of such a system, should it have worked, are obvious.

There are only two recorded authentic attempts to use hypnotism to create hypno-assassins along the lines of *The Manchurian Candidate*, and both turned farcical. The first, in 1963, was on a suspected Mexican double agent; the idea was to induce rapid trance, and then convince him to kill the local KGB head, but the hypnotist, codenamed 'Mindbender', at the last moment refused; perhaps he knew that such rapid induction was unlikely to be successful in an unwilling and unprepared subject. In the second the hypnotist was codenamed 'Dr Fingers'. His job was to hypnotize someone from the Cuban community in Miami to return to Cuba and assassinate Castro when triggered by the word 'cigar'. In 1966 Dr Fingers tried his skills on three men. The first refused to respond to the trigger word, except to say that he didn't smoke; the second could not be brought out of his trance; the third became violent at the mention of Castro's name and began to smash up the motel room where the meeting was taking place. (There is in any case an obvious difficulty with using trigger words or phrases in the creation of a super-spy. Suppose you want to trigger amnesia in a spy, so that he cannot confess when captured by the enemy. What trigger word do you use? The Russian for 'Halt! Police!'? But what guarantee is there that the arresting agents would use exactly these words?) At this point the CIA gave up using hypnotism as a means of creating a Manchurian Candidate lookalike. It remained in their arsenal only as a possible instrument of extracting information.

Any attempt to create a super-spy by hypnosis is doomed to failure. It simply is not possible to guarantee the kind of total amnesia the project requires, and the kind of reprogramming required to make people do things contrary to their deep conditioning would be both complex and hugely time-consuming. Claims that there have been such hypno-assassins run foul of their own implausibility. In his book, conspiracy-theory author William Bowart recounts the case of one Luis Angel Castillo, who was arrested in March 1967 in the Philippines on suspicion of conspiring to assassinate President Ferdinand Marcos. The case was eventually dropped, but not before Castillo had claimed to have been involved in an assassination plot three and a half years earlier, in November 1963, in Dallas, Texas. Castillo claimed not to know who the target of the assassination was. But he said that he arrived too late: the assassination had already taken place. He went into some detail about how he had been hypnotized, and hinted at Cuban involvement. His claims were checked by the Philippine authorities and the CIA, who were presumably less gullible than Bowart. Since Castillo was released without any charges being brought against him, for either assassination plot, we may assume that there was no reality to the claims of this petty criminal, whose most serious crime before this time was car theft.

Bowart similarly gives credence to the idea that Lee Harvey Oswald was hypnotized by David Ferrie, a former CIA agent, to be the fall guy in the JFK assassination; he hints that Jack Ruby, Oswald's killer, may have been hypnotized; he claims that George de Mohren-schildt, who allegedly knew all about the plot, committed suicide on having a post-hypnotic suggestion to do so triggered by a phone call. The fact that de Mohrenschildt had a history of suicide attempts is passed over. When Bowart also goes on to claim that James Earl Ray, who assassinated Martin Luther King, was a hypnotized dupe of the FBI, a fall guy like Oswald, and to repeat the idea floated by Robert Kaiser in his book *R.F.K. Must Die* that Bobby Kennedy's killer, Sirhan Sirhan, was also hypnotized, and that all these killings were the work of what Bowart calls 'the cryptocracy' – the various secret services of the USA – the whole conspiracy-theory edifice seems in danger of crumbling under the weight of its own idiocy. However, the kind of silliness that one finds in Bowart's book has not gone away. Through her website, Christian writer Carla Emery offers a book called *Secret, Don't Tell* which repeats many of the 'facts' perpetuated by Bowart and others.

Finally, a word must be said here about the incredible case of Candy Jones. In 1976 Donald Bain published *The Control of Candy Jones*, in which he claimed that under hypnosis Ms Jones (whose real name was Jessica Wilcox, but she had taken the name Candy Jones when she was a model) had revealed that she had, throughout the 1960s, acted as a courier for the CIA. The reason it took hypnosis to bring this out of her was that she had been hypnotized in the first place, by a doctor working for the CIA, who had effectively created an alternate personality. In a trance her other self had been sent off on all kinds of missions, on at least one of which she was tortured, and the plan was to induce her to commit suicide when her usefulness had run out.

Given the inherent implausibility of the creation by hypnosis of any such perfect tool, I read the book with considerable scepticism. My scepticism was only increased by a remarkable parallel. If I mention that Candy 'remembered' under hypnosis being prodded, poked and tested, often in a sexual fashion, by a Dr Gilbert Jensen (whom Bain tried and failed to locate), the reader will recall from Chapter 8 that tales of alien abduction invariably include exactly this element. The most plausible scenario seems to be this. A person's false memories, when they are tinged by fear, attach themselves to a spectre. This spectre will change according to culture and the

Zeitgeist. One would not expect such a bogeyman to be the same in a remote Pacific Island as in the USA, and one would not expect it to be the same in 1800 as in 2000. Nowadays, in the so-called space age, aliens are the great unknown; in Candy Jones's time the thing to fear was the secret police.

Scientists Respond

Fear and bemusement about brainwashing in the 1950s led, among other things, to the US Air Force sponsoring a study, by a number of distinguished scientists, of what really could be achieved. This study was later written up and published as *The Manipulation of Human Behavior*, edited by Albert D. Biderman and Herbert Zimmer. Although most of the articles in the book are written in that uptight and jargonese fashion many academics still use to protect their professional status, it is a pity that it is not better known, because it acts as a useful counterbalance to bestselling books that alarm the general public.

The scientists accept, of course, that one person can influence another. That is why we have the concepts 'influence', 'control', 'manipulation' and so on. But all their experiments and theories suggest that there are severe limitations on such influence, provided that the target person is unwilling to be influenced. The fictional or hysterical belief in the opposite, that one can be taken over despite one's best intentions, is an example of the syndrome whereby 'the aspirations and anxieties that not so long ago were projected onto conceptions of the wizard and witch are now directed to the scientist'. Interrogators are not supermen, no technique is infallible, and all require a responsive subject in order to be successful.

Suppose physiological methods are used, such as sensory deprivation or sleep deprivation. These methods are certainly guaranteed to impair the subject's brain functions. He will move from fatigue and inability to perform more complex tasks to irritability or depression, alternating with apathy, to lack of concern with manners and honesty and patriotism, until he ends with total confusion and disorientation, and even unconsciousness. At any point towards the latter end of this scale, he will be willing to cooperate with his interrogator, even to the extent of confessing to something he has not done: he can no longer separate fantasy from reality. In other words, ironically, the more cooperative a prisoner becomes, the less reliable his statements become at the same time.

Some people have the ability to hold out against such methods for a longer time than others. The chief factors here are the subject's personality and his attitude towards the experience. In other words, if you go in expecting that you will be able to resist whatever is thrown at you, you are more likely to be able to resist than if you go in scared and certain of your 'cowardice'. Personality and attitude are even more important when it comes to more direct methods such as torture, starvation and the threat of pain – that is, to methods which do not in themselves impair the functioning of the brain. Some people can resist such tortures to the bitter end, while others crack quickly. Torture is designed to 'soften people up' – to make them willing to impart information, because without that willingness the information will not be given. But again, the irony is that the longer the torture goes on, the less reliable the information given is likely to be. In any case, torture is not universally successful, because if a moral code of not giving information is deeply ingrained in the subject, he will not talk. It follows that no one can be made to give information against his will, and that information given under torture is not necessarily honest. It is merely a ploy to make the torture go away.

Drugs are also unreliable, since they are affected more than the layman would imagine by variable factors such as the attitude of the donor, and the attitude and physiological condition of the recipient. The popular press, fuelled by incautious statements by one or two early researchers, pounced on certain drugs as 'truth serums', and this notion has been perpetuated in many a movie and novel. But it is false: a confession induced by scopolamine or sodium amytal, for instance, might be nothing more than narcotically inspired babbling, or might be presented in an unintelligible fashion.

By now the reader will not be surprised to learn that the same or similar limitations also apply to the use of hypnosis in interrogation. Martin Orne's excellent essay in Biderman and Zimmer's book concludes that it would be extremely difficult to hypnotize a reluctant subject. The only situation in which hypnosis might be surreptitiously induced is if there is a relationship of trust between operator and subject – and it may safely be assumed that no such relationship exists between interrogator and prisoner. In any case, even if a prisoner could be hypnotized against his will, there is no guarantee that he would tell the truth. At the same time, it would be stupid to try to use hypnosis to strengthen someone's resistance in case he was ever captured and interrogated. The fact that a hypnotist had told a spy, for instance, to resist would actually have the opposite effect, since the spy would be better off relying on his own ego and strength of will.

In short, Bowart and his kind are living in a fantasy world. The suggestion that hypnotism is an all-powerful tool belongs to the pages of thrillers, not to books which are to be classified as nonfiction. This conclusion obviously meshes with the conclusion of Chapter 7 that you cannot be compelled by a hypnotist to do anything you would not otherwise have done. I can confidently say that there are no hypnotized secret assassins roaming the streets, waiting for the coded phrase that will galvanize them into action; and I can confidently say that there are serious limitations on the effectiveness of hypnosis in all conspiracy-theory contexts.

13

Self-improvement and the
New Age

Whatever consciousness is, it is not single or simple. There is, presumably, such a thing as full unconsciousness, the nearest approximation to which in reasonably common experience is the state of being anaesthetized for a surgical operation. There may, if the mystics are to be believed, be such a thing as full consciousness. But as well as these two extremes there are a number of different states, such as sleep (with its various depths and gradations), wakefulness, drunkenness, daydreaming, 'highway hypnosis', concentration and so on. Some of these states are known as 'altered states of consciousness' (ASCs) – altered because they vary from the paradigm state of waking consciousness. Apart from hypnosis, the most important ASCs are dreaming, daydreaming, creative states (especially the inspirational phase of the creative act), psychedelic states caused by mind-altering drugs, meditation, mystical rapture and shamanic ecstasy, states of dissociation and hallucinatory psychotic states. Even if all or most of these are odd states, it needs to be stressed that they are common. In fact, one study found that 89 per cent of the 488 societies for which there were adequate ethnographic data had institutionalized ways of entering trance states, chiefly through religious rituals.

Note that I have written 'as well as these two extremes' of full consciousness and total unconsciousness, where it would have been natural to write 'between these two extremes'. But this would perpetuate a false idea which impairs a great deal of thinking about consciousness. We tend to think in terms of a scale, with unconsciousness at one end and consciousness at the other. We would put sleep and hypnosis, for instance, closer to the unconsciousness end of the scale, and in fact one common professional definition of sleep is 'the natural periodic *suspension of consciousness* during which the powers of the body are restored'. That seems innocuous enough – until you remember that when you are asleep you dream, and that there is the phenomenon of lucid dreaming, in which we are conscious not just of our dreams, but of the fact that we are dreaming. So consciousness is not at one end of a scale, but is something that can be applied to the full range of mental states, including those like hypnosis which are generally thought to be unconscious.

I have maintained throughout this book that not every trance state is a hypnotic state: it is one ASC among others. Nevertheless, ASCs share a number of features. They commonly require focused attention, some means of cutting out distractions; as usual, focused attention leads to a degree of dissociation, since by narrowing things down other fields of attention seem to belong to another part of yourself. And so you acquire a certain freedom from your normal ego boundaries, and this leads to new ways of looking at things. Some ASCs refocus memory. What psychologists call 'implicit memory' is what allows us to walk and ride a bicycle without thinking about these activities at all; it is opposed to 'explicit' or 'declarative' memory, which is what enables us to recall facts and events. In some ASCs, you might find your attention being drawn to the way you walk or do some equally mundane and everyday task, previously stored in your implicit memory banks; in meditation you pay attention to your breath and/or to the arising of thoughts. ASCs are often induced by repetition, such as drumming, regular breathing or chanting. They involve time-distortion. Critical thought-processes are interrupted, with imagery and emotional expression taking their place (this may be characterized as a shift from left- to right-brain activity); you could say that thinking becomes pre-logical and pre-verbal to a certain extent, and so ASCs give access to what is normally unconscious. This is why the experiences are difficult to remember and give an account of afterwards. They commonly require trust, in a group or an individual, and the consequent willingness to allow oneself to be receptive to the coming experience. People in an ASC are often more suggestible than normal. ASCs may be produced by too much or too little sensory stimulus; a bored child in school retreats into daydreaming, whereas LSD increases sensitivity.

These are all subjective changes, but what about objective measures? Our brain is always giving out certain electrical impulses, called brainwaves. In a focused waking state, these waves fall in the range of 13–30 Hz, which is called the beta rhythm; when resting and relaxed, the alpha rhythm is prominent, between 8 and 13 Hz; when drowsy, the theta rhythm occurs, between 4 and 7 Hz; and very deep sleep is characterized by waves at roughly 1–4 Hz, which is called the delta rhythm. But objective physiological markers of ASCs are sometimes hard to find. You can hook someone up to an EEG machine and give him a massive dose of LSD, and his brain-wave patterns may look normal; on the other hand, the sometimes subtle difference between deep sleep and light sleep is invariably measurable on an EEG. Some ASCs involve a measurable state of relaxation, and so they will show alpha or even theta rhythms, and other physiological markers of relaxation.

In this chapter I will touch on some of the most important ASCs which to a casual observer seem similar to hypnosis, and also some methods of achieving altered states which are commonly used in conjunction with hypnotherapy. All of the states produced by these practices display *some* of the characteristics of the so-called hypnotic state; none of them display *all* of these characteristics. Therefore, none of them is the same as hypnosis.

Mesmer's practices were pounced on by the rhetoricians of the French Revolution as anti-aristocratic. In nineteenth-century Britain mesmerists sided with the poor against the rich, and with progressives against the establishment. Romantics in all periods have been attracted to hypnosis as part of their revolt against materialism. It's fascinating to see that the same thing is happening again today. However one characterizes the New Age movement, it is a rebellion, stemming from the hippies of the 1960s, against traditional and/or scientistic ways of doing things, in religion, medicine, business, technology, farming and so on and so forth. It is no coincidence that there is such a large number of hypnosis-like practices available in the New Age market-place.

Self-hypnosis

Winston Churchill is said to have used it. Countless New Age practitioners think it's the same as meditation. Hypnotherapists invariably teach it to their patients as a follow-up technique they can practise at home to reinforce the benefits of the therapy. Self-hypnosis is simply hypnosis carried out on one's own. A typical technique – this one is taken from Leslie LeCron's book – is to get into a position where you can be comfortable and stare at a lighted candle. Breathe quietly and deeply, and as you gaze at the flame of the candle, say to yourself: 'As I watch this candle, my eyelids will become heavier and heavier. Soon they will be so heavy that they will close.' Let them close, and as they do so, say to yourself: 'Relax now.' Relax your body systematically all the way from your toes up to the top of your head. Take your time over this. Once you have finished this phase, say to yourself: 'Now I will go deeper.' Visualize an escalator or a staircase, and go down it, counting backwards from ten to zero. By the time you reach the bottom, you should be in a light trance. After remaining there for a short while, you can seed any suggestions you want to make to yourself. When you want to wake up, you just say to yourself: 'Now I will wake up', and count back up from one to ten. The kind of trance you can get into through self-hypnosis varies in depth, but you won't go into a very deep state; an external hypnotist is needed for that.

One of the most common forms of self-hypnosis, though little known in English-speaking countries, is autogenic training (AT). Invented by Johannes Heinrich Schultz (1884–1970), a German neurologist who was interested in hypnosis, it is used widely by doctors in Germany for psychosomatic illnesses, and has also been extensively researched in Japan and Russia. It has solid medical credentials. The principle is one that we have met in Chapter 11. Relaxation makes the central nervous system passive, and so allows the autonomic nervous system to get on with its natural business of regulating the activity of the internal organs. Since these organs – the heart, lungs, liver and digestive system – are essential to health, then AT promotes health. But the healing process is not left to relaxation alone: in order to target the required internal organ, there are six verbal formulae to repeat, which are used in conjunction with visualization of the appropriate part of the body. The overall effect is to focus passive attention on to the required organ. First, for muscular relaxation, you focus on your dominant arm (the right arm if you're right-handed) and repeat: 'My arm is very heavy.' For vascular dilation, you again focus on the dominant arm, and say: 'My arm is very warm.' For the heart: 'My heartbeat is calm and strong.' For the lungs: 'It breathes me.' For the visceral organs, focusing on the solar plexus: 'Warmth is radiating over my stomach.' For the head: 'My forehead is cool.' It takes about eight weeks to become adept at the full set of exercises.

Those who are familiar with biofeedback will notice a resemblance between its methods and those of AT. In fact, the pioneers of biofeedback were influenced by Schultz's work. Biofeedback is a way of learning psychosomatic self-regulation by using sensitive instruments to monitor activity in some part of the body, until one learns to modify that activity. Both AT and biofeedback demonstrate what would have been unthinkable until as recently as the 1960s: that one can 'interfere' (I put the word in scare quotes, because the kind of interference involved should be passive) with the functioning even of physical processes previously thought totally instinctive and beyond one's control.

Although there is more to AT – adepts often go on to psychological visualization exercises – it is clearly physically and medically based. A good range of ailments has been treated by this means – basically, anything in which the nervous system is involved. Particular successes have been achieved with bed-wetting, asthma, stress, angina, infertility, insomnia, migraine and Raynaud's disease. But this physical and medical bias is unusual in the domain of self-hypnosis. Most of what passes as self-hypnosis has a quite different rationale. In a New Age context, it is a form of self-therapy that makes you feel good about yourself and the world, and is often combined with affirmations, which I will survey in a moment. One such New Age website has for sale tapes offering 'brain wave technology and subliminal audio/music programs for weight loss, jogging, yoga, meditation, relaxation, traditional-alternative medicine, and spiritual development'. That should just about cover it!

Self-hypnosis has been marginalized in this book because purely inner states and internalized practices are not accessible to the historian. In any case, self-hypnosis is just hypnosis with oneself acting as both operator and subject at once. But it is important to introduce it now, because most of the practices outlined in this chapter are carried on by oneself, and so knowing a little about self-hypnosis gives us a yardstick against which we can see whether these other practices are hypnotic.

Channelling

We've met the phenomenon of channelling, especially in the guise of the nineteenth-century mediumistic trance, often enough already in this book, but it needs bringing in once more here, in the context of New Age trance practices. Close to the beginning of his book on channelling, American anthropologist Michael Brown gives a description of J.Z. Knight at work. J.Z, as she is known, is one of the most famous and successful channels; the being who speaks through her is called Ramtha.

> J.Z.'s head drops. She breathes heavily ... Her head begins to rock. Slowly she brings up her arms until they are braced rigidly on the arms of the chair. Her feet drop to the floor, and she rises stiffly, hands balled into fists. She stamps her right foot, then her left. Gruffly, she shouts 'Indeed!' to one side of the ballroom, then the other. Each time, the audience responds, 'Indeed.' Her eyes open. She begins a series of geometric movements: bowing to the chair behind her, lifting her arms, profiling her body to the camera. She moves to a man sitting in a chair to her right, evidently her husband. 'Beloved Jeffrey, indeed how be you?' ... The strong angular body movements and twisted syntax signal that she is now Ramtha.

There exist a number of how-to books on channelling. One of the first channelled entities was Seth, whose medium was Jane Roberts. She wrote a book called *How to Develop Your ESP Power*, which was later retitled *The Coming of Seth*, once Seth had become a household name – at any rate, in certain households. In this book she describes the experiments in psychic powers that she and her husband undertook, and which resulted in her becoming a channel for Seth, and explains how the reader can do them for himself. The enterprise is commendable: many people who are interested in psychic powers expect them somehow to come naturally, forgetting that, as in every other sphere, practice makes perfect. The instructions contained in these books are basically instructions in self-hypnosis designed to put you into a passive state in which you are receptive to whatever voices may come – whether you regard them as part of yourself or as coming from an external source such as Seth or Ramtha.

Affirmations

Think of affirmations, and if you have any historical perspective on the subject, you think immediately of a man who was as famous in his time as Mesmer or Freud, but who will receive short shrift in this book, because although he was trained as a hypnotist, he gave it up. An adoring disciple left us this sketch of Emile Coué (1857–1926):

Thick-set; somewhat short. Quiet, compact strength. A remarkably high forehead; hair brushed back, a little thinned out and perfectly white for a number of years already, as also the short pointed beard. And set off by this white frame, a sturdy and youthful face, ruddy-cheeked, full of the love of life – a face that is almost jovial when the man is laughing, almost sly when he smiles. The eyes with their straight look reflect firm kindliness – small searching eyes which gaze fixedly, penetratingly, and suddenly become smaller still in a mischievous pucker, or

almost close up under concentration when the forehead tight-
ens, and seems loftier still.

I have described Coué as a student of hypnotism, and so he was,
but he was very clear that the method he taught, which he called
autosuggestion, was not hypnotism – and in fact was infinitely
superior to hypnotism. He was born in humble circumstances in
Troyes and after studying pharmacy in Paris returned there and
opened a drugstore. His in-laws came from Nancy, and on a visit
there in 1885 Coué heard a lecture by Liébeault on hypnosis. He was
very impressed, and he assisted Liébeault in some of his work. Back
in Troyes he held hypnotic clinics, but came to the conclusion that
any benefits his patients gained from hypnosis, and indeed from
the drugs he dispensed in his shop, were due to what we would
now call the placebo effect. Hence he came to develop the idea of
'conscious autosuggestion': it was autosuggestion that was doing
the business, in both hypnotism and drug-taking. And so by the end
of the century he gave up trying to hypnotize his patients and introducing suggestions from the outside, and instead taught them to give
themselves suggestions while fully awake. He was not the first to
practise or recommend autosuggestion, but he was a tireless crusader
and popularizer. His work was spread above all by his books and his
lecture tours, until he had achieved worldwide fame, with centres in
London, Paris and New York during his own lifetime. The craze for
'Couéism' had died out by the 1930s, however. He writes in a
breathless, crusading style:

> From our birth to our death we are all the slaves of suggestion.
> Our destinies are decided by suggestion. It is an all-powerful
> tyrant of which, unless we take heed, we are the blind instru-
> ments. Now, it is in our power to turn the tables and to
> discipline suggestion, and direct it in the way we ourselves wish;
> then it becomes auto-suggestion: we have taken the reins into
> our own hands, and have become masters of the most marvel-
> lous instrument conceivable. Nothing is impossible to us, except,
> of course, that which is contrary to the laws of Nature and the
> Universe.

He claims that even organic disorders can be cured, or certainly helped, by autosuggestion, let alone functional ones. We now know this to be true, thanks to the insights of psychosomatic medicine and psychoneuroimmunology. This was not a scientific study, but one woman in a long-term workshop run by George Leonard and Michael Murphy, co-founder of the famous California institute Esalen, cleared her eyes of incipient cataracts as a result of affirmations. It took two years, but it is a remarkable result.

But some of Coué's claims border on the extravagant – for instance, that a pregnant woman can determine the gender and characteristics of her unborn child by autosuggestion. And it has to be said that in his treatment of patients he displays an alarming rapidity and superficiality.

Coué had two great insights, which he expressed as follows: 'Firstly, that every idea that we put into the mind becomes a reality (within the limit of possibility, be it understood). Secondly, that contrary to what is generally believed, it is not the will which is the first faculty of man, but the imagination.'

The first insight he often expressed, in the context of health and healing, by showing that the mind and body are inextricably linked: imagine sucking a lemon and your mouth reacts. But the mind rules the body, so we actually cause our own health or illness by factors at work in the subconscious. As for the second, he said that whenever imagination and will come into conflict, imagination always wins. One of his stock examples was the old game of how easy it is to walk along a 6-inch plank which is lying on the ground, as opposed to how difficult it would be were the plank lying 1,000 feet over a gorge. The only difference between the two cases is that in the latter the imagination plays a decisive part, as you imagine yourself plummeting to your death. Or again, what came to be called the 'law of reversed effort' is the principle that an effort of conscious will has the opposite result to what it wants, as long as the imagination does not agree. For instance, you cannot force yourself, by mere exercise of will, to go to sleep. Therefore, he said, just be quiet and let your imagination go about its business unhindered. In order to get something done, seed it in your subconscious and let it grow by itself: the 'law of subconscious teleology' is the principle that when the end has been suggested, the subconscious finds means for its realization. The subconscious is a marvellous instrument that we have at our command. And the way to seed things in the subconscious is to use affirmations.

This is how he introduces the affirmation for which he is most famous:

> Every night, when you have comfortably settled yourself in bed and are on the point of dropping off to sleep, murmur in a low but clear voice, just loud enough to be heard by yourself, this little formula: 'Every day, in every way, I am getting better and better.' Recite the phrase like a litany, twenty times or more: and in order to avoid distracting your attention by the effort of counting, it is an excellent idea to tick the number off on a piece of string tied in twenty knots.

The affirmation is deliberately vague, so that it encompasses all ills, physical or mental. But he recommended using affirmations tailored for specific ailments as well.

Although he gave up hypnosis in favour of teaching people autosuggestion, there is something hypnotic about the way he treated people in his free clinics in Nancy. After explaining to them the general principles of autosuggestion, he got them to close their eyes and went through each of their worries and ailments, offering advice and encouragement. There is no doubt that his patients went into a light trance, and that Coué recognized it, because at the end of the talk he would say: 'I am going to count to three, and when I say "three" you will come out of the state in which you are, you will come out of it very quietly, you will be perfectly wide awake, not dazed at all, nor tired, but will feel full of life and health.'

Coué called his work, or allowed his follower, Professor Charles Baudouin, to call his work, the 'New Nancy School', after Liébeault and Bernheim. They, and especially Bernheim, had taught the importance of suggestion, even in the waking state; Coué taught the importance of autosuggestion in the waking state. Coué was not a sophisticated psychologist, but a pioneer and a lecturer who travelled around the world explaining his two insights. It was left to Baudouin to put his work on a more psychological basis, in *Suggestion and Autosuggestion*, which was hailed on its publication in 1920 as the most exciting book since *The Origin of the Species*.

Baudouin's theories are no more than an extended justification of the ideas of Coué we have already looked at. He spells out, at length, how many aspects of life are naturally governed by auto-suggestion, and deduces four laws (two of which have just been mentioned) which guarantee that such suggestions will be realized in the external world. At times he gets close to the mind-curists we looked at in Chapter 5: if autosuggestion produces an illness in the first place, then of course autosuggestion can remove it. His book provided, and still provides more thoroughly than any other, the psychological justification for the use of affirmations. He stresses the role of attention and emotion (as in faith healing) in effecting cures, and the importance of relaxation in releasing the subconscious to do its own work. Though the comparison with Darwin seems excessive, the importance of the book was that it emphasized, exhaustively, the importance of the subconscious in life. It rode on the wave of Freudian thought which was sweeping the Western world, especially America, and helped to disseminate and popularize the existence and nature of the subconscious.

As with self-hypnosis, so the practice of affirmations has been taken up and watered down by New Agers. A common form of affirmation practice today is known as 'prosperity consciousness', the idea being that the universe is a generous place, and so if you open yourself up to its generosity, a lot of money and material wealth will come your way. The kinds of affirmations you make, then, are: 'I am a good, healthy person, and I am open to whatever gifts the universe chooses to give me.' The Japanese Buddhist sect Nichiren Shoshu teaches its members a mantra which is also supposed to have the same effect. Although the mantra is supposed to be one's vehicle to take one to enlightenment, the sect encourages its use to gain prosperity for oneself and one's family along the way to enlightenment. The mantra, by the way, is 'Nam-myoho-renge-kyo', which roughly means 'Fusion with the ineffable source of all phenomena'.

Affirmations work by reframing. A bad self-image is self-fulfilling: it gives out bad vibes to others, making them dislike you, which increases your negative self-image and so on and on. This produces stress, and hence ill health. But affirmations can be criticized as too bland and Pollyanna-ish. They ignore all the difficulties of life, when it is arguably precisely these difficulties that put us on a learning curve. I stumble and fall, pick myself up, and learn to watch where

I'm going in the future. Sitting in on a session of New Age affirmations is somewhat like having warm marshmallow poured over your mind and body.

The difference between affirmations and self-hypnosis is often slight. But in hypnosis (including self-hypnosis) a suggestion should be seeded once or twice, and then left alone: the subconscious mind will do the rest. Affirmations, however, are to be repeated over and over again. Affirmations should always be spoken in the present tense, not the future, as if whatever is being affirmed was already present to you. Keep them short, keep them positive (e.g. not 'I will no longer oversleep in the morning', but 'I awaken at seven every morning').

After Emile Coué, the most famous prophet of affirmations is surely Norman Vincent Peale, whose book *The Power of Positive Thinking* has sold over 15 million copies since its publication in 1953. It is a wholesome, all-American book; every chapter would fit well in *Reader's Digest*. Describing the book as 'applied Christianity', Peale recommends a variety of practices for improving your life, gaining energy, dissolving anxieties and so on. One of these practices is the making of affirmations. As a Christian, Peale tends to use lines from the Bible as his affirmations, and recommends accompanying them with peaceful pictures formulated in the mind. One of the main affirmations is 'I can do all things through Christ which strengtheneth me', and this sums up the quality of the book: it is a combination of self-reliance and self-responsibility ('Who decides whether you shall be happy or unhappy? The answer – you do!'), and submission to God.

Affirmations require the kind of focused attention that you get in the hypnotic state, but otherwise there is little similarity between the two practices. Hence affirmations are often used along with hypnosis or self-hypnosis, as a route towards whatever goal you want the hypnosis to achieve.

Visualizations

There was a saying in the Middle Ages: 'A strong imagination begets the event itself.' As we have seen, Coué made the same claim for autosuggestion, while sensibly adding that there are natural limits to what kinds of events can be realized. I doubt, for instance, that through imagery or affirmation one could demolish a mountain or mend a broken leg (though one might accelerate the healing). Imagery is often used alongside hypnosis (and/or affirmations, and/or biofeedback) in therapeutic or New Age contexts.

Visualizations can be put to all sorts of uses. Shakti Gawain's rather glib bestselling book *Creative Visualization* teaches a method of achieving what you want by means of the imagination: you imagine that you have it, you invest that image with power, and you get it. This is also the kind of goal for which affirmations are commonly used, and indeed Gawain recommends using affirmations in conjunction with visualizations, literally to 'firm up' whatever it is that you are imagining. It is obvious that if you have a cheerful outlook, better things happen to you than if you are gloomy. So the idea behind visualization is that if you imagine good things, good things will happen to you. You picture something good happening to you, but the picturing alone is not enough. You have to want the event to happen and believe that it can happen.

The use of the imagination to accelerate or bring about healing has been known in the West since medieval times. In a psychotherapeutic context, it was revived in the modern era by Janet and others, but especially by Jung, the Swiss psychologist and philosopher. As he tells in his autobiography, *Memories, Dreams, Reflections*, Jung found visualizations extraordinarily revealing in his own life, and so he developed the technique of 'active imagination' as an intrinsic part of his therapy. In active imagination a patient allows her mind to float, without putting any preconceptions on what images may arise. When images do arise, she watches them without interfering with them, although she is allowed to interact with them: if she sees a person, for instance, she might offer him something or have him offer her something. Afterwards, the whole daydream is discussed with the therapist.

Visualization has a proven track record in psychotherapeutic contexts, and too many psychiatrists and psychologists have made use of it to list here. Techniques such as Guided Affective Imagery (GAI), which uses a series of ten imaginary situations, reach the parts other therapies find hard to reach. They allow the patient to daydream in a constructive fashion that quickly reveals layers of the subconscious to the therapist in a gentle, non-obtrusive way. Some techniques work with obviously symbolic images rather than normal pictures. In psychosynthesis, for instance, founded by Freud's associate Roberto Assagioli (1888–1974), one visualizes things like crosses, two hands clasping each other, a sword and a cup.

Visualizations are often used to help someone cope with anxiety, phobias, depression, insomnia, self-confidence and so on. The client is asked to visualize a scene in which whatever it is that is causing the anxiety is resolved or dissolved. Behaviourists use visualizations to acclimatize a person to something about which he is phobic. Suppose he is terrified of spiders; he is asked to visualize spiders in gradually closer proximity – starting out in the garden shed and ending crawling on his shoulder, perhaps – until the fear has been removed or reduced. Each image is introduced only once the previous one can be watched without fear. The opposite technique, designed to put someone off something rather than get them used to it, is aversion therapy. What strikes me about these kinds of therapies is that they empower the patient: she is doing the visualizing, and so it is self-help rather than imposed from outside.

The connection between emotion and image is familiar: stand in front of a great painting or watch a sentimental movie. So images arise, guided to a certain extent by the therapist, and emotional issues are worked through. Freud maintained that images were more primitive than verbal thought, and therefore reached layers of the mind that words gloss over. Psychotherapy is still biased towards verbal communication, but is increasingly having to recognize the value of imagery.

Visualization also helps physical healing. If you don't think that your imagination can have physical results, just imagine a beautiful woman (or man, according to preference) doing unmentionably sexy things to you, and see what happens! As with all psychosomatic techniques, visualization works because the CNS affects the ANS. The simplest experiment which has demonstrated this is one conducted by American scientist Edmund Jacobson: he found that when a person imagines himself running, the muscles used for running contract a little. In other words, the same neurological pathways are stimulated by imagining running as actually by running.

Perhaps the most striking use of visualizations for physical healing is the Simonton method of treating cancer. Physicians Carl and Stephanie Simonton noticed that spontaneous remission occurred far more frequently in people whose outlook was positive and life-affirming. They enhanced this attitude with a five-step programme. The patient is first taught to relax, and then to imagine a tranquil scene. She then pictures the cancer and visualizes the radiation treatment as bullets striking all the cells in her body, cancerous and healthy, with the cancer cells significantly weaker, so that they are killed by the radiation. Next she is to imagine her white blood cells carrying the dead cancer cells away through the kidney and liver. Finally, she imagines her body as healthy, with the tumors decreasing in size. The Simontons achieved some notable successes: even apart from downright remission, a good proportion of their patients with terminal cancer lived far longer than medical science could have expected. The same technique can be adapted to any part of the body and any illness.

Recreational Drugs

Recreational drugs such as alcohol, marijuana, ecstasy (methylenedioxymethamphetamine, or MDMA for short) and LSD produce almost archetypal ASCs. On the face of it, drug-induced ASCs resemble the hypnotic trance, and certainly a number of writers have assimilated these trances to one another. Also, for over 100 years, various drugs largely considered recreational (especially nitrous oxide, alcohol, LSD, hashish) have been used to deepen the hypnotic trance. But there are certain differences in the subjective experiences involved, and some drugs involve a wider range of experiences than hypnosis.

Let's deal with the major differences first. I discount physiological details, such as LSD's dilation of your pupils, or the need to snack which is stimulated by marijuana and hashish. Recreational drugs may involve unsolicited hallucinations (as opposed to hypnotic hallucinations, which are the product of the operator's suggestions), synesthesia (so that sound, say, is perceived in visual terms) and strong emotional changes from euphoria to anxiety. None of these are features of the hypnotic trance. While drug trances involve time-distortion, as hypnosis does, the results are different. On drugs, time goes slowly enough for you easily to observe your thoughts, which leads to increased creativity, as new and unusual connections are made in your mind. In the hypnotic trance, however, time just passes quickly, with no increased creativity as a side effect (unless you are involved in a creativity-enhancing hypnotic experiment).

The three chief features of the hypnotic trance are suggestibility, dissociation and a narrow field of attention. Tests have shown that all the usual recreational drugs involve an increase in suggestibility. If losing inhibitions is a sign of suggestibility, this is within everyone's experience. One only has to compare the behaviour of a hypnotized subject in a stage show with the outspokenness of a drunk or the love-making of a couple stoned on grass. Moreover, drugs certainly induce dissociation; the most familiar aspect of this is the ability to observe oneself and one's functions as if they belonged to someone else, and even to do so on several levels at once. But drugs open up, rather than concentrate, the field of attention. It is of course possible when stoned or drunk or high to become absorbed in some task or sensation, but the main subjective experience is one of heightened not dampened sensation. The hypnotic trance, if I can put it this way, is designed so that the only meaningful input is the operator's voice; the drug trance is such that everything has increased significance. You can be very sensitive to others' emotional states, and hallucinations start from heightened perceptions too: you pick out patterns in the carpet or the clouds that would not usually be perceived.

The differences make it clear that a different state is involved. There is little in any of following extracts that would be recognizable to hypnotized person:

> Throughout its duration, the intoxication will be nothing but a fantastic dream, thanks to the intensity of colours and the rapidity of the conceptions, but it will always retain the particular quality of the individual ... He is, after all, and in spite of the heightened intensity of his sensations, only the same man augmented, the same number elevated to a much higher power.

> I thought that I was near death; when, suddenly, my soul became aware of God, who was manifestly dealing with me, handling me, so to speak, in an intense personal present reality. I felt him streaming in like light upon me ... I cannot describe the ecstasy I felt.

> In that time we recognize life's deepest meaning; the opacity, the darkness is made bright. Like the lips of fresh and gentle girls, sound like kisses showers our bodies. In our spine, in our skull, colour and line buzz new, yet ancient and clear. And now, no longer resembling the colour and line to which we are accustomed, they reveal the grand secrets hidden in forms. That primitive and so very flawed knowledge of Life we had gained through sight, hearing, smell, taste and touch is now improved, and made whole. We are given the chance to learn the truth of Life inherent in each of us, all of truth, perfected, beyond the faculties of our senses.

The first extract is the French Symbolist poet Charles Baudelaire (1821–67) on hashish; the second is from a report by William James in *Varieties of Religious Experience* of the experiences of the English critic John Symonds (1840–93) on chloroform; the third is from a short story called 'Opium', first published in 1910, by the Hungarian doctor Géza Csáth (1887–1919).

Neurolinguistic Programming

NLP has been described as 'the art and science of personal excellence'. More precisely, it is a way of understanding people's behaviour patterns, and then influencing their behaviour. As a way of gaining power over your neighbour, it is popular among salespeople; as a way of gaining sensitivity to others, it is useful for, among others, social workers and businessmen (especially for conflict-resolution). It is a way of excellence, then, only if excellence is defined in terms of effectiveness. It owes a lot to the work of Milton Erickson. We saw in Chapter 10 how Erickson used language and precise observation of his patients to gain rapport with them and then to affect their present and future. Richard Bandler and John Grinder took the essential structures of Erickson's work (and that of Fritz Perls and Virginia Satir) and developed it into NLP. The central ideas are: first, there is no such thing as failure, only feedback. Every response is only information that can be used to tell you whether you are being effective. Second, people already have all the resources they need. All they have to do is access these resources at appropriate times. There are no problems, only results. Third, anything can be accomplished if the task is broken down into small enough pieces. Don't ask 'Why?', ask 'How?'. Fourth, the individual in any group with the most flexibility will also control that group. Look at what you can do rather than the limitations of the situation you're in. Remain curious.

Some people will be put off by the pretentious name and the slick packaging in which NLP is presented. Much given to mnemonics, snappy phrases (the 'blame frame'; 'what you resist persists', 'the swish pattern'), simple diagrams and tables (e.g. 'six-step reframing'), NLP offers a way of unlearning skills you think you have, and then re-learning them to do them better. It also develops in the practitioner a high degree of sensitivity to others' states of minds and body language. This is how it can help hypnotherapists (and other sorts of therapists too), because awareness of what the subject is experiencing enables a hypnotist to build trust more rapidly and securely, and, in a therapeutic context, to elicit emotions and resources, and tailor strategies for the subject's future. NLP is related to hypnosis historically, since Erickson was a hypnotist, and it can feed back into hypnosis by developing sensitivity to others, communications skills and confidence. But these skills are useful in any domain, so the relation of this aspect of NLP to hypnosis is purely accidental.

However, NLP has another aspect – what they call 'downtime' as opposed to the 'uptime' skills of using the senses to develop sensitivity to oneself and others. 'Downtime' is using all the Ericksonian skills we looked at in Chapter 10 (mirroring, ambiguities, etc.) to induce a light trance in others. Why would one want to do this? NLP is based on the belief, shared by Erickson and others, that the unconscious knows best. So you take someone down into her unconscious in order to tap into the resources hidden but available there. These unconscious resources can help a person reframe problems as opportunities, open up horizons and so on.

NLP arouses huge enthusiasm in its devotees. I was once standing in a queue and saw someone nearby holding one of Bandler and Grinder's books. With time to kill, I engaged him in conversation – and he would hardly let me go in the end, when we reached the front of the line. Academics are rather more sceptical. Scientific experiments have failed to validate most of the basic tenets of NLP, such as that there are ways, from a person's eye movements and speech patterns, to tell what his 'primary representational system' is – which of the sense modalities (visual, auditory, kinaesthetic, olfactory and gustatory) he is primarily oriented towards. If it works, then, it probably does so simply because it trains people in sensitivity. It's like the central controversy over astrology: is it a science or an intuitive divinatory practice? An astrological chart should trigger the reader's intuitions rather than be taken as a rigid system. NLP can develop interpersonal skills without being a science.

Meditation

There are so many different kinds of meditation that finding a common core is not easy. Psychologist Deane Shapiro's definition is broad enough to cover almost all techniques: 'Meditation refers to a family of techniques which have in common a conscious attempt to focus attention in a non-analytical way, and an attempt not to dwell on discursive, ruminating thought.' Hypnotic imperialists often assimilate meditation to hypnosis, and there are certainly enough superficial similarities to make things confusing from the outside. For instance, relaxation suggestions are likely to be given by both hypnotherapists and meditation teachers, and I have even heard a hypnotist tell his subject that if she noticed any extraneous sounds during the session she should just lightly let them go, without allowing them to disturb her state: this is a standard instruction in meditation.

But the practice of meditation involves repeatedly, over a period of twenty minutes or more, bringing one's attention back to the mantra or image or whatever the vehicle may be. You do not drop off into a full trance state; you do not let go into passivity; as in biofeedback, you monitor and regulate your performance. So the difference is one of will: the will remains active in proper meditation, but does not in self-hypnosis. In fact, this enables us to distinguish proper meditation from relaxation techniques, which are often wrongly called 'meditation', such as listening to tinkly music or Herbert Benson's 'relaxation response'. In other words, while hypnosis may look like meditation from the outside, it does not feel like it from the inside. Also, in so far as they can be trusted as evidence, the EEG characteristics of meditation and hypnosis are different: the former are far closer to the pattern of a sleeping person than the latter, which are hardly distinguishable from those of someone who is wide awake. In less experienced meditators, alpha waves predominate; the more experienced touch on the deeper theta state.

The differences between the two have been the subject of some scientific studies, not all of which are conclusive. For instance, some studies have shown that both meditation and hypnosis have similar effects on the autonomic systems: a reduced respiration rate, increased basal skin resistance, increased alpha rhythm activity in the brain, reduced blood lactate levels, reduced blood pressure and pulse rate. But these similarities are no more than one would expect. They are the typical changes brought on by relaxation, and both hypnosis and meditation involve relaxation (though neither of them stop there). However, the fact that two things involve relaxation does not make them the same, any more than the fact that both pancakes and bread contain flour makes them the same.

Going back to Hilgard's demonstration of the hidden observer, it is possible to describe one difference between hypnosis and meditation as follows. Hypnosis affects *output*: pain or other perceptions are perceived but evoke no response. Meditation affects *input*: in deeper meditative states the amount of sensory information received is limited. This is not just a subjective impression of meditators, but has been proved by scientific tests: the sensory parts of the brain are less stimulated.

Different meditation systems have different names for their ultimate goal (nirvana, bliss, enlightenment, etc.), and for the stages on the way, but they all both start and end with higher states than are recognized within a hypnotic context. The closest correlates within Western psychology to meditative experiences are the peak experiences described by psychologist Abraham Maslow (1908–70) in various books, drug-induced ecstasy and what Hungarian-born Mihaly Csikszentmihalyi, director of the Quality of Life Research Center at Claremont Graduate University in the States, calls 'flow'. Maslow insisted – especially against behaviourism – that as well as basic needs such as eating and drinking, people have higher needs, such as the need to be dignified. What he called 'peak experiences' are essentially the satisfaction of these higher needs, culminating in transcendent and ecstatic experiences which are marked by a detached, focused view of the interconnectedness of all creation. Csikszentmihalyi defines what he calls 'optimal experiences' in terms of 'flow'; they are times when we lose ourselves in whatever we are doing or experiencing, so that there is a suspension of the sense of time and a feeling of effortlessness. Sportsmen talk of being 'in the zone', others of being 'in the groove': this is flow, these are peak experiences – but they are not hypnotic experiences.

Shamanistic Drumming and Dervish Turning

A shaman is a master of spirits. He is the wounded healer, who has been threatened by chaos, insanity, death, but has mastered it, and this gives him the ability to heal or to make whole, to restore order to a body which is in the chaotic grip of disease. A shaman is possessed by a spirit (Polynesians call him a 'god-box'), but it is a stable bond, like a marriage. When possessed, he enters a trance, which he communicates to others by rhythmic methods such as chanting, stamping, dancing and drumming. This causes an abreaction in his congregation, and therefore psychological healing.

Whatever else a shaman may possess and use – a mask, for instance – he invariably has a drum:

> Its symbolism is complex, its magical functions many and various. It is indispensable in conducting the shamanic séance, whether it carries the shaman to the 'Center of the World', or enables him to fly through the air, or summons and 'imprisons' the spirits, or, finally, if the drumming enables the shaman to concentrate and regain contact with the spiritual world through which he is preparing to travel.

Mircea Eliade (1907–86), the Romanian-born professor of comparative religion, actually defined shamanism as a set of ecstatic techniques. Shamans go into trances to achieve their goals, whatever they may be. Obviously, these are not hypnotic trances in the narrow sense governing this book, because they are self-initiated (and often involve taking hallucinogenic drugs). But one could perhaps call them self-hypnotic trances. And the rhythm of the drum is essential to take them on their journey, just as the measured voice of the hypnotherapist takes her clients into the trance world. No other instrument is considered to have the same ability to transport its user, and such transport is vital to his function. As a healer, he has to travel in the spirit world, recapture the fugitive soul of the sick person, and restore it to its owner. The shaman has the ability to release his soul from his body – that is his special gift – and in many cultures it is trance-induced drumming that guides this ability, so much so that the drum is often seen as the vehicle that the shaman rides on his journey.

Repetitive and monotonous songs and dances are also common elements in shamanic ritual, and it is no coincidence that a certain kind of rhythmic, prolonged dancing in youth culture today is called 'trance dance'. Usually, it is the shaman himself who does the drumming, singing and dancing, but sometimes he has an assistant. Michael Harner, an anthropologist who gained a considerable following in the 1980s for his practical shamanic workshops, explains the rationale behind having an assistant doing the drumming:

> In the SSC [shamanic state of consciousness], part of the shaman's consciousness is usually still lightly connected to the ordinary reality of the physical or material environment where he is located. The lightness of his trance is a reason that a drumbeat often must be maintained by an assistant to sustain him in the SSC. If the drumming stops, he might come back rapidly to the OSC [ordinary state of consciousness], and thus fail in his work.

There have even been attempts to explain shamanistic drumming scientifically. One suggestion is that rhythmic sound stimulates unusual areas of the brain, because a drumbeat contains more frequencies than most instruments, so that it simultaneously stimulates a number of neural pathways. Another observation is that shamanic drumming is often in the region of four to seven beats per second, which corresponds to theta brainwaves, which would be good for inducing and maintaining a trance state.

With the assistant doing the drumming, we are getting closer to hypnotism, since we can see the assistant as a kind of operator and the shaman himself as subject. Sometimes it is explicit that the trance is induced by other people. The shaman often performs his rites in the presence of others – say, the family of the sick person he is trying to heal. Their chanting induces or deepens his trance: 'For I am a big dancer. Yes, I am a big dancer. I teach other people to dance. When people sing, I go into a trance. I trance and put n/um into people, and I carry on my back those who want to learn n/um. Then I go! I go right up and give them to God!'

Another traditional technique of inducing ecstasy is dervish turning. Although banned by Kemal Atatürk as part of his attempt to modernize and westernize Turkey in the 1920s and 1930s, it survives as a tourist attraction in some parts of Turkey, and as a living tradition underground all over the Islamic world. The dancers whirl around, their skirts forming a perfect circle around their ankles. They either have their arms folded on their chest, in which case the heart is the focus of attention, or spread out at shoulder height, with the right hand in a receptive gesture and the left thumb pointing down to earth, in which case the tip of the left thumb is the focus of attention, just as ballet dancers 'spot' in order to prevent getting dizzy. Since union with God is the goal of dervish turning, it is a kind of moving meditation, and the ecstatic nature of the goal, both of turning and shamanism, removes them from the sphere of hypnosis.

A Speculation: Rhythm and the Brain

The brain has a triune anatomy, which recapitulates our evolution. The oldest part of the brain is sometimes called the 'reptilian brain', since it resembles the brain of a reptile and is assumed to have developed about 500 million years ago. This part of the brain occupies the lowest part, the brain stem just above the spine. It is responsible for our most primitive and basic functions, such as the control of breathing and heart rate.

When reptiles left the water and took to the land, they faced a whole set of new challenges, and evolved a second part of the brain to cope with them. This is the 'mammalian brain'. It occupies the part of our skulls just above and to the front of the brain stem. It consists of two structures: the limbic system which is responsible for homeostasis – that is, for regulating things like temperature, blood pressure and the level of blood sugar – and the hypothalamus, which regulates eating and drinking, sleeping and waking, the hormonal balance of our bodies, and our emotions.

Pasted, as it were, on top of the mammalian brain is the final stage, the cerebral cortex, which developed about 50 million years ago. Its job is to look after those functions which make us peculiarly human: it thinks, plans, remembers, imagines and organizes, assesses sense data, communicates, appreciates art, constructs philosophies and so on. This is the part of the brain that is divided into two hemispheres: the right half which is characterized by holistic appreciation, and the left half which is logical, verbal and linear.

One of the things that is noticeable about all or most of the practices outlined in this chapter is that they involve rhythm. The shaman has his drumming, the dervish his whirling dance; meditators attend to their mantras and their breathing; self-hypnotizers and channellers (who also often rock back and forth) follow their breathing too. Drugs help you get into rhythm and pattern. Hypnotists employ a steady, measured tone, or ask their subject to fixate on a swinging watch; they get their subjects to move into a measured breathing.

My guess is that rhythm strikes a chord with a primitive part of the brain – more primitive than the cerebral cortex. Which part of the brain? The most rhythmical of human activities – music and dancing – are clearly emotional and sexual. These are functions of the mammalian brain, the limbic-hypothalamic system. We've briefly met the limbic-hypothalamic system before, in Chapter 11, since it is responsible for coordinating all the systems that go to make up mind–body interaction. We saw, following the ideas of Ernest Rossi, that hypnosis triggers the individual's own healing resources in the limbic-hypothalamic system. Since rhythm appears to be so important to inducing and maintaining trance states, I would guess that the way hypnosis triggers these resources is by means of rhythm. Even if this guess is off the mark, it serves to underscore the importance of rhythm to trance.

If this speculation were right, it would solve a major problem in hypnosis. It is clear *that* hypnosis affects the brain; if it didn't, hypnotherapy wouldn't work. But it is far from clear *how* it does so.

My suggestion is that short-term rhythm (as opposed to the longer ultradian rhythm) is, or is an important component in, the mechanism. There is certainly experimental evidence to suggest that one of the common features of ASCs is the slowing down of brainwaves in the limbic system, but there has been little research, to my knowledge, specifically on the way that rhythm affects the brain. Anthropologists, however, have long been aware that the rituals of the people they study often involve repetitive stimuli, especially through drumming and dancing (which affords the dancer a repetitive flicker effect due to shifting focus), and it is clear that these stimuli produce trances with a full range of neurophysiological indicators. I would think that further research might be interesting. Perhaps synchronizing the pulses of the brain – our brainwaves – with external pulses is fundamental to all ASCs, including hypnosis.

14

A Plea

Hypnosis has been in and out of favour over the last 200 or so years. Sometimes external factors, such as warfare or the discovery of chemical anaesthetics, have caused it to be neglected; sometimes internal factors, such as the extravagant claims of practitioners, have dismayed more sober-minded enquirers. Even now, for all the intensity and excellence of the academic research that has gone into the subject for the last fifty years, the prevalence of New Age forms of hypnotherapy is threatening to tarnish its reputation. And hypnosis has a fragile reputation: it doesn't take a lot for the general public to remember that it used to be thought of as a load of rubbish. But it simply refuses to go away. In the history of science and medicine in particular, countless theories have run out of fuel and become stranded on the highway, but all the many attempts to drive hypnosis off the road have failed. Its staying power is telling evidence not just of its fascination, but of the fact that it is real and effective.

In the eighteenth century and for most of the nineteenth century too, from Mesmer to Elliotson, hypnosis or its precursor, animal magnetism, was a religious experience. The subject often achieved some kind of ecstasy, and the mesmerist would present himself as a ritual magician, sometimes dressing the part and invariably making mysterious gestures with his hands. Braid, Charcot, Bernheim and others fitted hypnosis into a more scientific framework, and it became an important tool in the developing field of psychology. Then Freud cursed it, and along came Ted Barber and his peers, who attempted to prove that there is no such thing as hypnosis. Hypnosis is no longer as central to psychological research as it was at the end of the nineteenth century. The main impetus for hypnosis research nowadays comes from its value in medicine, and even if Barber were correct, hypnosis will continue to be employed by jobbing clinicians, who often have little time for the theories of experimental psychologists.

In the 1950s, both the British Medical Association and the American Medical Association at last acknowledged the efficacy of hypnosis. Here are the conclusions of the 1958 report of the Council on Mental Health of the American Medical Association:

> General practitioners, medical specialists, and dentists might find hypnosis valuable as a therapeutic adjunct within the specific field of their professional competence. It should be stressed that all those who use hypnosis need to be aware of the complex nature of the phenomena involved. Teaching related to hypnosis should be under responsible medical or dental direction, and integrated teaching programs should include not only the techniques of induction but also the indications and limitations for its use within the specific area involved. Instruction limited to induction techniques alone should be discouraged. Certain aspects of hypnosis still remain unknown and controversial, as is true in many other areas of medicine and the psychological sciences. Therefore, active participation in high-level research by members of the medical and dental professions is to be encouraged. The use of hypnosis for entertainment purposes is vigorously condemned.

Tentative, perhaps, but undoubtedly a step in the right direction. But this step was taken nearly fifty years ago, and still there is resistance. Why, in Britain and all the other countries with a National Health Service, can we rarely get it for free? Why is it totally ignored in the medical schools? The answer is a combination of factors, but they all boil down to one: ignorance. Too few people know enough about hypnosis for it to be more widely available; indeed, in the medical profession there are deep-rooted prejudices against it, stemming from the nineteenth century. If you ask a doctor why she doesn't use hypnosis, she will say that she never had the opportunity to learn it, but she will also say that she's heard that it is unreliable, erratic in its results. This is true, largely because it depends on the hypnotizability of the subject. But it is far less erratic than is commonly supposed, and for most ailments a light trance, of which about 90 per cent of the population are capable, is all that is needed.

Hopefully, one result of this book will be to bring the subject to the attention of a wider audience: doctors who might gain an interest in the subject, and lay people who might start to demand it as part of their medical service. I would like to see hypnosis more widely available and used, and the time is right, because now what used to be called 'alternative' medicine is no longer perceived as 'alternative', but as 'complementary', and hypnosis in particular is familiar: everyone knows someone who has had hypnotherapy for something. It goes without saying that checks and safeguards need to be put into place, so that only qualified people offer their services as hypnotherapists, but that is not hard to achieve. Hypnosis could be a great blessing to humankind. It's not the panacea that Mesmer thought his animal magnetism was, and I have certainly heard of cases of hypnotherapy failing to do what it set out to do, but it is a gentle, effective and empowering therapy for a surprisingly wide range of ailments. Instead of being a last resort, it should be used judiciously as the therapy of choice. Let's do it!

Philosophically and psychologically Cartesian thought is bankrupt. Its time has been and gone. It is time now to rediscover the holistic medicine of the ancient and medieval world, and to combine it with the genuine scientific and medical advances that have taken place in the last two centuries. Hypnosis could and should play an integral part in such a programme of reunification, because we now have enough scientific knowledge to understand, more or less, how it works, as well as a wealth of experiential and experimental evidence for its efficacy. The fields of psychosomatic medicine and psychoneuroimmunology are only going to grow over the next decades. They point the way to the medicine of the twenty-first century, and they reconnect us with practices that are as old as European history.

In Plato's *Charmides*, written probably in the 390s BCE, he has Socrates say:

> I learnt this charm while I was in Thrace on active service in the army from a Thracian healer, a priest of Zalmoxis. These healers are even said to make people immortal. Anyway, this Thracian told me that the Greeks were right to make the claim I mentioned a short while ago [that one should not try to cure

an eye disease without curing the head as a whole], and he said: 'But our lord and master, the divine Zalmoxis, tells us that just as one should not undertake to cure the eyes without also curing the head, or the head without also curing the whole body, so one should not go about curing the body either, without also curing the soul. And this is exactly why most ailments are beyond the capabilities of Greek doctors, because they neglect the whole when that is what they should be paying attention to, because if it is in a bad state it is impossible for any part of it to be in a good state.' He went on to say that the soul is the origin and source of everything that happens, good or bad, to the body and to every individual, just as the head is the origin and source of the eyes, and that therefore one should take care of the soul first and foremost, if the head and every other part of the body is to be in a good condition.

In Plato's day, the idea that the soul was the personality of the individual was new and startling. He used passages like this one to introduce the idea to the reading public, and to make a plea for holistic medicine. The plea worked, because in the Middle Ages it was taken for granted that imagination, charms and so on cured physical ailments – or rather, it was taken for granted that there is no such thing as a purely physical ailment, because the soul or mind was bound to be involved as well. That is the perspective that we need to rediscover today, in our post-Cartesian world.

Just as surgical hypnotism reached its heyday because it was not at the time possible to achieve anaesthesia through conventional or comprehensible means, so now hypnotherapy could and should become an antidote to the ever-increasing dependence on toxic drugs. There is no such thing as a magic bullet, no pharmaceutical pill that goes straight to the affliction and effects a cure without any side effects. Hypnotherapy cures without any pharmaceutical intervention, and without significant side effects. We have seen how the cultural absorption of hypnotic techniques, largely through fiction and film, has been to do with the manipulative and dangerous side of hypnosis. What we need now is a greater absorption of its positive, therapeutic side.

Any such programme designed to re-integrate hypnosis into the mainstream of medical practice and psychological research needs to be safeguarded by updated legislation. It should be made clear that there is a difference between the kind of hypnosis encountered in the theatre and the kind encountered in a doctor's surgery. This distinction can be maintained by reinforcing the current licensing strictures on stage hypnotists, while guaranteeing the accreditation of medical hypnotists. The various umbrella organizations in the European countries need to combine, and to graduate and regulate their members in accordance with guidelines laid down by legislation. The rules are simple: take a full medical and psychological history of each and every patient; make a good diagnosis of his condition; never ask him to do anything he doesn't want to do; make sure that he comes out of the trance refreshed and grounded. These are the kinds of rules that occur to me, but the professionals can add to them.

Although the therapeutic use of hypnosis is what I would most like to encourage for the future, at the same time I have no desire to restrict other forms of experimentation with it, or even stage hypnotism (though stage hypnotists should be more cautious than some of them are). I think, in fact, that it would be foolish to try to impose any such restrictions. If the history of hypnosis teaches us anything, it is that it will always attract rebels and those trying to push the envelope. There's no point in trying to outlaw lay use of hypnosis, as many medical practitioners want, because it will be an unenforceable law. And that is how it should be. Hypnosis has the ability to boggle our minds, and anything that has this ability is to be encouraged, because without new horizons we limit ourselves to little worlds, with no room for growth or expansion. It is no surprise to me that throughout its history hypnosis has attracted rebels, because they are precisely those who hate to find themselves in little boxes, and who therefore relish the expansive nature of hypnosis. If going to see a stage hypnotist can wake someone up to her own huge potential, then stage hypnotism should not be banned.

There is two-way traffic between the scientific world and the world of the general public. Ideas gradually filter through to the rest of us from high-flown scientific research, but also scientists are sometimes prompted by popular interest to take seriously a subject that would otherwise have been swept under the carpet. The history of hypnosis shows this clearly. Anyone interested in the further reaches of the mind has a responsibility to continue to explore altered states of consciousness by whatever means he finds to his taste. Our interest will continue to prod the scientists into action, and we will retain an interest in hypnosis and allied subjects provided we remember that the world is not dull, but is infused with magic.

But the traffic from the popular mind to the ivory towers of science works at a more subtle level as well. Advances in science do not happen until or unless the general population is ready for them. It is almost as if the impulse for a new scientific discovery came from the collective unconscious. A paradigm shift simply couldn't happen unless there was room in the group mind for the new material. In this sense we are all responsible for anything any scientist discovers, however benign or potentially destructive, and we all have to accept that responsibility. The last thirty or so years have seen the Cartesian paradigm whittled away from the bottom, by you and me, not initially by the scientists and philosophers. One of the scientific responses to this has been the development of mind–body sciences such as psychoneuroimmunology. As we have seen, it is within the power of PNI and new medical technology to explain the validity of hypnosis for the first time. This is our doing: we must unconsciously want new medical techniques, or the rediscovery of old ones. We already demand hypnosis unconsciously – from our collective unconscious – and so we have every right to move that demand into full consciousness.

Appendix: In Mesmer's Footsteps

There are a few alternative therapies around today which, consciously or unconsciously, imitate or echo mesmeric technique. Here is a rapid survey of four of them.

page(s) **Bioplasma**

In a brief essay in *The ESP Papers*, a collection of articles by Russian and other pre-glasnost Iron Curtain scientists on their researches into psychic and other fringe phenomena, Vladimir Masopust of Prague uses the term 'bioplasma' or 'biological plasma' for exactly what Mesmer used to call animal magnetism. By the use of hand passes, he claims to have evidence that something – bioplasma – is passed from the experimenter to the subject. He also claims to be able to use his own powers to draw the magnetic powers off a subject, leaving the subject weak and headachy, and causing in himself 'an indefinable emotion of superiority over the subject'. When the flow of energy is the other way round, from him to the subject, he often finds himself weakened – something which few of the early mesmerists found, to my knowledge. Masopust is clearly, like Mesmer, identifying 'bioplasma' with the vital force in humans, and regards it as a material substance, since he reports that in this experiment he loses over 300 grams of weight while the subject gains roughly the same amount. One subject gained clairvoyant abilities. But Masopust's experiments have not proved repeatable, and nothing significant has come of bioplasma.

page(s) **Magnotherapy**

Magnetic healing is especially popular in France, although it has invaded Britain too, especially in the form of little magnets worn on the wrist like watches (or as collars on pets). These are supposed to counter the harmful electromagnetic fields of overhead power lines and electricity in the home, and restore the natural healing effect of the earth's magnetic field, which has, according to one piece of publicity I've read, been depleted by up to 5 per cent in recent years.

Mesmer was of course working with fixed, solid magnets, but these days most magnotherapists work with devices that emit electromagnetic pulses. Nowadays, the kind of grandiose claims that Mesmer made for magnotherapy would not be tolerated, and so modern therapists are more modest. However, they do maintain that magnets are good for relieving pain and accelerating healing, and can reduce inflammation, ward off viruses, reduce stress and enhance athletic performance. More specifically, they are claimed to help with a range of ailments, but especially arthritis. There has been a surprising amount of respectable medical research on the subject, especially in Russia.

page(s)   **Orgone Therapy**

Wilhelm Reich (1897–1957) was one of Freud's most talented pupils, but disagreed with the master in fundamental ways. Reich held, for instance, that psychoanalysis had a material and even organic basis, and also that it could be used to improve social conditions. Freud was uncertain about Reich's materialism, and did not believe that psychoanalysis could or should be used to cure society's ills. After splitting from Freud, Reich settled in the States in 1934 and established his own laboratories to research his ideas. In the medical field, he believed, just like Mesmer, that he had discovered a new form of material energy, basic to the universe and especially to living creatures, which he called 'orgone'. Every living creature is maintained by orgone and gives a certain amount off as surplus to its own requirements. Orgone travels at the speed of light, in wave pulses, and usually from east to west.

Since he believed that orgone bounces off metal and is attracted by vegetable matter, Reich built a kind of accumulator – a modern *baquet*, as it were – consisting of layers of alternating metal and wood, which would concentrate orgone. An ill person sitting inside such an accumulator would be benefited, and in a number of trials some quite remarkable results were achieved. Details remain obscure, because in an act of extraordinary and shameful totalitarianism, reminiscent of the Nazism against which Reich had fought vehemently, his books and records were destroyed by US court order, but followers continue to report cures and alleviations. This act by a branch of the US government is unfortunately not unparalleled. At much the same time as its persecution of Reich, they were also hounding Ruth Drown, a pioneer of the alternative medical practice of radionics. Her equipment was destroyed as well, and she died shortly after being released from prison.

Towards the end of his life Reich seems to have become paranoid. He believed that radiation and orgone reacted together to create something called 'deadly orgone' and that this was building up in the atmosphere, especially around the sites of US nuclear weapons tests. He visited the Arizona desert to conduct experiments in rain-making, and to try to disperse these supposed clouds of deadly orgone. He also came to believe that UFOs were visiting the planet from elsewhere in the galaxy and poisoning the air. Subsequently, following an investigation that had been going on since 1947, he was forbidden by the Federal Food and Drugs Administration from selling orgone accumulators and ordered to destroy them – for no very good reason, it has to be said, since at their worst these accumulators are merely harmless. But Reich had received a great deal of bad press as a promoter of sexual freedom. Reich refused to destroy his life's work and was imprisoned in 1956 for two years. While in prison he died of a heart attack, increasing his followers' belief in a massive conspiracy against him and his work.

page(s) **Therapeutic Touch**

There was something of a craze for Therapeutic Touch in the 1970s and 1980s. The name is misleading, though, since there is no laying on of the therapist's hands. Instead, the unnamed vital force (which we might as well call animal magnetism as anything) is manipulated at a distance of a few centimetres from the patient's body. Disease is seen as the disorder of the subtle energy, and the purpose of the manipulation is to realign or re-balance the energy field, and to restore its uninterrupted flow through, around and in the body. All this is strongly reminiscent of Mesmer, except that the claims made for Therapeutic Touch are more modest, with practitioners claiming only that it accelerates the body's natural healing processes.

References

The numbers in square brackets refer to the bibliography that follows.

page(s)   **1. Hypnosis in Fact and Fiction**

8–9   *To the serious-minded . . . entertainment*: R.A. Nelson, *A Complete Course in Stage Hypnotism* (Columbus, Ohio: Nelson Enterprises, 1965), p. 3.

10   *A stage operator . . . knocked him down*: Estabrooks [16], p. 42.

12   *The ordinary . . . corruption of morals*: Quoted in Dingwall [99], vol. 3, p. 137.

17   *The business . . . or panic*: Stephen Fry, *Moab is My Washpot* (London: Hutchinson, 1997), p. 77.

17–18   *The process . . . to leave me*: Strieber [114], p. 59.

25   *The Unconscious . . . conscious of*: F. Jeffrey, quoted in Brian Lancaster, *Mind, Brain and Human Potential* (Shaftesbury: Element, 1991), p. 16.

26   *I could easily . . . was curious*: W.B. Yeats, *Autobiographies* (London: Macmillan, 1926), p. 103.

30   *The noise . . . but doing little*: Spiegel [169], p. 441.

39   *The hidden observer . . . It's just there*: From Ernest Hilgard, *Divided Consciousness* (1977); quoted in Crabtree [124], p. 32.

page(s)   **2. In the Beginning**

43   *You take a boy . . . that you wish*: F.L. Griffith and H. Thompson, *The Demotic Magical Papyrus of London and Leiden* (3 vols., London: Grevel, 1904).

46   *exegetically indefensible*: Letter to John Court, quoted in Court [31], p. 123.

54–5   *The significance . . . Jesus' home town*: Wilson [35], p. 93.

57   *that superior intelligences . . . camel into a pit*: *Speculum Astronomiae*, article 112.

page(s)   **3. Franz Anton Mesmer**

73   *The first patients . . . which Gassner did*: Quoted by Ellenberger [2], p. 54.

75   *Mesmer sat . . . up and down*: Adapted from the account in D.M. Walmsley, *Anton Mesmer* (London: Robert Hale, 1967), pp. 69–70.

90   *Science is . . . his need*: Robert White, 'A Preface to the Theory of Hypnotism', *Journal of Abnormal and Social Psychology*, 36 (1941), 477–505; reprinted in Shor and Orne [23], pp. 192–216. The quotation is taken from the start of the paper.

94   *After having attended . . . perfectly chimerical*: Quoted by Podmore [5], p. 55.

96   *Bergasse and Kornmann . . . proprietary rights*: Forrest [3], p. 59.

page(s)   **4. Magnetic Sleep and Victor's Sister**

109   *A young man . . . to be convinced*: A letter of M. Cloquet, an eyewitness, quoted in Podmore [5], p. 75.

110–11   *I no longer know . . . fluid exists*: Du Magnétisme animal (1820), pp. 155–6.

114   *He hypnotized her . . . to cure it*: Unknown translator, Daedalus edition, p. 255.

page(s)   **5. Crusaders and Prophets in the United States**

136   *Daily . . . outherod Herod*: Quoted by Fuller [45], p. 27.

137–8   *I use this term . . . are produced*: Pathetism (Boston: White and Potter, 1847), p. 3.

140   *Never has there been . . . space and spirit*: Quoted in Dingwall [99], vol. 4, p. 3.

143   *Dr Darling . . . to the life*: W. Gregory, *Letters to a Candid Inquirer on Animal Magnetism* (London: Taylor, Walter and Moberly, 1851), pp. 192–3.

149   *a deranged state of mind*: Horatio Dresser (ed.), *The Quimby Manuscripts* (Secaucus, NJ: The Citadel Press, 1976), p. 33.

150   *The poverty . . . nebula*: This is the summing-up by Podmore [5], p. 233.

156   *Before the discovery . . . passes for wisdom*: p. 85.

page(s)   **6. 'Mesmeric Mania' in the United Kingdom**

158–9   *small army . . . publications*: Parssinen [73], pp. 88–9.

161–2   *I looked . . . my hand*: Letter to her uncle John Welsh, 13 Dec. 1844.

162   *advocated . . . drop their h's*: *Journals and Correspondence of Lady Eastlake*, ed. C.E. Smith (London, 1895), vol. 1, p. 152, entry for 24 Dec. 1844.

162   *That in the nineteenth century . . . phreno-mesmerism*: Cooter [66], p. 158.

163   *in quarters . . . Phreno-Magnetism*: *Phreno-Magnet* (April 1843), 65–6.

164   *The new Mesmeric . . . the more respectable*: 'Mesmerism', n.d., n.p. Bod. Firth b. 27 (f. 242), Bodleian Library, Oxford, quoted by Cooter [66], p. 156.

165   *By the exercise . . . under the influence*: Barth [14], p. 6.

166–7   *In his body . . . senses cannot see*: From *La Magie dévoilée* (1852), translated by Crabtree [1], p. 196.

169   *in a state of philosophical doubt*: *Table Talk*, 31 March 1830.

180   *Mesmerism . . . civilized society*: *Lancet* (15 Dec. 1838), 450.

180–1   *Why has some knowledge . . . medical men*: Parssinen [74], p. 103.

182   *It is a measure . . . efficacy*: Ibid, p. 109.

186   *I have no hesitation . . . convince me*: *Human Physiology*, 5th edn (1840), pp. 679–80.

190   *And speaking of magnetism . . . rather alarmed*: Letter to John Forster, 1–4 April 1842, this section written on 2 April.

200   *your bigoted . . . your instruments*: *Zoist*, 1845, p. 206.

203   *Since it cannot . . . waking condition*: *Hypnotic Therapeutics* (1853), p. 12.

204–5   *But instead . . . sense of this*: Mary S. Lovell, *A Rage to Live: A Biography of Richard and Isabel Burton* (London: Little, Brown, 1998), p. 483.

207   *Now, I do not consider . . . testimony to the fact*: *Neurypnology*, in Tinterow [6], p. 284.

page(s)   **7. Murder, Rape and Debate in the Late Nineteenth Century**

219–20   *He would transfer . . . afflicted her*: Hacking [126], p. 173.

222   *The hypnotic condition . . . idea of a neurosis*: Bernheim [79], p. 418.

223   *The views . . . scientific men*: Bramwell [21], p. 437.

223   *forced to abandon . . . the subject*: Ibid, p. 323.

224   *I provoked . . . your own master*: Bernheim [79], pp. 57–8.

224–5   *On one occasion . . . out of hypnosis*: Owen [82], pp. 189–90.

228   *The subject . . . sleep condition*: John Watkins, 'Antisocial Compul-

sions Induced Under Hypnotic Trance', *Journal of Abnormal Psychology*, 42 (1947), 257–8.

230   *I felt heavy . . . my legs*: Quoted by Temple [19], p. 263.

232   *A certain patient . . . feared detection*: Cited in the translation by H.W. Armit of August Forel, *Hypnotism, or Suggestion and Psychotherapy* (1907; New York: Allied Publications, 1927), p. 296.

page(s)   **8. Psychic Powers and Recovered Memories**

247   *almost impossible . . . mesmerisation*: SPR *Proceedings*, 1 (1882–3), p. 257.

248   *The points . . . a murmur*: Ibid, p. 258.

255–6   *We discovered . . . English title*: Harold Rosen in Kline [108], pp. xvii–xviii.

260   *Did she put a fork . . . the fork*: Debbie Nathan and Michael Snedeker, *Satan's Silence: Ritual Abuse and the Making of a Modern American Witch Hunt* (New York: HarperCollins, 1985), pp. 141–2.

274   *Because . . . hypnotist as well*: Strieber [114], p. 55.

277   *Similarly . . . this burn*: Kline [108], p. 158.

page(s)   **9. Freud and Other Alienists**

282–3   *These sisters . . . everything afresh*: *Human Physiology*, 5th edn (1840), p. 1165.

286   *Gurney's . . . its importance*: From *William James on Psychical Research*, edited by Gardner Murphy and Robert Ballou (London: Chatto and Windus, 1961), p. 34.

287–8   *I believe . . . possession*: Crabtree [1], p. 290.

292   *The hypothesis . . . if it were true*: Gauld [4], p. 414.

292–3   *Well, Dr Wilbur . . . home going*: Schreiber [129], p. 172.

296–7   *a new way to be an unhappy person*: Hacking [126], p. 236.

296   *While I was still a student . . . hypnotic suggestion*: An Autobiographical Study, tr. James Strachey (London: Hogarth Press, 1948), pp. 206–7.

299   *I gave up . . . it returned*: Complete Works, vol. 6, p. 254.

301   *I held my finger . . . confusion*: Quoted in Kline [117], p. 23.

page(s)   **10. State or No State: The Modern Controversy**

308–9   *A resistant subject . . . into a trance*: Jay Haley, 'An Interactional Explanation of Hypnosis', *American Journal of Clinical Hypnosis*, 1

(1958), 41–57; reprinted in Shor and Orne [23], pp. 267–87. The quotation is from p. 281.

310–11 *The guideline . . . he's failed*: Grinder and Bandler [13], p. 25.

311 *A lot of people . . . he will talk*: quoted by Stanley Rosen, *My Voice Will Go with You: The Teaching Tales of Milton H. Erickson* (New York: Norton, 1982), pp. 58–9.

316 *The responsive . . . is receiving*: Barber, Spanos and Chaves [142], p. 5.

318 *Common sense . . . moral pressure*: Gibson [17], p. 27.

318 *that level . . . conscious mind*: In Leslie LeCron (ed.), *Experimental Hypnosis* (Secaucus, N.J.: Citadel Press, 1972), p. 80.

321 *I have every month . . . decide for themselves*: Esdaile [61], pp. 218–19.

323 *In summary . . . controversial issues*: Hilgard and Hilgard [151], p. 17.

324 *The view expressed . . . unique hypnotic process*: Graham Wagstaff in Naish [136], p. 78.

324 *postulates . . . from others*: Hilgard [149], p. 24.

page(s) **11. Hypnotherapy: Mind and Body**

330–1 *When I first heard . . . still under control*: Bowers [11], pp. 140–1.

334 *I feel relaxed . . . occasionally*: A hypnotized woman in labour, quoted by Hilgard and Hilgard [151], pp. 113–14.

335 *Hypnosis . . . past century or so*: Temple [19], p. 109.

346–7 *his method . . . patients about him*: Raginsky in Kline [108], p. 23.

348 *Genetic . . . scope of hypnosis*: H.M. Thomas in Heap [22], p. 142.

349–50 *Those two realms . . . immune system's business*: Sapolsky [186], p. 126.

350 *Your honour's players . . . lengthens life*: The Messenger, in *The Taming of the Shrew*, towards the end of the second part of the introductory Induction.

354–5 *There remains . . . How misleading!*: Court [31], p. 59.

357 *The great lesson . . . cures were effected*: W.R. Houston, quoted in Shapiro and Shapiro [194], p. 2.

359 *that when . . . will be effective*: Graham Wagstaff in Naish [136], p. 76.

360 *I am often asked . . . hypnotic patterns*: Yapko [12], p. 31.

page(s) **12. Mind Control**

362 *a rather . . . automaton*: G.I. Gurdjieff, *Views from the Real World* (New York: Dutton, 1973), p. 49.

364   *Motivation research . . . with the product*: Quoted by Packard [203], p. 5.

365   *Nike . . . emotional leverage*: Quoted by Klein [201], p. 21.

366–7 *The London . . . bear on him*: Packard [203], p. 35.

368   *In advertising . . . attitudinal predisposition*: Key [200], pp. 47–8.

369   *Media has . . . hypnosis*: Ibid, p. 187.

372   *What you say . . . logical argument*: Quoted by Serve Mosovici, *The Age of the Crowd: A Historical Treatise on Mass Psychology* (Cambridge University Press, 1985), p. 152.

374   *Gurus tend . . . impose them*: Anthony Storr, *Feet of Clay: A Study of Gurus* (London: HarperCollins, 1996), pp. xiii–xiv.

375   *groups . . . external constraints*: Kramer and Altstad [204], pp. 32–3.

376   *He is no longer conscious . . . reciprocity*: Gustave Le Bon, *The Crowd: A Study of the Popular Mind* (London: Unwin, 1896), p. 30.

380   *the ancient desire . . . spells and potions*: Marks [207], pp. 54–5.

380   *All he felt . . . anything wrong*: Ibid, p. 183.

388   *the aspirations . . . the scientist*: Biderman and Zimmer [196], p. 4.

page(s) **13. Self-improvement and the New Age**

396   *J.Z.'s head drops . . . she is now Ramtha*: Brown [216], p. 3.

397–8 *Thick-set . . . loftier still*: Charles Baudouin in [219], p. 9.

398   *From our birth . . . the Universe*: Coué, [220], p. 6.

399   *Firstly . . . the imagination*: Coué [219], p. 58.

400   *Every night . . . twenty knots*: Coué [220], p. 26.

400   *I am going . . . life and health*: Coué [219], p. 97.

407   *Throughout its duration . . . the faculties of our senses*: Mike Jay (ed.), *Artificial Paradises* (London: Penguin, 1999), pp. 16, 123, 187.

410   *Meditation . . . ruminating thought*: Shapiro [230], p. 14.

412   *Its symbolism . . . to travel*: Eliade [232], p. 168.

413   *In the SSC . . . fail in his work*: Harner [233], p. 64.

413–14 *For I am a big dancer . . . give them to God*: Part of the narrative of a !Kung Bushman, quoted from Joan Halifax, *Shamanic Voices* (New York: Dutton, 1979), p. 57. *N/um is at once divine power and healing medicine*.

page(s) **14. A Plea**

419–20 *I learnt . . . good condition*: Plato, *Charmides*, 156d–157a.

Bibliography

This is a severely restricted bibliography; it represents only a fraction of my reading, and of the hundreds of books and even more articles relevant to the subjects covered in this book. Whatever the category, I have tried to include the best and most accessible work, to create a reading list designed for the general reader; the focus is inevitably on books, with the occasional article added to fill gaps and bring things up to date. After a couple of general sections, I have broken the list up into sections relevant to each chapter. There are more detailed bibliographies especially in [1], [4], [12], [65] and [136].

The History of Hypnotism

Many general books on hypnotism will have a historical section too. The five most informative histories are:

[1] Adam Crabtree, *From Mesmer to Freud: Magnetic Sleep and the Roots of Psychological Healing* (New Haven: Yale University Press, 1993)
[2] Henri Ellenberger, *The Discovery of the Unconscious: The History and Evolution of Dynamic Psychiatry* (New York: Basic Books, 1970)
[3] Derek Forrest, *The Evolution of Hypnotism* (Forfar: Black Ace Books, 1998); repr. as *Hypnotism: A History* (London: Penguin, 2000)
[4] Alan Gauld, *A History of Hypnotism* (Cambridge University Press, 1992)
[5] Frank Podmore, *From Mesmer to Christian Science: A Short History of Mental Healing* (1909; New York: University Books, 1963)

And a number of original texts are reprinted or translated in:

[6] Maurice Tinterow, *Foundations of Hypnosis: From Mesmer to Freud* (Springfield, IL: Charles Thomas, 1970)

A swift, but well-informed historical survey is:

[7] Melvin Gravitz, 'Early Theories of Hypnosis: A Clinical Perspective' in Steven Jay Lynn and Judith Rhue (eds.), *Theories of Hypnosis: Current Models and Perspectives* (New York: Guilford, 1993), 19–42

And further relevant topics are covered in:

[8] Melvin Gravitz, 'Two Centuries of Hypnosis Specialty Journals', *International Journal of Clinical and Experimental Hypnosis*, 35 (1987), 265–76. See also the addendum in *American Journal of Clinical Hypnosis*, 39 (1996), 18–20
[9] ———— 'Etienne Félix d'Hénin de Cuvillers: A Founder of Hypnosis', *American Journal of Clinical Hypnosis*, 36 (1993), 7–11
[10] Melvin Gravitz and Manuel Gerton, 'Origins of the Term Hypnotism Prior to Braid', *American Journal of Clinical Hypnosis*, 27 (1984), 107–10

Hypnotism in General

The best two books with which to begin thinking about the nature of hypnotism are:

[11] Kenneth Bowers, *Hypnosis for the Seriously Curious* (New York: Brooks/Cole, 1976)
[12] Michael Yapko, *Essentials of Hypnosis* (Philadelphia: Brunner/Mazel, 1995)

The most instructive how-to book by far is:

[13] John Grinder and Richard Bandler, *Trance-formations: Neuro-Linguistic Programming and the Structure of Hypnosis* (Moab, UT: Real People Press, 1981)

And the following introductory works, from a spread of periods, are all good:

[14] George Barth, *The Mesmerist's Manual of Phenomena and Practice* . . . (London: Baillière, 1851)
[15] Fredrik Björnström, *Hypnotism: Its History and Present Development* (New York: Humboldt Publishing, 1887)
[16] George Estabrooks, *Hypnotism* (New York: Dutton, 1943)

[17] H.B. Gibson, *Hypnosis: Its Nature and Therapeutic Uses* (London: Peter Owen, 1977)

[18] F.L. Marcuse, *Hypnosis: Fact and Fiction* (Harmondsworth: Penguin, 1959)

[19] Robert Temple, *Open to Suggestion: The Uses and Abuses of Hypnosis* (Wellingborough: Thorsons, 1989)

[20] David Waxman, *Hypnosis: A Guide for Patients and Practitioners* (London: Allen & Unwin, 1981)

Somewhat more academic, but worth persevering with, are:

[21] J. Milne Bramwell, *Hypnotism: Its History, Practice and Theory* (London: Grant Richards, 1903)

[22] Michael Heap (ed.), *Hypnosis: Current Clinical, Experimental and Forensic Practices* (London: Croom Helm, 1988)

[23] Ronald Shor and Martin Orne (eds.), *The Nature of Hypnosis: Selected Basic Readings* (New York: Holt, Rinehart and Winston, 1965)

[24] Boris Sidis, *The Psychology of Suggestion* (New York: Appleton-Century, 1910)

[25] David Spiegel, 'Hypnosis and Implicit Memory: Automatic Processing of Explicit Content', *American Journal of Clinical Hypnosis*, 40 (1998), 231–40

[26] David Waxman *et al.* (eds.), *Modern Trends in Hypnosis* (New York: Plenum, 1985)

1. Hypnosis in Fact and Fiction

One of the topics that recurs throughout the book, but most prominently in the first chapter, is the fictional treatment of hypnosis. But there seems little point in giving bibliographical details for fictional works (or a filmography for the films I mention). There are a number of good books and articles in academic journals on the involvement with hypnosis or mesmerism of Poe, say, or Browning or Shelley, but the following more general works are more suitable for this bibliography:

[27] Arnold Ludwig, 'Hypnosis in Fiction', *International Journal of Clinical and Experimental Hypnosis*, 11 (1963), 71–80

[28] Maria Tatar, *Spellbound: Studies in Mesmerism and Literature* (Princeton University Press, 1978)

Here are a couple of the dozen or so how-to books on stage hypnotism:

[29] Kreskin, *The Amazing World of Kreskin* (New York: Random House, 1973)

[30] Professor Leonidas, *Secrets of Stage Hypnotism* (1901; Hollywood: Newcastle Publishing, 1975)

The best book on hypnotism and Christianity, with an informed and balanced approach, and a survey of and response to earlier literature, is:

[31] John Court, *Hypnosis, Healing and the Christian* (Carlisle: Paternoster Press, 1997)

2. In the Beginning

The early history of hypnotism in the West has scarcely been researched and a lot of inaccurate information is still being perpetuated, but the following works are useful:

[32] Emma and Ludwig Edelstein, *Asclepius: A Collection and Interpretation of the Testimonies* (2 vols., Baltimore: Johns Hopkins University Press, 1945; 1-volume edn, 1998)

[33] Henderikus Stam and Nicholas Spanos, 'The Asclepian Dream Healings and Hypnosis: A Critique', *International Journal of Clinical and Experimental Hypnosis*, 30 (1982), 9–22

[34] Lynn Thorndike, *A History of Magic and Experimental Science* (8 vols., Columbia University Press, 1923–58)

[35] Ian Wilson, *Jesus: The Evidence* (London: Weidenfeld and Nicolson, 1984)

3. Franz Anton Mesmer

Mesmer's own writings are available in various translations, but especially as follows:

[36] G.J. Bloch, *Mesmerism: A Translation of the Original Medical and Scientific Writings of F.A. Mesmer* (Los Altos, CA: Kaufmann, 1980)

There have been a good half-dozen books dedicated to Mesmer in English in the last 100 years, but the only two worth recommending are:

[37] Vincent Buranelli, *The Wizard from Vienna: Franz Anton Mesmer and the Origins of Hypnotism* (London: Peter Owen, 1976)

[38] Frank Pattie, *Mesmer and Animal Magnetism: A Chapter in the History of Medicine* (Hamilton, NY: Edmonston Publishing, 1994)

Then, on further topics in this chapter, see:

[39] Robert Darnton, *Mesmerism and the End of the Enlightenment in France* (Harvard University Press, 1968)

[40] Kevin McConkey and Campbell Perry, 'Benjamin Franklin and Mesmerism', *International Journal of Clinical and Experimental Hypnosis*, 33 (1985), 122–30

On Mesmer's twentieth-century descendants, summarized in the appendix, see (as well as [103]):

[41] David Boadella, *Wilhelm Reich: The Evolution of His Work* (London: Routledge & Kegan Paul, 1985)

[42] Janet Macrae, *Therapeutic Touch* (New York: Knopf, 1988)

[43] Gary Null, *Healing with Magnets* (New York: Carrol and Graf, 1998)

4. Magnetic Sleep and Victor's Sister

This important period, roughly between Mesmer and Braid, is rarely treated on its own, and so I simply refer the reader to the general histories listed at the start of this bibliography, apart from the following paper (which, however, largely repeats material from [2]):

[44] Henri Ellenberger, 'Mesmer and Puységur: From Magnetism to Hypnotism', *Psychoanalytic Review*, 52 (1965), 137–53

5. Crusaders and Prophets in the United States

For the early history of mesmerism in the United States the best single book is:

[45] Robert Fuller, *Mesmerism and the American Cure of Souls* (University of Pennsylvania Press, 1982)

Then see also:

[46] John Andrick, 'Hypnosis and the Emmanuel Movement: A Medical and Religious Repudiation', *American Journal of Clinical Hypnosis*, 20 (1978), 224–34

[47] Ruth Brandon, *The Spiritualists: The Passion for the Occult in the Nineteenth and Twentieth Centuries* (New York: Knopf, 1983)

[48] Eric Carlson, 'Charles Poyen Brings Mesmerism to America', *Journal of the History of Medicine and Allied Sciences*, 15 (1960), 121–32

[49] Robert Fuller, 'The American Mesmerists' in Heinz Schott (ed.), *Franz Anton Mesmer und die Geschichte des Mesmerismus* (Stuttgart: Franz Steiner, 1985), 163–73

[50] Melvin Gravitz, 'Early Uses of Hypnosis as Surgical Anesthesia', *American Journal of Clinical Hypnosis*, 30 (1988), 201–8

[51] ———— 'Early American Mesmeric Societies: A Historical Study', *American Journal of Clinical Hypnosis*, 37 (1994), 41–8

[52] Gail Parker, *Mind Cures in New England: From the Civil War to World War I* (Hanover, MA: University Press of New England, 1973)

6. 'Mesmeric Mania' in the United Kingdom

The most important original works relevant to this period are available in [6] and as follows:

[53] James Braid, *Satanic Agency and Mesmerism* (Manchester: Sims and Dinham, Galt and Anderson, 4 June 1842)

[54] ———— *Neurypnology, or the Rationale of Nervous Sleep Considered in Relation with Animal Magnetism* (London: John Churchill, 1843)

[55] ———— *The Power of Mind Over the Body* (London: John Churchill, 1846)

[56] ———— *Magic, Witchcraft, Animal Magnetism, Hypnotism, and Electro-biology* (London: John Churchill, 1852)

[57] ———— *The Physiology of Fascination and the Critics Criticised* (Manchester: Grant, 1855)

[58] John Elliotson, *Numerous Cases of Surgical Operations Without Pain in the Mesmeric State* (London: Baillière, 1843)

[59] ———— *Case of a True Cancer of the Female Breast* (London: Walton and Mitchell, 1848)

[60] ———— (ed.), *The Zoist* (London: Baillière, 1843–56)

[61] James Esdaile, *Mesmerism in India and Its Practical Application in*

Surgery and Medicine (London: Longman, Brown, Green and
Longmans, 1846; repr. New York: Arno, 1975); repr. as *Hypnotism in
Medicine and Surgery*, ed. William Kroger (New York: Julian Press,
1957)

[62] Fred Kaplan, *John Elliotson on Mesmerism* (New York: Da Capo Press,
1982)

[63] Harriet Martineau, *Letters on Mesmerism* (London: Moxon, 1845)

[64] Chauncy Hare Townshend, *Facts in Mesmerism with Reasons for a
Dispassionate Inquiry into it* (1840; repr. New York: Da Capo, 1982)

A great deal has been written about the period. The outstanding book is:

[65] Alison Winter, *Mesmerized: Powers of Mind in Victorian Britain*
(University of Chicago Press, 1998)

And particular topics are well treated in:

[66] Roger Cooter, 'The History of Mesmerism in Britain: Poverty and
Promise' in Heinz Schott (ed.), *Franz Anton Mesmer und die
Geschichte des Mesmerismus* (Stuttgart: Franz Steiner, 1985), 152–62

[67] ——— 'Dichotomy and Denial: Mesmerism, Medicine, and Harriet
Martineau' in Marina Benjamin (ed.), *Science and Sensibility: Gender
and Scientific Enquiry, 1780–1945* (Oxford: Basil Blackwell, 1991), 144–73

[68] Waltraud Ernst, ' "Under the Influence" in British India: James
Esdaile's Mesmeric Hospital in Calcutta and Its Critics', *Psychological
Medicine*, 25 (1995), 1113–23

[69] Fred Kaplan, 'The Mesmeric Mania: The Early Victorians and
Animal Magnetism', *Journal of the History of Ideas*, 35 (1974), 691–702

[70] ——— *Dickens and Mesmerism* (Princeton University Press, 1975)

[71] Jonathan Miller, 'Mesmerism in the London Medical Circle',
Transactions of the Medical Society of London, 106 (1989/90), 60–71

[72] Jon Palfreman, 'Mesmerism and the English Medical Profession: A
Study of Conflict', *Ethics in Science and Medicine*, 4 (1977), 51–66

[73] Terry Parssinen, 'Mesmeric Performers', *Victorian Studies*, 21 (1977/
8), 87–104

[74] ——— 'Professional Deviants and the History of Medicine:
Medical Mesmerists in Victorian Britain' in Roy Wallis (ed.), *On the
Margins of Science: The Social Construction of Rejected Knowledge*
(Sociological Review Monograph 27, University of Keele, 1979),
103–20

[75] Jacques Quen, 'Case Studies in Nineteenth-century Scientific

Rejection: Mesmerism, Perkinism and Acupuncture', *Journal of the History of the Behavioural Sciences*, 11 (1975), 149–56

[76] ——— 'Mesmerism, Medicine, and Professional Prejudice', *New York State Journal of Medicine*, 76 (1976), 2218–22

[77] Elizabeth Ridgway, 'John Elliotson (1791–1868): A Bitter Enemy of Legitimate Medicine?', *Journal of Medical Biology*, 1 (1993), 191–8; 2 (1994), 1–7

[78] Robert Weyant, 'Protoscience, Pseudoscience, Metaphors and Animal Magnetism' in Marsha Hanen *et al*. (eds.), *Science, Pseudoscience and Society* (Waterloo: Wilfrid Laurier University Press, 1980), 77–114

7. Murder, Rape and Debate in the Late Nineteenth Century

By the end of the nineteenth century, the most important research was being done on the Continent, especially in France:

[79] Hippolyte Bernheim, *Suggestive Therapies: A Treatise on the Nature and Uses of Hypnotism*, tr. C.A. Herter (New York: Putnam, 1900); repr. as *Hypnotism and Suggestion in Psychotherapy: A Treatise on the Nature and Uses of Hypnotism* (New York: University Books, 1964)

[80] Anne Harrington, 'Metals and Magnets in Medicine: Hysteria, Hypnosis and Medical Culture in Fin-de-siècle Paris', *Psychological Medicine*, 18 (1988), 21–38

[81] Robert Hillman, 'A Scientific Study of Mystery: The Role of the Medical and Popular Press in the Nancy-Salpêtrière Controversy on Hypnotism', *Bulletin of the History of Medicine*, 9 (1965), 163–82

[82] A.R.G. Owen, *Hysteria, Hypnosis and Healing: The Work of J.M. Charcot* (New York: Garrett, 1971)

[83] C.E. Schorer, 'The Later Bernheim: A Translation', *Journal of the History of the Behavioural Sciences*, 4 (1968), 28–39

In this chapter I digress on to the topic of hypnotism and crime:

[84] Heinz Hammerschlag, *Crime and Hypnotism* (North Hollywood, CA: Powers Publishing, 1957)

[85] Ruth Harris, 'Murder Under Hypnosis', *Psychological Medicine*, 15 (1985), 477–505

See also [19]

On forensic hypnosis, a number of cases are retailed with uncritical gusto in:

[86] Eugene Block, *Hypnosis: A New Tool in Crime Detection* (New York: McKay, 1976)

And of the many specialist works on the subject, I would recommend:

[87] Jean-Roch Laurence and Campbell Perry, *Hypnosis, Will, and Memory: A Psycho-Legal History* (New York: Guilford Press, 1988)
[88] Kevin McConkey and Peter Sheehan, *Hypnosis, Memory, and Behavior in Criminal Investigation* (New York: Guilford Press, 1995)
[89] Martin Orne, 'The Use and Misuse of Hypnosis in Court', *International Journal of Clinical and Experimental Hypnosis*, 27 (1979), 311–41
[90] Campbell Perry, 'Hypnotic Coercion and Compliance to It: A Review of Evidence Presented in a Legal Case', *International Journal of Clinical and Experimental Hypnosis*, 27 (1979), 187–218
[91] ———— 'Admissibility and Per Se Exclusion of Hypnotically Elicited Recall in American Courts of Law', *International Journal of Clinical and Experimental Hypnosis*, 45 (1997), 266–79
[92] Helen Pettinati (ed.), *Hypnosis and Memory* (New York: Guilford Press, 1988)
[93] Alan Scheflin *et al.*, *Repressed Memory, Hypnotherapy and the Law* (Des Plaines, IL: American Society of Clinical Hypnosis Press, 1994)
[94] David Spiegel and Alan Scheflin, 'Dissociated or Fabricated? Psychiatric Aspects of Repressed Memories in Criminal and Civil Cases', *International Journal of Clinical and Experimental Hypnosis*, 42 (1994), 411–32
[95] Roy Udolf, *Forensic Hypnosis: Psychological and Legal Aspects* (Boston: D.C. Heath, 1983)

These works necessarily deal with the topics of hypnotic coercion, confabulation and the reliability of memory. See also:

[96] Richard Ofshe and Ethan Watters, *Making Monsters: False Memories, Psychotherapy, and Sexual Hysteria* (New York: Scribner's, 1994)
[97] Kathy Pezdek and William Banks (eds.), *The Recovered Memory/False Memory Debate* (San Diego, CA: Academic Press, 1996)

Milgram's crucial experiments are recounted in:

[98] Stanley Milgram, *Obedience to Authority: An Experimental View* (New York: Harper & Row, 1974)

8. Psychic Powers and Recovered Memories

A lot of sober and well-researched studies on paranormal phenomena appear in the pages of two long-established journals: *Journal for the American Society for Psychical Research*; *Proceedings of the Society for Psychical Research*

The history of hypnotically induced paranormal phenomena is treated country by country, exhaustively and critically, by various authors, in:

[99] Eric Dingwall (ed.), *Abnormal Hypnotic Phenomena: A Survey of Nineteenth–century Cases* (4 vols., London: Churchill, 1967).

General books which cover the phenomena in the context of hypnotism include:

[100] Simeon Edmunds, *Hypnotism and Psychic Phenomena* (North Hollywood, CA: Wilshire, 1961)
[101] Michael Murphy, *The Future of the Body* (Los Angeles: Jeremy P. Tarcher, 1992)
[102] Sheila Ostrander and Lynn Schroeder, *Psi: Psychic Discoveries Behind the Iron Curtain* (London: Abacus, 1973)
[103] —————— *The ESP Papers: Scientists Speak Out from behind the Iron Curtain* (New York: Bantam Books, 1976)

Reincarnation, of course, has its own extensive bibliography. A fairly sober general study is:

[104] Hans TenDam, *Exploring Reincarnation* (London: Penguin Arkana, 1990)

And then books concerned with hypnotic past-life regression include:

[105] Morey Bernstein, *The Search for Bridey Murphy* (New York: Doubleday, 1956)
[106] Jeffrey Iverson, *More Lives Than One?* (London: Souvenir Press, 1976)
[107] Joe Keeton (with Simon Petherick), *The Power of the Mind: Healing through Hypnosis and Suggestion* (London: Robert Hale, 1988)

[108] Milton Kline (ed.), *A Scientific Report on 'The Search for Bridey Murphy'* (New York: Julian Press, 1956)
[109] Helen Wambach, *Reliving Past Lives: The Evidence Under Hypnosis* (New York: Harper & Row, 1978)
[110] —— *Life Before Life* (New York: Bantam, 1979)
[111] Ian Wilson, *Reincarnation?* (London: Penguin, 1982; first pub. as *Mind Out of Time* (London: Gollancz, 1981) and in America as *All in the Mind* (New York: Doubleday, 1982))

On alien abduction, you could try these:

[112] Courtlandt Bryan, *Close Encounters of the Fourth Kind* (New York: Knopf, 1995)
[113] Patrick Harpur, *Daimonic Reality: A Field Guide to the Otherworld* (London: Viking, 1994)
[114] Whitley Strieber, *Communion* (London: Century, 1987)

9. Freud and Other Alienists

On Freud's involvement with hypnotism, see:

[115] Melvin Gravitz and Manuel Gerton, 'Freud and Hypnosis: Report of Post-rejection Use', *Journal of the History of the Behavioural Sciences*, 17 (1981), 68–74
[116] —— 'Polgar as Freud's Hypnotist? Contrary Evidence', *American Journal of Clinical Hypnosis*, 24 (1982), 272–6
[117] Milton Kline, *Freud and Hypnosis: The Interaction of Psychodynamics and Hypnosis* (New York: Julian Press, 1958)
[118] —— 'Freud and Hypnosis: A Reevaluation', *International Journal of Clinical and Experimental Hypnosis*, 20 (1972), 252–63
[119] Jerome Schneck, 'Countertransference in Freud's Rejection of Hypnosis', *American Journal of Psychiatry*, 110 (1954), 928–31
[120] —— 'A Reevaluation of Freud's Abandonment of Hypnosis', *Journal of the History of the Behavioural Sciences*, 1 (1965), 191–5

On the history of the unconscious before Freud, see:

[121] Lancelot Whyte, *The Unconscious Before Freud* (New York: Basic Books, 1960)

On multiple personality disorder (MPD):

[122] Eugene Bliss, *Multiple Personalities, Allied Disorders and Hypnosis* (New York: Oxford University Press, 1986)

[123] Eric Carlson, 'Multiple Personality and Hypnosis: The First 100 Years', *Journal of the History of the Behavioural Sciences*, 25 (1989), 315–22

[124] Adam Crabtree, *Multiple Man: Explorations in Possession and Multiple Personality* (New York: Praeger, 1985)

[125] ———— 'Mesmerism, Divided Consciousness, and Multiple Personality' in Heinz Schott (ed.), *Franz Anton Mesmer und die Geschichte des Mesmerismus* (Stuttgart: Franz Steiner, 1985), 133–43

[126] Ian Hacking, *Rewriting the Soul: Multiple Personality and the Sciences of Memory* (Princeton University Press, 1995)

[127] Daniel Keyes, *The Minds of Billy Milligan* (New York: Random House, 1981)

[128] Morton Prince, *The Dissociation of a Personality*, 2nd edn (New York: Longmans, Green, 1908)

[129] Flora Rheta Schreiber, *Sybil* (Chicago: Henry Regnery, 1973)

[130] Christine Sizemore and Elen Pittilo, *I'm Eve* (Garden City, NY: Doubleday, 1977)

[131] Corbett Thigpen and Hervey Cleckley, *The Three Faces of Eve* (New York: McGraw-Hill, 1957)

10. State or No State: The Modern Controversy

There is an amazing quantity of modern research on hypnosis, much of it far too technical for inclusion in this bibliography, and much of it located within the covers of specialist academic periodicals, especially: *American Journal of Clinical Hypnosis*; *British Journal of Medical Hypnotism*; *Contemporary Hypnosis*; *International Journal of Clinical and Experimental Hypnosis*; *Journal of Abnormal Psychology*; *Journal of the International Society for Professional Hypnosis*

As an introduction to Milton Erickson's work, this one could hardly be bettered:

[132] William O'Hanlon, *Taproots: Underlying Principles of Milton Erickson's Therapy and Hypnosis* (New York: Norton, 1987)

Then see Erickson's own writings, especially:

[133] Milton Erickson and Ernest Rossi, *Hypnotherapy: An Exploratory Casebook* (New York: Irvington, 1979)
[134] Milton Erickson, Ernest Rossi and Shiela Rossi, *Hypnotic Realities: The Induction of Clinical Hypnosis and Forms of Indirect Suggestion* (New York: Irvington, 1976)

The most popular treatment of those psychologists who deny the existence of hypnosis is:

[135] Robert Baker, *They Call It Hypnosis* (Amherst: Prometheus Books, 1990)

Rather less strident than Baker's book is:

[136] Peter Naish (ed.), *What is Hypnosis? Current Theories and Research* (Milton Keynes: Open University Press, 1986)

A good but technical debate on neodissociationism (here in chronological order) is:

[137] Irving Kirsch and Steven Jay Lynn, 'Dissociation Theories of Hynposis', *Psychological Bulletin*, 123 (1998), 100–15
[138] John Kihlstrom, 'Dissociations and Dissociation Theory in Hypnosis: Comment on Kirsch and Lynn', *Psychological Bulletin*, 123 (1998), 186–91
[139] Erik Woody and Pamela Sadler, 'On Reintegrating Dissociated Theories: Comment on Kirsch and Lynn', *Psychological Bulletin*, 123 (1998), 192–7
[140] Irving Kirsch and Steven Jay Lynn, 'Dissociating the Wheat from the Chaff in Theories of Hypnosis: Reply to Kihlstrom (1998) and Woody and Sadler (1998)', *Psychological Bulletin*, 123 (1998), 198–202

The following works, mostly summaries rather than original research articles, are all worth consulting and will introduce the reader to a spread of views:

[141] Theodore Barber, *Hypnosis: A Scientific Approach* (New York: Van Nostrand, 1969)
[142] Theodore Barber, Nicholas Spanos and John Chaves, *Hypnotism, Imagination, and Human Potentialities* (New York: Pergamon, 1974)

[143] William Edmonston, *Hypnosis and Relaxation: Modern Verification of an Old Equation* (New York: Wiley, 1980)

[144] Erika Fromm and Michael Nash (eds.), *Contemporary Hypnosis Research* (New York: Guilford, 1992)

[145] Erika Fromm and Ronald Shor (eds.), *Hypnosis: Developments in Research and New Perspectives*, 2nd edn (New York: Aldine, 1979)

[146] Ernest Hilgard, 'Hypnosis', *Annual Review of Psychology*, 16 (1965), 157–80

[147] ———— *The Experience of Hypnosis* (New York: Harcourt, Brace and World, 1968)

[148] ———— 'Hypnotic Phenomena: The Struggle for Scientific Respectability', *American Scientist*, 59 (1971), 567–77

[149] ———— 'Hypnosis', *Annual Review of Psychology*, 26 (1975), 19–44

[150] ———— *Divided Consciousness: Multiple Controls in Human Thought and Action* (New York: Wiley, 1977)

[151] Ernest and Josephine Hilgard, *Hypnosis in the Relief of Pain*, 3rd edn (New York: Brunner/Mazel, 1994)

[152] Clark Hull, *Hypnosis and Suggestibility: An Experimental Approach* (New York: Appleton-Century, 1933)

[153] John Kihlstrom, 'Hypnosis', *Annual Review of Psychology*, 36 (1985), 385–418

[154] Irving Kirsch and Steven Jay Lynn, 'The Altered State of Hypnosis: Changes in the Theoretical Landscape', *American Psychologist*, 50 (1996), 846–58

[155] Theodore Sarbin and William Coe, *Hypnosis: A Social Psychological Analysis of Influence Communication* (New York: Holt, Rinehart and Winston, 1972)

[156] Peter Sheehan and Campbell Perry, *Methodologies of Hypnosis: A Critical Appraisal of Contemporary Paradigms of Hypnosis* (Hillsdale, NJ: Erlbaum, 1976)

[157] Nicholas Spanos and John Chaves (eds.), *Hypnosis: The Cognitive–Behavioral Perspective* (Buffalo, NY: Prometheus, 1989)

[158] Graham Wagstaff, *Hypnosis, Compliance, and Belief* (New York: St Martin's Press, 1981)

[159] ———— 'The Semantics and Physiology of Hypnosis as an Altered State: Towards a Definition of Hypnosis', *Contemporary Hypnosis*, 15 (1998), 149–65

[160] André Weitzenhoffer, *Hypnotism: An Objective Study in Suggestibility* (New York: Wiley, 1953)

On the neurophysiology of hypnosis:

[161] David Concar, 'You Are Feeling Very, Very Sleepy', *New Scientist*, 4 July 1998, 26–31

[162] Helen Crawford, 'Brain Dynamics and Hypnosis', *International Journal of Clinical and Experimental Hypnosis*, 42 (1994), 204–32

[163] Vilfredo DePascalis, 'Event-related Potentials During Hypnotic Hallucination', *International Journal of Clinical and Experimental Hypnosis*, 42 (1994), 39–55

[164] John Gruzelier, 'A Working Model of the Neurophysiology of Hypnosis: A Review of the Evidence', *Contemporary Hypnosis*, 15 (1998), 3–21

[165] Jean Holroyd, 'Hypnosis Treatment of Clinical Pain', *International Journal of Clinical and Experimental Hypnosis*, 44 (1996), 33–51

[166] Paul Jasuikaitis et al., 'Relateralizing Hypnosis: Or, Have We Been Barking Up the Wrong Hemisphere?', *International Journal of Clinical and Experimental Hypnosis*, 45 (1997), 158–77

[167] Stephen Kosslyn et al., 'Hypnotic Visual Illusion Alters Color Processing in the Brain', *American Journal of Psychiatry*, 157 (2000), 1279–84

[168] William Ray, 'EEG Concomitants of Hypnotic Susceptibility', *International Journal of Clinical and Experimental Hypnosis*, 45 (1997), 301–13

[169] David Spiegel, 'Neurophysiological Correlates of Hypnosis and Dissociation', *Journal of Neuropsychiatry and Clinical Neurosciences*, 3 (1991), 440–5

[170] David Spiegel and Paul Jasuikaitis, 'Hypnosis: Brain Basis' in G. Adelman and B.H. Smith (eds.), *Elsevier's Encyclopedia of Neuroscience*, 2nd edn (Amsterdam: Elsevier, 1999), 924–7

[171] David Spiegel et al., 'Hypnotic Hallucination Alters Evoked Potentials', *Journal of Abnormal Psychology*, 94 (1985), 249–55

[172] ———— 'Hypnotic Alteration of Somatosensory Perception', *American Journal of Psychiatry*, 146 (1989), 749–54

11. Hypnotherapy: Mind and Body

Most of the general books on hypnosis listed at the start of this bibliography will cover the topic, so I list here, out of hundreds of works, just a few that will help a general reader understand the present state of the art.

I haven't found a *really* outstanding introductory book, but this one is pretty good:

[173] Brian Roet, *Hypnosis: A Gateway to Better Health* (London: Weidenfeld and Nicolson, 1986)

A standard clinical textbook is:

[174] John Hartland, *Medical and Dental Hypnosis and Its Clinical Applications*, 3rd edn, ed. David Waxman (London: Baillière Tindall, 1989)

Two excellent scholarly books are:

[175] Daniel Brown and Erika Fromm, *Hypnotherapy and Hypnoanalysis* (London: Lawrence Erlbaum, 1986)
[176] H.B. Gibson and Michael Heap, *Hypnosis in Therapy* (London: Lawrence Erlbaum Associates, 1991)

Then see also:

[177] Joseph Barber, *Hypnosis and Suggestion in the Treatment of Pain* (New York: Norton, 1996)
[178] E. Thomas Dowd and James Healy, *Case Studies in Hypnotherapy* (New York: Guilford Press, 1986)
[179] Robert Lindner, *Rebel Without a Cause: The Hypnoanalysis of a Criminal Psychopath* (New York: Grune and Stratton, 1944)

On the possible after-effects of hypnosis:

[180] Lennis Echterling and David Emmerling, 'Impact of Stage Hypnosis', *American Journal of Clinical Hypnosis*, 29 (1987), 149–54
[181] Moris Kleinhauz and Ilana Eli, 'Potential Deleterious Effects of Hypnosis in the Clinical Setting', *American Journal of Clinical Hypnosis*, 29 (1987), 155–9
[182] Moris Kleinhauz *et al.*, 'Some After-effects of Stage Hypnosis: A Case Study of Psychopathological Manifestations', *International Journal of Clinical and Experimental Hypnosis*, 27 (1979), 219–26
[183] Frank MacHovec, 'Hypnosis Complications: Six Cases', *American Journal of Clinical Hypnosis*, 29 (1987), 160–5
[184] Tracie O'Keefe, *Investigating Stage Hypnosis* (London: Extraordinary People Press, 1988)

[185] Louis West and Gordon Deckert, 'Dangers of Hypnosis', *Journal of the American Medical Association*, 192 (1965), 9–12

Closely related to the topic of hypnotherapy is the topic of mind–body interaction. Again something of interest will often be found in academic journals, especially the following: *Advances: Journal of the Institute for the Advancement of Health*; *International Journal of Psychosomatics*; *Journal of the American Society of Psychosomatic Dentistry and Medicine*; *Journal of Psychosomatic Research*; *Psychosomatic Medicine*.

If you were to read only one book on the subject it would have to be:

[186] Robert Sapolsky, *Why Zebras Don't Get Ulcers: An Updated Guide to Stress, Stress-related Diseases, and Coping* (New York: Freeman, 1998)

But it would be a crime to omit the following too, which are all excellent:

[187] Franz Alexander, *Psychosomatic Medicine: Its Principles and Applications* (London: Allen and Unwin, 1952)
[188] Herbert Benson, *Timeless Healing: The Power and Biology of Belief* (London: Simon and Schuster, 1996)
[189] Howard and Martha Lewis, *Psychosomatics* (New York: Pinnacle Books, 1975)
[190] Steven Locke and Douglas Colligan, *The Healer Within: The New Medicine of Mind and Body* (New York: Dutton, 1986)
[191] Robert Ornstein and David Sobel, *The Healing Brain: Breakthrough Discoveries About How the Brain Keeps Us Healthy* (New York: Simon and Schuster, 1987)
[192] Robert Ornstein and Charles Swencionis (eds.), *The Healing Brain: A Scientific Reader* (New York: Guilford Press, 1990)
[193] Ernest Rossi, *The Psychobiology of Mind–Body Healing* (New York: Norton, 1986)

On the placebo effect in particular, see:

[194] Arthur and Elaine Shapiro, *The Powerful Placebo: From Ancient Priest to Modern Physician* (Baltimore: Johns Hopkins University Press, 1997)
[195] Margaret Talbot, 'The Placebo Prescription', *New York Times Magazine*, 9 Jan. 2000, 34–9, 44, 58–60

12. Mind Control

On mind control in general:

[196] Albert Biderman and Herbert Zimmer (eds.), *The Manipulation of Human Behavior* (New York: Wiley, 1961)

[197] James Brown, *Techniques of Persuasion* (Harmondsworth: Penguin, 1963)

[198] William Sargant, *Battle for the Mind: A Physiology of Conversion and Brainwashing* (London: Heinemann, 1957)

[199] Charles Tart, *Waking Up: Overcoming the Obstacles to Human Potential* (Boston: Shambala, 1986)

On advertising and selling:

[200] Wilson Bryan Key, *Subliminal Seduction: Ad Media's Manipulation of a Not So Innocent America* (New York: New American Library, 1973)

[201] Naomi Klein, *No Logo* (London: Flamingo, 2000)

[202] Donald Moine and Kenneth Lloyd, *Unlimited Selling Power: How to Master Hypnotic Selling Skills* (Englewood Cliffs, NJ: Prentice Hall, 1990)

[203] Vance Packard, *The Hidden Persuaders* (New York: David McKay, 1957)

On tyranny, gurus and cults:

[204] Joel Kramer and Diana Alstad, *The Guru Papers: Masks of Authoritarian Power* (Berkeley, CA: North Atlantic Books, 1993)

On the notorious CIA experiments:

[205] Donald Bain, *The Control of Candy Jones* (Chicago: Playboy Press, 1977)

[206] William Bowart, *Operation Mind Control* (New York: Dell, 1978)

[207] John Marks, *The Search for the Manchurian Candidate: The CIA and Mind Control* (New York: Times Books, 1979)

[208] Alan Scheflin and Edward Opton, *The Mind Manipulators* (New York: Paddington Press, 1978)

[209] Gordon Thomas, *Journey Into Madness: The True Story of Secret CIA Mind Control and Medical Abuse* (New York: Bantam, 1989)

13. Self-improvement and the New Age

Several of the practices surveyed in this chapter are associated with the movement known as 'New Age', on which an outstanding book is:

[210] Paul Heelas, *The New Age Movement* (Oxford: Blackwell, 1996)

A good anthology of essays covering a number of topics in this chapter is:

[211] Charles Tart (ed.), *Altered States of Consciousness: A Book of Readings* (New York: Wiley, 1969)

On the neurophysiology of trance states, see:

[212] Barbara Lex, 'The Neurobiology of Ritual Trance' in Eugene d'Aquili *et al.* (eds), *The Spectrum of Ritual: A Biogenetic Structural Analysis* (New York: Columbia University Press, 1979), 117–51
[213] Michael Winkelman, 'Trance States: A Theoretical Model and Cross-cultural Analysis' in *Ethos*, 14 (1986), 174–203

Of the many books on self-hypnosis, here are just a couple:

[214] Leslie LeCron, *Self-hypnotism: The Technique and Its Use in Daily Living* (New York: Prentice-Hall, 1964)
[215] Wolfgang Linden, *Autogenic Training: A Clinical Guide* (New York: Guilford Press, 1990)

On channelling:

[216] Michael Brown, *The Channeling Zone: American Spirituality in an Anxious Age* (Harvard University Press, 1997)
[217] Wouter Hanegraaff, *New Age Religion and Western Culture: Esotericism in the Mirror of Secular Thought* (Leiden: Brill, 1996)

On affirmations:

[218] Charles Baudouin, *Suggestion and Autosuggestion* (London: Allen and Unwin, 1920)
[219] Emile Coué, *My Method* (1923; Santa Fe: Sun Books, 1983)
[220] —— *How to Practice Suggestion and Autosuggestion* (1923; Santa Fe: Sun Books, 1992)

[221] Norman Vincent Peale, *The Power of Positive Thinking* (1953; London: Ebury Press, 1998)

On visualizations:

[222] Shakti Gawain, *Creative Visualization* (New York: New World Library, 1978)
[223] Mike and Nancy Samuels, *Seeing with the Mind's Eye: The History, Techniques and Uses of Visualization* (New York: Random House, 1975)
[224] Anees Sheikh (ed.), *Imagination and Healing* (Farmingdale, NY: Baywood, 1984)

On recreational drugs:

[225] Theodore Barber, *LSD, Marihuana, Yoga and Hypnosis* (Chicago: Aldine, 1970)

On neurolinguistic programming (NLP):

[226] Richard Bandler and John Grinder, *Frogs into Princes* (Moab, UT: Real People Press, 1979)
[227] Joseph O'Connor and John Seymour, *Introducing Neuro-Linguistic Programming*, 2nd edn (London: HarperCollins, 1993)

On meditation (not that this is something you can study through books):

[228] Herbert Benson, *The Relaxation Response* (New York: William Morrow, 1975)
[229] Joan Borysenko, *Minding the Body, Mending the Mind* (New York: Addison-Wesley, 1987)
[230] Deane Shapiro, *Meditation: Self-regulation Strategy and Altered State of Consciousness* (New York: Aldine, 1980)
[231] Deane Shapiro and Roger Walsh (eds.), *Meditation: Classic and Contemporary Perspectives* (New York: Aldine, 1984)
See also the massive bibliography in [101].

On shamanism:

[232] Mircea Eliade, *Shamanism: Archaic Techniques of Ecstasy* (New York: Pantheon Books, 1964)
[233] Michael Harner, *The Way of the Shaman* (New York: Harper & Row, 1980)

Index of Names

Index of Subjects